This book attempts a comprehensive analysis and re-evaluation of the first book of Hume's *Treatise of Human Nature*. Kant viewed Hume as the skeptical destroyer of metaphysics. Yet for most of this century the consensus among interpreters has been that for Hume skepticism was a means to a naturalistic, anti-skeptical end. The author seeks here to achieve a balance by showing how Hume's naturalism leads directly to a kind of skepticism even more radical – and more "Kantian" – than Kant imagined. In the process it offers the first systematic treatment of Humean associationalist psychology, including detailed exploration of his views on time-consciousness, memory, aspect-seeing, and the comparison with animal reason. Within this framework, Hume's views on language, belief, induction, causality, and personal identity emerge in a novel and revealing light.

Hume's theory of consciousness

Hume's theory of consciousness

Wayne Waxman

Assistant Professor of Philosophy,
The New School for Social Research, New York

CAMBRIDGE
UNIVERSITY PRESS

Published by the Press Syndicate of the University of Cambridge
The Pitt Building, Trumpington Street, Cambridge CB2 1RP
40 West 20th Street, New York, NY 10011–4211, USA
10 Stamford Road, Oakleigh, Melbourne 3166, Australia

First published 1994

Printed in Great Britain at the University Press, Cambridge

A catalogue record for this book is available from the British Library

Library of Congress cataloguing in publication data

Waxman, Wayne.
Hume's theory of consciousness / Wayne Waxman.
p. cm.
Includes bibliographical references and index.
ISBN 0-521-45381-X
1. Hume, David, 1711–1776. Treatise of human nature.
2. Knowledge, Theory of. I. Title.
B1489.W38 1994
128–dc20 93-29657 CIP

ISBN 0 521 45381 X hardback

à Béatrice

Mon Dieu! des mœurs du temps mettons-nous moins en peine,
Et faisons un peu grâce à la nature humaine;
Ne l'examinons point dans la grande rigueur,
Et voyons ses défauts avec quelque douceur.
Il faut, parmi le monde, une vertu traitable;
A force de sagesse, on peut être blâmable;
La parfaite raison fuit toute extrémité,
Et veut que l'on soit sage avec sobriété

Molière, *Le Misanthrope*

It is a history-book, sir, (Which may possibly recommend it to the world) of what passes in a man's own mind; and if you will say so much of the book, and no more, believe me, you will cut no contemptible figure in a metaphysical circle.

Sterne, *Tristram Shandy*

Contents

Preface

This book is a perpetuation "of the time honored and conventional myth enshrined in textbooks that present David Hume as the notorious negative and destructive thinker" (Capaldi). Hume's contemporaries, nearly every major thinker since, and most philosophers today are believers in this "myth." For them, as for me, Hume's importance as a philosopher derives from the challenge he levelled at rationalistic assumptions of the unrestricted validity of such notions as cause and effect, substance, space and time, and identity. They credit him further with developing the first thoroughgoing psychologistic skepticism, effectively reducing to associative imagination everything philosophers had formerly attributed to intellect. He is thus the first in a line of thinkers, extending through Kant, to treat the object of knowledge as its own construction, thereby shifting the focus of subjective philosophy from regulative principles of our experience of objects to constitutive principles of the objects we experience.

Why then have so many of those who ostensibly know Hume best turned their backs on the accepted view? The reasons are complex: the desire to re-examine orthodoxy and be original; Hume's elusiveness (he does not yield his secrets easily); developments like the rejection of subjectivism in twentieth-century philosophy which set the stage for those who would "rehabilitate Hume and make him one of our own; and recent trends in the history of philosophy which have transformed its methodology and focus. But, when all is said and done, an interpretation stands or falls by the quality of its textual analyses and its success in elaborating basic notions of Hume's system, like vivacity, custom, relation, association, etc. Whatever its shortcomings, the view of Hume "enshrined in textbooks seems to me preferable on both counts to the new revisionism. The Hume it portrays is a more powerful and coherent thinker, very much of his time, whose place in the great line of metaphysicians and antimetaphysicians from Descartes to Kant and beyond both makes sense and is deserved. Still, the revisionism undoubtedly creates the need for new work to probe Hume's basic concepts and to take the analysis deeper than before. The present book is intended as a contribution to this effort.

I owe an extra special debt of gratitude to Arthur Melnick and Wade Robison for their unstinting support and encouragement. I appreciate the invaluable comments and criticisms of David F. Norton and Fred Wilson. Additionally, I am grateful for important feedback on my work at various stages of development from Francis Dauer, Ken Gemes, Hidé Ishiguro, Béatrice Longuenesse, Patrick Murray, and the readers for Cambridge University Press. I am grateful to the editors of *Hume Studies* and Professors Robison and Malherbe, organizers of the 1992 Hume Conference in Nantes, for permissions to reprint, respectively, chapter 1-B and the conclusion. Judith Ayling, Gillian Maude, and others at the Press have performed their tasks splendidly and treated me with unfailing kindness and patience. Finally, I thank Alberto Hernandez-Lemus for his indispensable assistance in the production of the final manuscript, and my students for their many insightful questions and comments.

Abbreviations

Works by Hume

T	*A Treatise of Hume Nature.* Edited by L. A. Selby-Bigge, revised by P. H. Nidditch. Oxford: The Clarendon Press, 1978.
TApp	Hume's appendix published with Book III of the *Treatise*, Nidditch edition.
TAbs	Hume's abstract of the *Treatise*, Nidditch edition.
E	*Enquiries Concerning Human Understanding and Concerning the Principles of Morals by David Hume.* Edited by L. A. Selby-Bigge. Oxford: The Clarendon Press, 1902. The page numbers of passages excised by Hume from the final edition of *Enquiry Concerning Human Understanding* and which are omitted from the Oxford edition are preceded by "H" to indicate the page number in the edition by Charles W. Hendel (Indianapolis: The Bobbs-Merrill Company, Inc., 1955).
D	*Dialogues Concerning Natural Religion.* Edited by Richard Popkin. Indianapolis: Hackett Publishing Company, 1980.
EMPL	*Essays Moral, Political, and Literary.* Edited by Eugene Miller. Indianapolis: Liberty Fund, Inc., 1985.
LGFE	*A Letter from a Gentleman to his Friend in Edinburgh.* Edited by Mossner and Price. Edinburgh: The University Press, 1967.
L	*The Letters of David Hume.* Edited by J. Y. T. Greig, in two volumes. Oxford: The Clarendon Press, 1932.
ML	"My Own Life" in *An Inquiry Concerning Human Understanding.* Edited by Charles W. Hendel (see reference above).

Works by other authors frequently cited

ECHU	*An Essay Concerning Human Understanding*, by John Locke. Edited by P. H. Nidditch. Oxford: The Clarendon Press, 1975.
PHK	*Principles of Human Knowledge*, by George Berkeley, in

	Berkeley: *Philosophical Works*. Edited by M. R. Ayers. London: Dent and Sons, 1975.
CPR	*Kritik der reinen Vernunft*, by Immanuel Kant. Hamburg: Felix Meiner Verlag, 1956. All translations of Kant are my own.
AA	*Kants Gesammelte Schriften*. Berlin and Leipzig: Preussische Akademie der Wissenschaften, 1906–.

Introduction: a false reason or none at all

Hume's "dangerous dilemma"

Hume's survey of human understanding in *A Treatise of Human Nature* ends with a vertiginous descent into despair. "The intense view of these manifold contradictions and imperfections in human reason has so wrought upon me, and heated my brain, that I am ready to reject all belief and reasoning, and can look upon no opinion even as more probable or likely than another" (*T*268). Reason, which putatively sets man apart from and above his fellow creatures, exposes itself as nothing but "the general and more establish'd properties of the imagination" (*T*267); our sole and entire counterweight to "all the trivial suggestions of the fancy," which are so "often contrary to each other" and "lead us into such errors, absurdities, and obscurities, that we must at last become asham'd of our credulity," is thus simply fancy in another guise. Worse, this ostensibly "rational" brand of imagination," when it acts alone, and according to its most general principles, entirely subverts itself, and leaves not the lowest degree of evidence in any proposition, either in philosophy or common life. We save ourselves from this total scepticism only by means of that singular and seemingly trivial property of the fancy, by which we enter with difficulty into remote views of things, and are not able to accompany them with so sensible an impression, as we do those, which are more easy and natural" (*T*267f.). Human nature thus casts us into a nightmarish dilemma: sound reason can survive thanks only to a natural tendency to ignore its verdicts; yet to embrace this frivolousness as the principle of our reasoning is to "run into the most manifest absurdities" and so undermine sound reason. "We have, therefore, no choice left but betwixt a false reason and none at all" (*T*268).[1]

The "dangerous dilemma" (*T*267) confronting humankind on account of our dependence on trivial suggestions of the fancy is merely one, and by no means the most telling, of the "manifold contradictions and imperfections" that led Hume to brand ours a *false* reason. The dilemma we face in reasoning according to the relation of cause and effect is perhaps the most important. Of the "permanent, irresistable, and universal" principles of imagination, upon whose "removal human nature must immediately perish and go to ruin," the one closest to the heart of all reasoning and explanation bearing on matters of fact is "the customary transition from causes to effects, and from effects to causes" (*T*225). Without it," Inference and reasoning concerning the operations of nature would, from that moment, be at an end; and the memory and senses remain the only canals, by which the knowledge of any real existence could possibly have access to the mind" (*E*VIII/i.64). The internal world of the mind (see *T*261) and the external world of bodies (see *T*73f., *T*108 and *T*237) would be beyond our powers of conception; even demonstrative reasoning (especially mathematics) would lose all connection with matters of fact and carry no weight whatever in our thoughts and actions (see *T*414). Yet ...

> how must we be disappointed, when we learn, that this connexion, tie, or energy lies merely in ourselves, and is nothing but that determination of the mind, which is acquir'd by custom, and causes us to make a transition from an object to its usual attendant, and from the impression of one to the lively idea of the other? Such a discovery not only cuts off all hope of ever attaining satisfaction, but even prevents our very wishes; since it appears, that when we say we desire to know the ultimate and operating principle, as something, which resides in the external object, we either contradict ourselves, or talk without a meaning. (*T*266f.)

Experience, in disclosing to us causal relations, grants us no insight into the nature or relations of the objects we perceive; it is merely the occasion of certain feelings within us. The sole and entire source of our idea of cause is simply an amalgam of the *ease* felt in the transition from an impression to an associated idea and the *vivacity* which then characterizes our contemplation of the idea ("'Tis here that the real power of causes is plac'd, along with their connexion and necessity ... the customary transition is, therefore, the same with the power and necessity," *T*166). The feelings of facility and vivacity are the natural response of the human psyche to the repeated observation (constant conjunction) of perceptions, and, as such, are fully as hostage to the peculiar constitution of human nature as, say, the kind of sensation we receive from the touch of a velvet cushion. Were our senses constituted differently, the light refracted by a rose might produce a sensation like the taste of pineapple (or no sensation at all, as happens presently with ultraviolet stimuli). Likewise, a differently constituted imagination might *not* be predisposed to associate constantly conjoined perceptions (i.e. feel ease in the transition) or, even if it were, might still not respond to ideas thus associated to impressions with belief (= vivacity). Given an idea-enlivening imagination with quite different "general and more establish'd properties," not only would it never occur to us to ascribe objective significance to observed regularities, but also we might take no heed of them at all. We would attach significance to phenomena that, with our present natures, seem random and meaningless and pass unremarked.

The upshot of Hume's account of causal inference is that experiencing a world and seeing yellow are merely diverse expressions of basic animalian psychology; the one is no more capable than the other of yielding the least insight into independent realities ("all probable reasoning is nothing but a species of sensation ... a wonderful and unintelligible instinct in our souls," *T*103 and *T*179). Things we cannot help but believe and "must take for granted in our reasonings" (*T*187) – for example a cause to every beginning of existence, the existence of bodies – owe their immunity to doubt wholly to the fact that our imaginations are in thrall to the contingencies and blind dictates of human nature ("Nature, by an absolute and uncontroulable necessity has determin'd us to judge as well as to breathe and feel," *T*183). We therefore entirely undermine human reason – "contradict ourselves, or talk without a meaning" – when, as so often happens, we suppose it to be a source of objective truth or insight.

Nor did Hume deem his own causal account of the workings of the human mind immune to these considerations. The production of customs by the constant conjunction of perceptions; the power of an impression to enliven a customarily associated idea; the dependence of impressions of reflexion on ideas of sensation; the taking of an idea-copy from impression-originals; and the mind itself, as the recipient of perceptions and the agent of their relation: these causal relations are as imaginary as any others. The mind, this "system of different perceptions ... link'd together by the relation of cause and effect" (*T*261), is nothing "that really binds our several perceptions together," nor anything "really belonging to these different perceptions, and uniting them together," but simply "the union of their ideas in the imagination, when we reflect upon them," the fanciful contrivance of "uniting principles in the ideal world" (*T*259f.). "The identity, which we ascribe to the mind of man, is only a fictitious one" (*T*259).

If we query who – or what – observes perceptions and makes these "ideal" connections, Hume's answer, it seems, is no answer: our powers of reason simply do not equip us to explain or understand further. We may fancy that we penetrate its "infinite obscurities" (*T*232) when we "run into the notion of a *soul*, and *self*, and *substance*" (*T*254); yet, this is mere delusion:

We have no perfect idea of any thing but of a perception. A substance is entirely different from a perception. We have, therefore, no idea of a substance. Inhesion in something is suppos'd to be requisite to support the existence of our perceptions.

Nothing appears requisite to support the existence of a perception. We have, therefore, no idea of inhesion. (*T*234)

For Hume, perceptions are prior to, and independent of, mind:

what we call a *mind*, is nothing but a heap or collection of different perceptions, united together by certain relations, and suppos'd, tho' falsely, to be endow'd with a perfect simplicity and identity. Now as every perception is distinguishable from another, and may be consider'd as separately existent; it evidently follows, that there is no absurdity in separating any particular perception from the mind; that is, in breaking off all its relations, with that connected mass of perceptions which constitute a thinking being. (*T*207)

Causal explanation (implicating dependence, necessary connection) is no longer possible when one withdraws to the point *before* association forms our successive perceptions into "that connected mass of perceptions which constitute a thinking being." Yet, for Hume, to concede that causal inference is no longer possible is tantamount to saying there can be no explanation at all. If we try to advance further, our words outrun our ideas; we grope, invent principles with unfathomable meanings, and to no purpose but to blind ourselves with our own smoke and mirrors. As with the ultimate operating principles governing external objects (see *T*267f.), so, too, "any hypothesis, that pretends to discover the ultimate original qualities of human nature, ought at first to be rejected as presumptuous and chimerical" (*T*xvii): we must resist the urge to speculation, and accept that the ultimate sources and operating principles of that succession of perceptions which constitutes the "raw material" of associative imagination are veiled in impenetrable obscurity.

Nor is this yet the whole story. Hume explained necessary connections entirely in terms of imagination and its feelings: a reflexive impression comprised of feelings of facility (in the transition from one perception to its successor) and vivacity (if the transition is from an impression to an idea). This makes it possible to understand causal relations – or, rather, the customs of which they consist – in two quite distinct ways: from a *causal* point of view, as the *effect* of observed constant conjunction; or from an *introspective* viewpoint, as a transition of thought imbued with the aforementioned feelings. The second (which is an analysis of content, not a causal explanation) is independent of the first. In other words, the causal explanation, like any such, might well be falsified, and yet there be no loss of essential content to the idea of cause itself (and this could be so even if one lacked any memory of constant conjunction – as someone who had never been exposed to light might be given a sensation of red by using a probe to stimulate the appropriate nerve cells). Hume's independent introspective account thus opened the way to a safe skeptical haven to shelter him from the criticism that his own theory of association entails an observing, active, perduring mind. For, if pressed, he could reply: according to my analysis of the idea of cause and effect, its sole contents are (i) the immediately perceptible relation of temporal succession plus the feelings of (ii) vivacity and (iii) ease of transition. How causal relations arise I have explained so far as experience (= causal explanation) permits. Appeal to principles of real connection lying beyond experience I *will* not engage in for I *can*not, as there is no possible source or warrant for ideas other than experience; I must therefore plead the privilege of the skeptic and avow my ignorance.

Skeptic or naturalist?

For more than a century, the falseness of reason as portrayed by Hume – the ideal, illusory nature of its principles and productions – was accepted at face value.[2] This changed, however, thanks especially to a series of articles by Norman Kemp Smith, culminating in his 1941 book, *The Philosophy of David Hume*.[3] To Kemp Smith, the traditional portrait of Hume as the exponent of a radical, destructive skepticism was not simply a caricature, but a distortion, even an inversion, of his true position. Kemp Smith's Hume is more interested in answers than in questions, more concerned with action than knowledge, content to believe even where he is ignorant, and far keener to avoid than to seek out skeptical culs-de-sac:

> Which is the more fundamental in his thinking, the naturalism or the scepticism? ... Nature, through the beliefs to which it gives rise ... acts as an arbiter. It defines the conditions of health, and the regimen suitable for its maintenance. Scepticism serves as an ally, but in due subordination, not an equal ... Man, he insists, while a creature of Nature, is yet a being in whom reflexion plays so large a part, and operates so extensively in the formation of *artificial* beliefs, that nothing short of the dispassionate questionings of a sceptical philosophy can avail to keep him in wholesome conformity with Nature's ends ... He had no intention of proving – quite the contrary – that there is no such thing as rational necessity. For consciousness of it, as he recognised, is implied in the proof that in particular instances it is absent ... Hume's manner ... shows very clearly that he does not mean to deny the objective reality of material bodies or their mutual influence.[4]

Some recent interpreters have gone even farther than Kemp Smith, claiming that Hume did not merely take for granted, but expressly set out to affirm, the mind-independent reality of causation and physical objects.[5] Yet, such a view does not do justice to the insight at the heart of Kemp Smith's break with the past: it was not that Hume took anti-skeptical positions on the same, traditional metaphysical issues earlier interpreters had supposed him to have treated skeptically, but that such issues were not his true concern. Hume employed skepticism as a weapon to break others of their metaphysical commitments, not for the purpose of replacing these with new ones, but in order to shift the focus of philosophy away from metaphysics to all and only those questions that can be dealt with entirely naturalistically. On the Kemp Smith view, therefore, Hume's originality and greatness lay in the emphasis he placed on rationally inexplicable, unwarrantable beliefs, rooted in human nature, which serve to regulate the conduct of our lives; and this emphasis on naturalism over skepticism remains, in one form or another, the majority view in Hume interpretation today.[6]

To exponents of this view, the notion of a "false reason" is a non-sequitur. For while our reason may lack the divine guarantees demanded by Descartes, since we have no other with which to compare or contrast it, how – except by relying on the veracity of this same reason – could we demonstrate or discover its falsehood? All we can legitimately ask is whether it is possible that one could ever come to *believe* it to be false – for example, actually convince oneself of the non-existence of bodies, real relations of cause and effect, etc. – and so actually become a skeptic in life. To this, of course, the answer is all too obviously and uninterestingly no; with the exception of those brief moments when we are caught in the throes of philosophical speculation (see *T*217), no one is capable of disbelieving these things ("Whoever has taken the pains to refute the cavils of this *total* scepticism, has really disputed without an antagonist, and endeavour'd by arguments to establish a faculty, which nature has antecedently implanted in the mind, and render'd unavoidable," *T*183). So, interpreters of a naturalist bent would caution us against taking talk of "false reason" literally: we are misreading the message at the heart of Hume's philosophy if we suppose him ready to countenance the notion that the only kind of reason we know is, or could be, "false" – so far as this word may have any meaning at all.

The present work is a challenge to the naturalistic consensus in Humean scholarship. The position defended in it is that Hume's naturalism, far from being incompatible with radical skepticism, actually dovetails into it, so that the proposition that human reason is false possesses the same irresistible authority of natural belief as does its contrary. The key to recognizing this is that not all the natural beliefs identified by Hume are beliefs of reason (= imagination). For what seems to have escaped interpreters in the tradition of Kemp Smith is that beliefs founded on the immediate data of sense have precisely the same nature and authority as the beliefs he ascribed to idea-enlivening imagination; each alike owes its dominion over us not to what they *reveal* or enable us to *discover*, but simply and solely to the *feeling* of vivacity they engender in the contemplating mind:

> the *belief* or *assent*, which always attends the memory and senses, is nothing but the vivacity of those perceptions they present; and ... this alone distinguishes them from the imagination. To believe is in this case to feel an immediate impression of the senses, or a repetition of that impression in the memory. (*T*86)

Since Hume made clear that the testimony of immediate consciousness gainsays all the ideas and beliefs of imagination (for example, *T*188ff.), we are all possessors of two sets of diametrically opposed, yet equally natural and irresistible, beliefs, between which we are powerless to choose. Put another way, each of us is as certain (on the basis of the senses) of the falsity of natural beliefs founded on imagination as we are powerless to disbelieve them (as is true too of conflicts of natural beliefs internal to imagination – see, for example, *T*266). And to maintain that all beliefs founded on custom and other propensities of imagination are mere natural *illusions* is nothing other than to believe that human reason is a false reason.

What saves us then from total skepticism? Only the aforementioned "singular and seemingly trivial property of the fancy, by which we enter with difficulty into remote views of things, and are not able to accompany them with so sensible an impression, as we do those, which are more easy and natural." The possession of contradictory beliefs poses problems for us only if they are brought into actual opposition, within a single purview. Yet, no attitudes or modes of awareness are less suitable to be brought together in this way than those of immediate consciousness and imagination: the one persuades us that reality consists of disparate, instantaneous perceptions in perpetual flux, while the other discloses an orderly world of dynamically interconnected, enduring objects (the two systems of *T*108). Although it is immediately evident that perceptions and objects are identically the same existents, we are preserved from the paradoxes this entails by the mere fact that great difficulty and exertion are required to unite the two views in one. Were our natures different, if our imaginations found it easy to adopt this perspective, we would surely succumb to a skeptical despair from which we could never extricate ourselves. But this nightmare human nature spares us by depriving such conflicts of any ability to make a strong, enduring impact on us. This, above all, the philosopher must recognize. For then, when the "manifold contradictions and imperfections in human reason" are brought to light, he will not be led to question his methods and results by the fact that something seemingly so grave and dire as the falsity of reason affects him far less than the sickness of a loved one or a humiliation. Such a ranking of priorities may not seem reasonable, but neither is it contrary to reason (after all, "'Tis not contrary to reason to prefer the destruction of the whole world to the scratching of my finger," *T*416). It simply is so. Trivial suggestions of the fancy, and they alone, save human reason from the precipice; and, recognizing this, the philosopher will not be tempted to turn his back on reason in favor of a quasi-fideistic naturalism. This, in my view, is the position of Hume: a "mitigated skepticism" not on account of its content, but on our unruffled reaction to it ("A true sceptic will be diffident of his philosophical doubts, as well as of his philosophical conviction; and will never refuse any innocent satisfaction, which offers itself, upon account of either of them," *T*273).

With the thesis stated, let us proceed to the means employed to develop and defend it. My purpose is to show that Hume's naturalism leads to a most extreme skepticism. As purely a matter of textual interpretation, the means throughout must be exegetical: painstaking, detailed analysis of the main components of Hume's naturalistic account of human understanding (association, belief, causal inference, identity, etc.). Implicit in such an approach is the need to identify and respect the basic lines of the theory as laid down by Hume himself. For, if an interpretation is to have any claim to being a precise rendering of the positions and unifying standpoint actually present in a text, fixed points to moor, guide, and establish its parameters are indispensable. In their absence, attempts to resolve ambiguities, eliminate obscurities, extract arguments, etc., are bound to seem makeshift and idiosyncratic. Yet, therein lies the difficulty facing us: there is little agreement where the fixed points in Hume's philosophy lie.[7] Apparent inconsistent formulations of principle, or principles belied by practice, abound in his writing, obliging one sometimes to sacrifice the letter of his philosophy to one's sense of its spirit. And here the choices one makes are determined, above all, by whether one believes its spirit to be fundamentally skeptical or naturalist.

There is no better example of how an interpreter's confidence that he has penetrated into the true spirit of Hume's philosophy can shape the way he traces its basic lines – even in conscious opposition to the text and without corroborating evidence – than the case of Kemp Smith. If for no other reason than the deep and lasting mark his views have stamped on subsequent Hume interpretation, they merit detailed consideration:

(1) *The vivacity of impressions*. Hume was quite explicit that the single feature constitutive of the distinction between ideas and impressions is their differing degree of vivacity. Further, as a difference solely of degree, it follows that, when Hume explains the vivacity of an *idea* as belief in the real existence of its content, we must understand the vivacity of impressions *in precisely the same way*: as belief in the real existence of the content present in them. Kemp Smith, however, rejects this implication. While

conceding that Hume employed the term "vivacity" to characterize both impressions and ideas, he claims that this usage must be "reinterpreted, and understood in a non-literal, indeed metaphorical, sense";[8] hence, "vivacity" as applied to impressions has a different meaning than when applied to ideas, and, in particular, does *not* connote naturalistic belief. Accordingly, the distinction between impressions and ideas is based not on difference in vivacity – "the seemingly explicit character of many of his statements notwithstanding"[9] – but on the relation of original to copy. Kemp Smith gave numerous arguments in defense of his position; yet, quite clearly, his bold decision to draw the fundamental lines of Hume's philosophy elsewhere than Hume himself saw fit to do was ultimately a matter of "gut feeling" – his sense that Hume's naturalism was the primary determinant in his philosophy. For, if a uniform sense of "vivacity" were admitted, how could the naturalism possibly be detached from the theory of ideas, and thence from subjectivist skepticism?

Besides limiting the equation of vivacity with belief to ideas, Kemp Smith also restricted the equation of belief with vivacity to beliefs founded on iterated experience. It seems never to have occurred to him that Hume may have held that beliefs founded on immediate consciousness owe their infallibility precisely to their partaking of that very feeling of vivacity. Instead of taking Hume at his word, that *all* belief is merely vivacity, he took for granted that the infallibility of immediate consciousness was the same for Hume as for Descartes, Locke, or Berkeley: a matter purely of insight, or intuition. This completely ignores the fact that infallible knowledge implies not simply the *absence* of doubt but the *presence* of belief – a belief so powerful as to *exclude* doubt – and Hume offered only one theory of belief: vivacity.[10] Because of this oversight, Kemp Smith excluded immediate consciousness from the scope of naturalistic belief, and so, like every interpreter since, overlooked precisely that which, above all, distinguishes Hume's theory of ideas from that of his predecessors. We thus arrive at the view that the skepticism to which the naturalism would otherwise lead is subservient to it:

> Not only ... is Hume unshaken in his adhesion to Locke's doctrine of ideas by the sceptical consequences to which it leads, this is one main reason why he values the doctrine so highly ... His purpose, from the start, has been to give prominence to those negative consequences, and to push them as far as they can be made to go. The more negative their character, the more evident must it become that "ideas" cannot afford a sufficient basis for belief, and that belief must therefore be accounted for in some other, very different, manner ... He perceived very clearly that the theory of ideas, in being retained, would in his system have to subserve uses very different from any to which it had hitherto been put, and that it was not therefore merely in his supplement to the theory of ideas but also even in respect of

his treatment of the theory itself that he must rest his philosophy on a foundation almost entirely new.[11]

By contrast, the view I advance here – that the theory of ideas was for Hume neither subordinate nor superior to naturalism but one and the same with it – is grounded on a thesis derivable directly from the text: *all vivacity is belief (including that of impressions), and all belief vivacity (including that founded on immediate consciousness)*. Hume did not have two theories of belief, one for ideas made vivid in consequence of iterated experience, another for immediate consciousness independent of any reference to vivacity; rather, all belief without exception *is* a feeling of vivacity. If anything can be identified as the single founding insight of Hume's theory of understanding, informing and uniting all its elements, it is this.

However, to understand my claim correctly, it is essential to recognize that Hume's sense of "belief" should not be equated with "believe to be true," i.e. affirmation. This is in effect to treat belief as inherently propositional which, in my view, is incompatible with Hume's psychological conception of belief/vivacity applicable to infants and animals. We should consider "believe to be true" to be, from Hume's perspective, secondary and derivative by comparison with its primary sense of "believe to be real," i.e. belief in the real existence of a content present in sensation, reflexion, or thought. For the beliefs most fundamental to and characteristic of understanding, and so of most concern to the philosopher – a cause of every beginning of existence, an external world, the self – are precisely those that, in Hume's view, humans share with animals. "Belief" in this sense contrasts not with denial (affirmation of the falsity of), but with fantasy (the fictitious, the unreal). For example, while the same content, say, an object of fear like a charging tiger, may present itself immediately to consciousness either in sensation or in fancy (as an idea-copy), it is only in the former case that evasive action is taken. The reason, as I understand Hume, is that human nature ordains that only the sensation shall create in us a maximal feeling of vivacity, and so engender belief in the real existence of that present in it. Degree of belief/vivacity constitutes the sole difference between the effects of sensation and mere thought. And since there is here no implication of the propositional, we can easily see why Hume saw fit to extend it to infants and animals (as he did the principles of association, whose importance to human understanding derives solely from their ability to enliven otherwise unbelieved ideas).

(2) *Relations*. In Humean nomenclature, *perceptions* are the immediate objects of consciousness. Such objects are of two kinds: impressions and ideas. Notably absent from their ranks are *relations*. Hume ascribed relations to the imagination; hence, instead of being objects *before*

consciousness, they fall within the province of the *consciousness* contemplating the objects. Why? Hume does not tell us; but there is no claim he repeated more frequently or with such insistence than that the objects present immediately before us are, one and all, distinct, independent existents; each is therefore capable of existing in the absence of any – or, for that matter, every – other (see *T*207). So, if relations were to be included among such objects, this principle would have to apply to them as well; that is, we would be faced with the absurdity of supposing that relations like "is to the left of," "is the same color as," or "is the cause of" might exist entirely on their own, separate even from the objects standing in them. Faced with the alternative of renouncing his principle or avoiding the absurdity, Hume presumably chose the latter and so denied that relations stand on a par with perceptions as objects of consciousness.

Nevertheless, Hume left unclear whether he believed that all relations must be internally felt (in imagination) in order to be said to exist; and certain passages, as well as his practice, have led many to deny this, among them Kemp Smith. He claimed that Hume departed from the letter of his position ...

> in his treatment of time and space, and in his attempted denial of abstract ideas – to mention only two instances. His way of circumventing problems confronting him in such cases is to contend that the new non-sensational factors are not *constituents* of what is apprehended, and are due solely to the *manner* in which it is apprehended – an obvious evasion of the difficulties, and a virtual recantation of his fundamental hypothesis.[12]

The anti-skeptical significance of Kemp Smith's assertion that relations, space and time, and other abstractions (for example, distinctions of reason) were, for Hume, apprehensible objects is unmistakable. By endowing them with an objectivity equal to that of impressions and ideas, we may not only suppose them to obtain whether or not we take notice of them, but also, as "non-sensational factors," regard them as capable of relating things other than perceptions ("things in themselves"). For then, even if one grants that we have no *idea* of objective relations of cause and effect other than the constant conjunctions of perceptions, there is no reason to suppose that objects specifically different from perceptions are any less capable of standing in relations of constant conjunction than perceptions. Thus, the door is opened to metaphysical realism, or at least a naturalism in which the ultimate reality of causes, bodies, etc., is never brought into question.

Realism has obvious attractions; yet, the problem remains that it ill accords with Hume's expressed positions. In my view, Hume was for all intents and purposes agnostic about the consciousness-transcending reality of "non-sensational factors." He had no need to commit himself, since the question has nothing to do with his real concern: the nature and workings of human understanding. What mattered to him, and alone entered into his theorizing, were factors capable of influencing human thoughts and actions; and, since nothing can do so which is incapable of producing belief (a feeling of vivacity), his sole and entire concern with relations derived from their power to engender belief. Unobserved relations obviously lack this power, and so too observed relations that fail to excite a feeling of vivacity in the observing consciousness. Because imagination had traditionally been deemed responsible for the relating of distinct perceptions, this species of consciousness naturally became the locus for Hume of any feelings of vivacity which relations may occasion (i.e. they are literally *felt in the imagination*). Consequently, even if there were a sense in which relations might be said to exist independently of imagination, they could have no role in the explanation of human understanding, and so are of no interest to the philosopher of human nature.

In Hume's view, three relations so excel every other in their power to inspire belief that, "upon their removal human nature must immediately perish and go to ruin": resemblance, contiguity, and, above all, cause and effect (see *T*10 and *T*225). He held that our natures are so constituted as to bias imagination in favor of these relations through a concomitant feeling of pleasureful ease in the transition from one perception to another. Since vivacity-producing powers were ascribed to none of the other relations of perennial concern to philosophers (identity, quantity, etc.), the fact that they none the less have significance for us (weigh in our thoughts and actions) can only be explained by their being parasitic on relations of resemblance, contiguity, and cause and effect. In other words, if the support of the latter were withdrawn and all links to them severed, these relations (which Hume termed "philosophical") would be without any influence upon us at all, and so could have no place in a science of human nature. Since even philosophical relations are of concern to the science of human nature and have objective significance only in and for idea-relating and -enlivening imagination, it is impossible for their import, thus restricted, to carry over into consciousness-transcending contexts (the same is true of relations of constant conjunction, which are merely an amalgam of natural resemblance and contiguity relations: the former weigh in our thoughts and actions only because the latter have belief-engendering effects – see chapter 2-D). Hume's doctrine of relations makes them important in the analysis of understanding only in so far as they are capable of engendering feelings of vivacity and ease of transition in the idea-relating imagination; so, *pace* Kemp Smith, if it leads anywhere, it is clearly in the direction of psychologism, from which it is but a short way to skepticism. Condensed into a thesis: *philosophical relations are parasitic on the belief-engendering power of natural relations; and because belief in the reality of an idea is itself nothing more than a feeling in imagination, no relation can be accorded reality except in and for idea-enlivening imagination.*

(3) *Association.* So far as Hume himself was concerned, nothing in his philosophy is more pervasive, important, or original than the theory "of the connexion or association of ideas" (*T*10):

> Thro' this whole book, there are great pretensions to new discoveries in philosophy; but if any thing can intitle the author to so glorious a name as that of an *inventor*, 'tis the use he makes of the principle of the association of ideas, which enters into most of his philosophy (*TAbs*661f). Here is a kind of ATTRACTION, which in the mental world will be found to have as extraordinary effects as in the natural, and to shew itself in as many and as various forms. (*T*12)[13]

Kemp Smith, however, took great pains to show that association is only a "secondary plot" in the *Treatise* that soon fizzles out. The main plot is, of course, the naturalism, where belief is viewed not "mechanically" but "normatively," and the moral is that "The beliefs which ought to be accepted are... beliefs that Nature itself marks out for us."[14] Unfortunately, it sometimes happens that "psychology, as exposing the mechanisms through which belief is causally produced, usurps upon logic, as defining the conditions under which it can be intelligently regulated."[15] It is therefore necessary, in the interests of saving Hume from himself, to spare no effort to separate the indigestible psychological chaff from the wholesome naturalistic germ.

It is not at once evident why naturalistic-minded interpreters tend to be so keen to denigrate Hume's reliance on association. Its immense appeal to Hume no doubt stemmed, in large part, from its capacity to operate in infants, simpletons, inarticulate savages, and even animals. No language, acculturation, or social interaction of any kind is implicated. Hence, it is just the sort of operation whereby we might plausibly be supposed, independently of others and almost from the first moments of our conscious lives, to acquire beliefs in an external world, a cause of every beginning of existence, specific necessary connections (as between the sun and heat), etc., as naturally and inevitably as we cut our milk teeth. Admittedly, it is non-normative; yet, it is difficult to see why natural beliefs should stand in need of being "intelligently regulated": they are, by definition, not subject to whim; our nature guarantees that we acquire them virtually from the first onset of mental activity and never afterwards lose them (no matter how persuasive our philosophy professors). So why does Hume's theory of association, so clearly tailor-made to suit understanding "in a state of nature," evoke such resistance from precisely those who champion his naturalism?

Kemp Smith justified his decision to detach Hume's naturalism from the theory of association as follows:

> the self operates ... in a twofold capacity. First, as "human nature," i.e. as that which in reaction upon external stimuli is determinant of the impressions of sensation, and, through them, also of the impressions of reflexion. In these respects it exhibits (to employ Hume's terms) ... "a productive faculty, [which] gilding or staining all natural objects with the colours borrowed from internal sentiment, raises in a manner a new creation." Secondly, the self operates ... as observer, i.e. as exercising the acts of awareness which give it access to the impressions of sensation and to the consequent impressions of reflexion.
>
> When Hume is endeavouring to establish a statics and dynamics of the mind, on analogies derived from Newton's natural philosophy, the self in this second capacity as observer recedes into the background; as not required for the operation of the associative processes, it is treated as otiose, indeed so much so that there is considerable excuse for those who have been led to suppose that Hume is actually denying its existence ... When he is proceeding on Newtonian lines, belief is a quality of this and that perception ... When he is proceeding more on Hutchesonian lines, belief is ... an attitude of mind, and rests on a fundamental distinction between the mind in its character as observer, and the items observed ...
>
> When the really distinct features, whether in the complex ideas of relations, modes and substances, or in the "natural beliefs," are squarely faced (as in Part iv of Book I), it is Hutchesonian, not Newtonian concepts (i.e. biological not physical analogies) which prove to be the more fundamental in Hume's thinking. The processes of mind, as Hume recognizes, are adaptive, not mechanical in character, and in final outcome it is in the resources of human nature, as exhibited in the instincts, passions and affections, not in the operation of association that he finds the solution of his chief problems.[16]

Kemp Smith based his decision to detach Hume's naturalism from the theory of association on the thesis that the latter does away with the conscious, feeling observer, replacing him with a blind, sheerly reactive mechanism. This is a widely held view but, in my judgment, patently implausible. For it is no mechanism but *imagination* that, according to Hume, is responsible for the association of ideas;[17] and what is imagination if not a species of *observing, feeling consciousness*? Though in principle free to relate ideas any way whatever, the imagination is subject to a certain "gentle force, which commonly prevails" (*T*10; see also *E*V/ii.41), thus tipping the scales in favor of certain relations and against others. This "associating quality, by which one idea naturally introduces another" (*T*10) amounts to nothing more than this: "our imagination runs easily from one idea to any other"(*T*11) that resembles it, is contiguous to it, or is causally related to it ("the very essence of these relations consists in their producing an easy transition of ideas," *T*260). To interpret this ease not as a *feeling*, but as the operation of some *unconscious* mechanism seems wholly unwarranted. To be sure, in comparison with more deliberative, calculating mental activity, the operation of associating imagination may be characterized as "blind," "automatic," "unthinking," etc.; but it would be a crude distortion to infer from this that association is not a conscious activity, or even that imagination lacks the freedom to resist its gentle forces when so inclined (a freedom Hume believed it to possess – see *T*92f.). Like Locke before him, Hume believed that much mental activity escapes our notice because, through long usage, it becomes ingrained habit (see chapter 2-A); still, it does not entirely escape our consciousness and we are constantly undergoing feelings (of facility and vivacity) in sync with it. Activity of this sort is, of course, precisely that one would wish to invoke if, like Hume, one's objective were to explain not only the beliefs of acculturated adults but of infants and animals as well – beliefs preserved until the end of our lives whether we will or not. It is also the most plausible alternative to innatism for explaining how, though beginning life a *tabula rasa* (so far as concerns matters of fact), we acquire the framework (belief in causes, in an external world, etc.) and initial stock of information necessary for more complex forms of mental activity (including the capacity to be trained in the use of language).

Another respect in which Kemp Smith misrepresented Humean association is the enlivening of ideas. Hume spoke of vivacity sometimes as if it were a quality of perceptions themselves, and at other times as if it were an attitude the perceiver adopts towards them. But it simply is not true, as Kemp Smith claims, that the former usage falls neatly and systematically within associative Newtonian contexts and the latter within naturalistic Hutchesonian ones.[18] More importantly, he neglected the very feature that distinguishes resemblance, contiguity, and cause and effect from all other relations capable of yielding customary associations: *their unrivalled capacity to enliven ideas* (i.e. engender beliefs). This is the characteristic that makes the attractive power of these relations so special: relations lacking this feature, even if they can produce customs, have no part to play in the explanation of objective understanding; only those capable of affecting our convictions regarding matters of fact hold out the promise of something resembling a Newtonian science of the mental world. Association is not distinct from natural belief, introduced by Hume *ad hoc*, from outside, to explain it. On the contrary, he conceived association quite specifically, and imagination generally, with the *conscious feelings* of vivacity (= belief) and ease of transition uppermost in mind (this is the basis, I believe, of the thesis that "Reason is, and ought only to be the slave of the passions, and can never pretend to any other office than to serve and obey them," *T*415). Association is, therefore, first and foremost what might be termed a *phenomenological* operation: it is essentially comprised of feeling-data immanent to consciousness.[19]

Nothing in Kemp Smith's interpretation of Hume has exerted greater influence or been echoed more frequently than his belief that Hume's naturalism may be detached from the theory of association. Though notions and reasons vary, the unanimity on this point is striking, as is the consensus that this detached naturalism is by far the most important and original idea in Hume's theory of understanding. Perhaps this is due, more than anything else, to the philosophical temper of the times: while psychologistic approaches to philosophical questions, especially those relying on the theory of ideas (first-person subjectivism), tend to be viewed with disfavor, naturalism has never been more in vogue. In this climate of opinion, the way pointed by Kemp Smith is bound to seem attractive, all the more so since he packaged it as textual interpretation. Although neither he nor other naturalist-minded interpreters would deny that their theses conflict with many of Hume's own statements about where the fixed points of his philosophy lie and in what its true importance and originality consist, most nevertheless are willing – far too readily – to attribute the confusion to Hume himself rather than to shortcomings of their own interpretive approach. It is difficult to argue against such convictions. The only criterion to which one can, in the end, appeal is the outcome to which a particular approach leads: Is the style of the portrait of Hume's philosophy anachronistic or suited to its temper and times? How well does it do justice to the sense most of us have that Hume ranks among the greatest philosophers? And, above all, how much of the sitter's character and complexity are captured on the canvas? A principal aim of this book will be to show that these criteria are best satisfied by a portrayal in which Hume's associationalism is seen not only as integral to his naturalism, but even identical with it. What this means is that *Hume's naturalistic conclusions about understanding are one and all consequences of his theory of ideas, particularly the application of his conception of belief as vivacity to relations in imagination, so that the naturalism not only is undetachable from the skepticism, but actually dovetails into it.*

Hume's skepticism

"Skepticism" is one of those words that tend to vary in meaning as often as they are used.[20] That which interests me here is the skepticism which, ever since Kant, has become almost synonymous with the name of Hume. Within it, however, three strands may be distinguised, as well as a fourth species of skepticism which stands more or less outside this conception and has hitherto escaped notice. The first might be termed *metaphysical agnosticism*. There may be things to whose existence and/or nature we are utterly blind owing to the lack of senses to be affected by them and/or faculties to comprehend them. Furthermore, there may be much about even those perceptions we are equipped to have of which we are ignorant. Hume's position regarding such possibilities was agnostic. His scientific interest in perceptions ranged no farther than their psychological and epistemological dimensions, leaving the ontological to take care of itself (see chapter 6-B).

The second strand in Hume's skepticism is the *anti-metaphysical.* It is founded on the examination of the *origins* of concepts traditionally held to have mind-independent objective validity. For example, Locke, Berkeley, and other thinkers prior to Hume took for granted the objective validity of general principles of necessary connection: that every beginning of existence must have a cause, everything that exists must be self-subsistent or inhere in something else that is, etc. By contrast, Hume argued that nothing has to *be* as our natures oblige us to *conceive* and *believe* it to be, that reality is under no constraints to conform to the laws of human nature. In particular, investigation of the origin of the idea of necessary connection reveals that metaphysical principles are derived not from the objects present to consciousness, but from the consciousness contemplating them: the feelings of vivacity and the easy transition of thought in idea-relating and -enlivening imagination. Since these feelings are the originals of our ideas of necessary connection – the source of their very content – Hume could go so far as to assert the impossibility of their applying to anything imperceptible. For, they lack validity even with respect to perceptions themselves (sensations, reflexions, thoughts), and hold only in and for the imagination contemplating them. So too our ideas of constant conjunctions – the regularities that give rise to customs – since these too are merely products of association (contiguity and resemblance); they weigh in our thoughts and reasoning (including those of philosophers) solely because of their capacity to engender feelings of vivacity and smooth transitions between ideas. We must resist the temptation to transfer to the objects (perceptions) before us a "reality" and "objectivity" the true grounds and nature of which are subjective: an imagination disposed by nature to experience certain feelings while observing or thinking of them. Likewise, since abstraction and generality have no extralinguistic reality beyond the natural human inclination to attach significance to resemblances, Hume could even go so far as to question whether there is any real basis for distinguishing a separate faculty of understanding over and above "the imagination, or the vivacity of our ideas"(*T*265; see chapters 2-D and 3-B).

Third, there is a *self-nullifying* strand within Humean skepticism, in which Hume applied his general account of causal relations to those utilized in his own theory of ideas (that impressions give rise to ideas, ideas to other impressions, perceptions call to mind customary associates, etc.), together with the idea of the mind (personal identity) that results from the constancy of these relations. Presumably, he delayed subordinating these relations to associative imagination until the second to last section of *Treatise* I in order to prevent his skeptical juggernaut from crashing to a halt prematurely. For its upshot is clear: the means employed in Hume's (causal) explanation of causal and other imagination-based beliefs regarding matters of fact, as well as of general principles traditionally accepted in metaphysics, turn out to be mere expressions of the very feelings they were invoked to explain (see chapter 6-C).

The final strand of Humean skepticism I term the *dialectic of natural belief*. Hume's theory of ideas having devoured itself in the penultimate section, the conclusion of *Treatise* I represents an attempt to assess and come to terms with conflicts between opposed beliefs each of which is grounded in human nature and so equally impossible to renounce. For example, immediate consciousness inspires the conviction (= feeling of vivacity) that our senses present only fleeting existents, no necessary connections or external objects, and that the content of our ideas of these latter is derived in part from phenomenological feelings in our consciousness of them. Idea-associating imagination nevertheless leaves us powerless to disbelieve in necessary connections and external objects. Both alike have the force of natural belief, and so are impossible to cast off or overcome; thus, we have only good fortune (natural selection?) to thank for "the trivial suggestions of the fancy" that prevent us from taking much notice of these conflicts. Still, this brand of skepticism is perhaps the most important because it is the common lot of mankind, not just that of the philosopher (see conclusion).

Definitions and premises

I. I call *phenomenological* those data of immediate consciousness that, unlike other immediate data, are not perceptions. Hume employed the term "perception" to signify the *object* of immediate consciousness, and distinguished three general kinds: sense data, data of reflexion,[21] and thoughts. Towards these objects, Hume supposes that consciousness (especially in the guise of imagination) adopts various attitudes, or has certain special feelings, for example, belief (vivacity). Such feelings in the contemplation of perceptions I shall term *phenomenological* data. In addition to belief, there are two other such feelings that play important roles in Hume's analysis of understanding: the *ease* of transition from one idea to another associated with it, and the *discomfort* felt when confronting obstructions to easy transitions (together with the attendant *satisfaction* in overcoming them – for example, *T*205f.).

Another type of datum that figures prominently in my interpretation is that of *experience*. These data are imperceptible and non-introspectible; they require several perceptions or mental actions in order to come to light. The most important either derive from or presuppose custom of the sort characteristic of causal inferences. Chief among them for Hume's purposes are the experiential data which make possible a naturalistic explanation of the nature and workings of human understanding itself, for example, the knowledge that constantly conjoined perceptions produce customs, that customary transitions from an impression to an idea engender belief in that idea, that ideas derive from resembling impressions (i.e. the relation of copy to original), that impressions of reflexion depend on ideas of sense, etc.[22] By contrast with description of phenomenological data (which is restricted to first-person, present-time reports), the expression of experiential data may employ reference to past and future time as well as third-person reports and behavior (including animal behavior). Thus, in the analysis of causal relations, there are, on the one hand, the experiential data of constant conjunctions generating customs and, on the other hand, the phenomenological data of the ease felt in the transition from the impression to an associated idea and the vivacity felt in contemplating that idea. The experiential therefore differs from the phenomenological in the same way as the *cause* of a perception does from its *content*.[23]

II. Although it is generally assumed that the philosophers who had the greatest influence on Hume were Locke and Berkeley, some commentators have disputed this. Kemp Smith deemed Hutcheson an even more important influence than either Locke or Berkeley, while others give the nod to Butler, Bayle, or even Huet; some even contend that Hume's philosophy shows hardly any influence by Berkeley at all.[24] Yet, it seems improbable that any but a philosopher of comparable gifts and achievement could have exercised a fundamental influence on a philosopher of Hume's calibre. Undoubtedly, he borrowed a great deal from lesser thinkers and found considerable stimulus in their writings; some he even saw fit to mention by name (for example, Malezieu). But the only instances of acknowledged major influences on Hume's theory of understanding – avowed cases of the wholesale adoption or adaptation of important doctrines identified with a single philosopher – are Locke's account of succession (see *T*35) and Berkeley's critique of abstraction (see *T*17). This, of course, does not prove that other philosophers did not exercise an unacknowledged influence as great or greater; establishing a negative is difficult. Nor does it mean that his debt to Locke and Berkeley is limited to what he acknowledges (that, to Locke especially, can hardly be exaggerated). Yet, I do not believe it an accident that Hume chose to single out succession and abstraction for explicit recognition. In adopting these doctrines, he also transformed them: from Locke's account of succession he eliminated everything presupposing abstraction, while Berkeley's account of generality he greatly extended and enriched by the addition of his own theory of association. What emerges is, in my view, the quintessence of Hume's thought. In developing my interpretation, it struck me that virtually everything in his philosophy follows directly from the combination of Locke's theory of succession and Berkeley's criticism of abstract ideas with his own notion of idea-enlivening association (which helps explain why he singled out the latter as his special innovation). And, as will emerge below, it is just this combination that makes possible the transformation of Hume's naturalism into the more radical forms of skepticism outlined above.

III. The principal text on which the present interpretation is based is *A Treatise of Human Nature*. Hume's later survey of many of the same topics, *An Enquiry Concerning Human Understanding*, will be relied on mainly to corroborate and supplement it. Admittedly, this practice conflicts with Hume's own expressed view. Near the end of his life, he excluded the *Treatise* from the collected edition of his works and issued a statement requesting that all future judgments concerning his philosophy be based on the *Enquiry*. Whether, in denying Hume his wish (as nearly all of us do), we are committing only a venial sin or a great one depends on whether the differences between the two works are important. Yet, aside from the greater concision of the *Enquiry*, and its restriction of detailed analysis solely to causation, their difference seems essentially stylistic. As its original titling as a set of essays suggests, the *Enquiry* was aimed at a broader, less philosophically savvy reading public than the *Treatise*; and its narrower focus, simpler conceptual scheme, and less rigorous and exacting style of argument are the natural result.[25] Nor is there any evidence to suggest that Hume significantly altered or watered down any of his views in the interval separating the *Treatise* from the *Enquiry*.

One reason Hume distanced himself from the *Treatise* was its failure to win a readership (it "fell deadborn from the press, without reaching such distinction as even to excite a murmur among the zealots").[26] He responded to its poor reception by treating it, apparently quite sincerely, as his own failure as a writer rather than the closed-mindedness or heedlessness of the public. Since the reception given to the *Enquiry*, if not overwhelming, was far more favorable than that accorded to the *Treatise*, his disavowal of the latter may have been partly a matter of deference to his public. Yet, almost certainly he was also motivated by a long history of suffering on account of material present in the *Treatise* but absent from the *Enquiry*: a professorship denied, hounded from his position as librarian, a victim of innumerable scurrilous attacks (culminating in Beattie's diatribes) – the distress of the dying man evident in his public declaration disowning the *Treatise* no doubt owed much to this history. If these were the causes that led Hume to issue his statement, then one may well ask what his attitude would have been had the *Treatise* met with the same acclaim during his lifetime that it has received subsequently. It is difficult to believe that one with his readiness to defer to the judgment of readers would not have been persuaded to re-embrace the child of his youth could he have known the verdict of posterity. So, while conceding the desirability of obtaining corroboration from the *Enquiry* whenever possible, there is no reason not to make the *Treatise* one's principal guide and ultimate arbiter.

IV. The *Treatise* is more than a study of human understanding: its second book is devoted to the passions and the third to morals. The compass of Hume's philosophy as a whole is far broader still. In confining myself to his views on understanding, I make no pretence of offering a synoptic view of the integral whole of his thought. Yet, one may question whether one can do justice to the theory of understanding advanced in *Treatise* I by taking it in isolation. Some scholars maintain that "the very problems which could not be solved by the sort of thinking Hume enacted in Book I are later by him resolved in the fuller human accounts of Book II and Book III: For example, how causal thinking can be placed beyond the reach of skepticism; how things – self and others – have identity over time; what serves as Hume's model for the association of ideas."[27] I do not question that there is much in later books of the *Treatise* that is useful in comprehending the first, and shall often rely on them to fine-tool, amplify, and corroborate my analyses. I would also be the last to deny that Hume was a quintessentially systematic thinker. Nevertheless, in my judgment, the account of understanding in *Treatise* I is, in all its essentials, self-sustaining and self-contained. Its relation to the two subsequent books does not seem to me that of the way of error to the way of truth, or a trial run to what is for keeps, but that of a *distinct*, *independent* branch of Hume's science of human nature to the others. I would go further: just as the science of human nature *as a whole* furnishes "a foundation almost entirely new" for "a compleat system of the sciences ... and the only one upon which they can stand with any security" (*T*xvi), so too that *branch* of it dealing with knowledge is the indispensable foundation and warrant for all the rest.

Hume recognized that an inquiry into the passions, emotions, and desires (language too – see chapter 3-C) is of interest only if it sets them within the public context of selves, others, and external objects. A purely subjectivist account would be as impoverished and jejune as an analysis of politics confined to the contents of politicians' mental states. Nevertheless, if, as Hume supposed, passions, emotions, and desires have a foundation in human nature, so too must selves, others, and external objects; that is, selves et al. must exist not only in our talk and social practices, but also as ideas in understanding. So, if reference to these ideas in explaining passions and morals is not to be rendered suspect, and we are not always to be at risk of misinterpreting their role in our lives, then we must seek to apprise ourselves of their precise *contents* and the *conditions* of their acquisition. Accordingly, it was necessary for Hume to consecrate the first portion of his science of human nature to ascertaining "the extent and force of human understanding, and ... explain the nature of the ideas we employ, and of the operations we perform in our reasonings" (*T*xv).

A case in point is the self, the object of the passions of pride and humility and the presupposition (in the form of *other* selves) of the passions of love and hatred. Before pretending to be able to account for its role in our lives in terms of human nature (as something each of us *by nature* is concerned for, takes pride in, etc.), Hume deemed it necessary first to ascertain (i) *that* an idea corresponds to our words, (ii) *what* its contents are, and (iii) *how* it is obtained. After achieving this, and in the process having shown it to be rooted in the most fundamental principles of human nature, he could then utilize it in his account of the passions and morals without fear of lapsing into error or obscurity. For if ever, in either context, a question arose which turned on the content of the idea or the limits of its validity, he could always "unpack" it in light of the *Treatise* I analysis (to show, for example, that we have no idea in our understanding of anything which answers to the expression "immortal soul").

There is, in my view, a clear division of labor between *Treatise* I and the two subsequent books: the former focuses chiefly on the origins and contents of our ideas, the latter on their role in human life. At the center of the first is the isolated individual (human or animal), respecting which at least equal weight must be assigned to first-person data as to third-person. The object of concern in the two later books is, from the very outset, an inhabitant of the external world and a member of a group; the isolated mind and the first-person data pertinent to it become almost wholly irrelevant.[28] Accordingly, the "human nature" examined in *Treatise* I is not quite the same as that dealt with in *Treatise* II and III. This difference can best be highlighted by reference to animal nature: the account of human understanding in *Treatise* I can apply equally well to the understanding of asocial animals like tigers; by contrast, Hume's study of the passions and morals, though independent of any *particular* social structure, demands at least *some* such. If this view is correct, then it is quite impossible for problems and solutions peculiar to the subject matter of

Books II and III to have any bearing whatsoever on problems and solutions arising within the context proper to Book I. The concluding section of *Treatise* I effectively terminates discussion centered on the individual, isolated consciousness; and, with the shift to the social and uniquely human, I take my leave of Hume.

Part I

The elements of Hume's philosophy

'Tis very difficult to talk of the operations of the mind with perfect propriety and exactness; because common language has seldom made any very nice distinctions among them, but has generally call'd by the same term all such as nearly resemble each other. *T*105

It becomes, therefore, no inconsiderable part of science barely to know the different operations of the mind, to separate them from each other, to class them under their proper heads, and to correct all that seeming disorder in which they lie involved when made the object of reflexion and enquiry. *E*I.8

The first part of this work is consecrated to what Hume "consider'd as the elements of this philosophy" (*T*13). They include: the division of perceptions into *impressions* and *ideas* by virtue of their differing *force and vivacity;* the *simplicity* and *complexity* of perceptions; the relations in which impressions stand to ideas (viz. their *resemblance*, their relation as *originals* and *copies*, and the *production* of impressions of reflexion by ideas of sensation); the distinction between ideas of *memory* and *imagination*; the *association* of ideas in imagination by means of the relations *resemblance*, *contiguity*, and *cause and effect*; the distinction between *natural* and *philosophical* relations; *substance* and *mode*; and *abstract ideas*.

Since it is unusual to devote so great a portion of a book on Hume to the discussion of these topics, a word of explanation may be in order. The aforementioned notions together form the framework in which Hume identified, formulated, and attempted to solve philosophical problems; the terms in which he reasoned; and the means he believed necessary and sufficient to arrive at an ordered, coherent, persuasive account of the nature and workings of human understanding. It is imperative to make every effort to comprehend them in all their aspects, leaving nothing out, before proceeding to consider their application by Hume to problems like space and time, causality, and identity. In my view, not to do so, or to be unable to, is virtually to guarantee that the philosophy one presents as his will appear artificial, inconsequential, and ill-organized.

Yet, whether it is because the elements of Hume's philosophy are thought not to require detailed consideration or not to merit it, in most writing on Hume they are unceremoniously dispatched after only a cursory review, while others imported from twentieth century philosophy are often summarily set in their place. No doubt, it is the sincere belief of those authors who do so that not only their readers and themselves, but Hume too, are best served by such a procedure. This, in my view, is mistaken and misguided. If Hume's philosophy still deserves study two centuries after his death, it is quite likely that its principal use and benefit for us lies in its essential *difference* from contemporary ways of thinking. There can be no more valuable antidote to philosophical complacency – the inclination to take things for granted in the absence of any sense of crisis about fundamentals – than a confrontation with a powerful thinker working from a quite different standpoint. He can reveal our most basic, unarticulated assumptions and impel us to scrutinize them critically; oblige us to shore up defenses that otherwise might fall into neglect; challenge us to re-examine our standpoint in the most fundamental ways; and, all in all, afford us an invaluable opportunity to gain self-understanding. Nothing seems to me more wrongheaded than the practice of downplaying or obscuring a past philosopher's differences from us by recasting his thought in a modern mold (which then, almost inevitably, makes it appear in a poor light by comparison with the genuine article). In order to gain the greatest benefits from the study of Hume, it therefore seems to me imperative to accustom ourselves to working with and within the elements of his thought; only by taking them as seriously as he did can we hope to understand him as he would have us do.

1 Impressions and ideas

A. Difficulties understanding "force and vivacity"

To comprehend the difference between impressions and ideas, it is crucial to distinguish those features of perceptions which are "immediately present to us by consciousness" (*T*212) from those that become evident only through *experience* and *custom.* For example, the supreme principle of Hume's theory of ideas – that every idea is *copied* from an antecedent impression – is experiential in nature. For the *existential dependence* of one perception on another, like any assertion of necessary connection, is a matter of experience: "the constant conjunction of our resembling perceptions, is a convincing proof, that the one are the causes of the other; and this priority of the impressions is an equal proof, that our impressions are the causes of our ideas, not our ideas of our impressions" (*T*5). The only elements of Hume's principle that are independent of experience (i.e. known by immediate perception) are the *resemblance* between impressions and ideas and the temporal *precedence* of one *vis à vis* the other (see *T*73 and *T*168f.);[1] Yet, even these, as natural relations, are products of associative imagination (see *T*10ff.). So, the question is this: is there any immediately perceptible difference between impressions and ideas, prior to, and independent of, both experience and associative imagination, that warrants their distinction?

Hume's answer is that there is: we are immediately aware of a difference in *force and vivacity* among our perceptions. Experience is of no use to discover a quality such as this; and imagination, though capable of enlivening ideas to the point where they approach impressions, presupposes the vivacity of impressions as given. In light of Hume's view that "our perceptions are our only objects" (*T*213) and "The perceptions of the mind are perfectly known" (*T*366), it thus is no surprise that, in positing an original, fundamental division among perceptions, he should prefer to rely on some quality that can be directly sensed or felt:

The difference betwixt these consists in the degrees of force and liveliness, with which they strike upon the mind, and make their way into our thought or consciousness. Those perceptions, which enter with most force and violence, we may name *impressions;* and under this name I comprehend all our sensations, passions and emotions, as they make their first appearance in the soul. By *ideas* I mean the faint images of these in thinking and reasoning; such as, for instance, are all the perceptions excited by the present discourse, excepting only, those which arise from the sight and touch, and excepting the immediate pleasure or uneasiness it may occasion. I believe it will not be very necessary to employ many words in explaining this distinction. Every one of himself will readily perceive the difference betwixt feeling and thinking. (*T*1)

Hume has often been criticized for thinking vivacity sufficient by itself to distinguish impressions from ideas.[2] Quite apart from the question of whether it is an adequate criterion, it is far from clear just what quality of our perceptions he had in mind.[3] One possibility is that it is something like the difference between scarlet and brick red; or between red and purple; or perhaps that between blinding light and dim. But it is equally possible that its sense lies in a different direction altogether, say, a difference between *actual seeing* – even in a pitch black room (i.e. uniformly black visual *sensation*) – and mere *recollection* (even that of an intensely bright, sharply delineated scene, viewed only a moment before, i.e. an *image* of sensation). Or perhaps in yet another direction: a directly discernible feature not of the objects present to consciousness themselves (i.e. *perceptions*) but of our *consciousness* of them (i.e. a kind of primitive intentional attitude adopted towards perceptions). It is even unclear whether impressions and ideas are not simply diverse *aspects* of perceptions, so that a perception counts as an impression if it is regarded as a *present* content of consciousness and an idea if deemed a *representation* of something distinct from it.[4] Such doubts may well prompt one to wonder why Hume should have thought it germane to his purpose to replace more readily comprehensible terms like "sensation," "feeling" ("passion," "emotion"), and "thought" ("conception," "fancy," "memory," "reflection," "judgement," "reason") with novel ones like "impression" and "idea," distinguishable only by means of so very obscure and ambiguous a criterion as "force and vivacity." Why did he think it necessary? Does it achieve his aims? And at what price?

One might seek to avoid such difficulties by finding in Hume some other distinguishing mark between impressions and ideas than force and vivacity. But although there are many such,[5] Hume never tired of repeating that the *essential*, truly *fundamental* difference is vivacity:

Impressions and ideas differ only in their strength and vivacity. (*T*19) The component parts of ideas and impressions are precisely alike. The manner and order of their appearance may be the same. The different degrees of their force and vivacity are, therefore, the only particulars, that distinguish them. (*T*319)

Vivacity is something "'tis impossible by words to describe" but "every one of himself will readily *perceive*" (*T*1) and "must be conscious of in his own breast" (*TAbs*654); it denotes the "*feeling to the mind*" (*TApp*629) "with which [perceptions] *strike upon the mind*, and make their way *into our thought or consciousness*" (*T*1), and so an original quality of human consciousness.[6] There is thence no need for remembrance, imagination, experience and custom, judgment, or reason in order to discover it: from the very first moment of conscious life, their difference in vivacity makes it impossible for us to regard a thought as we do sensations or reflexions. In short, the distinguishing features of vivacity are the immediacy, which renders it as directly evident to us as yellow or pain, and its freedom from any presupposition of imagination (relation or enlivening of ideas) or iterated experience. It therefore seems reasonable to conclude, given that Hume placed vivacity at the very center of his theory of ideas, that the immediacy which singles it out from every other feature differentiating impressions from ideas was somehow vital for his philosophical purposes.

Having accepted that the only way properly to comprehend Hume's distinction between impressions and ideas is in terms of force and vivacity, one naturally turns back to the text for illumination. Here one is likely to be disappointed. Hume himself complained of the inadequacy of the terms "force" and "vivacity" to convey his meaning, be it to distinguish impressions from ideas or, as here, to distinguish believed ideas from unbelieved:

> even when I think I understand the subject perfectly, I am at a loss for terms to express my meaning ... I scarce find any word that fully answers the case, but am oblig'd to have recourse to every one's feeling, in order to give him a perfect notion of this operation of the mind. An idea assented to *feels* different from a fictitious idea, that the fancy alone presents to us ... And this different feeling I endeavour to explain by calling it a superior *force*, or *vivacity*, or *solidity*, or *firmness, or steadiness*. This variety of terms, which may seem so unphilosophical, is intended only to express that act of the mind, which renders realities more present to us than fictions, causes them to weigh more in the thought, and gives them a superior influence on the passions and imagination. (*TApp*629–30)[7]

Despite the difficulties, Hume struggled to articulate the "feeling" he had in mind (the citation above being a case in point). Unfortunately, several of his attempts appear to conflict and so only make matters worse. One such instance relates to the crucially important question of whether a difference in vivacity is a difference *in kind* or *in degree*. One might assume that it is the latter, both for linguistic reasons (the ordinary usage of "vivacity" as well as Hume's frequent use both of it and its cognates as comparatives –

"stronger," "firmer," "more intense," etc.) and because a central tenet of Hume's philosophy is that the vivacity of ideas admits of being increased (to the point of certainty) and diminished (to incredulity). But before one infers from this that "impression" simply signifies the maximum possible degree of vivacity (on a scale extending from conception through various degrees of conviction), one has to reckon with passages like this:

[Memory and imagination] may mimic or copy the perceptions of the senses; but they never can entirely reach the force and vivacity of the original sentiment. The utmost we say of them, even when they operate with greatest vigour, is, that they represent their object in so lively a manner, that we could *almost* say we feel or see it: But, except the mind be disordered by disease or madness, they never can arrive at such a pitch of vivacity, as to render these perceptions altogether undistinguishable ... The most lively thought is still inferior to the dullest sensation. (*E*II.11)

This passage makes the gulf between impression and idea seem wellnigh insuperable, and so points to a true difference in kind. The caveat regarding madness, as well as another form of debility mentioned in the corresponding passage of the *Treatise* ("it sometimes happens, that our impressions are so faint and low, that we cannot distinguish them from our ideas" – *T*2), do not seem to be true exceptions. For, by presenting them as a failure or inability to *distinguish* idea from impression, Hume makes it seem as if they were merely cases of mistaken identification (mistaking a thought for a sensation or reflexion) – as typically happens when one is deluded, heedless, or otherwise impeded from marking differences that might otherwise be discerned.[8] If so, the difference between impressions and ideas cannot be eliminated simply by an increase or diminution of vivacity; that is, never can *the idea itself* become an impression or *the impression itself* an idea. Hume, therefore, may well have taken the view that a thought can no more become a sensation or reflexion (emotion, passion, desire) than a visual sensation can become a tactile sensation or transmutate itself into pride.

Unfortunately, Hume seems also to have affirmed the contrary: that ideas *do* sometimes become impressions and vice versa. This is never more apparent than when he enunciates his doctrine of sympathy in *Treatise* II:

The idea of ourselves is always intimately present to us, and conveys a sensible degree of vivacity to the idea of any other object, to which we are related. This lively idea changes by degrees into a real impression; these two kinds of perception being in a great measure the same, and differing only in their degrees of force and vivacity. But this change must be produc'd with the greater ease, that our natural temper gives us a propensity to the same impression, which we observe in others, and makes it arise upon any slight occasion. In that case resemblance converts the idea into an impression, not only by means of the relation, and by transfusing the original vivacity into the related idea; but also by presenting such materials as take fire from the least spark. (*T*354; see also *T*317)

Elsewhere, Hume again credits both sympathy and the natural relations of *Treatise* I with the power to transform ideas into impressions:

And since these relations [i.e. resemblance and contiguity] can entirely convert an idea into an impression, and convey the vivacity of the latter into the former, so perfectly as to lose nothing of it in the transition, we may easily conceive how the relation of cause and effect alone, may serve to strengthen and inliven an idea. In sympathy there is an evident conversion of an idea into an impression ... sympathy is exactly correspondent to the operations of our understanding. (*T*320)[9]

And in Book I itself one finds a text dealing with madness which has a quite different import than the one discussed earlier:

When the imagination, from any extraordinary ferment of the blood and spirits, acquires such a vivacity as disorders all its powers and faculties, there is no means of distinguishing betwixt truth and falshood; but every loose fiction or idea, having the same influence as the impressions of the memory, or the conclusions of the judgment, is receiv'd on the same footing, and operates with equal force on the passions. A present impression and a customary transition are now no longer necessary to inliven our ideas. Every chimera of the brain is as vivid and intense as any of those inferences which we formerly dignify'd with the name of conclusions concerning matters of fact, and *sometimes as the present impressions of the senses.* (*T*123; emphasis mine)

Here Hume appears to be maintaining that certain figments of the deranged imagination do not merely *seem* to have, but *actually attain*, the vivacity characteristic of "present impressions of the senses."[10] Remarks like this, when contrasted with those cited earlier, make it difficult to believe that he was very clear or decided as to whether the vivacity which distinguishes impressions from ideas represents a difference in kind or degree.

There are other apparent inconsistencies in Hume's presentation of impressions and ideas as well. Impressions can be calm or dull to the point almost of insensibility:

The raptures of poetry and music frequently rise to the greatest height; while those other impressions, properly call'd *passions*, may decay into so soft an emotion as to become in a manner, imperceptible. (*T*276)

'Tis natural for one, that does not examine objects with a strict philosophic eye, to imagine, that those actions of the mind are entirely the same, which produce not a different sensation, and are not immediately distinguishable to the feeling and perception ... Hence it proceeds, that every action of the mind, which operates with the same calmness and tranquility, is confounded with reason by all those, who judge of things from the first view and appearance. Now 'tis certain, they be real passions, produce little emotion in the mind, and are more known by their effects than by the immediate feeling or sensation. (*T*417) 'Tis evident passions influence not the will in proportion to their violence, or the disorder they occasion in the temper; but on the contrary, that when a passion has once become a settled principle of action, and is the predominant inclination of the soul, it commonly produces no longer any sensible agitation. (*T*418)

One can only wonder how anything could be an *impression*, have the full force and vivacity proportionate to this species of perception, and yet seem to consciousness *dull*, *calm*, *soothing*, even *insensible* – to the point of being "confounded with reason" by those who judge "from the first view and appearance." For was it not Hume's view that perceptions "must necessarily appear in every particular what they are, and be what they appear"? (*T*190).

The same gap between the being and the appearance of perceptions insinuates itself in the case of ideas too. An idea can be "so strong and lively as to support itself" (*T*422), and may even induce a person to "confound his judgment with sensation" (*T*112). If so, what warrant is left for calling it "idea" at all? Though Hume has an answer to this question, it raises another problem:

But how great soever the pitch may be, to which this vivacity rises, 'tis evident, that in poetry it never has the same *feeling* with that which arises in the mind, when we reason, tho' even upon the lowest species of probability. The mind can easily distinguish betwixt the one and the other; and whatever emotion the poetical enthusiasm may give to the spirits, 'tis still the mere phantom of belief or persuasion ... Where the vivacity arises from a customary conjunction with a present impression; tho' the imagination may not, in appearance, be so much mov'd; yet there is always something more forcible and real in its actions, than in the fervors of poetry and eloquence. The force of our mental actions in this case, no more than in any other, is not to be measur'd by the apparent agitation of the mind. A poetical description may have a more sensible effect on the fancy, than an historical narration ... But still the ideas it presents are different to the *feeling* from those, which arise from the memory and the judgment. There is something weak and imperfect amidst all that seeming vehemence of thought and sentiment, which attends the fictions of poetry ... [T]he great difference in their feeling proceeds in some measure from reflexion and *general rules*. We observe, that the vigour of conception, which fictions receive from poetry and eloquence, is a circumstance merely accidental, of which every idea is equally susceptible; and that such fictions are connected with nothing that is real. (*TApp*630–31)

If poetic ideas, however great the fervor and agitation they excite, still "feel" differently than ideas of memory and experience-based belief, then how much more differently, one presumes, must *ideas generally* feel than *impressions*. But just what is this "feeling"? How is it analogous to the poetry/history distinction? According to Hume, when taken as history, even a humdrum recitation is more "forcible and real" than the most stirring fiction, while a captivating, moving narrative, if taken as fiction, is "connected with nothing that is real" and is unbelieved. Might not the same be true of the difference between an impression and an idea?

B. Vivacity as verisimilitude

The key to solving the problems arising from Hume's decision to base his distinction between impressions and ideas on vivacity is, in my view, to understand vivacity and its cognates (force, firmness, steadiness, etc.) as *verisimilitude.* In a text considered earlier, Hume explained that "This variety of terms, which may seem so unphilosophical, is intended only to express that act of the mind, which renders realities, *or what is taken for such*, more present to us than fictions, causes them to weigh more in the thought, and gives them a superior influence on the passions and imagination" (*E*V/ii.40, emphasis mine).[11] In this passage, Hume was not concerned with the difference in vivacity between impressions and ideas, but rather that between two kinds of ideas: beliefs and mere conceptions (= "perfect ideas,"[12] i.e. unbelieved thoughts). Nevertheless, there seems to me ample warrant to believe that its gist applies to the former distinction as well. For Hume did not restrict his notion of "belief," defined as the vivacity of a perception, to ideas:

> the *belief* or *assent*, which always attends the memory and senses, is nothing but the vivacity of those perceptions they present; and ... this alone distinguishes them from the imagination. To believe is in this case to feel an immediate impression of the senses, or a repetition of that impression in the memory. (*T*86)

Here, the vivacity *specifically* of "an immediate impression of the senses" is expressly equated with belief; moreover, it is clearly stated to be belief of the very same sort which characterizes memory, and by virtue of which memories are distinguished from mere fictions of the imagination. The implication is that the vivacity of impressions earns for them a place in the spectrum of beliefs alongside believed ideas – a place at the top end, below which come memories, then products of associative imagination, and finally other habits and relations (see *T*153f.). Accordingly, just as with believed ideas, the vivacity of impressions is what renders them more *real* to us than fictions; and, since their vivacity exceeds that of even the liveliest idea, theirs is the *non plus ultra*, and so the standard, of *all* believed reality among perceptions. Moreover, like believed ideas,[13] the verisimilitude of impressions is not, as so often is supposed, a quality of *the perceptions themselves*, but of our *consciousness* of them, an intentional *regarding-as-real.* Hume, lacking any such vocabulary (or perhaps spurning jargon), could express this only by having "recourse to every one's feeling" upon the occasion of "that *act of the mind*, which renders realities, or what is taken for such, more present to us than fictions, causes them to weigh more in the thought, and gives them a superior influence on the passions and imagination."[14] Human nature is such that when sensations and reflexions "*strike upon the mind*, and make their way into *our thought or consciousness*," we instinctively regard them as *actual presences*, as *there* (by contrast with unenlivened thoughts). It is this phenomenological quality in the regarding of something that renders even the dullest impression more "forcible and real" (*TApp*631) than the most finely delineated, powerfully evoked idea. It renders the fire we see raging before us more terrifying than a fire we merely infer in imagination from the sight of smoke filling the room. And it explains what renders the images of the madman so terrifying to him: his disordered nature permits some of his thoughts actually to attain the perfect verisimilitude – the degree of presence and reality – which, in the sane, only sensations and reflexions (passions, emotions, and desires) ever attain; he thus flees the mere thought of, say, a dragon, as if there were a dragon he was actually seeing. He has lost that vital function of human nature whereby thoughts are dampened (kept quiescent, wavering, and weak); and his images are able to impose themselves upon him with the same verisimilitude (fixity, steadfastness, strength, etc.) as actual sensation, and therewith, without ceasing to be thoughts, literally *become* impressions.

The interpretation of vivacity as verisimilitude will for some be sure to recall James' conception of belief, which (wittingly or not) may have been derived from Hume:

> In the case of acquiescence or belief, the object is not only apprehended by the mind, but is held to have reality. Belief is thus the mental state or function of cognizing reality ... In its inner nature, belief, or *the sense of reality*, is a sort of feeling more allied to the emotions than to anything else.[15]

Russell objected to this, querying: "Is mistaken belief cognizing of unreality? Is not the whole conception of 'existence' inapplicable to just the objects of which we are most certain, namely those given in present acquaintance? And are not imagined objects also 'something,' with a 'reality' of the kind appropriate to such objects?"[16] Whether or not these questions represent genuine difficulties for James, it seems to me that, where Hume's distinction between impressions and ideas is concerned, Russell completely misses the point. For, implicit in Hume's notion of vivacity, as I interpret it, is that the mere *presence* of a perception before consciousness does not suffice for us to *regard* it as real, *believe* in its real existence. The mere *presence before the mind* of a perception and the *belief* in its real existence are for him utterly distinct, and this seems to me no less true of our *regarding* sensations and reflexions as *impressions* than our believing in the real existence of something we merely *think* (for example, fire) because it comes to mind in connection with an impression (smoke filling the room) associated with it by constant conjunction (see *T*86ff.). Before there can be belief in the existence of *any* perception, consciousness must respond to it with the *feeling* that it is real ("the ... quality, call it firmness, or solidity, or force, or vivacity, with which the *mind reflects upon it*, and is *assur'd of its present existence*," *T*106 – emphasis mine). This feeling is grounded in human nature and reflects its constitution just as surely as our having sensations of color, texture, odor, etc., rather than other kinds. For, just as we might have had different senses or been so constituted as to respond to sound waves by perceiving colors and shapes, so, too, our natures might either not have equipped us with the feeling of verisimilitude (possibly having some other in its stead) or have keyed it to thoughts rather than sensations and reflexions. Evolution would undoubtedly have soon done away with creatures who gave their thoughts the same weight we give to our sensations and reflexions, and their sensations and reflexions that of perfect ideas. But the point remains: for Hume, human nature is such that thoughts, albeit objects of acquaintance like sensations and reflexion, fail to arouse in us the same pitch of vivacity (see also chapter 2-B). And it is thus that the latter first become the reality with which thoughts must then be brought into agreement lest they be "mistaken."[17]

Construing vivacity as verisimilitude enables us to understand why having only the categories "sensation," "reflexion," and "thought" would have been insufficient for Hume's purposes, and a further dichotomization of perceptions as "impressions" and "ideas" was necessary. For he had need of two axes of description: one to represent the qualities proper to *perceptions themselves*, such as those which demarcate sensations from thoughts and both alike from reflexions (or, more particularly: emotions from passions from desires; sounds from colors from odors; dream images from dream feelings from dream inferences; etc.); another to represent phenomenological qualities of our *consciousness* of perceptions like vivacity/verisimilitude or the ease felt in the customary transition of ideas.[18] For vivacity, as he construed it, must be able to vary independently of any and all changes in the perceptions themselves: thoughts, sensations, and reflexions may gain or lose vivacity/verisimilitude in any degree without thereby ceasing to *be* a thought or a sensation. Gains and losses of vivacity imply no change in our stock of perceptions – they merely alter the way we *regard* those we already have. Among other things, the ability of the vivacity of a perception to vary independently[19] enabled Hume to affirm a strict difference *in kind* between thoughts (memories, images, etc.) and sensations or reflexions *as perceptions*, and, at the same time, to treat the difference *in vivacity* between them as merely one of *degree*. In other words, without two axes of description for perceptions, he would have had no alternative but to assert that, when a thought gains in vivacity, it ceases to be a thought and becomes something intermediate between thought and sensation or reflexion (rather than simply a more verisimilar thought).[20] With vivacity an independent variable, however, a thought can be enlivened to the point where it *actually becomes* an impression (as in madness) *without thereby ceasing to be a thought*. Likewise, sensations and reflexions may be weakened to the point of *actually becoming* ideas without ceasing to be sensations or reflexions (as when "our impressions are so faint and low, that we cannot distinguish them from our ideas," *T*2: for example, the effects of a strong sedative or when lapsing into a coma). For, in both cases, only the *feeling* characteristic of our consciousness of the perception will have undergone any change. It is noteworthy, however, that, on either supposition, it is necessary to postulate some deformation of human nature. For the same nature that, in our present condition of wakefulness and health, determines us to regard some kinds of perception as more verisimilar than others, could, if changed, cause us to regard them in different, even opposite, lights (for example, our natures might have been such that we feared the *image* of a charging rhino but remained placid when having *sensation* of the beast).[21]

The principal presupposition of my interpretation of Hume's conception of vivacity as verisimilitude is that there are directly discernible qualitative distinctions between thoughts and sensations no less marked than those between visual and tactile sensation or between these and passions like love. Were this not the case, we could never distinguish between our present sensations and the thoughts we have concurrently with regard to them. For although, according to Hume, our thought of a sensation is in every way like the sensation ("a copy taken by the mind, which remains after the impression ceases" – *T*8), if there were nevertheless not *some* discernible difference in their appearance to the mind, we should just take them to *be* the same, and so accord them the same degree of vivacity (i.e. we would be unable to react to the one as an *impression* and the other as an *idea*). Thus, a phenomenologically based dichotomization of perceptions into impressions and ideas entails immediately discernible qualitative differences in the *appearance* of perceptions whereby to distinguish them as *sensations*, *reflexions*, or *thoughts*.[22] For example, I must be no less aware of the qualitative difference between a cube I imagine or dream and one I actually see, than of that between the cube I see and one I touch with my hand; nor can I mistake the thought-image of its red coloring for the red of the cube I actually see, however poor the lighting ("the most lively thought is still inferior to the dullest sensation" – *E*II.11). Or, again, though the visual experience of a cellar in near pitch black is incomparably less intense and detailed than a minute-old memory of a brilliantly lit ballroom, the quality of the former as *sensation* (its *vivacity* aside) remains unmistakable; and it is only as a consequence of this discernible difference in its appearance that the sensation can then be felt by consciousness in a more forceful (verisimilar) manner than the memory ("force ... is not to be measur'd by the apparent agitation of the mind," *TApp*631). Similarly, if dreams and hallucinations are in fact thoughts and not sensations, then they too should be recognizable as such by their appearance; hence, only a dysfunction or impairment of our faculties can induce us to conceive them with a pitch of vivacity approaching – or, in the madman's case, equalling – that of sensations (the assumption being that if one could summon up one's healthy, wakeful powers of discernment, one would react differently to what is, after all, in appearance, a mere thought: "All the operations of the mind depend in a great measure on its disposition, when it performs them; and according as the spirits are more or less elevated, and the attention more or less fix'd, the action will always have more or less vigour and vivacity," *T*98).

Ryle advanced what is perhaps the most trenchant criticism of Hume's distinction between impressions and ideas as heretofore interpreted, and may serve as an object lesson on the effect of neglecting the two axes of description in Hume:

> Hume notoriously thought that there exist both "impressions" and "ideas," that is, both sensations and images; and he looked in vain for a clear boundary between the two sorts of "perceptions." Ideas, he thought, tend to be fainter than impressions, and in their genesis they are later than impressions, since they are traces, copies or reproductions of impressions. Yet he recognised that impressions can be of any degree of faintness, and that though every idea is a copy, it does not arrive marked "copy" or "likeness," any more than impressions arise marked "original" or "sitter." So, on Hume's showing, simple inspection cannot decide whether a perception is an impression or an idea.[23]

Although failing to distinguish the appearance-axis (sensations/images) from the phenomenology axis (impressions/ideas), Ryle is quite right to say that impressions and ideas do not arrive marked "original" and "copy": this is the result of experience and association (see section E below). But I think it mistaken to infer from this that impressions cannot be distinguished from ideas by direct inspection: while inspection of the *perceptions themselves* cannot do so, inspection of the phenomenological feeling in our *consciousness* of them cannot fail to demarcate impressions from the ideas: the *feelings* in the two cases are as discernibly different as the sensations of blue and red differ in *appearance*. Hence, I disagree also with Ryle's contention that

> the crucial difference remains between what is heard in conversation and what is "heard" in day-dreams, between the snakes in the Zoo and the snakes "seen" by the dipsomaniac, between the study that I am in and the nursery in which "I might be now." His mistake was to suppose that "seeing" is a species of seeing, or that "perception" is the name of a genus of which there are two species, namely impressions and ghosts or echoes of impressions. There are not such ghosts, and if there were, they would merely be extra impressions; and they would belong to seeing, not to "seeing."

In cases like these, the need to distinguish two axes of description is critical: "seeing" and "hearing" designate thoughts, discernibly different in appearance from actual sensations of seeing and hearing; yet, in a dysfunctional mind, the former, without becoming *sensations*, may indeed become *impressions*, or the latter, without becoming *thoughts*, may indeed become *ideas*. Only in the absence of these distinctions would Hume be confronted by the dilemma Ryle so well described:

> Hume's attempt to distinguish between ideas and impressions by saying that the latter tend to be more lively than the former was one of two bad mistakes. Suppose, first, that "lively" means "vivid." A person may picture vividly, but he cannot see vividly. One "idea" may be more vivid than another "idea," but impressions cannot be described as vivid at all, just as one doll can be more lifelike than another, but a baby cannot be lifelike or unlifelike. To say that the difference between babies and dolls is that babies are more lifelike than dolls is an obvious absurdity. One actor may be more convincing than another actor; but a person who is not acting is neither convincing nor unconvincing, and cannot therefore be described as more convincing than an actor.

Ryle, restricting his consideration to only one axis of description, can see no alternative to supposing that certain *perceptions themselves* are somehow more lifelike than others. He overlooks the possibility that *we*, in accordance with human nature, *consciously regard* certain perceptions as more verisimilar than others even though all alike are *present* to the mind. That is, like Russell, Ryle left no place for a distinction between the mere *presence* of something before the mind (i.e. *appearance*) and our *sense* (feeling, belief) of its reality. He also neglected the possibility that Hume's main purpose in characterizing vivacity as a "feeling" was to distance his notion from the sense of belief as a propositional attitude (Ryle's sense). Rather, Hume had in mind a far more primitive kind of intentional stance, such as might plausibly occur in infants and animals (Ryle's analogies are all far too sophisticated to bear on so elementary a distinction as that between impressions and ideas).[24] So, if the vivacity of impressions is understood simply as the feeling constitutive of the attitude of verisimilitude we *naturally* adopt towards contents in sensation but not towards (qualitatively identical – save for their quality *as* thoughts) contents in imagination, Ryle's criticism is effectively neutralized.

So too the other horn of the dilemma:

> Alternatively, if Hume was using "vivid" to mean not "lifelike" but "intense," "acute" or "strong," then he was mistaken in the other direction; since, while sensations can be compared with other sensations as relatively intense, acute or strong, they cannot be so compared with images. When I fancy I am hearing a very loud noise, I am not really hearing either a loud or a faint noise; I am not having a mild auditory sensation, as I am not having an auditory sensation at all, though I am fancying that I am having an intense one. An imagined shriek is not ear-splitting, nor yet is it a soothing murmur, and an imagined shriek is neither louder nor fainter than a heard murmur. It neither drowns it nor is drowned by it.

Equipped with two axes of description, however, Hume has plenty of room to accommodate the qualitative difference *in kind* between sensing and thinking a sound, and the mere difference *in degree* between regarding the one as verisimilar in the highest degree (i.e. an impression) and the other as having less verisimilitude (if a memory) or nearly none at all (if a fiction). Thus, the interpretation advanced here, in which we carefully distinguish characteristics pertaining to the *appearance* of perceptions from those pertaining to our *consciousness* of them, not only has the strongest textual support, but also is most resistant to standard criticisms.[25]

So long as we recognize that their difference in vivacity relates not to the perceptions themselves but only to our consciousness of them, there is no difficulty explaining how ideas can be confounded with, or even become, impressions, and vice versa. The difference between impression-consciousness and idea-consciousness is as great, and immediately evident, as that between the appearance of scarlet red and royal blue. Under normal circumstances, the distinction between impression and idea and that between conviction and conception are separated by no less great an order of magnitude than that demarcating a difference of color from a mere difference in shade (of the same color). Indeed, rather than a difference of shade, it would be fairer to compare the difference between a belief and a perfect idea to a variation in the *brightness* of a single shade of color. For, according to Hume, "any colour may acquire a new degree of liveliness or brightness without any other variation. But when you produce any other variation, 'tis no longer the same shade or colour" (*T*96). The same holds true of an idea: it too can increase in vivacity all the way to an unshakable conviction and then diminish again to a mere conception; yet, no matter how much it may change in liveliness, it neither ceases to be the same idea it was at the outset, nor *a fortiori* does it cease being an idea and become an impression. A change capable of making it a different idea corresponds to a change in the *shade* of color; but nothing less than a change all the way from red to blue could equal the magnitude of change required to transform an idea into an impression (i.e. a qualitative change no less momentous than – *but not the same as* – one capable of converting a thought into a sensation or reflexion). For such a change is possible only in cases where human nature has been dramatically deformed or impaired (for example, when the madman treats thoughts as impressions he is like the victim of jaundice who sees all objects in various shades of yellow).[26] But this does nothing to negate or mitigate the stark, immediately evident difference between perceptions in the case of normal, fully functional individuals, which Hume denominated by the terms "impression" and "idea"; and with respect to such persons, if ever any difference among perceptions were tantamount to a difference in kind, it is surely the gulf in vivacity/verisimilitude between their impressions and corresponding ideas.[27]

It might be objected that to understand Hume as I suggest conflicts with his view that, in sympathy, "ideas become impressions." For, unless he meant merely that ideas are supplanted by exactly resembling impressions, this would be a case of the actual transformation of a mere *thought* (for example, of another's anger at an injustice inflicted upon him) into an actual *emotion* (one's own anger at the injustice). But surely this cannot be what he intended. It would wreak havoc with one of Hume's most fundamental principles (hereafter, *the separability principle*):

> We have observ'd, that whatever objects are different are distinguishable, and that whatever objects are distinguishable are separable by the thought and imagination. And we may here add, that these propositions are equally true in the *inverse*, and that whatever objects are separable are also distinguishable, and that whatever objects are distinguishable are also different. (*T* 18)

Aside from the thesis that all ideas are copied from impressions, there is no more important or frequently cited principle in Hume's account of human understanding than this.[28] Now, among other things, it implies that nothing can "run the several different perceptions into one, and make them lose their characters of distinction and difference, which are essential to them" (*T* 259). Since I obviously am able, in imagination, to *separate* the mere *contemplation* of anger from the actual *emotion* (*reflexion*), these have to be regarded as *distinct* perceptions. That is, unless Hume had been prepared to say that sympathy only *supplants* the idea of the emotion with an exactly resembling impression (i.e. the actual emotion), he would undermine the whole basis of the claim, axiomatic to his system, that an impression and its resembling idea are distinct perceptions (not merely distinct aspects of one and the same perception). This claim presupposes some prior, directly discernible difference between *thoughts*, on the one hand, and *sensations* and *reflexions*, on the other. Since Hume would surely not have countenanced an alchemy capable of transforming the one (thoughts) into the other (sensations/reflexions), he cannot have wished us to construe his claim concerning sympathy with undue literalism. By contrast, since the thought of the emotion as a perfect idea and the thought of the same emotion as, say, a memory, are both *thoughts*, here there is a genuine sense in which the one, as identical in content with the other, can be said to *become* the other.[29] But if vivacity were a feature of the perceptions themselves, on a par with the qualitative difference that demarcates a reflexion from a thought or a tactile sensation from a visual one, then the memory and the mere thought could not be identical in content. For them to be identical while both alike are distinct from the actual emotion, two separate axes of description are indispensable. The case of sympathy is therefore actually a confirmation of the interpretation offered here.

No one can deny that Hume's theory of consciousness is sketchy and obscure. He said so little in fact that one may suspect him of intentionally ignoring it (perhaps because description can only falsify feelings which, as immediate, convey their nature to us directly or not at all). Still, this much at least is certain: Hume deemed consciousness, including imagination, susceptible to feelings, most notably vivacity and facility (felt in the transition of thought from one perception to another associated with it). Vivacity, in particular, distinguishes what we deem actual both from what we regard as memory or inference (i.e. lively ideas) and what we regard as mere thought or fancy (minimal verisimilitude, "perfect ideas"). The difference lies not in the *violence* of the feeling, but only in its peculiar *quality*, its "flavor," as it were ("The force of our mental actions ... is not to be measur'd by the apparent agitation of the mind," *TApp*631; "the most lively thought is still inferior to the dullest sensation," *E*II.11). It is, therefore, in this qualitative, phenomenological sense alone that the differences in verisimilitude of our perceptions depend entirely on "the degrees of force and liveliness, with which [perceptions] strike upon the mind, and make their way into our thought or consciousness" (*T*1), "their feeling to the mind ... or manner of conception" (*TApp*629).

Yet, it is precisely here that the analogy of phenomenological feelings with what are ordinarily called "feelings" seems to break down. For, while I may well be a witness not only to sensations, but equally to imaginings, emotions, and so forth, can I ever be a witness to this *very witnessing itself* – and, *a fortiori*, the "feeling" of verisimilitude that attends or "colors" it? Can this feeling ever *itself* be perceived? If by "perception" we understand what Hume did – an object present to consciousness but distinct from it –

then clearly it is not a perception. Situated on the hither ("noetic") rather than the thither ("noemic") side of awareness, it is more like an attitude, or bearing towards a present content, than a content in its own right. But although it is neither itself a perception nor a quality of perceptions, it is sufficiently primitive in character (pertaining to infants and animals as to the rest of us) that words like "feeling" and "quality" are perhaps, in the end, the most appropriate. For Hume supposes us to be aware of the feeling of vivacity/verisimilitude simply in being aware at all; it is an original quality of our consciousness of perceptions exactly as yellow, red, blue, etc., are original qualities of visual perceptions (i.e. part of its "logical space"). No descriptive term could fully capture this, and too much weight should not be placed on any one; instead, we are "oblig'd to have recourse to every one's feeling, in order to give him a perfect notion of this operation of the mind ... which renders realities more present to us than fictions, causes them to weigh more in the thought, and gives them a superior influence on the passions and imagination" (*TApp*629; see chapter 5-E for further discussion).

C. Simplicity

In shifting from the topic of the vivacity of perceptions to their simplicity, we are moving from what may be known of them directly by the senses (immediate consciousness) to what requires imagination (though still only *sense-imagination*, i.e. an operation performable directly on immediately perceived data of sense without requiring repeated observation, custom, or inference of any kind). This is clear from the fact that simplicity is introduced by way of the separability principle (= what is distinct *in fact* is separable *in imagination*):

> Simple perceptions or impressions and ideas are such as admit of no distinction nor separation. The complex are the contrary to these, and may be distinguished into parts. Tho' a particular colour, taste, and smell are qualities all united together in this apple, 'tis easy to perceive they are not the same, but are at least distinguishable from each other. (*T*2) [W]hen we analyze our thoughts or ideas, however compounded or sublime, we always find that they resolve themselves into ... simple ideas. (*E*II.14)

Though an object of much criticism, the division of perceptions into simple and complex was common right into the present century. Yet, Hume's version of the distinction has often been singled out as especially naïve, ill-defined, and more than usually beholden to inconclusive examples.[30] This seems excessive; in my view, his is among the more nuanced and sophisticated attempts at such a distinction. Hume's *criterion* of simplicity, implicit in his separability principle, is a case in point: *if a perception cannot be separated into others or otherwise analyzed – or, in so far as it can, if these others cannot actually be represented singly and separately by the imagination – then that perception is simple.*[31] Hence, a sensation of color does not count as complex simply because its particular hue can be mentioned independently of its intensity; nor can a note sounded on a piano be deemed complex because its pitch can be referred to independently of its timbre. For neither hue and intensity nor pitch and timbre can occur in consciousness alone, without the other; it is impossible to *imagine* a hue without intensity or a pitch without timbre. Hume's criterion is clearly evident in the following:

'Tis certain that the mind wou'd never have dream'd of distinguishing a figure from the body figur'd, as being in reality neither distinguishable, nor different, nor separable; did it not observe, that even in this simplicity there might be contain'd many different resemblances and relations. Thus when a globe of white marble is presented, we receive only the impression of a white colour dispos'd in a certain form, nor are we able to separate and distinguish the colour from the form. But observing afterwards a globe of black marble and a cube of white, and comparing them with our former object, we find two separate resemblances, in what formerly seem'd, and really is, perfectly inseparable. After a little more practice of this kind, we begin to distinguish the figure from the colour by a *distinction of reason*; that is, we consider the figure and colour together, since they are in effect the same and undistinguishable; but still view them in different aspects, according to the resemblances, of which they are susceptible ... By this means we accompany our ideas with a kind of reflexion, of which custom renders us, in a great measure, insensible. (*T*25)

Distinguishing shape from color "by reason" is no guarantee of being able to eliminate it from the image itself; and if one cannot imagine the one in the absence of the other, then there can be no *real* distinguishability and difference (for perceptions are in every respect what they appear to be – see *T*190). That which can only be distinguished by a distinction of reason Hume terms *aspects*, by contrast with genuine (and thence distinct) *perceptions*. Confounding mere distinctions of reason with genuinely distinct perceptions was, in Hume's view, a major source of philosophical error and illusion (see chapter 3). His keen awareness of this risk led him to devise a very specific, well-defined notion of simplicity: all one has to do to decide of something whether it is a simple perception or a mere aspect is to ask oneself whether anything distinguished in it can be imagined to exist in consciousness on its own, separately and singly. Something that cannot potentially be the only content ever present to one (for example, "Suppose the mind to be reduc'd even below the life of an oyster," *TApp*634) is a mere aspect.

Nevertheless, Hume recognized that, in application, his criterion of simplicity is far from infallible. In theory, the only items genuinely to qualify as "simple and indivisible" (*T*27) are perceptible *minima*:

Put a spot of ink upon paper, fix your eye upon that spot, and retire to such a distance, that at last you lose sight of it; 'tis plain, that the moment before it vanish'd the image or impression was perfectly indivisible. 'Tis not for want of rays of light striking on our eyes, that the minute parts of distant bodies convey not any sensible impression; but because they are remov'd beyond that distance, at which their impressions were reduc'd to a *minimum*, and were incapable of any farther diminution. (*T*27)

One can extend this to all sensory fields (their temporal dimension included) and imagination as well: at the point just before a perception vanishes or the time becomes too brief for it to be remarked, one arrives at the simple, indivisible minimum of sound, touch, et al. However, in practice, we still have to contend with

the natural infirmity and unsteadiness both of our imagination and senses, when employ'd on such minute objects. Put a spot of ink upon paper, and retire to such a distance, that the spot becomes altogether invisible; you will find, that upon your return and nearer approach the spot first becomes visible by short intervals; and afterwards becomes always visible; and afterwards acquires only a new force in its colouring without augmenting its bulk; and afterwards, when it has encreas'd to such a degree as to be really extended, 'tis still difficult for the imagination to break it into its component parts because of the uneasiness it finds in the conception of such a minute object as a single point. This infirmity affects most of our reasonings on the present subject, and makes it almost impossible to answer in an intelligible manner, and in proper expressions, many questions which may arise concerning it. (*T*41f.)

When appearing only at intervals, the spot is so vague, unsteady, and ephemeral one can hardly even be sure it is there, much less discriminate its color; one might almost say it is colorless since, at this stage, it is wellnigh impossible to discern the difference between a red and a yellow spot, a green and a blue, etc. It is presumably only at the stage when the spot is *always* visible that one can do this; yet, even then, the color may still be so lacking in force as to render it impossible to distinguish red of such-and-such hue and intensity from red of another, or even red from orange or perhaps green. Certain features of visual sensation may still not become discernible until the spot has expanded into a colored region, divisible by the imagination: if not hue or intensity, then possibly such features as matte/gloss, smooth/protuberant, etc. Hume's remarks suggest that he was aware that there are aspects of perceptions that pertain only to complex perceptions, never to simple ones: aspects that may, therefore, be deemed simple (= irreducible) and original (= underived from anything which pertains to simple impressions), but which, nevertheless, are still only aspects, not perceptions in their own right, and thus fail to meet his criterion of a simple perception. Hence, although a person whose *entire* visual field, due to some infirmity, consisted of no more than a single, vaguely discernible minimum would find it impossible to reconstitute in imagination a significant portion of that with which we are visually familiar, there would still be no simple visual perception he could not have.[32]

The preceding should not be thought to cast doubt on the *existence* of minima; it simply raises a question as to their *utilizability* as elements from which to assemble the complexes we encounter in perceptual fields. The following remark concerning the equality of composite objects seems to me to apply with equal force to the analyzability of complex perceptions into simple ones (my substitution of "complexity" for "equality" is indicated by brackets):

> tho' this answer be *just*, as well as obvious; yet I may affirm, that this standard of [complexity] is entirely *useless*, and that it never is from such a comparison we determine objects to be [complex] or [simple] ... For as the points, which enter into the composition of any line or surface, whether perceiv'd by the sight or touch, are so minute and so confounded with each other, that 'tis utterly impossible for the mind to compute their number, such a computation will never afford us a standard, by which we may judge of proportions. (*T*45)

Hume's theoretical standard of simplicity, like that of equality, is often useless in application – true, but useless. For example, "The impressions of touch are simple impressions, except when consider'd with regard to their extension" (*T*230–31). Is our lack of an imagination able to split up the touch of a table beneath a finger into minimally perceptible extensions an argument against Hume's criterion? Hume would surely have acknowledged the infirmity of human imagination in this regard (which has no practical need for such fine discriminations of touch), and would probably have reminded us of something of which he was quite cognizant: in psychology, no criterion, however sound in theory, is ever exact or universal in application. The spot discerned with difficulty, true-but-useless standards, the missing shade of blue (*T*6), the acknowledgment that the "permanent, irresistable, and universal" (*T*225) principles of association are nevertheless "neither the *infallible* nor the *sole* causes of an union among ideas" (*T*92), and numerous other instances of this kind attest to this awareness, and indicate that Hume had a considerably more sophisticated appreciation of the difficulties posed by the introduction of the simple/complex dichotomy into a theory of perceptions than he is often given credit for.[33]

Given Hume's sober awareness of the limits of the inquiry in which he was engaged, the question still remains, whether these difficulties do not prevent him from using the simple/complex dichotomy for the purposes that led him to introduce it. He relied on it principally in order to retain a modified version of his claim that all ideas derive from antecedent impressions; for since some clearly do not (for example, the idea of the New Jerusalem – *T*3), he needed to show that such ideas are complex and can be analyzed into simple ideas that clearly do derive from impressions. To achieve this, did he have need of any very rigorous or universally applicable standard of simplicity? Perfection never being a prime concern of his, the modest psychological test of endeavoring to resolve a perception into parts that are themselves free-standing, separable, distinct perceptions – if yes complex, if no simple – seems quite practicable. If one retains any doubt that the parts originated from impressions and cannot have been dreamed up, then one need merely continue subdividing until one arrives at parts (disjunct colors, sounds, smells, etc.) whose derivation from impressions one does not doubt. I think it was Hume's belief that his readers could analyze their perceptions sufficiently far towards simplicity to be convinced of the basic empiricist tenet that the components of our images of sensations and reflexions are always (excepting odd cases like the missing shade of blue) copied from antecedent impressions. The only thing truly essential to this process is that one be careful not to confuse mere distinctions of reason with genuinely distinct elements of complex ideas. Hume's psychological notion of simplicity was fully adequate for his purposes, and the lack of a rigorous, exact method of reduction presents no insuperable obstacles to his procedure (see also chapter 3-C and -D).[34]

D. The resemblance between impressions and ideas

Having applied the simple/complex dichotomy to perceptions, Hume set out to discover the relations holding between impressions and ideas:

> The first circumstance, that strikes my eye, is the great resemblance betwixt our impressions and ideas in every other particular, except their degree of force and vivacity. The one seem to be in a manner the reflexion of the other; so that all the perceptions of the mind are double, and appear both as impressions and ideas. When I shut my eyes and think of my chamber, the ideas I form are exact representations of the impressions I felt; nor is there any circumstance of the one, which is not to be found in the other. In running over my other perceptions, I find still the same resemblance and representation. Ideas and impressions appear always to correspond. (*T*2f.)

Resemblance, as a relation holding *generally* of impressions and ideas, Hume forthwith restricted to simple ideas and impressions, with complex ideas dealt with as indicated above. It should however be noted that resemblance, though a relation of associative imagination, is a matter of immediate perception, not experience and custom (see *T*73). Hence, so long as the focus is restricted to resemblance, and until causality is factored in (i.e. the observed constant conjunction of impressions and their resembling ideas together with the recognition of the regular temporal priority of the former *vis à vis* the latter), it is impossible to say which – impression or idea – is the representation (copy) and which the original: this can only be found "by constant experience" (*T*5).

The natural question concerning the resemblance between impressions and ideas is whether, like simplicity, Hume's position is more nuanced and sophisticated than it initially appears. It certainly *needs* to be, since the problems it occasions are even more recalcitrant than those raised by simplicity. Resemblance is not a real relation between things as causality is; two things can seem resembling to us without actually being related (whereas objects related as cause and effect have a necessary connection, i.e. the existence of the one depends on that of the other). Any notion that there is something in perceptions themselves corresponding to the resemblances we find in them risks degenerating into absurdity, since virtually anything can be found to resemble anything else *in some respect.* Hume seems to have been aware of this. Resemblances must be present wherever comparison is possible: "no objects will admit of comparison, but what have some degree of resemblance" (*T*14); "'tis impossible to found a relation but on some common quality," (*T*236). Simple ideas too "admit of infinite resemblances upon the general appearance and comparison, without having any common circumstance the same" (*TApp*637). Even the only two genuinely contrary ideas – existence and non-existence – "are plainly resembling, as implying both of them an idea of the object" (*T*15). Since even the most disparate things admit of comparison in *some* respect (aspect), it follows that, in this sense, all things without exception resemble one another. Moreover, the problem is aggravated by the fact that, in one context or respect, I might find it natural to relate X and Y as resembling but not Z, whereas in another X and Z might immediately strike me as resembling while X never would come to mind (for example, let X = baseball bat, Y = baseball glove, and Z = a Louis XV commode; let one context be "baseball equipment" and the other "wooden artifacts"). So how are the problems of arbitrariness and context-dependence to be overcome? Why and how should the likeness between impressions and ideas be accorded a special significance (validity, reality) that sets it apart from all the other resemblances that might be found among perceptions? And which of the countless possible likenesses between impressions and ideas deserves to be assigned this special import?[35]

Since Hume seems never to have had occasion to address these questions directly, our task is to determine whether he could have done so if called upon. Now, in all probability, his response would have been to invoke the same distinction he used to such good effect in establishing criteria for simplicity and complexity: real distinctions among perceptions vs. mere distinctions of reason (aspects). For so long as we are concerned with aspects, we cannot fail to find *some* point of resemblance between any one thing and any other. But aspects are the result of comparisons repeated so often as to become habitual (see chapter 3-B); so, before it is possible to compare perceptions according to their aspects with an eye to their resemblances, we must first have found the perceptions themselves resembling. In other words, being blind at the outset to their aspects, we have no option but to set out by comparing perceptions, both simple or complex, with an eye to their resemblance as *wholes*; for, while imagination can separate the complex or combine the simple, it cannot immediately, without a history of comparing individual perceptions, discern their aspects. This narrows the range of possible resemblances dramatically, and does so at just the stage where discrimination of the resemblances between impressions and ideas in associative imagination must be supposed to take place: immediately subsequent to our having distinguished perceptions according to their appearance (as sensations, reflexions, and thoughts) and their phenomenological quality (as impressions and ideas).

Subject to the constraint that aspects be excluded from comparison we could not, for example, compare a sensation of a certain shade of red having a particular configuration to a tactile sensation (in virtue of their agreeing in *respect* of being sensations), to a like-configured sensation of blue (in *respect* of color), a differently configured sensation of red of the same shade, a similarly configured red of a different shade, or even a like-configured, like-shaded sensation of red of a different apparent size.[36] For all these comparisons involve distinctions of reason (aspects), and so presuppose both a history of comparison of (genuinely separate and so distinct) perceptions and the development of habits of association. The sensation in question, considered as a whole perception, can therefore be related by resemblance only to (i) another like-shaded, like-configured sensation of red, of the same apparent size, and (ii) its correspondent copy in thought (though surely so exacting a standard would be one Hume would have classified as true-but-useless, for our imaginations are rarely so scrupulous or heedful of minute differences).

How can perceptions so radically disparate in quality as a sensation and a thought partake of strict resemblance relations when sensations which differ from other sensations even in only a single respect cannot? Must we not have resort to distinctions of reason in order to find them resembling (i.e. ignore those *aspects* in which they differ so as to focus solely on those in which they agree)? To navigate these shoals, we need to discover what, for Hume, is the true (if perhaps useless) standard of resemblance. We can avoid searching vainly in the wrong place by recognizing at the outset that he neither affirmed nor needed any *objective* standard of resemblance or any other relation ("a relation ... is not, strictly speaking, a property in the figures themselves, but arises merely from the comparison, which the mind makes betwixt them," *T*46). Resemblance was important for him, first and foremost, as a *natural relation.* Natural relations do not hold between perceptions directly, but only in and for the consciousness (imagination) contemplating them. Natural relations entail phenomenological feeling of some kind – "some associating quality, by which one idea naturally introduces another ... nature in a manner pointing out to every one those simple ideas, which are most proper to be united into a complex one." (*T*10) The two principal feelings are, of course, an *easy transition* from one idea to another related to it ("our imagination runs easily from one idea to any other that *resembles* it, and ... this quality alone is to the fancy a sufficient bond and association," *T*11); and, under certain circumstances, a feeling of *vivacity* ("when of two objects connected together by any of these relations, one is immediately present to the memory or senses, not only the mind is convey'd to its co-relative by means of the associating principle; but likewise conceives it with an additional force and vigor," *T*107). Hence, just as the mere presence before the mind of a perception must not be mistaken for belief in its real existence, so too the *mere qualitative identity* between perceptions should not be mistaken for a *natural resemblance relation.* The presence or absence of qualitative identity would not interest us in the least – would not "weigh more in the thought" or have "a superior influence on the passions and imagination" (*TApp*629) – if human nature were not such that we directly respond to its presence with certain, quite specific feelings ("This easy transition is the effect, or rather essence of relation," *T*224). Moreover, since what Hume termed *philosophical relations* are "the effects of this union or association of ideas" (*T*13), and so effects of natural relations, philosophical resemblances too would cease to matter for us if the support of human nature were removed from them. Once stripped of its natural power to facilitate transitions of ideas or affect belief, resemblance – and the philosophical generality founded on it – would cease to have any bearing for us on matters of fact, and so could play no role in our inferences (see chapter 2-D). In sum, resemblances do not so much strike the *eye* (as said on *T*2) as the *mind* (the corrected formulation on *T*70); their true locus is *consciousness.*

As only gradually emerges over the course of the first book of the *Treatise*, there are three factors involved in resemblance relations: the perceptions themselves (sensations, reflexions, thoughts); their idea-copies associated by the imagination; and the feeling, or disposition of imagination, in contemplating these ideas. In the first instance, with only the single exception described on *T*283,[37] all association is a union of ideas in imagination:

[The question whether] we observe some real bond among ... perceptions, or only feel one among the ideas we form of them ... we might easily decide, if we wou'd recollect what has been already prov'd at large, that the understanding never observes any real connexion among objects, and that even the union of cause and effect, when strictly examin'd resolves itself into a customary association of ideas ... [There is only] the union of their ideas in the imagination, when we reflect upon them. Now the only qualities, which can give ideas an union in the imagination, are these three relations [resemblance, contiguity, and causation]. These are the uniting principles in the ideal world, and without them every distinct object is separable by the mind, and may be separately consider'd, and appears not to have any more connexion with any other object, than if disjoin'd by the greatest difference and remoteness ... [T]he very essence of these relations consists in their producing an easy transition of ideas. (*T*259–60; see also *TAbs*662)

Resemblance is a comparison of ideas; but the ultimate arbiter of the comparison is the feeling in the imagination contemplating them. Association concerns not the objects observed, but the imagination that does the observing; how *it* reacts, what *it* feels in the transition *it* makes, are, for Hume, what determines whether a relation of ideas exerts an influence on our thoughts and actions. So, being no less a matter of the operation of the mind than of the perceptions to which it is directed, resemblance exerts a twofold associative effect: "it ... not only causes an association of ideas, but also of dispositions, and makes us conceive the one idea by an act or operation of the mind, similar to that by which we conceive the other" (*T*203).[38] From this, one may infer that if, in the "act or operation" of contemplating one perception, the imagination did *not* feel anything which prompted it to recall the contemplating of another perception, then *those two perceptions themselves* would not be found resembling, regardless of their properties (congruity, etc.). Conversely, whatever disparity in qualities or relations two perceptions might have, they would be found resembling if the *action* of the mind in contemplating the one were felt by the imagination to resemble that in contemplating the other. In the particular case of sensations/reflexions and thoughts, it therefore would not matter that they are qualitatively disparate *if* it happened that *this particular disparity* did not eliminate or at least significantly mitigate the feeling of resemblance in respect of the actions of the mind in contemplating them. Since, in Hume's view, our psyches furnish ample testimony that such associations are the rule of our mental life virtually from the moment of its commencement, the contemplative actions in both cases must be for all intents and purposes indistinguishable to feeling. Moreover, since the ease felt in the transition from the idea of one action to the other is an immediate response to their qualitative identity, requiring no prior history of comparison, no distinctions of reason are entailed. This immediate instinctive brand of resemblance is therefore the first relation between impressions and ideas and the ground of all the others.[39]

E. Truth: impression-originals and idea-copies

If the resemblance between impressions and ideas is understood in the manner described above, we may begin to see why Hume attached such importance to it as a touchstone of *truth*. For, so long as resemblance is restricted to *whole* perceptions (as distinct from aspects), the resemblance between a thought and a sensation or reflexion must invariably be (felt as) a *perfect correspondence*. The very same operation by which the mind apprehends the impression in external or internal sense (sensation or reflexion) also serves for producing a perfect idea-copy in the qualitatively incommensurate medium of thought; hence, despite the disparity of their objects, the *consciousness* in the one case (sentience) maintains a complete and entire agreement with that in the other (memory, imagination, reason).

This by itself does not suffice to give us truth: it has still to be determined by *experience* which – the impression or the idea – is the representation and which the original. To do this:

> I consider the order of their *first appearance*; and find by constant experience, that the simple impressions always take the precedence of their correspondent ideas, but never appear in the contrary order ... The constant conjunction of our resembling perceptions, is a convincing proof, that the one are the causes of the other; and this priority of the impressions is an equal proof, that our impressions are the causes of our ideas, not our ideas of our impressions. (*T*5)

On this purely empirical basis – *and no other* – Hume determined that ideas are *representations* and impressions their *originals*. In no sense is it of the "essence" of ideas to be copies; on the contrary, Hume clad his thesis in the full panoply of an ordinary causal inference, to be understood, like any other, on the model of his general account of such inferences in *Treatise* I/iii: viz. a custom engendered by the observed constant precedence of perceptions. Hume was, in my view, a complete agnostic both as to *why* ideas and impressions occur in duplicate, and *why* the impressions invariably precede their correspondent ideas; it mattered to him only that they *do* ("their ultimate cause is, in my opinion, perfectly inexplicable by human reason ... Nor is such a question any way material to our purpose," *T*84) Even if these reasons were not unknowable, they would still be irrelevant to comprehending the bases of our *belief* that ideas represent impressions. This can only be understood by consulting *experience* and recognizing its effect on *imagination*: for, our nature being what it is, the *constant conjunction* of an idea preceded by an impression which it exactly resembles induces us to relate them, i.e. *believe* the idea to be the image in thought (copy, representation) of the impression. There is nothing "intrinsic" to ideas, nor any a priori structure discoverable by pure consciousness or intellectual intuition, that renders them representations by *metaphysical necessity*. To uphold the contrary is to suppose that thoughts are inherently dependent on sensations and reflexions, and so contradict Hume's iterated assertion that no perception depends on any other for its existence (see *T*207, *T*233, *T*244, *T*252, and *TApp*636).[40] Clearly, for him, *thoughts are not inherently representational, but stand originally on a par with sensations and reflexions as perceptions* (*objects of consciousness*). The necessary connection responsible for the representation relation arises in exactly the same manner in which we associate two converging billiard-balls: both alike are a matter of the union of ideas in imagination, and so of felt ease of transition and vivacity. Psychology supersedes logic, and considerations of a metaphysical character nowhere intrude (distinctions of reason, aspects, forms of representation, etc.).

To overlook the empirical origin and nature of Hume's concept of a representation is to misunderstand both his criteria for meaning and truth[41] and his standard of clarity and distinctness regarding both conception and reasoning:

> Since all impressions are clear and precise, the ideas, which are copy'd from them, must be of the same nature, and can never, but from our fault, contain any thing so dark and intricate. (*T*72; see also *T*75)

> Now since all ideas are deriv'd from impressions, and are nothing but copies and representations of them, whatever is true of the one must be acknowledg'd concerning the other. Impressions and ideas differ only in their strength and vivacity. The foregoing conclusion is not founded on any particular degree of vivacity. It cannot therefore be affected by any variation in that particular. An idea is a weaker impression; and as a strong impression must necessarily have a determinate quantity and quality, the case must be the same with its copy or representative. (*T*19)

> [W]henever any idea is ambiguous, [the author of the *Treatise*] has always recourse to the impression, which must render it clear and precise. And when he suspects that any philosophical term has no idea annexed to it (as is too common) he always asks *from what impression that pretended idea is derived*? And if no impression can be produced, he concludes that the term is altogether insignificant. (*TAbs*648f.; see also *E*II.17)

"All ideas are deriv'd from, and represent impressions" (*T*161); and, since they may represent or be applied only to that "from which they are deriv'd" (*T*37), we "can never go beyond these original perceptions" (*T*85); that is, the meaning and truth of our ideas is confined exclusively to the impressions they represent. There can never be an occasion where it is necessary to go *beyond* impressions to explain the meaning or truth of an idea. Nor could we avoid undermining the foundation on which truth itself rests were we to admit even so much as the *possibility* of an idea having application to anything other than an impression: *for the foundations of truth are empirical/causal.* This should not be forgotten, especially when seeking to ascertain his position on the applicability (i.e. sense, not truth) of ideas like that of cause and effect, external objects, substance, and the mind (including the mind posited by his own theory of ideas).

Yet, the frequency with which the experiential basis of the status of ideas as representation is overlooked or misunderstood by commentators is surprising. Flew, for example, finds it "scandalous" that Hume was willing to countenance exceptions to his general principle that simple ideas are copied from antecedent impressions, since "Any universal generalization is decisively falsified by even one single genuine counter-example."[42] The exception in question is the missing shade of blue:

> Suppose therefore a person to have enjoyed his sight for thirty years, and to have become perfectly well acquainted with colours of all kinds, excepting one particular shade of blue, for instance, which it never has been his fortune to meet with. Let all the different shades of that colour, except that single one, be plac'd before him, descending gradually from the deepest to the lightest; 'tis plain, that he will perceive a blank, where that shade is wanting, and will be sensible, that there is a greater distance in that place betwixt the contiguous colours, than in any other. Now I ask, whether 'tis possible for him, from his own imagination, to supply this deficiency, and raise up to himself the idea of that particular shade, tho' it had never been conveyed to him by his senses? I believe there are few but will be of opinion that he can; and this may serve as a proof, that the simple ideas are not always derived from the correspondent impressions; tho' the instance is so particular and singular, that 'tis scarce worth our observing, and does not merit that for it alone we should alter our general maxim. (*T*6; see also *E*II.16)

True to his empiricist credo and the experiential nature of the claim, Hume attached no greater warrant to the idea-as-copy thesis than that experience could supply. Far from giving any indication of wanting his reader to interpret the thesis as a "universal generalization," he could hardly have made its status as an inductive generalization clearer. Four times in the course of its proof on *T*4f. he refers to "constant conjunction" or "constant experience." The real question is whether a principle having this status is adequate for his purposes. Stroud thinks it is not. Although recognizing that Hume "puts forward his 'general maxim'... as a straightforward causal hypothesis ... to be taken as contingent, as something that might well have been, or might even be found to be, false," he finds that "Hume's rather cavalier attitude towards the exception is unsettling" because "it is difficult to see how far he would allow it to be generalized. Could ideas of a whole range of shades – in fact, all the shades of a certain colour – spring into the mind as a result of impressions of the other colours?"[43] Is Stroud justified in feeling unsettled? To describe Hume's maxim as contingent means that its certainty falls somewhere between "The sun will rise in the morning" and "The mail will arrive early." What makes the former as certain for us as "2+3 = 5" is that it has been confirmed innumerable times and there is not a single known exception; for the mere *conceivability* of its not happening – for example, the sun suddenly going dark – is not a sufficient basis for real doubt, in any degree. But is the same not true of Hume's principle as well? The case of the shade of blue is not a *known* exception, only a *conceivable* one; and since it is not the sort likely ever to occur to, much less influence, the vulgar, it can no more count against what is, after all, a thesis about vulgar understanding than any other recondite philosophical supposition. For against it stands the constant experience of our every waking moment: we can imagine only what we have previously seen or felt (i.e. simple ideas are always found to be preceded by exactly resembling simple impressions). His maxim therefore has a certainty *at least* the equal of "The sun will rise in the morning,"[44] and cannot be in any way diminished by the mere possibility of imagining exceptions.[45]

Hume distinguished two kinds of truth:

> Truth is of two kinds, consisting either in the discovery of the proportions of ideas, consider'd as such, or in the conformity of our ideas of objects to their real existence. (*T*448)

> Reason is the discovery of truth or falshood. Truth or falshood consists in an agreement or disagreement either to the *real* relations of ideas, or to *real* existence and matter of fact. Whatever, therefore, is not susceptible of this agreement or disagreement, is incapable of being true or false, and can never be an object of our reason. (*T*458)

The first species of truth comprises *intuition* and *demonstration* (notably mathematical proof); they are not founded on experience and no experience could ever refute them. By the same token, their application to reality is dependent on conditions of the second variety of truth, above all the natural associative relation of cause and effect, on which the relation of ideas to impressions as copies to originals is founded (i.e. our association-based belief that ideas are representations of impressions). For "real" must here be understood as "verisimilar;" hence, only an idea-enlivening relation whereby ideas, as copies, are connected to impression-originals can extend truths concerned with the former to the latter. Our belief that reality (the verisimilar world of the senses) is subject to the same laws our thought is therefore mediated by associative imagination (see chapter 4).

Even within the framework of immediate consciousness, there can be no *belief* in a relation of ideas without a feeling of vivacity; for while it may be impossible for us to *think* otherwise than, say, that $2+2 = 4$, this relation of ideas can only weigh in our thoughts and influence our actions if buttressed by verisimilitude ("the *real* relations of ideas"). If we consent to take Hume's theory of belief/vivacity at face value, as we should, it seems to me that we have no choice but to suppose that, for him, even the sort of certainty founded on immediate consciousness is, without exception, a matter of the vivacity of our conception. Take, for example, the infallible awareness exploited in the theory of ideas by philosophers before and after Hume:

> since all the actions and sensations of the mind are known to us by consciousness, they must necessarily appear in every particular what they are, and be what they appear. Every thing that enters the mind, being in *reality* a perception, 'tis impossible any thing shou'd to *feeling* appear different. This were to suppose, that even where we are most intimately conscious, we might be mistaken. (*T*190)

The infallibility of immediate consciousness described here is of particular importance since it concerns not only the relations of ideas but the nature, situations, and *relations* of all perceptions, impressions included. I see no reason to exempt it from Hume's general thesis that all belief is a matter of the vivacity of perceptions; nor do I see how one might reconcile such an exemption with the claim that "to feel an immediate impression of the senses" is to believe, and this belief is "nothing but the vivacity of those perceptions [the senses] present" (*T*86). Only by overlooking or annulling Hume's explication of the vivacity of impressions in terms of belief, and highhandedly restricting vivacity to ideas, can belief *qua* felt vivacity be excluded from immediate consciousness. The reasons against such a restriction are compelling (see introduction and section B above). There is no evidence whatever to suggest that Hume had a separate theory of belief for immediate consciousness; hence, the "assent" to which he refers in claiming that "our perceptions ... being immediately present to us by consciousness, command our strongest assent, and are the first foundation of all our conclusions" (*T*212) is no different in nature than the assent accompanying relations of identity or cause and effect. Despite the absence of explicit textual confirmation, we do Hume a service and almost certainly conform to his real wishes if we interpret the certainty pertaining to relations of ideas, and immediate consciousness generally, in accordance with a single general theory of belief as felt vivacity.

The second, experiential variety of truth is undoubtedly a more rickety and haphazard affair than the first: if the operation of delineating the thought "feels" the same to consciousness as that involved in apprehending the corresponding situations and relations of sensation or reflexion, then the thought will be regarded as true. This truth is simply a *felt* accord; and finding falsehood therefore amounts to nothing more than a lack of this feeling, or some other feeling of the wrong quality. Were Hume to be accused of ignoring the propositional nature of truth and of advancing highly subjective, inexact criteria of truth, he would probably have concurred wholeheartedly, and said in his defense that this is precisely what we should expect of a truth criterion whose sole and entire foundation is human nature. *Human* (like animalian) truth is not founded on some "pure and intellectual view, of which the superior faculties of the soul are alone capable" (*T*72); nor is it rooted in any a priori, crystalline-pure isomorphism between thoughts and sensations/reflexions. It is not even a relation between these *perceptions themselves* (i.e. ideas and impressions), but one that exists only in and for *consciousness* – that certain "je-ne-scai-quoi" *feeling* each sensation or reflexion occasions in its apprehension, and likewise each thought in the act of delineating its object. Such feelings (whereof we are usually, according to Hume, quite insensible, owing to settled habits) are literally *constitutive* of truth in all matters of fact. Apart from the associative propensities rooted in human nature, it simply would never occur to us to compare our thoughts and sensations/reflexions with an eye to their resemblance or representational correspondence; nor, *a fortiori*, would imagination have any impulse to direct itself so as to promote such correspondence. For, given the qualitative disparity between our thoughts and our sensations/reflexions, as well as the great gulf separating them in respect of verisimilitude, it is quite conceivable that our imaginations might lack the inclination to associate (connect, relate) them, leaving the senses and imagination to carry on independently of the other, the twain never meeting.[46]

Before leaving the subject of truth, it is important to remark that impressions have no truth, only ideas do. Hume made this point most explicitly about impressions of reflexion, but since his reason for deeming it impossible for the predicates "true" or "false" to apply to them is their status as *original* existents, it may be presumed to apply likewise to the no less original impressions of sensation:

> A passion is an original existence, or, if you will, modification of existence, and contains not any representative quality, which renders it a copy of any other existence or modification. (*T*415) Now 'tis evident our passions, volitions, and actions, are not susceptible of any such agreement or disagreement; being original facts and realities, compleat in themselves, and implying no reference to other passions, volitions, and actions. 'Tis impossible, therefore, they can be pronounced either true or false, and be either contrary or conformable to reason. (*T*458)

The basis of this "impossibility" is no doubt entirely empirical: since there are no perceptions which exactly resemble and constantly precede impressions, there is nothing in our experience to cause us to regard them as copies, or representations, of anything else. On the contrary, since experience shows them to be the originals of all other perceptions, nothing could be more opposed to our nature than the supposition that they are copies, or representations, of anything. It is thus experience which establishes that we "can never go beyond these original perceptions" (*T*85). This simply means that, as a matter of empirical fact, our perceptions occur in duplicate; and since the sensations and reflexions are found always to precede their likenesses in thought, the former are *naturally believed* to be the originals and the latter the copies. Had ideas been found constantly to precede the resembling impressions, we no doubt would have come to the opposite belief. Hence, what holds for causal relations generally presumably holds likewise of the original-copy relation:

> as no beings are ever present to the mind but perceptions; it follows that we may observe a conjunction or a relation of cause and effect between different perceptions, but can never observe it between perceptions and objects. 'Tis impossible, therefore, that from the existence of any of the qualities of the former, we can ever form any conclusion concerning the existence of the latter, or ever satisfy our reason in this particular.(*T*212) And I shall further add, that even tho' they cou'd afford such a conclusion, we shou'd never have any reason to infer, that our objects resemble our perceptions. (*T*216)

Since the supposition that impressions are representations can have no foundation in experience, it is incapable of rousing the slightest belief in us, and so can never be regarded as truth (notwithstanding protestations to the contrary – see chapter 7). To overstep the bounds of experience with our concepts of an original and its representation is therefore to deprive them of all meaning.[47]

2 Imagination and the vivacity of ideas

A. The originality of Hume's conception of imagination

Imagination is the focal point of Humean psychology. It is the seat of principles "which are permanent, irresistible, and universal ... the foundation of all our thoughts and actions, so that upon their removal human nature must immediately perish and go to ruin" (*T*225). Without imagination, there would be only "those perceptions, which are immediately present to our consciousness" (*T*265); there would be neither activity[1] nor connection,[2] no "compounding, transposing, augmenting, or diminishing the materials afforded us by the senses" (*E*II.13), and no idea could acquire the vivacity/verisimilitude of belief. If perceptions happened not "to strike upon the mind, and make their way into our thought or consciousness" *together*, there would be nothing that could unite them (nor, conversely, if they occurred together, could they be separated). Imagination is the bridge which alone enables us to pass from the self-less, object-less flux of disjointed perceptions and unvivified ideas of the senses (immediate consciousness) to the world of objective order and regularity, minds and bodies, and well-founded belief and inference. The imagination *is* our self, its pespective our *own* ("the present situation of the person is always that of the imagination," *T*430; see *T*261). The subjectless flux of perceptions before immediate consciousness is, by contrast, an alien world into which we cannot venture without literally leaving our selves behind. *Being* imaginations, we are no more free to abandon ourselves than to disbelieve in the existence of the material objects we see and touch; we are therefore condemned to remain almost wholly oblivious to the only reality ever present before us: fleeting appearances.

In this chapter, I will endeavor to (i) show that the preceding is an accurate portrait of Humean imagination, (ii) sketch in some of the details, and (iii) reckon with doubts to the contrary. But, assuming for the moment that it is accurate, one question likely to arise is whether immediate, pre-imaginative consciousness is not merely a figment of the philosopher's imagination. For the notion that the actual given of the senses is in fact a flux – random congeries of perceptions which neither refer nor relate beyond themselves – is, in the view of many philosophers, not a datum of unprejudiced observation, much less a belief as natural and irresistible as its contrary, but a mere rational construct. One has only to try to reproduce it in oneself to see the problem: perhaps, after considerable effort, one might momentarily succeed in convincing oneself that the only thing immediately present to one is, say, a sensation of grainy brown, not an actual table top. Even with the best will in the world, however, it does not seem possible to follow Hume in regarding the continued consciousness of this sensation as the result of a union in the imagination of a succession of distinct, momentarily existing qualitatively identical sensations (viz. Hume's fiction of perfect identity – see chapter 6-A); nor, still less, follow him in ascribing to imagination the feeling of vivacity through which alone the ideas thus united are "receiv'd as true pictures of past perceptions" (*T*265).[3] For this means that pre-imaginative consciousness is devoid of memory and so confined to the present instant (i.e. the temporal minimum of perception); and I, for one, am incapable of segmenting my consciousness in this manner, even in a thought experiment. So, one can only wonder how a consciousness we seem unable to detect even in ourselves can possibly be the basis of an empiricism such as Hume professed, much less a source of "perfect knowledge" (see chapters 1-E and 6-B). For, if it is so elusive as *always* and *invariably* to evade our grasp, does not that put even the most sympathetic reader of Hume in the position of having to feign having it? Would we not be doing him a greater service by explaining it away rather than defending it – perhaps even extending him the benefit of the doubt and sparing him the burden of so much subjectivist baggage (as Livingston, Baier, and many others advocate)?

The premise on which this work is based is that Hume should be taken at his word. Where his statements seem at cross purposes, we should give precedence to those texts in which the issue is addressed most directly and explicitly. For example, in order to decide whether Hume meant to affirm the mind-independent reality of causes, we should not rely on casual asides or passages in which references are made to such causes solely in order to state that they are not his present concern (such as *T*86), but look rather to those texts in which the task of determining the nature and scope of the idea of cause is Hume's declared order of business (see chapter 5-F). So too in the case of immediate consciousness. Even if Hume often drew his examples from the material world and common life, it does not mean that perceptions as given to immediate consciousness were not the true objects of his theorizing. This certainly is made clear enough when he actually came to examine external objects and mind (see Part III), and it is especially important to recognize when considering his theory of cause and effect (see chapter 4). Moreover, before we think twice about ascribing to Hume the affirmation of a pre-imaginative consciousness of a bare flux, it behooves us to reflect on what he would have us understand by it. It has no "object" in the sense of something it is possible to regard with the attitude of a spectator, to scrutinize, cast a reflective glance upon, etc. Locke's metaphor of reading our sensations as we read characters on a page (*ECHU* II/ix/§9) has no application to *immediate* consciousness. For characters may themselves become objects for us if we direct our attention to them, but the very notion of immediacy precludes the possibility of anything we might read *as* sensation, reflexion, or thought. Only in this sense may we legitimately be said to *perceive* perceptions: we must *first* have collected them together in consciousness in order *then* to read (imagine or judge) something through them – be it the characters on this page or passers-by outside the window. They are therefore not so much *before* our eyes as they are *our very eyes themselves* – the *medium* in which the objects of our attentive, directed gaze present themselves to us, the *materials* of which their appearance is composed. The objects of an immediate consciousness neither require nor are capable of being "perceived" in the ordinary sense of this term. As Locke explained in a passage which must surely have met with Hume's approval:

Because Sight ... conveying to our Minds the *Ideas* of Light and Colours, which are peculiar only to that Sense; and also the far different *Ideas* of Space, Figure, and Motion, the several varieties whereof change the appearances of its proper Object, *viz.* Light and Colours; we bring ourselves by use to judge of the one by the other. This in many cases, by a settled habit, in things whereof we have frequent experience, is performed so constantly, and so quick, that we take that for the Perception of our Sensation, which is an *Idea* formed by our Judgment; so that one, *viz.* that of Sensation, serves only to excite the other, and is scarce taken notice of it self; as a Man who reads or hears with attention and understanding, takes little notice of the Characters, or Sounds, but of the *Ideas*, that are excited in him by them. Nor need we wonder that this is done with so little notice, if we consider how *quick* the *actions of the Mind* are performed. For, as it self is thought to take up no space, to have no extension; so its actions seem to require no time, but many of them seem to be crouded into an Instant ... How frequently do we, in a day, cover our Eyes with our Eye-lids, without perceiving that we are at all in the dark? Men, that by custom, have got the use of a By-word, do almost in every sentence pronounce sounds which, though taken notice of by others, they themselves neither hear nor observe. And therefore it is not so strange, that our Mind should often change the *Idea* of its Sensation, into that of its Judgment, and make one serve only to excite the other, without our taking notice of it ... I ... leave with my Reader, as an occasion for him to consider, how much he may be beholding to experience, improvement, and acquired notions, where he thinks, he has not the least use of, or help from them. (*ECHU* II/ix/§§8–10)

It ought to be a byword of anyone seeking the key to gain entry to the thought of British empiricists: the actions of the mind no more occupy time than they do space. There can be no other way to discover them other than analytically and experimentally (introspection is, for all intents and purposes, useless). At first, when learning, we are halting and awkward in reasoning; but, long before we attain the mastery of our native tongue and acquire the capacity for reflective self-consideration, we have become masters of the sorts of judgment we then, through long practice and habit, mistake for perception. The latter, properly understood (i.e. stripped of the accretions of higher level reflexivities), is so primitive that, "from the Make of an *Oyster*, or *Cockle* ... I cannot but think, there is some small dull Perception, whereby they are distinguished from perfect Insensibility" (*ECHU* II/ix/§§13f.). So too, I believe, in the case of Hume: ordinary usage of "perception" can only mislead us when it comes to understanding what he meant by it, and we only make matters worse by struggling to make it an *object* of scrutiny in the manner of a sense-datumist or phenomenologist (see for example, *T*374f., *T*417, *E*I.8f.). Perception, as he understood it, is precisely that which can never be an object of our judgment because it is prior to all the effects of experience and training, and we only deceive ourselves if we believe we can "bracket out" the latter by means of any introspective, or quasi-introspective, technique. So long as we abstain from seeking to isolate perceptions and tag them with names drawn from the stock of a private language, there need be no fear of weaving the sort of mythology around immediate consciousness which invites the suspicion that empiricism has been supplanted by rational constructs. "Immediacy" then emerges as exactly what we should expect in the absence of all judgment, culture, language, even the attentive gaze: *the senses*, both internal and external, as purely receptive, unobjectifiable, inert, oblivious of both mind and world.

Traditionally, imagination has been defined in relation to the senses. It was as true for Hume as for Descartes before and Kant after him that imagination depends on the senses for the provision of its materials: "we shall find, upon a nearer examination, that it is confined within very narrow limits, and that all this creative power of the mind amounts to no more than the faculty of compounding, transposing, augmenting, or diminishing the materials afforded us by the senses and experience" (*E*II.13; see also *E*V/ii.39 and *TAbs*648). One ought never to overlook the fact that Hume's concern for resolving ideas not copied from impressions of sense into products of imagination almost surely derived from its anti-innatist implications, undermining any claim that we have in our possession a *literally* creative power, a source of ideas *ex nihilo*. This certainly is how we should understand Hume's assertion at the end of

Treatise I, that "The memory, senses, and understanding are, therefore, all of them founded on the imagination, or the vivacity of our ideas" (*T*265). For, having by that time established that ideas previously thought to arise independently of imagination are in fact founded on it, Hume could invoke its non-creative character as a basis for claiming that everything present in our thought is in fact nothing more than congeries of sensations, reflexions, and/or copies of these in thought, combined and organized in imagination.

But it was not simply to propound a sounder, more sophisticated proof strategy than had been employed by Locke and others against innatism that prompted Hume radically to recast the relation between imagination and the other faculties. The conception of "imagination, or the vivacity of our ideas," (*T*265) on which so much of his theory of understanding is based, requires a reference to pre-imaginative original sensory consciousness by which to orient its idea-enlivening activity. It is only because consciousness, in its *pre-imaginative* receptivity, naturally regards sensations and reflexions as impressions, and thoughts as mere ideas, that associative imagination instinctively inclines to enliven ideas which stand in associative relation to sensations and reflexions. An idea lacking any association with an impression is regarded with indifference rather than belief – a "mere" thought, weighing little, if at all, in our reasonings and actions. Take, for example, the relation of identity: human nature predisposes the imagination to identify successive resembling *sensations*, even if their perception is interrupted, and so fancy itself an observer of really existing, continued and distinct objects, but does not do so in the case of successive resembling fancies (interrupted or not).[4] Unless linked to sensations by a causal relation which makes us believe in their present reality (for example, the *thought* of fire that comes to mind when we *see* smoke pouring through the door of the room), it would be literally *unnatural* to identify a series of resembling thoughts: having no "life" (verisimilitude) of their own as impressions to command the assent and orient the activity of imagination, we are content to leave them be in the wavering, gappy manner in which they actually appear (and this would remain true even if they exhibited the properties of constancy and coherence). The same is true of the relation of cause and effect, whether imputed to external objects or, as in volition and personal identity, to perceptions themselves: since only that to which reality is ascribed can be regarded in imagination as a bearer of efficacy, impressions alone can stand in relations of cause and effect, or ideas in so far as an associated impression (of sense, volition, etc.) induces us to regard the idea as real as well; otherwise, the imagination cannot but regard a thought as an idea, without real existence, and thence as inert. So, too, contiguity: we do not hesitate to situate an aspatial *sensation* like the taste of a fig in the spatial (i.e. visual and/or tactile) fig itself (see *T*236), whereas it would never occur to us to externalize the thought-copy of this sensation (save insofar as thoughts are events of internal sense, and so are situated in the brain – but they are not naturally situated "in" the brain as the flavor of an apple is vulgarly believed to be "in" the fruit; thoughts, vulgarly, have no "natural" place). And resemblance is again no exception, as the case of memory shows: only by virtue of their exact resemblance to and causal dependence on prior impressions are ideas "ever receiv'd as true pictures of past perceptions" (*T*265; see *T*4f.), that is, beneficiaries of a belief that fancies, lacking association with impression-originals, are denied.[5] Thus, the presupposition by imagination of sensory immediacy has a quite special character and significance in Hume's theory of ideas that it lacks in any preceding: not confined solely to an oyster-like passive reception of perceptions, the vivacity-feeling native to immediate consciousness bequeathes to imagination the realities (impressions) towards which all its idea-enlivening activity is directed and, in the absence of which, it would be rendered impotent ("reality-blind").

B. The metamorphoses of imagination: memory

It should come as no surprise that Hume described imagination in disparate, sometimes incompatible ways, depending on whether he was considering it from the standpoint of immediate consciousness or that of experience. Matters are further complicated by the fact that he deemed imagination the source of the very experience and modes of reasoning by means of which he proposed to understand its operations (see Part II). But the greatest difficulty facing us is posed by the various metamorphoses undergone by imagination over the course of *Treatise* I, so that what is initially a marginal faculty conventionally conceived becomes, by the end, the foundation of all our knowledge.

In examining Hume's theory of imagination, let us take as our guide his assertion that "The memory, senses, and understanding are, therefore, all of them founded on the imagination, or the vivacity of our ideas" (*T*265). I shall begin with memory because it was in connection with it that Hume first introduced imagination into his system:

> We find by experience, that when any impression has been present with the mind, it again makes its appearance there as an idea; and this it may do after two different ways: either when in its new appearance it retains a considerable degree of its first vivacity, and is somewhat intermediate betwixt an impression and an idea; or when it intirely loses that vivacity, and is a perfect idea. The faculty, by which we repeat our impressions in the first manner, is called the MEMORY, and the other the IMAGINATION. (*T*8f.)

Here, in stark contrast with the meaning it later acquires, imagination is the faculty of *unenlivened* ideas, devoid of all verisimilitude. Moreover, since a difference in vivacity is "a sensible difference betwixt one species of ideas and another" (*T*9), its distinction from memory in particular cases seems to bear the imprimatur of immediate consciousness (only the general thesis do "We find by experience"). So, what is it that eventually led Hume to supplant his initial notion with that of "imagination, or the vivacity of our ideas"?

Perhaps a clue may be gleaned from Hume's second point of contrast between imagination and memory in *Treatise* I/i/§3:

> There is another difference betwixt these two kinds of ideas, which is no less evident, namely that tho' neither the ideas of the memory nor imagination, neither the lively nor faint ideas can make their appearance in the mind, unless their correspondent impressions have gone before to prepare the way for them, yet the imagination is not restrain'd to the same order and form with the original impressions; while the memory is in a manner ty'd down in that respect, without any power of variation ... The chief exercise of the memory is not to preserve the simple ideas, but their order and position ... Where-ever the imagination perceives a difference among ideas, it can easily produce a separation. (*T*9f.)

If Hume's first contrast between memory and imagination seemed to favor the former, the second is clearly to the benefit of the latter. Imagination alone can depart from the original order and form of impressions, and separate conjoined ideas or combine separated ones. It would be difficult to overstate the importance for Hume's philosophy of this power of separation and combination. I have already remarked on the importance of the separability principle to Hume's analysis of understanding (see chapter 1-B). But what of the separability and combination of *impressions*? Having no power to separate or combine impressions in sensation or reflexion, our only means of distinguishing simple impressions from complex ones, or, in general, of recognizing any impression as distinct from any other, is by distinguishing in *thought* (imagination) the ideas copied from them. For the flux of impressions is in itself seamless; its contents are distinct only *in* and *for* the imagination which separates them (albeit "in idea" only). Only the experiential principle that ideas are exact copies of previous perceptions can warrant the extension of the separability principle from ideas in thought to impressions in sensation and reflexion, and so give it a validity with respect to *all* of our perceptions (the same is true of relations of ideas – see section D below and chapter 4-C).

Yet, Hume eventually abandoned this second way of distinguishing the ideas of imagination and memory:

> When we search for the characteristic, which distinguishes the *memory* from the imagination, we must immediately perceive, that it cannot lie in the simple ideas it

presents to us; since both these faculties borrow their simple ideas from the impressions, and can never go beyond these original perceptions. These faculties are as little distinguish'd from each other by the arrangement of their complex ideas. For tho' it be a peculiar property of the memory to preserve the original order and position of its ideas, while the imagination transposes and changes them, as it pleases; yet this difference is not sufficient to distinguish them in their operation, or make us know the one from the other; it being impossible to recal the past impressions, in order to compare them with our present ideas, and see whether their arrangement be exactly similar. Since therefore the memory is known, neither by the order of its *complex* ideas, nor the nature of its *simple* ones; it follows, that the difference betwixt it and the imagination lies in its superior force and vivacity. (*T*85)

Clearly, Hume's "Attempt to introduce the experimental method of reasoning into moral subjects" (*Treatise* subtitle) involves at least the appearance of a proceeding by trial and error, so that conclusions the reader supposes to be final turn out to need revising or even to be discarded in the light of subsequent findings.[6] The first hint that vivacity too fails adequately to differentiate between memory and imagination occurs in Hume's analysis of belief. He distinguishes memory-based belief from that founded on imagination in the following manner:

it appears, that the *belief* or *assent*, which always attends the memory and senses, is nothing but the vivacity of those perceptions they present; and that this alone distinguishes them from the imagination. To believe is in this case to feel an immediate impression of the senses, or a repetition of that impression in the memory. 'Tis merely the force and liveliness of the perception, which constitutes the first act of the judgment, and lays the foundation of that reasoning, which we build upon it, when we trace the relation of cause and effect. (*T*86)

At this juncture, the species of belief "which attends the memory" has yet to be ascribed to imagination. The idea-enlivening powers of imagination first come to the fore in Hume's account of belief in connection with the three associative relations. They figure here not because they carve out the grooves along which our thought most readily travels; other relations too, whether native to our minds or acquired through education, are capable of ingraining habits no less firmly (see *T*115ff.). What singles them out from all others is their unrivalled power to *enliven* ideas. When an idea is associated with an impression by one of these relations, it is imbued with a verisimilitude sufficient to "approach an impression in force and vivacity ... and bestow on it a like influence on the passions" (*T*119);[7] and since ideas can enter into these relations irrespective of the order and position of their original impressions, it was necessarily to imagination, not memory, that Hume attributed the associative power to enliven ideas.[8]

The implication is that the two features by which Hume originally distinguished ideas of memory from ideas of imagination on *T*9 are clearly incompatible: if imagination, construed as the power to depart from the order and form of impressions, can sometimes yield ideas just as vivacious as those of memory, then superior vivacity alone is not an adequate standard by which to distinguish the memory from imagination. Hence, the conception of imagination as a means of bestowing verisimilitude upon ideas developed in *Treatise* I/iii precludes the possibility of *any* sensible (immediate, non-experiential) criterion to distinguish the ideas of memory and imagination. This left Hume only two alternatives: he could either look beyond consciousness to *experience* for some new mark by which to distinguish them, or he could *deny the difference altogether* and argue that the one sort of idea is actually only a species of the other. Why the first option is unworkable can perhaps best be seen by reflecting on the limits to which scientific investigation of such matters is subject. In order to determine the relevant differences in the central nervous system between, say, vision and olfaction, researchers are dependent on the testimony of consciousness, that is, on their subjects' immediate awareness of the contents of both sensory fields and their native ability to distinguish them (were they unable to do this, scientists would have no phenomenon to investigate). So too with ideas of memory and imagination: if one could not *already* discriminate them immediately, by the testimony of consciousness, there would be nothing for which to seek *experiential* criteria. It is this that makes physiological investigation of the psychological so treacherous an undertaking: differentiating modes of consciousness such as memory and imagination by ostensibly objective, rigorous procedures is always, in the end, hostage to subjective testimony and the quicksands of introspection. Hume therefore had no option but to subordinate memory, as species, to imagination, so that the difference between recollection and conception becomes one of enlivened and unenlivened ideas of one and the same faculty.[9]

As it happens, one can pinpoint the metamorphosis of memory into imagination with a high degree of certainty since there is only one extended discussion of memory in the sections immediately subsequent to *Treatise* I/iii/§5, where Hume says, for the last time, that vivacity alone suffices to distinguish memory from imagination: *T*105f. This text is prefaced with the remark "that 'tis very difficult to talk of the operations of the mind with perfect propriety and exactness; because common language has seldom made any very nice distinctions among them, but has generally call'd by the same term all such as nearly resemble each other." Hume's concern is "a little ambiguity in those words *strong and lively*" as applied to belief which might seem to leave him open to an objection. What commonly is confounded, but which his own theory requires be kept scrupulously apart, is the *presence* of an idea and its *verisimilitude*. When a thought appears before the mind, it is just as clear and distinct as a sensation or reflexion: its entire contents are laid bare, nothing is hidden. Yet, it is one thing for a thought to be present to consciousness and quite another to *believe* in its *real existence* before the mind. Before it can be "consider'd ... as a real perception in the mind," it must be imbued with the requisite degree of verisimilitude, that "quality, call it *firmness, or solidity, or force, or vivacity*, with which the mind reflects upon it, and is assur'd of its present existence." The implication of this for memory, which Hume believes must be treated "upon the same principles," is that no idea can represent a *past* existence until it is enlivened; and since vivacity is a feature not of perceptions themselves but of our consciousness of them, "In thinking of our past thoughts we not only delineate out the objects, of which we were thinking, but also conceive the action of the mind in the meditation, that certain *je-ne-scai-quoi*, of which 'tis impossible to give any definition or description, but which every one sufficiently understands." Memory involves not only the idea itself, but also an idea of the mind's contemplation of it. For the difference between the recollection of a past perceiving and a past fantasizing lies solely in the idea of the *consciousness* attending each: if it has the "vigour and firmness" characteristic of perceiving a content in sensation or reflexion, the idea will *now* be regarded as a memory; but if the consciousness has the weak and wavering feel of contemplating a content in thought, it will be regarded merely as an idea of a past fantasizing.

Hume's account of memory almost certainly derives from Locke: "Memory, signifies no more than this, that the Mind has a Power, in many cases, to revive Perceptions, which it has once had, with this additional Perception annexed to them, that it has had them before" (*ECHU* II/x/§2). The additional perception Locke had in mind appears to be a retention of *the mind's past contemplation* of the recollected idea.[10] Hume's account is identical save for one element, which serves to make good a notable shortcoming in Locke's theory. For what is the difference between recalling a past fancy and recalling a past sensation when both alike, *in recollection*, are merely thoughts, and it is "impossible to recal the past impressions, in order to compare them with our present ideas, and see whether their arrangement be exactly similar" (*T*85)? One possible answer is that the actions of the mind in the two cases are discerned to be different so that, in recollecting these actions, we can directly read off which was the actual perceiving and which the imagining. Yet, this solution carries too high a price: scrutinizing each recollected idea with the aim of discerning the particular mental act attending it conflicts with Locke's insistence, echoed by Hume after him, that habits deeply ingrained from our infancy render us insensible to the actions of the mind, so that we regularly mistake higher intellectual activity for lower (see section A above). The second possibility is that endorsed by Hume: in recalling the action of the mind, we recall with it the accompanying feeling of vivacity/verisimilitude, and can therefore immediately read off, from the recollected feeling, the difference in having contemplated a sensation/reflexion or a thought. No minute discriminations of thought processes are requisite, merely the noticing of the phenomenological feeling.[11]

Direct inspection of the idea presently before our minds (i.e. the memory of our feeling in contemplating the perception) reveals whether the recollected perception was an impression (sensation or reflexion), a lively idea (as in causal inference), or a mere fancy (conception). We simply consult the *phenomenological* quality of our idea of "the action of the mind in the meditation" and observe the degree of verisimilitude characterizing it to determine which sort of perception the mind had formerly been meditating upon (just as we consult features of the appearance of the idea of that meditated upon to determine that the recollected day was sunny, the fantasy island was girded with palms, etc.). Factors like coherence do not enter in at all; indeed, by Hume's criterion, one could straightaway distinguish, presently or in memory, the most coherent of dreams – even a Rip van Winkle affair of twenty years duration – from the most kaleidoscopic of appearances before the senses. As he viewed it, memory is distinguished from fantasizing solely by its associative relation to sensation or reflexion, and this we must be able to determine well before objectifying relations like cause and effect, identity, etc., extend our purview beyond the memory and senses and introduce coherence into mental life (see chapter 4-A). Even if the remembered object has grown fuzzy, dim, and detached from its context, so long as the idea of the consciousness accompanying it includes enough detail to discern its feeling of vivacity, it will still be treated as a memory: "'tis no objection to the present doctrine, that we can reason upon our past conclusions or principles, without having recourse to those impressions, from which they first arose. For even supposing these impressions shou'd be entirely effac'd from the memory, the conviction they produc'd may still remain" (*T*84). By contrast, no matter how clear and finely detailed the recollection of the object, if all traces of the vivacity should vanish from our idea of the action of the mind in the meditation, then, even if the object was sensed only an instant previously, its idea-copy would not be deemed a memory. So, while not yet the whole story of Hume's view on memory, this should suffice to show that, *pace* certain critics,[12] it was not without warrant that he declared, "After this any one will understand how we may form the idea of an impression and of an idea" (*T*106).

At this juncture, an objection is likely to arise in connection with the identification of force and vivacity with verisimilitude: since the thought I am having now is regarded as *real thinking*, must it not too have a full degree of verisimilitude? But if so, should it count not as an idea but as an impression? In other words, if the identification with verisimilitude is correct, we should expect Hume to treat everything of which we are immediately conscious, thoughts included, as realities in the fullest sense, and thence as impressions. A clue to how he solved this puzzle may be gleaned from his other remark on memory on *T*105–6:

suppose I form at present an idea, of which I have forgot the correspondent impression, I am able to conclude from this idea, that such an impression did once exist; and as this conclusion is attended with belief, it may be ask'd, from whence are the qualities of force and vivacity deriv'd, which constitute this belief? And to this I answer very readily, *from the present idea.* For as this idea is not here consider'd, as the representation of any absent object, but as a real perception in the mind, of which we are intimately conscious, it must be able to bestow on whatever is related to it the same quality, call it *firmness, or solidity, or force, or vivacity,* with which the mind reflects upon it, and is assur'd of its present existence. The idea here supplies the place of an impression, and is entirely the same, so far as regards our present purpose. (*T*105f.)

That the idea is said only to *supply the place* of an impression and not to *be* one, and to be the same as an impression only "as regards the present purpose," suggests that, for Hume, a *thought* can never be anything to one of sound mind other than an *idea*, however much *like* an impression it may be in respect of its influence on the imagination.[13] More precisely, Hume's concern is to explain why we *believe* an impression to have preceded an idea currently in our possession even if we have no recollection of the impression. The answer, in part, is obvious since Hume here invokes his "principle, that all our ideas are deriv'd from correspondent impressions." This principle rests on a habit more deeply ingrained than any other, since from our earliest moment, and every moment since, we have, according to Hume, witnessed the constant conjunction of impressions with resembling ideas. With its uniquely high frequency and the complete absence of counterexamples (once the simple/complex dichotomy is taken into account), the causal relation yielded by this constant conjunction produces a belief so strong that, without a moment's hesitation, we ascribe an origin in sensation or reflexion to every thought.[14] But what if we have no recollection of having encountered it in sensation or reflexion? The answer, one would assume, is that we would still unthinkingly refer it to a forgotten impression and that would be that. But this is incorrect. The mere presence of a thought before consciousness is not sufficient to trigger the custom: before we can feel a need to refer a thing to a cause, we must first believe it to really exist (for causes are invoked only to explain existents). The idea can trigger the custom only after it has been imbued with that "quality, call it *firmness, or solidity, or force, or vivacity*, with which the mind reflects upon it, and is assur'd of its present existence," whereby alone it can be "consider'd ... as a real perception in the mind." This, however, is not to say that the thought has to be enlivened to the point of becoming an actual *impression*. For, while it must acquire a verisimilitude sufficient to trigger any relevant customs, it does not require the maximal verisimilitude of an impression simply in order to be considered a real perception in the mind. Human nature is such that pre-imaginative consciousness imbues thoughts with an inferior degree of vivacity to that with which it favors sensations and reflexions, but does not deny them vivacity altogether. Were our nature such that we lacked this feeling, all perceptions would be on a par, and would lack the reality even of a perception of the mind (we would be reality-blind, as those who saw only undifferentiated white light would be visually blind). Or if we were so constituted as to regard our thoughts with the maximal verisimilitude of impressions instead of our sensations and reflexions, then thoughts would be the prime beneficiaries of our belief and concern. But, constituted as we are, all perceptions are received by consciousness with the verisimilitude of real perceptions of the mind (i.e. real presences), and only some with that of realities in the fullest, *non plus ultra* sense of impressions. Our thoughts, lacking this *n*th degree of vivacity, consequently have a far weaker claim on our assent and an inferior grade of reality (the sole exceptions are thoughts conjoined to sensations or reflexions in associative imagination, especially by relations of cause and effect). Accordingly, an idea unattended by an idea of a past contempation of a sensation or reflection still carries the verisimilitude of a real perception of the mind; and this enables it to trigger the habit which refers it back to an impression-original, giving it the status of a memory (again with the caveat that if not the idea itself then its simpler constituents are subject to the custom).

For a faculty to be said to be founded on imagination it must be shown to depend on one or more of the natural relations of associative imagination: resemblance, contiguity, and cause and effect. Having examined Hume's theory of memory in considerable detail, it should not now be difficult to see that memory is dependent on all three. True memory, by contrast with mere retention, involves representing something *as* past, that is, as an image of something that *actually* occurred (as distinct from merely *fancying* that it *might* have occurred).[15] Its dependence on resemblance is evident: "For what is the memory but a faculty, by which we raise up the images of past perceptions? And ... an image necessarily resembles its object" (*T*260). An idea (or, rather, the contemplation thereof) not felt by imagination to resemble any (the contemplating of an) impression would, *ipso facto*, not be regarded as a memory. Hence, without "imagination, or the vivacity of our ideas," "those lively images, with which the memory presents us" could never be "receiv'd as true pictures of past perceptions" (*T*265).

The dependence of memory on cause and effect is no less evident, for we consider an idea a memory not merely because it resembles something that actually existed or occurred, but because it derives from it, is copied from it, and so depends upon it.[16] Temporal contiguity, however, poses a variety of problems. Present impressions are believed to be more closely related to ideas of perceptions immediately preceding than to those distant in time (one does not refer something happening now *directly* to a cause years in the past, without a chain of intervening causes to connect them). But what accounts for our disposition to respect the time order of perceptions in associating them and biases the imagination in its relation of ideas in favor of more recent predecessors? Moreover, since it is impossible to recall past perceptions themselves for purposes of comparison, how is the imagination able to determine which of its memories are remote and which proximate in the first place? Finally, ideas, including those of past actions of the mind, do not wear their pastness on their sleeves; temporality is not an immediately discernible feature like shape. So, how does the imagination determine which among its lively ideas are memories (i.e. representations of the past as past) and which representations of present existents lying beyond the purview of the senses (the cake baking in the oven recalled to mind by a burning smell)?

Temporal contiguity is a relation of ideas, and so not something given that appears but an affair strictly of the imagination. Since there can be no relation of ideas except via feelings of easy transition and vivacity in imagination, it follows that, if the imagination were constituted differently, and temporal contiguity failed to inspire these feelings, its appearance would pass totally unremarked and not in any way affect our reasoning or actions (see section D). So, idea-enlivening imagination, and it alone, is responsible for arranging perceptions in a temporal sequence. It is an ongoing activity of which we are scarcely conscious,[17] but which, for Hume, is fundamental not only to memory, but also to our time-sense in general (see section C). This, however, is merely the precondition for our sense of, and respect for, the *order* of time in all our judgments. The focal point of all time-consciousness is the idea of the self (itself a product of idea-enlivening imagination – see *T*259ff.):

> There is an easy reason, why every thing contiguous to us, either in space or time, shou'd be conceiv'd with a peculiar force and vivacity, and excel every other object, in its influence on the imagination. Ourself is intimately present to us, and whatever is related to self must partake of that quality ... 'Tis obvious, that the imagination can never totally forget the points of space and time, in which we are existent; but

receives such frequent advertisements of them from the passions and senses, that however it may turn its attention to foreign and remote objects, it is necessitated every moment to reflect on the present ... Here then we are to consider two kinds of objects, the contiguous and remote; of which the former, by means of their relation to ourselves, approach an impression in force and vivacity. (*T*427f.)

Since "the present situation of the person is always that of the imagination" (*T*430), temporal ordering, like all other natural associations of ideas, is oriented in relation to that which, for imagination, is most real of all: present impressions. Since associative relations convey the vivacity of impressions to related ideas (see *T*10, *T*107, and *T*109), it follows that the more closely an idea is related to an impression by contiguity, the greater its share of vivacity; in consequence, our thought is more likely, *ceteris paribus*, to proceed to (and be influenced by) an idea the more temporally contiguous it is to present impressions ("Contiguous objects must have an influence much superior to the distant and remote," *T*428). The graduated diminishing of vivacity as imagination proceeds from the present to the past explains why we find it repellent to make leaps when relating ideas (never, for example, tracing a present impression back to a cause five years in the past without supposing a succession of intermediate causes):

'Tis also remarkable, that in the conception of those objects, which we regard as real and existent, we take them in their proper order and situation, and never leap from one object to another, which is distant from it, without running over, at least in a cursory manner, all those objects, which are interpos'd betwixt them. When we reflect, therefore, on any object distant from ourselves, we are oblig'd not only to reach it at first by passing thro' all the intermediate space [or time] betwixt ourselves and the object, but also to renew our press every moment; being every moment recall'd to the consideration of ourselves and our present situation. 'Tis easily conceiv'd, that this interruption must weaken the idea by breaking the action of the mind, and hindering the conception from being so intense and continu'd, as when we reflect on a nearer object ... Here then ... [are] two kinds of objects, the contiguous and remote; of which the former, by means of their relation to ourselves, approach an impression in force and vivacity. (*T*428).

The differing degrees of vivacity accorded to memories in accordance with their relative contiguity to present impressions keeps our reasoning tightly affixed to their temporal order, and nothing more. Since nothing but the continuous proportional diminishing of their vivacity with each passing moment can give us immediate awareness of the *passage* of time, idea-enlivening imagination is responsible also for the direction of time and our respect of it in reasoning (for example, the repugnance of reverse causation):

We always follow the succession of time in placing our ideas, and from the consideration of any object pass more easily to that, which follows immediately after it, than to that which went before it ... An equal distance ... in the past and in the future, has not the same effect on the imagination; and that because we consider the one as continually encreasing, and the other as continually diminishing. The fancy antipates the course of things, and surveys the object in that condition, to which it tends, as well as in that which is regarded as the present. (*T*430ff.)

The only way the recession of memories into the past can be immediately felt is by a dynamic process of vivacity diminishment (an action that occurs spontaneously and to which habit renders us insensible). Since imagination, like a moth to flame, tends always toward the more vivacious and finds great difficulty in proceeding otherwise, this dynamic points it toward the present away from the past and toward the future away from the present:

When the object is past, the progression of the thought in passing to it from the present is contrary to nature, as proceeding from one point in time to that which is preceding ... in opposition to the natural course of the succession. On the other hand, when we turn our thought to a future object, our fancy flows along the stream of time, and arrives at the object by an order, which seems most natural, passing always from one point of time to that which is immediately posterior to it. This *easy* progression of ideas favours the imgination, and makes it conceive its object in a stronger and fuller light, than when we are continually oppos'd in our passage, and are oblig'd to overcome the difficulties arising form the natural propensity of the fancy. (*T*430f.)

Memory would have a completely different character if temporal ordering were subject to different principles of association. If our nature were such that imagination failed to enliven memories in proportion to their proximity to the present, a memory twenty years distant would be neither more nor less vivid than one five minutes past, and, with no determination to adhere to the sequence in causal explanations, we might find it quite acceptable to posit an *immediate* causal relation between that ancient remembrance and a perception present to us in sensation currently; even reverse causation would lose its repugnance. If imagination enlivened past ideas according to their *distance from* the present and the recent past seemed as distant memories do to us now, then ideas of the most distant past would be believed to bear most directly on our present situation; since this would have the effect of reversing our sense of the direction (but not of the order) of time, reverse causation would become the only sort tolerable in our reasoning. Or, if imagination enlivened ideas in proportion to their proximity not to present impressions, but to ideas of ten years past, ideas situated in the intervening years would not be taken as memories, but as the part of the future we already know.

The only alternative to attributing to idea-enlivening imagination the function of favoring ideas of perceptions temporally more contiguous to present impressions over ones less so would be to suppose that perceptions, once past, still retain a portion of their vivacity as real presences (much as a light-bulb filament continues glowing for a brief interval after the current is switched off).[18] However, even were it conceded that an idea of a consciousness one second earlier than the present is somehow *objectively* more real than another of an hour before (i.e. that greater temporal contiguity translates into a difference of *appearance* among perceptions), it would still have to be *felt* in consciousness to be so before it could be expressed in a *belief* as to its closer effective relation to present reality. For Hume did, after all, classify temporal contiguity as an association of ideas, a natural relation. So, unless there were a predisposition of associative imagination to respond to this appearance of greater temporal proximity with a heightened feeling of verisimilitude (giving it preference to others lacking that appearance), it would be without significance for us, and so be useless to account for memory. Certainly, there is no evidence that Hume recognized any such predisposition, and quite properly so: temporal characteristics of perceptions cannot simply be read off from appearances; they are not perceptible features of their appearance in the way the timbre or loudness of aural perceptions are, or the intensity or shade of visual, etc. But, in the absence of anything pertaining to the appearance of an idea in virtue of which its temporal contiguity in relation to the present might be discovered, then it cannot be appearances that induce us to regard an idea as more or less verisimilar than otherwise. Hence, only through the application of a natural associative function of the mind, which enlivens ideas according to their temporal contiguity with respect to present consciousness can memory, in the fullest sense, come into being.

C. The metamorphoses of imagination: the senses

According to Hume, the senses too are "founded on the imagination, or the vivacity of our ideas." Yet, it is impossible to believe he deemed them dependent on imagination in so far as they furnish us with sensations and/or reflexions; nor could he have ascribed to imagination the immediate *appearance* of perceptions to consciousness or the vivacity of *impressions*. In my view, the most plausible candidate for an ostensible "datum" of the senses which Hume could have claimed to be founded on imagination is our consciousness of perceptual succession ("that succession, which is obvious to the senses," *T*65; "*perceivable* succession," *T*35). Immediately prior to declaring that the senses are founded on imagination on *T*265, Hume asserted that the "succession of perceptions, which constitutes our self or person" – described one sentence earlier as "dependent on the senses" – is so dependent on idea-enlivening imagination that, in its absence, "we cou'd only admit of those perceptions, which are immediately present to our consciousness." We would be prisoners of the present, each new instant of consciousness being, in effect, the first and only perception of our conscious lives; and, with no sense of the succession of perceptions, nor able to receive "those lively images, with which the memory presents us ... as true pictures of past perceptions," we would necessarily lack all sense of continued existence through time, and have no idea of self or of identity generally (memory-resemblances and causal relations are the basis of "the true idea of the human mind," *T*261). Such a view would represent a radical break with tradition since philosophers thitherto took consciousness of this succession to be a datum of the senses and retention; they never even so much as considered the possibility that association-engendered phenomenological feeling might be an essential component.[19] So, by espousing such a view, Hume could legitimately claim to have shown that even the senses, *as then conceived*, are in fact founded on the imagination, without thereby falsifying the very notion of imagination by supposing it actually to *supply* sensations and reflexions, or to be responsible for the vivacity of impressions no less than of ideas.

Against this interpretation, it might be argued that there is no need to resort to anything so recondite in order to make sense of Hume's claim that the senses are founded on imagination. More probably, he simply meant to have his reader recall the conclusions reached in *Treatise* I/iv/§§2–6, that bodies and the self – which we vulgarly (naturally) take to be objects of our external and internal senses – are actually fictions of the imagination. Since there is no other text in the *Treatise* (or his other writings) which suggests that the awareness of perceptual succession is not wholly an affair of the senses and retention, this reading seems to have the added recommendation of modesty: it does not ascribe views to Hume more original and radical than the text can firmly support.

Now, while there is much to be said for adopting a modest approach to *T*265, it still has to be shown that the text supports such a reading. To see why it cannot, consider the entire passage here in question:

After the most accurate and exact of my reasonings, I can give no reason why I shou'd assent to it; and feel nothing but a *strong* propensity to consider objects strongly in that view, under which they appear to me. Experience is a principle, which instructs me in the several conjunctions of objects for the past. Habit is another principle, which determines me to expect the same for the future; and both of them conspiring to operate upon the imagination, make me form certain ideas in a more intense and lively manner, than others, which are not attended with the same advantages. Without this quality, by which the mind enlivens some ideas beyond others (which seemingly is so trivial, and so little founded on reason) we cou'd never assent to any argument, nor carry our view beyond those few objects, which are present to our senses. Nay, even to these objects we cou'd never attribute any existence, but what was dependent on the senses; and must comprehend them entirely in that succession of perceptions, which constitutes our self or person. Nay farther, even with relation to that succession, we cou'd only admit of those perceptions, which are immediately present to our consciousness, nor cou'd those lively images, with which the memory presents us, be ever receiv'd as true pictures of past perceptions. The memory, senses, and understanding are, therefore, all of them founded on the imagination, or the vivacity of our ideas.

This text is clearly carefully constructed, exposing its several points in a quite definite sequence. It proceeds in three stages, with each successor bringing under the ægis of imagination something that, in the previous, seemed to be independent of it. For example, reasoning, which one presumes to depend solely on understanding, in fact owes its power to influence us solely to experience-bred habits of imagination. Memory, which at first seems the very antithesis of imagination, turns out instead to be merely one of the more primitive species of associative imagination. To complete the pattern, therefore, one would expect Hume to contend that a species of perception commonly thought to depend solely on the senses in fact involves imagination. But the ostensibly modest reading of *T*265 contradicts this expectation. For it portrays Hume as claiming that the senses are founded on imagination because external objects, *present* to the senses but expressly deemed to be *independent* of them, are products of the imagination. To demonstrate that something present to the senses yet *not* dependent on them is a product of the imagination is, however, no basis for claiming that the senses are founded on imagination. *T*265 requires that ideas and beliefs putatively founded on the senses entail association. A claim that the awareness of perceptual succession – which *seems* to depend solely on the senses – is *in fact* founded on idea-enlivening imagination quite clearly satisfies this condition. The objects comprehended "entirely in that succession of perceptions, which constitutes our self or person," are explicitly stated to be "dependent on the senses." Moreover, in referring "the true idea of the human mind" to causal connections between successive perceptions (*T*261), Hume asserted that they are not real bonds, but merely a "union of... ideas in the imagination, when we reflect on them," "an easy transition of ideas," relations we "only feel... among the ideas we form" (*T*259ff.). Causal association, together with the other natural relations, give what otherwise would be a disconnected succession, lacking progress and continuity, a history, a direction (causation based anisotropy), and a future that connects up with the past (hence the commonwealth analogy of *T*261). Without these associative bonds, our ideas, lacking any relation to one another or to impressions, would in effect have neither predecessors nor successors; all sense of time-order would be lost. Images, however lively, could not then be "receiv'd as true pictures of past perceptions," and "we cou'd only admit of those perceptions, which are immediately present to our consciousness." Here then is something – the causally determined temporal ordering of perceptions ("a system of different perceptions ... link'd together by the relation of cause and effect") – that thitherto had invariably been conceived as a given of the senses but Hume ascribed to associative imagination ("the uniting principles in the ideal world," *T*260).

A last line of defense for those inclined to resist this conclusion is what later philosophers called "the specious present."[20] The specious present is, in my view, just specious psychology;[21] nor is it easy to reconcile with other tenets of Hume's psychology.[22] But, more importantly, it is irrelevant to the issue whether the succession of *associatively related* perceptions presupposed by our idea of self is or is not a product solely of the senses. For *this* succession is one that Hume indisputably characterized as dependent on the senses yet explained in terms of associative imagination. The specious present might suffice to convey to us an idea of temporal succession (contiguity) itself, but only causal relations can transform this appearance into belief in the reality of the *ordering* of preceptions as precedessors and successors.

D. The metamorphoses of imagination: the understanding

There is a third metamorphosis of imagination recapitulated in the conclusion to *Treatise* I: imagination as understanding. This, for Hume, was undoubtedly the most important of the three, for empirical reasoning was the central concern of his writings on knowledge. Still, the pattern is the same as that followed in the cases of memory and the senses: the reduction to imagination achieved by demonstrating that functions traditionally ascribed to understanding and thought to set it apart from the "lower" faculties are simply exercises of associative imagination. The targets for reduction are these: those relations Hume denominated "philosophical"; substance and mode; and abstraction. Over the course of *Treatise* I, we duly discover that judgment and reasoning "resolve themselves into [conception], and are nothing but particular ways of conceiving our objects ... the only remarkable difference, which occurs on this occasion, is, when we join belief to the conception, and are perswaded of the truth of what we conceive" (*T*96n.). Since enlivening conceptions is the distinctive function of associative imagination, it comes as no surprise to find Hume treating understanding as equivalent to it ("understanding, that is ... the general and more establish'd properties of the imagination," *T*267). Moreover, since abstraction and generality turn out to be nothing more than habitudes of comparison with an eye to resemblance, there is no basis for distinguishing a special kind of consciousness requiring "a pure and intellectual view, of which the superior faculties of the soul are alone capable" (*T*72). That is, since concepts and generality irreducible to the particular have no existence outside of language (see chapter 3-B), the warrant for positing a separate faculty of understanding over and above imagination is cancelled. Accordingly, idea-relating and -enlivening imagination suffices for wellnigh everything traditionally comprehended under the terms "concept," "judgment" (referred to custom on *T*108), "understanding," and "reason," so that the latter, so far as Hume was concerned, are merely imagination operating in a particular guise.[23]

The key to understanding Hume's theory of relation is to recognize that perceptions, considered in themselves, lack relation. They are "interrupted, and perishing, and different at every different return" (*T*211). "They ... succeed each other with an inconceivable rapidity, and are in a perpetual flux and movement ... [they] make their appearance; pass, re-pass, glide away, and mingle in an infinite variety of postures and situations" (*T*252f.). In respect of existence, they "are different, and distinguishable, and separable from each other, and may be separately consider'd, and may exist separately, and have no need of anything to support their existence" (*T*252). So, perceptions – the only objects immediately present to us by consciousness – are a random jumble, the very antithesis of order and relation. They become related only via the mediation of consciousness, and in particular through the union of their *ideas* in imagination. It is true that some relations are said to be perceived (for example, *T*73f. and *T*168f.); but the context makes clear that Hume's intention was not to exclude imagination as such, but solely those functions of it which depend on experienced constant conjunction (for no one can doubt that, for Hume, resemblance, contiguity, and identity are relations of imagination). Accordingly, all shaping, structuring, ordering, and uniting of perceptions must be understood to occur within the medium of thought, and so to exist only in and for idea-relating and -enlivening imagination. This is not to say that Hume was anything other than agnostic about the independent reality of relations: he would deny only that any relation *of which we have an idea* can exist outside imagination; and if we choose to call "relation" that of which we have *no* idea, he would deem it "of little consequence to the world" (*T*167). *For part of the content of the complex idea of any relation is the disposition of imagination in contemplating the related perceptions and the phenomenological feelings characterizing (or failing to characterize) that contemplation.*

It is sometimes thought that Hume reserved some relations for reason *in contradistinction to* imagination, in particular those falling within the province of knowledge (i.e. intuitive or demonstrative certainty). Yet, here again, context suggests that this simply is not the case. Hume's first example of an intuitive relation is resemblance, which clearly is an affair of imagination. It is true that, in considering demonstration, he seems to contrast reason with imagination. But the reference to "The loose judgments of the senses and imagination" (*T*71) does not exclude imagination in the sense of understanding (see *T*265 and *T*267). His aim, on the contrary, was not to encourage, but to deflate the pretensions of mathematicians and others to free themselves from all dependence on "fancy":

I shall here take occasion to propose a second observation concerning our demonstrative reasonings, which is suggested by the same subject of the mathematics. 'Tis usual with mathematicians, to pretend, that those ideas, which are their objects, are of so refin'd and spiritual a nature, that they fall not under the conception of the fancy, but must be comprehended by a pure and intellectual view, of which the superior faculties of the soul are alone capable. The same notion runs thro' most parts of philosophy, and is principally made use of to explain our abstract ideas ... 'Tis easy to see, why philosophers are so fond of this notion of some spiritual and refin'd perceptions; since by that means they cover many of their absurdities, and may refuse to submit to the decisions of clear ideas, by appealing to such as are obscure and uncertain. But to destroy this artifice, we need but reflect on that principle so oft insisted on, *that all our ideas are copy'd from our impressions.* (*T*72) The first principles [of mathematics] are founded on the imagination and senses: The conclusion, therefore, can never go beyond, much less contradict these faculties. (*TApp*638; see also *T*51)

Why should the imagination be requisite to such arcane disciplines as algebra and arithmetic? Quite apart from the obvious factor of comparison with an eye to resemblances by which quantities are related and distinguished, there is the simple fact of belief, which for Hume is never anything other than a feeling of vivacity. Our "reasoning and belief is some sensation or peculiar manner of conception" (*T*184), and "the conviction, which arises from a subtile reasoning, diminishes in proportion to the efforts, which the imagination makes to enter into the reasoning, and to conceive it in all its parts. Belief, being a lively conception, can never be entire, where it is not founded on something natural and easy" (*T*186). It is in this sense that "Even *Mathematics, Natural Philosophy, and Natural Religion*, are in some measure dependent on the science of MAN" (*T*xv), and understanding is always only "the general and more establish'd properties of the imagination" (*T*267). We should therefore be careful to take Hume at his word when he treats as analogous these two claims: (i) that "the necessity, which makes two times two equal to four, or three angles of a triangle equal to two right ones, lies only in the act of the understanding," and (ii) that "the necessity or power, which unites causes and effects, lies in the determination of the mind to pass from the one to the other ... [and] belongs entirely to the soul, which considers the union of two or more objects in all past instances" (*T*166). Both relations lie equally in the considering no less than in the considered, and are products of the mind's one and only relating faculty, imagination.

A related, far more malignant, misinterpretation of Hume's theory of relations is the view that philosophical relations are independent of the phenomenological feelings of easy transition and vivacity, and so are wider in scope than natural relations. When so construed, it becomes permissible to suppose that causal relations, identical objects, space and time (as the mathematician conceives them), etc., may obtain in the absence of any observing feeling consciousness, and the way is opened to the sort of unbridled metaphysical speculation, untethered by experience, against which Hume pronounced himself with such vehemence ("If we take in our hand any volume; of divinity or school metaphysics ... Commit it then to the flames: for it can contain nothing but sophistry and illusion," *E*XII/iii.132). However, a few brief reflections employing Hume's theory of belief should suffice to nip this approach in the bud.

Hume contrasted philosophical relations with the natural relations responsible for "the connexion or association of ideas" as follows:

> As all simple ideas may be separated by the imagination, and may be united again in what form it pleases, nothing wou'd be more unaccountable than the operations of that faculty, were it not guided by some universal principles, which render it, in some measure, uniform with itself in all times and places. Were ideas entirely loose and unconnected, chance alone wou'd join them; and 'tis impossible the same simple ideas should fall regularly into complex ones (as they commonly do) without some bond of union among them, some associating quality, by which one idea naturally introduces another. This uniting principle among ideas is not to be consider'd as an inseparable connexion; for that has been already excluded from the imagination: nor yet are we to conclude, that without it the mind cannot join two ideas; for nothing is more free than that faculty: but we are only to regard it as a gentle force, which commonly prevails, and is the cause why, among other things, languages so nearly correspond to each other; nature in a manner pointing out to every one those simple ideas, which are most proper to be united into a complex one. The qualities, from which this association arises, and by which the mind is after this manner convey'd from one idea to another, are three, *viz.* RESEMBLANCE, CONTIGUITY in time or place, and CAUSE and EFFECT. (*T*10f.)

Philosophical relations lack even this gentle force. In them, ideas do not naturally introduce one another but are artificially united via "that particular circumstance, in which, even upon the arbitrary union of two ideas in the fancy, we may think proper to compare them" (*T*13). Resemblance underlies all comparison (*T*14), and since anything may be found to resemble anything else, no two things are devoid of *some* philosophical relation (even "existence and non-existence, which are plainly resembling, as implying both of them an idea of the object," *T*15). It is precisely because they are both omnipresent and indifferent to the general forces governing phenomenological feeling, that so many commentators presume them to be independent of natural relations, or even presuppositions of them. After all, how else could our imaginations associate perceptions if we did not first "philosophically" perceive them as resembling, contiguous, or constantly conjoined? Yet, the very appellation "philosophical" should serve to put us on our guard when it is suggested that Hume regarded them as preceding and making possible natural relations. It seems completely antithetical to the tenor of his philosophy to suppose him to have set the natural, or vulgar, on a philosophical foundation. On the contrary, his constant refrain was that philosophical understanding is not only rooted in, but, in respect of belief, entirely parasitic upon, the natural sort (thus not even mathematics was spared the ignominy of being deemed a form of fancy). Nor does one have to look far for textual evidence to support the priority of natural relations *vis à vis* philosophical. It is hard to imagine a more explicit declaration than Hume's preamble to the section on relations:

> Amongst the effects of this union or association of ideas, there are none more remarkable, than those complex ideas, which are the common subjects of our thoughts and reasoning, and generally arise from some principle of union among our simple ideas. These complex ideas may be divided into *Relations*, *Modes*, and *Substances*. (*T*13)

The principles of association in imagination – resemblance, contiguity, and cause and effect – are here explicitly termed the *causes* of the "complex ideas, which are the common subjects of our thoughts and reasoning," among which he lists *relations*. This clearly suggests that, for him, it is not until ideas have been associated in natural relations that comparison, and so all manner of philosophical relation, is possible.

According to Hume, resemblance "is a relation, without which no philosophical relation can exist; since no objects will admit of comparison, but what have some degree of resemblance" (*T*14). This resemblance may be either natural, if resulting from association, or philosophical, as is the case if, "When a quality becomes very general, and is common to a great many individuals, it leads not the mind directly to any one of them; but by presenting at once too great a choice, does thereby prevent the imagination from fixing on any single object" (*T*14). Only what we have previously *naturally* associated in relations of resemblance is available, as species, for more general comparisons, and this well before the point is reached where the influence of association can no longer be felt and we are left to our own *philosophical* devices. In other words, without initial, instinctive resemblances to supply the raw material, we would lack the material necessary to carry out more general, abstract comparisons, and so could never arrive at fully non-associative philosophical resemblances.

The dependence of philosophical on natural relations is easiest to recognize when we recall that only the latter possess the power to engender belief. As such, they *constitute*, and are our *sole and exclusive* guide to, the "real" (verisimilar) affinities of nature. Sortings may strike us as "natural" and impose themselves on us as "true" reflections of the "facts" only if, and so far as, we so *regard* them, and such regarding is entirely a matter of the phenomenological feelings of vivacity and facility in the transition from the impression to the idea. Were human nature different and relations of qualitative disparity came easier to imagination – or were its associating activity governed by qualitative ordering principles so remote from our own that we have no names for them and, if we paid heed to them at all, would consider them entirely random and void of significance – then it is quite inconceivable that *philosophical* resemblances should have the least weight in our thoughts and reasonings or exert any influence on our actions. Philosophical relations are wholly parasitic on natural: lacking any belief-engendering powers of their own, they must rely on that of the natural relations from which they spring. If this foundation were removed, it is quite clear, given Hume's conception of belief, that philosophical relations could have no persuasive force whatever, and quite simply would *never* be employed in inferences ("philosophical decisions are nothing but the reflections of common life, methodized and corrected," *E*XII/iii.130). The whole point of Hume's theory of relation is that the "common subjects of our thoughts and reasoning" are *common* subjects only because they are rooted in associative propensities grounded in human nature. In the case of natural resemblance, this means that, irrespective of the perceptual arrays and sequences before us, or any relational property capable of being read off directly from them (for example, congruity), nothing of significance to human understanding – that is, no *relation* of ideas – exists unless and until the imagination *feels* an easy transition in successively contemplating them and, in the transition from an impression to an idea, *feels* heightened verisimilitude in the idea. In the absence of such feelings, or, in the case of philosophical relations, the lack of any foundation in natural relations featuring them, such arrays and sequences are wholly incapable of influencing our thought or action; whereas, in their presence, imagination will relate them however incongruous their appearance. Thus, resemblances are never *simply* read off from appearances; and if not themselves felt in imagination, then they must be rooted in others that are.

Since Hume's criteria for distinguishing philosophical from natural relations are wholly psychological, nothing prevents one from becoming the other. For example, if scientists discover that certain stellar behavior is indicative of the presence of a black hole, they are likely to develop a habit such that, upon seeing a photograph showing such behavior, they will immediately form the idea of a black hole and believe in its probable existence. All that is required to make the relation natural is the habit and the consequent enlivening of an idea associated with an impression. Conversely, a savage set in front of a television for the first time will believe in the contiguity of the person he sees in the box; only gradually will he understand that the person may be remote in place or even time, and so come to regard his relation to the person philosophically.

To my knowledge, no interpreter who has asserted the primacy or independence of philosophical relations over natural in Hume's philosophy has ever managed to explain, in a manner consistent with Hume's conception of belief, how the least credence could be attached to such relations. For, without the benefit of "that act of the mind, which renders realities, or what is taken for such, more present to us than fictions, causes them to weigh more in the thought, and gives them a superior influence on the passions and imagination" (*E*V/ii.40), such relations could have no place in an account of human understanding. There is probably no single interpretive lapse responsible for more ill-founded criticism and unnecessary controversy than the failure to appreciate this. For example, perhaps the most written-about issue in all of Hume criticism is whether or not he reduced causality to regularity, and, if so, whether he supposed causal relations in this sense to obtain unobserved. But a question that few address, and which those that do generally treat unsatisfactorily, is whether philosophical causal relations could retain any of their weight in our reasonings and influence on our actions if supposed to obtain prior to, or independently of, natural causal relations. A philosophical causal relation is defined as "an object precedent and contiguous to another, and where all the objects resembling the former are plac'd in like relations of precedency and contiguity to those objects, that resemble the latter" (*T*170). Rarely noticed is the fact that contiguity and resemblance – the ingredients of constant conjunctions – are themselves natural relations of associative imagination. Is it conceivable that, if human nature were different and these were not natural relations, constant conjunctions would have the least significance for us, or even be taken notice of? So, even if philosophical causation did reduce to regularity, as some suppose, that would not make it any the less dependent on a foundation in natural relations for its power to inspire belief. However, the true force of philosophical causation stems from its rootedness in natural relations of cause and effect. These are unrivalled by anything else in the repertoire of imagination in their capacity to endow an idea with a verisimilitude approaching that of impressions; in their absence, deprived of that "quality, by which the mind enlivens some ideas beyond others (which seemingly is so trivial, and so little founded on reason)" (*T*265), we would never dream of assigning the least objective worth to relations of constant conjunction, observed or otherwise. Philosophical causation, including our belief in the uniformity of nature and the maxim that every beginning of existence has a cause, is therefore merely an outgrowth of the natural relation of cause and effect (see Part II).

In addition to philosophical relations, Hume saw fit to distinguish two other effects of the association of ideas: substances and modes. That he deemed it necessary to devote an entire section to the topic had more to do with the favor shown them by other philosophers than any interest of his own, for he seems chiefly to have been concerned to debunk them:

> I wou'd fain ask those philosophers, who found so much of their reasonings on the distinction of substance and accident, and imagine we have clear ideas of each, whether the idea of *substance* be deriv'd from the impressions of sensation or reflexion?... I believe none will assert, that substance is either a colour, or a sound, or a taste... But the impressions of reflexion resolve themselves into our passions and emotions; none of which can possibly represent a substance. We have therefore no idea of substance, distinct from that of a collection of particular qualities, nor have we any other meaning when we either talk or reason concerning it. (*T*15f.)

Substance is segregated from relation in Hume's review of "the elements of this philosophy" (*T*13) because, of the latter, even the philosophical variety, we have a clear idea. Relations begin with a transition from one perception to another which the imagination may find easier or harder; and, in this way, various circumstances of resemblance are in due course brought to light in respect of which ideas may be further compared in the fancy. Complex ideas of philosophical relations are compounded from the particular *circumstance* of comparison (founded on habit) together with the residual vivacity and ease of *transition* inherited from the natural relations on which they are grounded. In the case of our complex ideas of substance, however, there is no circumstance in virtue of which the accidents are compared and united, and so no special comparison of any kind whatever (an action "necessary to all philosophical relation," *T*14). For this reason, it seems, Hume concluded that, apart from the (natural) contiguity and causal interrelation of the qualities concerned, we have no idea whatever of substance and the term "is altogether insignificant" (*TAbs*649).[24]

3 Words and measures

A. Abstract ideas: the legacy of Locke and Berkeley

Never did Hume express such a deep sense of obligation, or more warmly endorse the work of another, than at the outset of *Treatise* I/i/§7, "Of Abstract Ideas":

> A very material question has been started concerning *abstract* or *general* ideas, *whether they be general or particular in the mind's conception of them.* A great philosopher has disputed the receiv'd opinion in this particular, and has asserted, that all general ideas are nothing but particular ones, annexed to a certain term, which gives them a more extensive signification, and makes them recall upon occasion other individuals, which are similar to them. As I look upon this to be one of the greatest and most valuable discoveries that has been made of late years in the republic of letters, I shall here endeavour to confirm it by some arguments, which I hope will put it beyond all doubt and controversy.

The philosopher was George Berkeley. Since Hume's own treatment of the subject presupposes an acquaintance with Berkeley's, it will behoove us briefly to review and assess Berkeley's views on generality.

Although Berkeley directed his critique of abstract general ideas at all preceding philosophers (particularly materialists), his special target was Locke. This was not because Locke was more culpable in his eyes than others; he was perhaps closer to Locke and more deeply indebted to him than to any other thinker. Rather, it was probably the very proximity of their position, his belief that Locke had stopped just short of the truth, that made him the ideal stepping stone for Berkeley. There is doubt, however, that an additional step was even necessary. Prolix and prone to ambiguity as he was, Locke is one of the philosophers most liable to being misrepresented by the selective use of quotations, and Berkeley has been accused of just this, quite rightly I believe, in the case of abstract general ideas.[1] Locke's position, in overall conception and thrust, is simplicity itself. Rejecting nominalism on the one side[2] and the possibility of the mind-independent existence of universals on the other,[3] he sought to blaze a new, intermediate trail by explaining generality in terms of directly discernible resemblances. For example, when people contrive to produce a general idea of man,

> they make nothing new, but only leave out of the complex *Idea* they had of *Peter* and *James*, *Mary* and *Jane*, that which is peculiar to each, and retain only what is common to them all ... By the same way, that they come by the general Name and *Idea* of *Man*, they easily *advance to more general Names* and Notions. For observing, that several Things that differ from their *Idea* of *Man*, by retaining only those Qualities, and uniting them into one *Idea*, they have again another and a more general *Idea* ... Which new *Idea* is made, not by any new addition, but only, as before, by leaving out the shape, and some other Properties signified by the name *Man*, and retaining only a Body, with Life, Sense, and spontaneous Motion, comprehended under the Name *Animal*. (*ECHU* III/3/§§7–8)

Armed with abstract ideas, the mind is in a position to relate different particulars by means of a feature common to all. Its commonness signifies no more than the possibility of comparing any of them with the abstract idea and finding a perfect resemblance *as far as the comparison goes*. That is, since my *idea* of man is without specification as to sex, age, nationality, etc., there is nothing in it to diminish or oppose its accord with any *actual man* who has these together with other individuating features but otherwise agrees with the idea. For Locke, a perfect resemblance in one direction (of the idea with individuals) is sufficient for the individuals concerned to be found resembling; and, in this way, via the mediation of an abstract idea, things that might otherwise never strike us as resembling come to be related (transitively). The universality of an abstract idea consists, therefore, in its enabling the mind to sort out and collect various particulars via their relation to it ("Standards to rank real Existences into sorts, as they agree with these Patterns," *ECHU* II/xi/§9); and this, in turn, enabled Locke to explain general terms as particular sounds or other sensible marks annexed to such ideas for purposes of communication.

Berkeley took exception to a single element of Locke's account: that a universal can exist as even so much as an *idea* in the mind. It was Berkeley's view that the mind is furnished solely with singular, completely determinate ideas, and this is true no less of images in thought than of sensations, passions, and emotions. His main evidence for ascribing the opposite view to Locke is the following passage (excerpted from neither the analysis of abstraction in *ECHU* Book II nor that of general terms in Book III, but a chapter on maxims in Book IV, "Of Knowledge in General"):

> Thus particular *Ideas* are *first* received and distinguished, and so Knowledge got about them: and next to them, the less general, or specifick, which are next to particular. For abstract *Ideas* are not so obvious or easie to Children, or the yet unexercised Mind, as particular ones. If they seem so to grown Men, 'tis only because by constant and familiar use they are made so. For when we nicely reflect

upon them, we shall find, that general *Ideas* are Fictions and Contrivances of the Mind, that carry difficulty with them, and do not so easily offer themselves, as we are apt to imagine. For example, Does it not require some pains and skill to form the *general Idea* of a *Triangle*, (which is yet none the most abstract, comprehensive, and difficult,) for it must be neither Oblique, nor Rectangle, neither Equilateral, Equicrural, nor Scalenon; but all and none of these at once. In effect, it is something imperfect, that cannot exist; an *Idea* wherein some parts of several different and inconsistent *Ideas* are put together. (*ECHU* IV/vii/§9)[4]

We may regard with a certain skepticism Berkeley's contention that Locke was so poor or careless an observer of the contents of his own mind that he believed he could picture to himself a triangle that is neither equilateral, equicrural, nor scalenon. The problem may be simply one of nomenclature, arising from Locke's (deliberately) comprehensive use of the term "idea" to include not only sensations and their images in thought, but also ideas of reflexion which acquaint us with consciousness and its doings – including operations like perceiving, retaining, comparing, and abstracting as well emotions, passions, etc. Locke seems to have used the term "abstract idea" to designate a complex "idea" comprised of a *particular* image in imagination plus certain operations of the mind, whereby the idea is *regarded* in abstraction from "all other Existences, and the circumstances of real Existence, as Time, Place, or any other concomitant *Ideas.*" (*ECHU* II/x/§9) In other words, it is not from the perceived image itself that the features we abstract are removed, but from our consideration of the image; we *abstract* simply by ignoring them and heeding only some one or few selected aspects of the image. For Berkeley, any such considering, as an act of the mind, ought not be termed "idea" but "notion" (see *PHK* §27).[5]

Nomenclature aside, Berkeley's interpretation would be correct only if it had been Locke's intent to explicate the *nature* of abstract ideas in this passage, and so affirm that there exists a species of idea that somehow, quite miraculously, is exempt from the law of non-contradiction. But it was obviously no such thing. Locke's concern was strictly with the question of their origin, not their nature, and specifically whether they are innate or acquired. He recognized that it would be strong evidence that such ideas are innate if children showed special ease and facility with ideas the more general and abstract they were; but, of course, experience shows quite the reverse: it is only with great difficulty, and after considerable training, that most children show any facility with abstract general ideas at all; and, in general, the more abstract and universal the idea, the more difficulty any of us has in grasping it. The general idea of a triangle employed by geometers is a perfect example of an idea beyond the reach of children whose innate possession it supposedly is. That was Locke's point; if his language left him open in some measure to readings such as Berkeley's, we have only to look back at what he actually says about abstraction and generality in *ECHU* II and III to see that this interpretation does not hold water:

the Mind ... considers that Appearance alone, makes it a representative of all of that kind ... and thus Universals, whether *Ideas* or Terms, are made. (*ECHU* II/xi/§9) Words are general ... when used for Signs of general *Ideas*; and so are applicable indifferently to many particular Things; And *Ideas* are general when they are set up, as the Representatives of many particular Things: but universality belongs not to things themselves, *which are all of them particular in their Existence, even those ... Ideas, which in their signification, are general.* When therefore we quit Particulars, the Generals that rest, are only Creatures of our own making, their general Nature being nothing but the Capacity they are put into by the Understanding, of signifying or representing many particulars. For the signification they have, is nothing but a relation, that by the mind of Man is added to them ... From whence it is easy to observe, that the essences of the sorts of things, and consequently the sorting of Things, is the Workmanship of the Understanding, since it is the Understanding that abstracts and makes those general *Ideas*. (*ECHU* III/iii/§11 and §13 – emphasis mine)

Abstraction, for Locke, was a matter not of the idea itself, but of the manner in which the understanding regards it: the *separate consideration* of what cannot actually *exist separately* (for example, equilaterality and equiangularity) or the *conjoint consideration* of what cannot *exist together* (equiangularity and scalenity). Thus, Lockean abstraction relates not to a content before the mind, but solely to an intellectual operation, the performance of which carries with it no implication at all for what can and cannot be given separately or together in idea (thought or sensation) or reality.

It is not difficult to see that the views of Locke and Berkeley on abstraction are essentially identical. Consider the circularity evident in Berkeley's definition of generality: "an idea, which considered in itself is particular, becomes general, by being made to represent or stand for all other particular ideas of the same sort" (*PHK* Intro. §12). How *in the first place* does one know they are "particular ideas of the same *sort*"? A given particular idea, say, of a teacup perched upon a table, may be used to represent a host of different things: white things, round-rimmed things, drinking implements, porcelain, things set atop items of furniture, all cups other than this cup, etc. How can one know unless one already has in mind a particular *sort*? For example, if there were nothing in one's mind but the thought of this particular cup plus the sensation of a particular book lying on a particular chair, how could one tell whether, not to say how, the book on this table agrees or disagrees in any way with the thought of the cup? No mere comparison of the thought with the sensation could enable one to decide whether or not there is agreement. It is only if one *abstracts* from every feature of the image of the cup save its being atop a piece of furniture and then compares it *in this respect* with the book that one can determine that they agree. But is this not just to say that one must already know the *sort* of thing one is seeking *before* being able to make use of a particular idea for comparison? One must have in mind a certain *standard*, or "abstract general idea," to which to refer particular ideas if they are to function as general representatives; and, while this certainly need not be an abstract image, it at least has to be a mental operation if one is to have something prior to, and independent of, both language and particular images whereby to comprehend how the latter come to represent *generally*.

It is not unlikely that, by the time of the second edition of the *Principles*, Berkeley realized that his position may not have been so very different from Locke's after all. This would explain the addition he made to a passage which, in the first edition, appeared as follows:

For example, having demonstrated that the three angles of an isosceles rectangular triangle are equal to two right ones, I cannot therefore conclude this affection agrees to all other triangles which have neither a right angle nor two equal sides. It seems therefore, that, to be certain this proposition is universally true, we must either make a particular demonstration for every particular triangle, which is impossible; or once for all demonstrate it of the abstract idea of a triangle, in which all the particulars do indifferently partake, and by which they are all equally represented. To which I answer, that, though the idea I have in view whilst I make the demonstration be, for instance, that of an isosceles rectangular triangle whose sides are of a determine length, I may nevertheless be certain it extends to all other rectilinear triangles, of what sort or bigness soever. And that because neither the right angle, nor the equality, nor determinate length of the sides are *at all concerned in* the demonstration. It is true the diagram I have in view includes all these particulars; but then *there is not the least mention of them in the proof of the proposition*. It is not *said* the three angles are equal to two right ones, *because* one of them is a right angle, or *because* the sides comprehending it are of the same length. Which sufficiently shews that the right angle might have been oblique, and the sides unequal, and for all that the demonstration have held good. And for this reason it is that I conclude that to be true of any obliquangular or scalenon which I had demonstrated of a particular right-angled equicrural triangle, and not because I demonstrated of a particular right-angled equicrural triangle, and not because I demonstrated the proposition of the abstract idea of a triangle. (*PHK* Intro. §16 – emphasis mine)

One cannot help but be struck by how very like Lockean abstraction Berkeley's account of the generality of the proof is! The idea (image) of the triangle may be particular, but little in the way it is *considered* by the understanding is: various features of the triangle are simply ignored, omitted (*left out*, Locke would say – for example, *ECHU* III/iii/§7) from the train of thought that constitutes the demonstration. So, it is little wonder that, in the second edition, Berkeley seems finally to have consented to call a spade a spade:

> And here it must be acknowledged that a man may *consider* a figure merely as triangular; without attending to the particular qualities of the angles, or relations of the sides. So far he may abstract. But this will never prove that he can frame an abstract general inconsistent idea of a triangle. In like manner we may consider Peter so far forth as man, or so far forth as animal, without framing the forementioned abstract idea, either of man or of animal; inasmuch as all that is perceived is not considered.

Evidently, having re-read Locke's account of the acquisition of the general idea of man from the particular ideas of Peter and James, Mary and Jane in *ECHU* III/iii/§7, he tacitly admitted, however grudgingly, that his triumph over Locke was neither so clear-cut nor complete as he had supposed. Since the triangularity of the figure obviously could not *exist* without particular qualities of its angles and particular relations of its sides, we see that Berkeley has also been brought explicitly to affirm the existence of a special mental operation of abstraction, a kind of aspect-seeing, over and above the ability to separate perceptions in imagination in so far as they are likewise capable of existing separately in sense (to which he purported to limit abstraction in *PHK* Introduction §10 and Part I §5: the texts from which Hume's own separability principle and criterion of simplicity probably derive).

One reason for estimating how original was Berkeley's position with respect to Locke is to prize out what precisely it was that so impressed Hume. But an even more important reason for returning to Locke is that, in so doing, we can get a clear grasp of the basic inspiration behind the approach to generality common to Locke, Berkeley, and Hume: its reduction to empirical psychology (especially comparison and abstraction). The attraction of such an approach for the empiricist is that, to the extent it succeeds in explaining generality in terms of empirical psychology, it renders any intellectualist or linguistic explanation redundant. The whole apparatus of quantificational logic (the fully fledged version of Frege no less than its Aristotelian ancestor) would then be put in question. For, whatever its utility in formalistic inquiry, it could no longer be supposed (as many philosophers today continue to do) to reflect what actually goes on either in thought or common language, and its appeal as a technique by which to explore (make perspicuous) the workings of human understanding would be seriously compromised.

The reliance on abstractive mental operations to explain generality by both Locke and Berkeley seems to me incapable of attaining the goal of a genuinely naturalistic alternative to logical analysis. It is quite conceivable that one might abstract from various properties of a triangle and demonstrate a relation between it and two right angles *while never suspecting that this procedure has any implication for figures other than these.* One might repeat the procedure on different figures, or the same figure at different times, and still never suspect that it has implications for anything else; for one has yet to take the leap from aggregates to true generality, to *all* and *some*, to *indifferent* denotation (Berkeley's phrase – see *PHK* Introduction §12). Abstraction and comparison can get us only so far as the recognition that *similar* particular simple ideas exist in different complexes; this does not, however, suffice for an awareness that a particular idea has a possible representative use extending far beyond the peculiar circumstances of its experienced occurrence to *indefinitely* many other possible circumstances. Both Locke and Berkeley seem to have presupposed this awareness, as being somehow obvious to anyone who performs the abstraction and makes the comparisons. But to assume this is to assume the very thing they set out to explain: how we are able to grasp the use of an idea or term to represent *generally*.

By way of illustration, consider Locke's claim that "the same Colour being observed to day in Chalk or Snow, which the Mind yesterday received from Milk, it considers that Appearance alone, makes it a representative of all of that kind; and having given it the name *Whiteness*, it by that sound signifies the same quality wheresoever it be imagin'd or met with; and thus Universals, whether *Ideas* or Terms, are made" (*ECHU* II/xi/§9). There is an unexplained gap between the consideration of the appearance alone and the use of it to represent generally. For it is one thing for experience to present us with various things and the mind to take note of the resemblances, but quite another for it to leap beyond the resemblances to the conception of a feature *common* to different things, to an idea as "representative of *all* of that *kind.*" Abstraction seems to be of no help in bridging the gap, for it merely allows one to ignore certain features of *the particular complex* before the mind while focusing attention on others; it does not, of itself, point beyond the *particular* object or aspect in sensation or thought to a *kind* of object. Abstraction simply makes it possible to compare and relate two, three, or however many particular ideas one possesses which share the abstracted feature or features. But what of all the myriad other exemplars of the kind which happen not to have been encountered in one's experience, and may never be: how can the abstraction be supposed to encompass them? Even if infinitely many ideas could be held before the mind, that by itself promises only the possibility of infinitely many *individual* resemblance relations; it is not sufficient, in and of itself, to furnish the idea of a single feature or group of features as *common* to them all. At the very least, Locke and Berkeley fail to explain how one first comes to use a particular idea to make comparisons in the *open-ended* manner characteristic of a genuine universal, that is, with an application extending to *all possible* resembling individuals. This use of an idea or term is instead left a mystery, each seeming merely to assume an acquaintance with it. The principal criterion by which to judge of the success of a psychological account of universals, it seems to me, is its ability to bridge the gulf between a mere associative tie between particulars and the use of a particular to represent universally; and, by this reckoning, both Locke and Berkeley fall short.

According to Kemp Smith, Hume too "presupposes abstract ideas in his account of the mechanism which provides their imagery":

> Now clearly the "resemblance" that is found [among several objects], and when found marked by a name (to distinguish it from "the many respects" in which varying particulars differ), is not a particular, completely determinate image; it is that in which certain determinate images, while otherwise different in degrees of quantity and in quality, agree with one another. And since it cannot be equated with any particular image, it follows that if *all* ideas are particular images, there can be no idea of it whatsoever. In allowing it here, and in insisting that its apprehension is antecedent to the process of naming, and therefore also antecedent to the operation of custom, Hume is cutting the ground from under his own theory. The associative machinery may play its part in supporting the processes of abstract thinking through a supply of appropriate imagery; it cannot be made to account for what it thus itself presupposes – the apprehension which has led the mind to feel the need for a general name, and which in confining the use of the name to the "resemblance" is what alone enables the mind to distinguish between images which are appropriate and those which are not.[6]

There seem to be two distinct components of Kemp Smith's criticism of Hume. First, echoing Maund,[7] he claims that Hume surreptitiously adds resembling respects (aspects) to his stock of objects of consciousness, which earlier he had expressly confined to impressions and ideas. Second, by augmenting our stock of data in this way, Hume is guilty of presupposing abstractions in the very attempt to explain generality wholly in terms of individual, fully determinate ideas.

In my view, Kemp Smith is mistaken on both counts. Natural relations, and therefore relations generally, are indissoluble from phenomenological feelings, and so from consciousness. A relation is thus never something "out there" before the mind, which can be apprehended; it exists only *in the apprehension itself*, in the transition of imagination from one perception to any associate ("the very essence of these relations consists in their producing an easy transition of ideas," *T*260; "a relation ... arises merely from the comparison, which the mind makes," *T*46). Once this is appreciated, there is no difficulty recognizing the limits within which it is permissible, within the confines of Hume's system, to talk in terms of "apprehending" relations: never in such a way that relations are accorded the same independence *vis à vis* imagination that perceptions have. The mere fact that we *imagine*, and *believe*, perceptions to be related does not mean that they *can be* so or that relationships are *apprehensible realities* before consciousness. Even if perceptions were in some factual sense related, such relations would be of no concern to Hume's science of human understanding, since it is only in so far as the *imagination* feels an easiness and vivacity in the transition from one perception to another that relations become a factor in our reasonings and actions. Thus, so far as what appears before the mind is concerned, Hume should be taken at his word: "all our perceptions are different from each other, and from every thing else in the universe" (*T*233); they are "interrupted, perishing, and different at every return" (*T*211); and, despite the efforts of imagination to disguise it, they "appear as such" (*T*194).

Yet, in my view, Kemp Smith makes an even more basic mistake when he supposes that relations, simply as such, are universals. For there is one respect in which an associative tie, be it resemblance or any other, is like a perception: it is singular until *used* generally (i.e. as a representation common to many different things – a *conceptus communis*). Natural relations *felt* by consciousness are as particular as the perceptions themselves to which the resemblances are ascribed, since, for Hume, the felt ease of transition *is* the relation. There is merely *this* perception *felt* in present consciousness to relate to *that*. Not until the idea of *this* transition of thought is *used* open-endedly as a representative for *any* pair of perceptions – so that variables, as it were, replace the particular perceptions related – does it take on a value greater than that of a single, isolated relational consciousness of perceptions. Take for example the relation between a triangle and two right angles discussed by Berkeley. I draw the figures on a piece of paper, and go through the steps necessary to discerning the relation. Once this is done, need it ever occur to me that the relation I have just discovered does, or even can, hold for other figures, much less all *possible* figures amenable to this process of reasoning? I might at a later date perform a like abstraction on different figures and fail even to notice (feel) any *resemblance* (be it between the two sets of figures, which might differ greatly in appearance, or the operations I carry out upon them, or the relations discovered thereby), let alone apprehend it with the *universality* characteristic of mathematical demonstration (i.e. the extension of the relation to all *possible* figures of a certain *kind*). In short, just like Locke and Berkeley, Kemp Smith failed to realize that resemblances have no *intrinsic* generality (respects too, in that Hume reduced aspects to resemblances – see below).[8]

Before proceeding to the detailed examination of Hume's position, one final problem should be mentioned in connection with the views of Locke and Berkeley. Neither offers a satisfactory analysis of *abstraction*, that is, the intellectual operations of *discerning* aspects and leaving some out while including others in one's consideration of an idea which in itself is particular. These operations are, at the very least, suspect; for, without a proper clarification, it may well seem that, in expelling abstraction out the front door of images and sensations, they then immediately readmit it through the backdoor of mental activity. If I am supposed to lack the power to form abstract images, how can I still be supposed to have the power to *conceive* them abstractly? If aspects, in particular, are not really separate and distinct in the image (as Berkeley in particular contended), then how can I in any sense separate them in my conception of the image? For example, if I cannot imagine the angles of a triangle without also imagining sides of determinate length, then how can I be supposed to apprehend them separately? It is one thing to claim to be able to refer separately, *in language*, to the pitch of a sound and its timbre; but quite another to suppose that it is possible to conceive them separately *in consciousness*. Berkeley, no less than Locke, seems to endow us with a mental capacity that would permit us to discern the color of an image from its shape *even if we never had experience of different shapes or colors* (i.e. on a first presentation, with no prior history of comparisons). If so, then this is simply another faculty of non-sensible insight akin to Cartesian intellectual intuition; and such a power is quite incompatible with the methods and aspirations of a thoroughgoing empiricism such as Hume's (see especially *T*72).

B. Generality as associative propensities and habits

If generality cannot be reduced to comparison and abstraction and left at that, then clearly a more rigorous and powerful psychologistic theory than Locke or Berkeley were able to offer is required. In what follows, I shall contend that Hume's theory of generality is just such a theory. In particular, I will try to show (i) that Hume recognized the significance of the fact that generality lies not in ideas themselves, but in the representative use made of them, (ii) employed his theory of association (i.e. principles of natural relation), first (iii) to reduce generality to abstraction (aspects, distinctions of reason), and then (iv) to reduce abstraction itself to habitudes of comparison and resemblance.

Everyone recognizes that Hume would not have generality be construed as a feature of ideas themselves. However, what in my view is rarely if ever realized is that the reason for this is not that ideas, as copies of *individual* impressions, must themselves be individual, but rather their status as *representations*. Far from being an *intrinsic* quality, ideas may become even so much as *singular* representations of impressions only through their *constant conjunction*, and consequent *association* with them. In particular, *causal relations* are the basis of their status as singular representatives (copies) of impressions. Resemblance, by contrast, is an indiscriminate relation, incapable of coupling ideas specifically with impressions. For example, tactile sensations may be found (i.e. felt by consciousness) to resemble olfactory sensations in some respect, and either or both may be found to resemble an emotion in the same or another respect; but such resemblances are no more (or less) reason to suppose one to be the representation of the other than the resemblance of ideas to impressions is a basis for supposing the former to represent the latter. Since any two ideas may be compared in *some* respect, and "no objects will admit of comparison, but what have some degree of resemblance" (*T*14), there is no perception that could not then be considered the representation of any other (impressions might even be deemed representations of ideas). Resemblance is simply too weak a relation to underpin representationality. Even if aspects are excluded and the comparison is confined to whole perceptions, resemblances would still relate perceptions across all manner of boundaries: the visual triangle and the tactile triangle, five notes played on a flute and five definitions of justice, grief and disappointment (see *T*283), etc. Since, of all relations, resemblances have the least respect for differences of kind among perceptions, they can hardly be deemed sufficient to fix the very precise boundary demarcating representation from all other resemblance relations. Thus, it is only in combination with causal relations that resemblances can become representations (see chapter 1-D and -E).

The examination of ideas as general representatives must take the causal relation between impression-originals and idea-copies as its point of departure: this is the Humean condition *non plus ultra* for mental symbolism. This means, above all, that the generality of ideas must be explicated in the same *natural*, *associative*, *wholly empirical* manner in which they acquire their status as singular representatives. So, the resemblance relations at the center of Hume's account of generality must be construed simply as yet another expression of that "gentle force" (*T*10) or "attraction, which in the mental world will be found to have as extraordinary effects as in the natural, and to shew itself in as many and as various forms" (*T*12f.). The instinctive character of such a relation – our propensity to take note of resemblances at nearly all times and under almost any circumstances – furnishes the essential ingredient of a psychological theory of generality missing from the accounts of Berkeley and Locke. For it is one thing, for example, to say that the demonstration of the connection between this image of a triangle and these two right angles *can* be extended to all other possible triangles and pairs of right angles, but quite another to account for why and how it actually *is*. Equally, to repeat it on other figures and to recognize in it an altogether new use for ideas as representatives *common* to *indefinitely* many others quite another are quite different things.[9] It cannot be left to chance, so that we merely happen upon this use, nor can it be serendipity that accounts for the pervasiveness of generality in our thinking. Education cannot account for it, since the ability to use ideas in this way is suggested in the behavior of infants and animals (see section C), and presumably was evinced in that of our adult, prelinguistic ancestors as well. Hume's associationalism seems tailor-made to furnish an account of generality within these parameters. For, given a natural human propensity to extend resemblance relations as far and wide as possible, ingrained *habitudes* of comparison with an eye to resemblances must inevitably arise; and these habitudes have precisely the *open-ended* character – the same extension to all *possible* things and situations an individual might encounter – implied by general representation. The use of an idea as a general representative, and the possession of such habitudes are, for Hume, not merely coextensive, but the same, the former *being* nothing but the latter. When we would conceive of universality in terms of abstract ideas or abstractive mental operations, the vacuum left by the absence of any idea (or "notion") is filled – without our consciously realizing it – by the conception of particular habitual operations of comparison performed with an eye to resemblances: they are the "original" of our notion that the representative power of an idea may extend beyond past and future experience to all *possible* occasions of perception. Berkeleian indifferent denotation is, for Hume, simply this: idea-representatives governed by acquired associative propensities. The explanation of generality in terms of such propensities is therefore, from a Humean perspective, simply another confirmation of the truth and explanatory power of association ("as these are the only ties of our thoughts, they are really *to us* the cement of the universe, and all the operations of the mind must, in a great measure, depend on them," *TAbs*662).[10]

We may now proceed to the details of Hume's account of generality. Since natural resemblance relations are the heart of the theory, it is clear, given their nature, that its true focus is the *action of the mind*, and, in particular, the resemblances *felt* between various operations such as delineating out an object in thought and apprehending one in sensation. Perhaps the most illuminating example of the preeminence of this facet of resemblance relations in Hume's theory of generality is his analysis of distinctions of reason (aspects) on *T*25. It begins as follows:

'Tis certain that the mind wou'd never have dream'd of distinguishing a figure from the body figur'd, as being in reality neither distinguishable, nor different, nor separable; did it not observe, that even in this simplicity there might be contain'd many different resemblances and relations.

There is no immediately perceptible distinction between a figure and that of which it is the figure, or such items as color and shape, timbre and pitch, etc. We could not, even if we would, suppose such distinctions to exist did we not afterwards proceed to *compare* these perceptions to *others*, and so come to associate them in natural relations of resemblance:

Thus when a globe of white marble is presented, we receive only the impression of a white colour dispos'd in a certain form, nor are we able to separate and distinguish the colour from the form. But observing afterwards a globe of black marble and a cube of white, and comparing them with our former object, we find two separate resemblances, in what formerly seem'd, and really is, perfectly inseparable. After a little more practice of this kind, we begin to distinguish the figure from the colour by a *distinction of reason*; that is, we consider the figure and colour together, since they are in effect the same and undistinguishable; but still view them in different aspects, according to the resemblances, of which they are susceptible.

Aspects, or distinctions of reason, are not "seen" or "intuited," but are rather by-products of comparison, and so inextricably bound up with imaginative activity directed upon particular (distinct) perceptions. But, just as Locke stressed in the case of judgment and perception (see chapter 2-A), habit blinds us to the true, relational nature of aspects:

When we wou'd consider only the figure of the globe of white marble, we form in reality an idea both of the figure and colour, but tacitly carry our eye to its resemblance with the globe of black marble: And in the same manner, when we wou'd consider its colour only, we turn our view to its resemblance with the cube of white marble. By this means we accompany our ideas with a kind of reflexion, of which custom renders us, in a great measure, insensible.

It is no more possible to *think* an aspect in isolation (i.e. independently of acts of comparison) than to encounter it alone in sensation or form an isolated image of it in imagination:

A person, who desires us to consider the figure of a globe of white marble without thinking on its colour, desires an impossibility; but his meaning is, that we shou'd consider the colour and figure together, but still keep in our eye the resemblance to the globe of black marble, or that to any other globe of whatever colour or substance.

To interpret the injunction to "*keep in our eye* the resemblance" in a manner consistent with the impossibility of *considering* "the figure... without thinking on its color," I see no alternative but to suppose Hume to be referring to the habitual transition, the custom, which alone connects the figure with the black globe in our imagination. Hence, aspect-seeing (i.e. abstractive mental operations), which both Locke and Berkeley made central to their accounts of generality, is supplanted in Hume's theory by habits founded on associative propensities.

The core of Hume's theory of generality is the custom ingrained in us by numerous comparisons of resembling individuals. This "custom, which we have acquir'd by surveying them" enables us to produce "any other individual one, for which we may have occasion" (*T*20f.). Those individuals not presently before the mind are "*represented* by means of that *habit*, by which we recall them, whenever any present occasion requires it" (*T*22 – emphasis mine). The habit is triggered by an encounter with a perception having the relevant aspect (i.e. a perception suited to the comparison on which the habit is grounded); and, being mere habit, we do so without deliberation, without having to go through the motions of recalling previous perceptions and carrying out the comparisons ("They are not really and in fact present to the mind, but only in power ... we keep ourselves in a readiness to survey any of them, as we may be prompted by a present design or necessity," *T*20). The custom alone is enough; without needing to recall past perceptions to compare with a present one in order to feel whether they are resembling, the recognition occurs with the practiced ease and effortlessness (but also the obliviousness) characteristic of all habitual routines (hence the mysterious seeming power whereby imagination "suggests its ideas, and presents them at the very instant, in which they become necessary or useful," *T*24).

The real importance of habitudes for Hume's theory of generality is their ability to convert the reflective operations of comparison from representations merely of the aggregate of previously apprehended and imagined perceptions into a representation of every *apprehensible* or *imaginable* (= every *possible*)[11] perception in which that aspect can be discerned: "If ideas be particular in their nature, and at the same time finite in their number, 'tis only by custom they can become general in their representation, and contain an infinite number of other ideas under them" (*T*24). The acquisition of a habit so that the performance of an operation of comparison becomes routine and automatic gives a particular idea (or term) connected with it the open-ended character of a genuine universal; the idea acquires the status of a representative *common* to all *possible* perceptions, however different otherwise, which, if presented to consciousness, would be felt to resemble it. Differences of aspect are, correspondingly, nothing more than the various habitudes any given perception may, depending on one's present train of thought, trigger in the imagination. Despite falling well short of the archetypes favored by the platonist, Humean "universals" are therefore at least adequate to the representative task required of general ideas and/or terms ("Tho' the capacity of the mind be not infinite, yet we can at once form a notion of all possible degrees of quantity and quality, in such a manner at least, as, however imperfect, may serve all the purposes of reflexion and conversation," *T*18).

It should now begin to be clear why association, the single point distinguishing Hume's theory of generality from those of Locke and Berkeley, is of such paramount importance: *unless the repeated observation of the resemblance of individuals led to the formation of a habit, comparison by itself would never take us beyond aggregates of resemblance relations to true universality.* The operation of comparison with an eye to particular resemblances permits us to distinguish aspects. When the operation becomes a habit of mind (and so insensible to us), it will then not only enliven any idea subsequently found to incorporate the relevant aspect, but also induce in us a belief that the object it represents bears, or is capable of bearing, any of the qualities and relations previously met with in things having that aspect; we thus come to regard an object not just as an isolated individual, but as a new *instance* of a previously encountered *sort*. The awareness of a habitude in ourselves (i.e. of the habitual performance of a particular operation of comparison), plus the feeling of recognition characteristic of its exercise, are, for Hume, identical with the awareness of the universality of an idea. So, too, higher universals: when representations already rendered universal are found resembling, and these resemblances become for us both *natural* (i.e. the verisimilitude of the one will, *ipso facto*, enliven the other) and *habitual* (an easy transition from the presence of the one to the thought of the other), new aspects are distinguished, i.e. higher natural kinds. For example, we begin by noticing a resemblance in respect of action between different causal relations, A does *this* to B, C does *that* to D, and E *that* to F; it then becomes *customary* to expect and believe things *like* A, C, and E to do this *sort* of action – say, *warm* – things *like* B, D, and F. Our consciousness of *to warm* as a universal and the custom-based expectation/belief felt in imagination when it performs this (now routine) comparison are, for Hume, one and the same. Once acquired, however, this complex idea too may be compared and found to resemble other universals, for example, *to clean*, *to cover with soft materials*, *to fix a drink*, etc. If the occurrence of warming *naturally* prompts one to think of these other actions and a new habitual comparison is infixed, a new *natural* sort may be recognized, say, *to make oneself comfortable*. In this way, we eventually arrive at highly general ideas like *to alter*, *to exercise a power*, *to depend on*, etc., and, ultimately, the single most general form of action, *to cause*. Well before this, the resemblance will have become too general, too "philosophical" to yield an habitual, idea-enlivening association ("the more general and universal any of our ideas are, the less influence they have upon the imagination," *T*425). Yet, imagination is "like a galley put in motion by the oars, [which] carries on its course without any new impulse" (*T*198). So, although these higher universals are conceived long after the influence of habit has ceased, they retain a residue of appeal to imagination, a kind of after-life, as outgrowths or extensions of association-based universals.[12]

An excellent illustration of the paramountcy for Hume of habit and the merely marginal importance of both the particular idea and the general term annexed to it is the following:

> so entire is the custom, that the very same idea may be annext to several different words, and may be employ'd in different reasonings, without any danger of mistake. Thus the idea of an equilateral triangle of an inch perpendicular may serve us in talking of a figure, of a rectilineal figure, of a regular figure, of a triangle, and of an equilateral triangle. All these terms, therefore, are in this case attended with the same idea; but as they are wont to be apply'd in a greater or lesser compass, they excite their particular habits, and thereby keep the mind in a readiness to observe, that no conclusion be form'd contrary to any ideas, which are usually compriz'd under them. (*T*21f.)

Although different ideas or terms may be conjoined with the same habit and the same idea or term with different habits, generality is wholly a function of the habit. Ideas like the equilateral triangle of an inch perpendicular are needed only for the *acquisition* of the habit, that is, for the initial comparisons whereby the mental routine for discovering a given aspect becomes infixed (see *T*22). But, just as a child is able to dispense with its walker once it has acquired a certain competency in walking, so the imagination ceases to depend on individual ideas once a comparison has become habitual:

> I believe every one, who examines the situation of his mind in reasoning, will agree with me, that we do not annex distinct and compleat ideas to every term we make use of. (*T*23) For it [is] usual, after the frequent use of terms, which are really significant and intelligible, to omit the idea, which we wou'd express by them, and to preserve only the custom by which we recal the idea at pleasure. (*T*224)[13]

Once the initial stage of infixing a habit of comparison is passed, the role of particular ideas in universal representation is merely to "excite their particular habits," for which purpose terms will do just as well.

Hume's debt to Berkeley went beyond the thesis that an abstract idea is no idea at all to the reasoning behind it:

> I own myself able to abstract in one sense, as when I consider some particular parts or qualities separated from others, with which though they are united in some object, yet, it is possible they may really exist without them. I deny that I can

abstract from one another, or conceive separately, those qualities which it is impossible should exist so separated. (*PHK* Intro. §10)

Thus, I imagine the trunk of a human body without the limbs, or conceive the smell of a rose without thinking on the rose itself. So far, I will not deny, I can abstract; if that may properly be called *abstraction* which extends only to the conceiving separately such objects as it is possible may really exist or be actually perceived asunder. But my conceiving or imagining power does not extend beyond the possibility of real existence or perception. (*PHK* §5)

For Berkeley, "abstract idea" is an oxymoron. Nothing can be termed "idea" which is incapable of presenting itself in consciousness on its own and exists only in relation to an attentive gaze (aspect-seeing). Now, while Berkeley himself strayed from this credo in practice,[14] Hume stood fast against abstraction in all its guises. By treating the imagination as a necessary condition of relations, he inseparably linked these complex ideas, as well as their habit-based products (especially aspects), to the consciousness that considers perceptions. This enabled him to affirm the *T*18 separability principle adapted from Berkeley unqualifiedly, and apply it to perceptions so as not to admit even a single exception.

Hume did not cease to utilize abstract language (how could he?), including even the locution "abstract idea." This should, however, be seen against the background of a psychology that permits each and every abstract idea to be explicated in terms of habitudes of comparison.[15] In particular, there seems to me no warrant for the view of several recent commentators that Hume readmitted full-blown abstractions through the backdoor in the guise of distinctions of reason. There is nothing in the passage in which Hume analyzed distinctions of reason to support this contention. When we first see the white globe, "we receive only the impression of a white colour dispos'd in a certain form, nor are we able to separate and distinguish the colour from the form." The *illusion* of their separability derives from the fact that we compare, and find resembling, the white globe and, on the one hand, a black globe, a green globe, or a silver globe, and, on the other hand, a white cube, a white pyramid, or a white cloud. For it then is quite natural to presume that what is separable in view of our comparisons must be *really* separable *in itself*. This is precisely the mistake we make when we suppose, say, that the *very same* figure we *see* can be distinguished in the medium of *tactile* sensation – or, for that matter, in that of a bat's *echo-sonar* or any other sensation medium with the requisite acuity. For it is plainly only a short, easy step from this level of abstraction to that where a figure common to all these sensory media is supposed also to be capable of existing independently of the senses, and so of bestowing a shape on mind-independent – albeit not directly knowable (Descartes, Locke), or even inconceivable (Berkeley) – media such as "matter" (of which some interpreters of Hume suppose him to have accorded us a "relative idea"). For Hume, as I understand him, such suppositions are sheer fantasy. If figure and color were truly separable in the way prescribed, it would be possible to distinguish them at the outset, without having to go to all the trouble of comparing the sensation of the white globe with other sensory data with an eye to their resemblances. But such abstractive powers are, in Hume's view, merely a myth of philosophers. He would regard it as impossible to discern any difference at all between the color of the globe and its figure merely by inspecting and reflecting on that one isolated perception. Without other perceptions with which to compare it, or with no prior history of making comparisons of the relevant sort, we would find the figure and color of the globe "the same and undistinguishable" (*T*25). There is thus no such thing as a power of *abstraction*, an intellectual capacity *really* to conceive the color and figure separately (see *T*72f.).

The issue of how Hume is to be interpreted on the objectivity of distinctions of reason ultimately hinges on how one understands his theory of relation. The white globe, over time, becomes enmeshed in a wide and varied network of habit-driven resemblance relations: not only black globes and white cubes, but geographical implements, tennis balls, planets, the texture of polished stone, the coldness of snow, the flavor of coconut, rolling pins (i.e. things that roll), and innumerably many other things the imagination even of a child might find to resemble it. Can it plausibly be supposed that all these myriad aspects of our consciousness of the white globe reflect actual distinctions in the perception itself? Only the most die-hard realist would be inclined to suppose this true of *all* of them; and, in my view, Hume would deny that *any* of them correspond to a real difference in the perception of the white globe. He stated quite explicitly that "a relation ... is not, strictly speaking, a property in the figures themselves, but arises merely from the comparison, which the mind makes betwixt them" (*T*46). He also made clear that distinctions of reason are "founded on the different resemblances, which the same simple idea may have to several different ideas" (*T*67; see also *TApp*637). So, "having regard to the color of the white globe" amounts simply to situating it in a series of perceptions which includes the white cube but not the black globe (a series the "rule" for which is neither concept nor social practice but a psychological habitude of association). It is as if there were a number of different axes ramifying in all directions from the idea of the white globe: color-resemblances, shape-resemblances, tactile-resemblances, geography-resemblances, etc. Yet, these axes are constituted not by anything intrinsic to the idea of the white globe, but by various graduations in the *feeling* to consciousness attendant upon the transition of the attentive gaze from one to the next. Resemblances naturally partition themselves into different groupings in accordance with their "feeling" to imagination. For example, having moved from the resemblance of the white globe to the white cube, the transition to a white pyramid *now* feels more natural to imagination than otherwise, and certainly more so *at that moment* than a transition to the black globe. Considered sequentially, the white globe, white cube, and white pyramid "feel" like they belong together in a special, almost familial way, and virtually repel, by main force, black globes, red spheres, and brown eggs from their company. But if the same perceptions were considered in a different order, starting, say, with the white globe and proceeding to the black globe, an entirely different family of resemblances results, with a repellent force no less great. In this way, whole networks of distinct associative habitudes are formed; and it is solely of such natural groupings of resemblances that "aspect-seeing" consists (we "view them in different aspects, according to the resemblances, of which they are susceptible," *T*25).[16] Thus, distinctions of reason imply no power literally to see an aspect ("A person, who desires [this] ... desires an impossibility"); and their true, purely associative nature escapes our notice only because it is "a kind of reflexion, of which custom renders us, in a great measure, insensible" (*T*25).

By reducing aspect-seeing to a matter purely of comparisons and resemblances, Hume achieved three things. (i) By dispensing with the need for ideas "of so refin'd and spiritual a nature, that they fall not under the conception of the fancy, but must be comprehended by a pure and intellectual view, of which the superior faculties of the soul are alone capable" (*T*72), there is no longer any basis for positing a special mode of intuition by which to perceive distinctions in what otherwise would be "the same and undistinguishable." (ii) The figure and color of the white globe are indissolubly bound up with the whole visual datum and have no bearing on its simplicity or complexity as a perception. Besides sparing Hume the problems inherent in Locke's abstractive distinction between simple and complex ideas (see chapter 1-C), this implies that what we call "figure" in the case of the visible white globe cannot be identified with what we call the "figure" of a *tactile* globe, much less be deemed (even problematically) a representation of a globe of pure Aristotelian matter. Hence, the possibility of even so much as a relative idea of an imperceptible existent is precluded: aspects like figure, motion, color, etc., are merely shorthand for comparisons that natural relations have rendered habitual and, so, insensible; they are neither perceptions in their own right nor representations of a reality beyond. In this, Berkeley was quite clearly Hume's inspiration; yet, Hume's account of generality so far outstripped this inspiration in depth, rigor, and explanatory power, that the theory may legitimately be ascribed to him alone.

(iii) But perhaps the greatest philosophical consequence of Hume's elimination of abstraction (intuitive apprehension of aspects) from the capacities of the mind is to annul the basis for distinguishing a special faculty of discursive understanding over and above imagination, so that what we call "understanding" signifies merely "the general and more establish'd properties of the imagination" (*T* 267). Here a brief glance forward to Kant is in order. Hume's attempt to supplant strict logical universality with psychological habitudes endangered not only the objectivity, but the very existence *as concepts* of cause, substance, quantity, etc. Kant recognized and set out to overcome, the empiricist challenge to vindicate the extra-linguistic reality of concepts and furnish a new, sounder basis for distinguishing understanding from imagination that involves neither abstract images nor abstractive mental operations. To begin with, going part way to meet Hume, he concurred that the categories (cause, substance, et al.) are not, in and of themselves, concepts; but, instead of reducing them to psychological principles of associative imagination, he traced them to logical forms of judgment.[17] In Kant's view, the logical forms and pure understanding are one and the same: "We can trace back all actions of the understanding to judgments, so that the *understanding* can be represented as *a capacity for judging*... The functions of the understanding can therefore all be found by exhaustively enumerating the functions of unity in judging" (*CPR* A69/B94). Since logical forms lack all conceptual content and objective relation, they are metaphysically so barren that even Hume could countenance them; yet, by tracing the categories to this source, Kant could at least claim to have secured them against psychological reduction. The second, transcendental stage of Kant's attempt to rescue generality from the prison of language is far more complicated. It concerns the demonstration that the objectivity of the logical forms is a necessary condition for both possible experience and its objects (as derivative, the categories are only of secondary concern: they express the *relation* of pure understanding to sensibility, the mere thought of sensible appearances in conformity with the logical forms). For reasons we cannot go into here, part of this demonstration involves establishing that "the representation *I think* ... be capable of accompanying all other representations" (*CPR* B132). This means that the *I think* has a relation to all possible representations, and so a genuinely *universal* reference; hence, any particular representation, in being thought, is able itself to partake of this universal relation as well. The key to Kant's account, I believe, is the claim that the *I think*, in and of itself, is the mere *copula* of judgment, that is, the sheer act of uniting different representations in accordance with logical form ("The logical form of all judgments consists in the objective unity of apperception of the concepts they contain," *CPR* B140).[18] Accordingly, the universal relation in which a representation partakes by virtue of being thought is a *logical* one: that of a predicate of a possible judgment with potentially *universal* validity. For even if, as a matter of empirical fact, it should happen to hold of few other representations, or even none, it still, logically and a priori, has universal applicability (i.e. it ranges over the domain of all possible representations). In other words, the *universal* relation of representations to a possible representation *I think* gives every representation, as *my* representation, a potential application not just to every empirical consciousness I have had or will ever have, but every one I could *possibly* have ("a representation which is to be thought of as common to *different* representations ... must previously be thought in synthetic unity with other, though it may be only possible, representations, before I can think in it the analytic unity of consciousness, which makes it a *conceptus communis*," *CPR* B133n.). There is, accordingly, a kind of universality proper to consciousness itself, independent of language, yet logical in nature; and on this basis Kant believed himself warranted in affirming a faculty of discursive understanding over and above imagination.

Kant's conception of generality is inextricably bound up with the possibility of experience and its objects. The synthetic unity presupposed by the analytic unity of a *conceptus communis* is *singular* and belongs to *sensibility*, and is none other than pure space and time (see *CPR* B136n., B140, and B160n.). That is, the *use* of a perception, in itself singular, as a *conceptus communis*[19] entails the subordination of the manifold to conditions of space and time as that which makes possible unity of apperception. Accordingly, the production of this network of singular relations through synthesis in imagination of the manifold in conformity with the logical forms of judgment not only makes possible universal representation, but also yields a universe of dynamically interconnected objects constituted wholly of spatial and temporal relations. In this way, Kant sought to re-establish understanding as an autonomous faculty and to overcome Hume's skepticism concerning causality with one bold stroke.[20]

C. Philosophy and common language

Hume's account of generality is, in part, an essay in the philosophy of language. But is it so primarily, even essentially? Given the way he framed the issue, one might well suppose generality to be inherently linguistic (language dependent):

> A particular idea becomes general by being annex'd to a general term; that is, to a term, which from a customary conjunction has a relation to many other particular ideas, and readily recalls them in the imagination. (*T*22)

> [A]ll general ideas are, in reality, particular ones, attached to a general term, which recalls, upon occasion, other particular ones, that resemble, in certain circumstances, the idea, present to the mind. (*E*XII/ii.125n.)

On the basis of such remarks, many commentators ascribe to Hume the view, that, as Baier puts it, "Without language... there would be no generality, no abstraction, no ideas of the sort that have *a priori* knowable 'relations.'"[21] However, this seems to me mistaken. Language plays only a marginal role in Hume's account of generality. Only two factors, both psychological, are for him essential to generality: (i) the native propensity of human imagination to compare perceptions with an eye to their resemblance, and (ii) the establishing of customs (habitual transitions) by the repeated performance of such comparisons. General terms are essential to neither process (by contrast with ideas which are needed for comparison *before* a habit can be instilled). General terms are as dispensable to Hume's account of generality as proper names, demonstratives, et al., are to his equally psychological account of singular representation (ideas as copies of impression originals). That Hume chose to frame the problem in linguistic terms is probably just a carry over from Berkeley, who, believing he was correcting Locke (falsely, as *ECHU* III/iii/§11 shows), insisted that ideas are always particular ("a word becomes general by being made the sign, not of an abstract general idea but, of several particular ideas, any one of which it indifferently suggests to the mind," *PHK* Introduction §11). Berkeley traced the contrary view to the naïve linguistics of his opponents. By wrongly treating all nouns on the model of proper names, they suppose that a general term can only have meaning if there is something general either in thought or reality which it "names" (see *PHK* Introduction §19). Yet, while Berkeley may have stressed the linguistic dimension of the traditional problem of universals, it must not be overlooked that he did so only in order to expel language from the domain of true philosophy:

> Since therefore words are so apt to impose on the understanding, whatever ideas I consider, I shall endeavor to take them bare and naked into my view; keeping out of my thoughts, so far as I am able, those names which long and constant use hath so strictly united with them... We need only draw the curtain of words, to behold the fairest tree of knowledge, whose fruit is excellent, and within the reach of our hand. (*PHK* Introduction §21 and §25)

For all his prescient comments relating to language, Berkeley's concern with generality, like Locke's before him, centered on what is present in the *mind* when we have general *ideas*: whether, when our ideas are general, there are other than singular contents present in or before consciousness. Language was of interest to him only in so far as reflecting upon it might shed light on this issue, and so merely as a means, not an end. So too, I believe, in Hume's case. One only need recall the terms in which he lauded Berkeley at the outset of the section on abstract ideas to recognize that he too conceived the problem psychologically rather than linguistically: "A very material question has been started concerning *abstract* or *general* ideas, *whether they be general or particular in the mind's conception of them*" (*T*17). Hume's problem was the mind's conception of its ideas, that is, the contents of consciousness; mention of language was not even required to formulate it. Moreover, as he made clear shortly afterwards, far from desiring to alter or supersede Berkeley's treatment of the question, his aim was the more modest one of endeavoring "to confirm [Berkeley's discovery] by some arguments, which I hope will put it beyond all doubt and controversy." So, to interpret Hume as seeking a linguistic account of generality, though surely tempting, is highly anachronistic and almost certainly mistaken.

There is one consideration that seems to me decisive in this regard as in so many others. Hume was keen to avoid succumbing to the tendency of most philosophers "to foster the predominant inclination, and push the mind, with more determined resolution, towards that side which already *draws* too much, by the bias and propensity of the natural temper" (*EV*/i.34). Since the hallmark of higher intellect is undoubtedly the ability to think in general ideas (to conceptualize, judge, and reason), it is all too easy to treat this capacity as unique to man, as setting him apart from everything else in nature. As language is the most obvious and compelling evidence of human uniqueness,[22] it suffices to prove that generality is the exclusive province of the language-user to gain a warrant for asserting the fundamental intellectual superiority of man with respect to animals. Were Hume's account of generality of this kind, however, it would represent a signal failing on his part to satisfy the criterion he declared to be "a kind of touchstone, by which we may try every system in this species of philosophy" (*T*176): that no philosophy should attribute to human understanding any capacity that cannot also be seen to operate in what he pointedly described as "the reason of animals" (title to both *Treatise* I/iii/§16 and its *Enquiry* counterpart). The *full* satisfaction of this criterion he saw as "an invincible proof of my system" (*T*178), whereas even a partial failure to do so he deemed a sure indication of error:

The common defect of those systems, which philosophers have employ'd to account for the actions of the mind, is, that they suppose such a subtility and refinement of thought, as not only exceeds the capacity of mere animals, but even of children and the common people in our own species ... Such a subtility is a clear proof of the falshood, as the contrary simplicity of the truth, of any system. Let us therefore put our present system concerning the nature of the understanding to this decisive trial, and see whether it will equally account for the reasonings of beasts as for these of the human species. (*T*177; see also *E*IX.82)

We must ask ourselves why Hume would have gone to such great lengths to reduce human understanding to purely psychological functions of association capable of operating in animals only to readmit human uniqueness through the backdoor by treating generality – which on the face of it he makes a purely psychological affair of habit-governed associative imagination – the exclusive province of the language-user?

Animal behavior permits us to infer that (i) they too regard as impressions their sensations and reflexions, and as ideas their thoughts, images, and dreams ("there [is] some impression immediately present to their memory or senses, in order to be the foundation of their judgment," *T*177f.); they are therefore, presumably, endowed with phenomenological consciousness as well. We may further suppose that (ii) animals have associative imaginations which enliven certain of their ideas in preference to others, and (iii) that they do so on the basis of the very same principles of association operative in humans (their "actions ... proceed from a reasoning, that is not in itself different, nor founded on different principles, from that which appears in human nature," *T*177). In particular, as with humans, (iv) their reasoning is constituted by habitual natural relations: "It is custom alone, which engages animals, from every object, that strikes the senses, to infer its usual attendant, and carries their imagination, from the appearance of the one, to conceive the other, in that particular manner, which we denominate *belief*" (*E*IX.84). (v) Since "the animal infers some fact beyond what immediately strikes his senses" (*E*IX.83), these principles clearly include cause and effect and the uniformity of nature (see *T*327 and *E*IX.84). (vi) Just as humans "always suppose an external universe ... the animal creation are governed by a like opinion, and preserve this belief of external objects, in all their thoughts, designs, and actions" (*E*XII/i.118). Accordingly, there is no reason to believe (vii) that Hume would have thought animals less capable than ourselves of representation: they need only observe that all their perceptions come in duplicate, and, since the impression always precedes the idea, associate them in imagination as original and copy. So, if any fundamental difference between humans and animals exists, it is not to be found in the possession of idea-representatives as such, but only in the ability to make use of them as *general* representatives.

Hume never directly addressed the issue of generality in animals; yet, since general representation involves no capacity of mind he did not also ascribe to animals, there is no basis on which he could have denied that they possess this power. We may take it as a rule of thumb, that if he did not expressly deny a capacity of mind to animals, then, if their behavior gives evidence of it, they should be supposed to possess it (though not, perhaps, in the same degree or to the same ends as humans). Is there any warrant for believing that Hume saw evidence of a capacity for general representation in animals? According to him, "This application of ideas beyond their nature proceeds from our collecting all their possible degrees of quantity and quality in such an imperfect manner as may serve the purposes of life" (*T*20).[23] From this one may reasonably infer that if the purposes of an animal's life were served by forming habitudes of comparison with an eye to resemblances, and its behavior gave evidence of such mental dispositions, then, since it is as well equipped as we are to represent universally, it would do so. And the following strongly suggests that, in Hume's view, universalizing is no less useful to animals than to humans:

> It seems evident, that animals as well as men learn many things from experience, and infer, that the same events will always follow from the same causes. By this principle they become acquainted with the more obvious properties of external objects, and gradually, from their birth, treasure up a knowledge of the nature of fire, water, earth, stones, heights, depths, & c., and of the effects which result from their operation ... A horse, that has been accustomed to the field, becomes acquainted with the proper height which he can leap, and will never attempt what exceeds his force and ability. An old greyhound will trust the more fatiguing part of the chace to the younger, and will place himself so as to meet the hare in her doubles; nor are the conjectures, which he forms on this occasion, founded in any thing but his observation and experience. (*E*IX.83)

The mature horse has learnt how to gauge the *height in general* he is able to jump; for he takes account of the lay of the ground, the angle of approach, the speed required, etc., while having learned to ignore other features like where (in what field) the obstacle happens to be, what material it is made of, whether it is covered with moss, whether birds are perched on it, etc. Likewise, the veteran hunting dog, expert in the predator-eluding tactics *general* to hares (as distinct from other *sorts* of prey), has developed habits that lead him to anticipate, under a given *set* of circumstances, that his prey will double back, and, furthermore, what is the best sort of place to lie in ambush; and this is possible only because he has learned to regard certain features (aspects) of the chase as inessential (which fool novice dogs). How, except as generalization of their ideas of physical entities, could Hume explain these behaviors? If animals can reason from the *sameness* of events to the *sameness* of their causes, then are they not, in exactly the same manner Hume described in humans, treating events as *instances* of *types* (natural kinds)? If animals may be said to have knowledge of the *nature* and *effects* of fire, water, etc., then are we not talking of more than just their cumulative past experience, but of true generalizing of the habit-driven sort, that is, of representation that extends to *all possible* instances of the kind (= all perceptions able to trigger the habitude)? This capacity may be different in certain respects from our own, and it may be outside either their power or their purposes of life to generalize as we do (the discovery of aspects which emerge only at the level of philosophical resemblance, and so where habit no longer exerts any influence). Yet, when one reflects on Hume's horse and hound, animal understanding comes to seem so similar to our own to warrant accusations of anthropocentricity if one refuses to impute to them powers of generalization (understood to involve solely the capacity to form habits of comparison). If we bear in mind that the generalizing of a horse or a hound is bound to be adapted to its species' peculiar purposes and observe how remote these are from human ones, we may come to suspect our belief in the superiority of human understanding to be a mere prejudice.

Anthropomorphizing is not a danger so long as we may plausibly suppose that higher animals are sufficiently like humans to feel resemblances as we do, and to form similar basic habitudes; for then there would be a large stock of shared basic natural kind concepts, e.g. *fire*, *water*, *hare*, *evasion of capture*, *hiding place*, *leapable height*, etc. That they lack words for their general ideas can only be deemed a sign of deficient intelligence if their purposes of life would be better served by having them, and, Kipling notwithstanding, who could say whether words would be of benefit to the tiger or the cobra? So, however unpalatable some may deem it, there seems little doubt that Hume would have extended his psychologized universals to animals rather than make them the exclusive province of language-users, and, moreover, would have done so unashamedly, regarding it as rebounding to the credit of his philosophy.[24]

Clearly, the uses and forms of language are as incidental to Hume's account of generality as to those of Locke and Berkeley. In both inspiration and essentials, Hume's account is *psychological*. Before a term can be affixed to a particular idea and become general by virtue of an habitual operation of comparison, it is necessary to form another, quite distinct sort of habit, one derived not from natural relations grounded in our native propensities, but from education. The use of terms as proxies for ideas is not natural, but artificial, and motivated by the particular purpose of communication. General terms, for Hume, are the result of special training, the goal of which is to inculcate an habitual relation of a general idea with a sensible sign so that the latter may eventually circumvent the former and be able itself to trigger the relevant habitude of comparison ("it being usual, after the frequent use of terms, which are really significant and intelligible, to omit the idea, which we wou'd express by them, and to preserve only the custom by which we recal the idea at pleasure," *T*224).

Once it is accepted that the uses and forms of language are marginal to Hume's psychological account of generality, one may wonder how he proposed to deal with language. Did he regard it as falling within the compass of psychological explanation as well, or did he think it irreducibly societal? And, if the latter, was he cognizant of just how ill-adapted and hazard-laden a tool our language is for the investigation of private mental experience? Livingston has tried to furnish answers to such questions. He contends, quite correctly in my view, that both champions and critics of Hume are wrong to assume that ideas are, for him, not merely *criterial* for, but *identical* with, the meanings of words: "Hume's first principle – that ideas are derived from past impressions – is not a theory of how words have meaning. Hume does, however, intend for it to be employed as a norm for bringing cognitive order into our use of language."[25] Equally importantly, Livingston shows that Hume was cognizant that language derives its sense from its use, citing in evidence a letter in which Hume states that "the continual Application of the Words and Phrazes teaches at the same time the Sense of the Words and their Reference to each other" (*L*II.157). In addition, he cites abundant evidence in both the *Treatise* and the two *Enquiries* that Hume had a remarkably sophisticated appreciation of the social dimension of language. For example, "two men pull the oars of a boat by common convention for common interest, without any promise or contract: thus gold and silver are made the measures of exchange; thus speech and words and language are fixed by human convention and agreement" (*EApp*III.257). To understand language, Hume recognized the need to broaden one's purview beyond the isolated individual:

> General language ... being formed for general use, must be moulded on some more general views, and must affix the epithets of praise or blame, in conformity to sentiments, which arise from the general interests of the community ... [W]e every day meet with persons who are in a situation different from us, and who could never converse with us were we to remain constantly in that position and point of view, which is peculiar to ourselves. The intercourse of sentiments, therefore, in society and conversation, makes us form some general unalterable standard, by which we may approve or disapprove of characters and manners. (*E*V/ii.186; see also *T*581f.)

Hume's recognition that common language "must be moulded on some more general views" and "some general unalterable standard" is indicative of an awareness that language and psychology march to the beats of different, often clashing, drummers. Of the two worlds distinguished in

Treatise I/iii/§9 – the private world of the memory and senses and the external world of judgment (see *T*108) – language belongs to the second:

The judgement ... corrects the inequalities of our internal emotions and perceptions; in like manner, as it preserves us from error, in the several variations of images, presented to our external senses. The same object, at a double distance, really throws on the eye a picture of but half the bulk; yet we imagine that it appears of the same size in both situations; because we know that on our approach to it, its image would expand on the eye, and that the difference consists not in the object itself, but in our positions with regard to it. And, indeed, without such a correction of appearances, both in internal and external sentiment, men could never think or talk steadily on any subject; while their fluctuating situations produce a continual variation on objects, and throw them into such different and contrary lights and positions. (*E*V/ii.185). Such corrections are common with regard to all the senses; and indeed 'twere impossible we cou'd ever make use of language, or communicate our sentiments to one another, did we not correct the momentary appearances of things, and overlook our present situation. (*T*581f.; see also *T*591 and *T*603)

The possibility of objective judgment depends on an imagination able to conjure up the fiction of a general point of view which transcends the vagaries of time and position peculiar to any particular point of view. Left to their own devices, the senses would continually be embroiled in conflict; no balance could be struck between divergent appearances, no means found between the extremes. Only in imagination can this want be made good and the sort of steady, unvarying network of relations necessary to objective judgment achieved. Similarly, the possibility of *communicating* our judgments requires a comparable correction and the formation of general views in order to reconcile divergences of judgment due to individual differences of situation and sentiment. But there is this difference between the two cases: while it may be possible to gauge distances and such like without reconciling the general views of different individuals, this is not the case with language, which, as Hume well realized, is possible only by means of conventions: established standards adhered to by the group.

Hume's recognition of the need for common standards led him to speculate on the origin of conventions:

I observe, that it will be for my interest to leave another in the possession of his goods, *provided* he will act in the same manner with regard to me. He is sensible of a like interest in the regulation of his conduct. When this common sense of interest is mutually express'd, and is known to both, it produces a suitable resolution and behaviour. And this may properly enough be call'd a convention or agreement betwixt us, tho' without the interposition of a promise ... [E]xperience assures us ... that the sense of interest has become common to all our fellows, and gives us a confidence of the future regularity of their conduct: And 'tis only on the expectation of this, that our moderation and abstinence are founded. In like manner are languages gradually establish'd by human conventions without any promise. (*T*490)

From individual interest and natural inclination, people unite in various forms of social organization (family, tribe, etc.) and become sensible of their *mutual* interest. Social cohesion, and the common sense of interest it brings with it, lead people to institute various norms of conduct, to mesh their behavior in a variety of ways, and to form expectations regarding the conduct of others that simply could not exist in a natural (i.e. non-societal) context. It is this "confidence in the future regularity of their conduct" that makes possible the development and transmission of conventions of word use, and so language; and the extraordinary usefulness of language in connection with all manner of individual and common interests eventually makes complex social organization wellnigh inconceivable without it. Since language, as Hume conceived it, is not merely useless, but impossible, outside the context of human organization – the pursuit of the common interest and instituted regularity of conduct – it is not as "bundles of perceptions" that we are speaking beings, but as creatures whose needs, predispositions, and natural endowments impel them to develop and sustain the most intimate and intricate relationships with fellow members of their species.

However, Hume's account of language extends beyond socio-anthropology to the natural endowments a speaking being must have, especially those of a psychological character:

'tis impossible the same simple ideas should fall regularly into complex ones (as they commonly do) without some bond of union among them, some associating quality, by which one idea naturally introduces another. This uniting principle among ideas is ... a gentle force, which commonly prevails, and is the cause why, among other things, languages so nearly correspond to each other; nature in a manner pointing out to every one those simple ideas, which are most proper to be united into a complex one. (*T*10f.) [T]he faculties of the mind are supposed to be naturally alike in every individual; otherwise nothing could be more fruitless than to reason or dispute together. (*E*VIII/i.62)

These uniting principles – resemblance, contiguity, and causation – are, as we have seen, essential even to the status of ideas as *representatives* of impression originals. It should thus come as no surprise that Hume held that men's "words or discourses ... have an intimate connexion with certain ideas in their mind; and these ideas have also a connexion with the facts or objects, which they represent" (*T*113). It is at just this point that I part company with Livingston. For, according to him, Hume's use of ideas and their relations as criteria for the meaning of words and the truth of statements cannot be understood without supposing him to have given up "hopelessly trying to build a public world out of private mental images or public language out of private language."[26] In my view, this is only half right: he is correct that Hume never dreamed of attempting to build public *language* out of a private one; nevertheless, it seems clear, on any reasonably straightforward reading of his philosophy, that his preeminent objective was to account for our *consciousness* of a natural and interpersonal realm (the world of judgment of *T*108) entirely in terms of private perceptual contents and psychological associative propensities. That he could not thereby explain language would not have worried him in the least, since the cognitive beliefs that interested him – the reality of the external world, causal efficacy, the self, etc. – are precisely those that cannot plausibly be supposed to depend on possession of a language or passing one's life in the society of humans. Livingston's position, like all "common life" readings of Hume, suffers because it does not attach sufficient importance to Hume's fondness for the analogy with animal reason, and so fails to be *common* enough.

Consciousness and language were, for Hume, two quite distinct subject matters. Language is intrinsically a social phenomenon and should be understood accordingly. Not unlike Wittgenstein after him, Hume would likely have regarded efforts to understand private thought through the forms and structures of public language as bound to lead only to error and confusion. For example, just because "belief" ("want," "hope," "desire," etc.) typically takes a subordinate clause and so, from a logico-linguistic point of view, may properly be termed a propositional attitude, in no way implies a parallel ("intentional") structure of thought. The hunting dog believes the hare will double back and so lies in wait, expecting its return; but does that give its thought a structure isomorphic with propositional attitudes? If we refrain from making such an inference in the case of dogs, however, why should we suppose we have any less reason for restraint in the case of our pre-linguistic ancestors, infant children, or even ourselves? We should no more expect to find a grammar in thought than we should a bank charter. A language of thought is a very tempting picture, all the more so because it encourages us to tear down the barriers separating our social selves (actors in human life) from our private selves (passive spectators of a flux of perceptions). Yet, so far as Hume was concerned, simply because these selves are never experienced distinctly in common life does not mean that they are not in fact distinct; and, in order to understand either properly, a strict separation must be maintained (i.e. completely different kinds of investigation need to be conducted).

Hume would in all likelihood have been aghast to learn that twentieth-century philosophers like Quine have extrapolated a theory of language from his associationalist account of the relations between ideas and impressions. Had it been his intent to develop a semantics of natural language, he would have been unlikely to undertake the sort of inquiry he did, nor to have employed descriptive categories like "impression" and "idea" (of course, one cannot know since he seems not to have given the matter much thought). His science of knowledge was concerned with understanding "in a state of nature," a brief which obliges its practitioner to strip away all effects of socialization and acculturation (as these tend to separate rather than unite us with infants, the retarded, higher animals, early hominids, etc). That humans form themselves into social organizations and develop languages is, *pace* Livingston, of only marginal importance to Hume's study of understanding. It is true that we would not give names to our ideas did we not have the ability, need, and desire to communicate with others, and equally true that these names would not be accepted by others as genuine currency in the exchange of ideas if their use did not connect up with the inter-human world (common forms of life) and respect accepted norms. Nevertheless, the fundamental fact for Hume is that the true and only *raison d'être* of language is the exchange of *ideas*: however steeped we are in human forms of life, and however scrupulously established rules are followed, neither the sounds we make nor the figures we inscribe can have the least sense or signification if, in exchanging them with one another, no *ideas* changed hands in the process (a charge he regularly laid at the door of philosophers, for example, *EApp*IV.261, *T*61f., *E*II.17, *T*72f., and *TAbs*649).

D. Inexactitude in mathematics and language

Hume, philosopher of ideas though he was, was as dependent as the rest of us on language and the conditions of its use. Accordingly, he had no option but to conform to the bounds and conditions accompanying the use of *common* language to describe a *private* world independent of, and, ostensibly, the source of, the public. Whether he recognized this challenge and how well he grasped its nature is far from clear. Such concerns were not in the forefront of eighteenth-century thought, and we should not expect to find any explicit or extended thematization of it in any philosophical work of the period. Still, it is difficult to believe that a thinker as gifted and thorough as Hume would not at least have sensed the problem. We thus should be prepared to find him reckoning with it in what, to our eyes, is a strange and indirect manner, yet sufficiently akin to contemporary approaches to be adaptable to the purpose. There is even an indication of where to look. In the course of Hume's analysis of the custom in which the generality of our ideas consists, after remarking that "The most proper method, in my opinion, of giving a satisfactory explication of this act of the mind, is by producing other instances, which are analogous to it, and other principles, which facilitate its operation" (*T*22), he offered the following example: "when we mention any great number, such as a thousand, the mind has generally no adequate idea of it, but only a power of producing such an idea, by its adequate idea of the decimals, under which the number is comprehended. This imperfection, however, in our ideas, is never felt in our reasonings; which seems to be an instance parallel to the present one of universal ideas." Magnitudes exceeding the powers of imagination are analogous to representations that do likewise in that both alike are known to us only as *acquired mental powers*. Hume's purpose is not to offer an explanation ("To explain the ultimate causes of our mental actions is impossible," *T*22), but merely to suggest that if mathematical thought gets along quite well without adequate ideas of anything but the simplest, most readily imaginable things, then why not philosophical thought as well? The implication of this analogy is that, by correctly gauging what is and is not needed for philosophical psychology, we may well discover that its requirements and the available means at hand (i.e. common language in its common signification) are not perhaps so disproportionate as one might fear. So, to follow up this hint at a resolution of Hume's methodological problem, let us proceed in the direction indicated by it: his analysis of unimaginable magnitudes, and, chief among them, space and time.

It is remarkable how frequently commentators have failed to recognize that the whole thrust of Hume's analysis of space and time is to show that they are merely *abstract ideas*, and thence *no ideas at all*. Space and time are regularly held up as awkward exceptions to Hume's rule that all ideas are copied from antecedent impressions (being copied instead from the *manner* in which perceptions make their appearance in consciousness).[27] While it is true that he entitled *Treatise* I/ii, "Of the Ideas of Space and Time," this hardly amounts to a commitment to their genuineness as ideas. That he saw fit to brand them with the deprecatory epithet "abstract idea" should serve to eliminate all doubt on this score:

Suppose that in the extended object, or composition of colour'd points, from which we first receiv'd the idea of extension, the points were of a purple colour; it follows, that in every repetition of that idea we wou'd not only place the points in the same order with respect to each other, but also bestow on them that precise colour, with which alone we are acquainted. But afterwards having experience of the other colours of violet, green, red, white, black, and of all the different compositions of these, and finding a resemblance in the disposition of colour'd points, of which they are compos'd, we omit the peculiarities of colour, as far as possible, and found an abstract idea merely on that disposition of points, or manner of appearance, in which they agree. Nay even when the resemblance is carry'd beyond the objects of one sense, and the impressions of touch are found to be similar to those of sight in the disposition of their parts; this does not hinder the abstract idea from representing both, upon account of their resemblance ... The idea of time, being deriv'd from the succession of our perceptions of every kind, ideas as well as impressions, and impressions of reflection as well as of sensation, will afford us an instance of an abstract idea, which comprehends a still greater variety than that of space, and yet is represented in the fancy by some particular individual idea of a determinate quantity and quality. (*T*34f.)

After our analysis of Hume's account of distinctions of reason, it should be clear that he was no friend of abstraction; and, in claiming of space and time that "All abstract ideas are really nothing but particular ones, consider'd in a certain light" (*T*34), he was in effect saying they amount to no more than acquired habitudes of comparison with an eye towards particular resemblances. Space and time, construed as manners in which perceptions present themselves before consciousness, are therefore not genuine ideas but mere aspects of perceptions, explicable in terms of natural associative propensities.

Hume's underlying premise throughout *Treatise* I/ii – a version of the classical empiricist thesis – is that nothing incapable of appearing to the senses or of delineation in imagination is conceivable. So, in addressing the question of infinite divisibility in section 1, he contends that "Nothing can be more minute, than some ideas, which we form in the fancy; and images, which appear to the senses; since there are ideas and images perfectly simple and indivisible" (*T*28). Divisibility becomes a problem only when we unwittingly make the mistake of "taking the impressions of those minute objects, which appear to the senses, to be equal or nearly equal to the objects, and finding by reason, that there are other objects vastly more minute, we too hastily conclude, that these are inferior to any idea of our imagination or impression of our senses" (*T*28). In other words, the tendency to identify the impression immediately present to our *senses* with the physical object discovered by *reason* results in the contradiction that the same thing is both simple and complex.[28] From this conflation of perceptible points with physical, we are led to conclude that our senses and imagination are limited in their powers of discrimination, so that their apparently "simple" objects contain, beyond our threshold of perception, a whole world of minute parts and features. The power of the senses and imagination to put a stop to division is thereby nullified, and the abyss of infinite divisibility – replete with the paradoxes involved in either affirming or denying it – yawns before one.

Hume's analysis of the error as one of mistaking the magnitude of the impression for that of the physical spot of ink might appear clearer and more persuasive if viewed as a prototype of modern criticisms of the failure to appreciate the radical disparity between the natural "geometry" of perceptual spaces (especially visual) and full-fledged *scientific* geometry (pure or applied).[29] The closer one considers his treatment of space and time, the more credible it seems that this was exactly the point at which he was driving, and only the paucity of descriptive resources then available, as well as the need to make himself understood to a readership accustomed to dealing with them in purely objective (mathematical, physical and/or metaphysical) terms, stands in the way of our appreciating this better than his contemporaries could. Of all the disparities between psychology and geometry that concerned him, the most important is also the one most liable to be overlooked, owing to his manner of considering it: the possibility of producing a visual extension through a combination of points that are, in themselves, simple and indivisible (i.e. minima). For the geometer, generating an extension from a plurality of non-extended points is a contradiction, tantamount to getting something from nothing. Nevertheless, for Hume, this "contradiction" is a fundamental principle of *perceived* space:

I first take the least idea I can form of a part of extension, and being certain that there is nothing more minute than this idea, I conclude, that whatever I discover by its means must be a real quality of extension. I then repeat this idea once, twice, thrice, *&c.* and find the compound idea of extension, arising from its repetition, always to augment, and become double, triple, quadruple, *&c.* till at last it swells up to a considerable bulk, greater or smaller, in proportion as I repeat more or less the same idea. (*T*29; extended to time on *T*31) I ask anyone ... does he not evidently perceive, that from the union of these points there results an object, which is compounded and divisible, and may be distinguish'd into two parts, of which each preserves its existence distinct and separate, notwithstanding its contiguity to the other? (*T*41)

It has often been maintain'd in the schools, that extension must be divisible, *in infinitum*, because the system of mathematical points is absurd; and that system is absurd, because a mathematical point is a non-entity, and consequently can never by its conjunction with others form a real existence. This wou'd be perfectly decisive, were there no medium betwixt the infinite divisibility of matter, and the non-entity of mathematical points. But there is evidently a medium, *viz.* the bestowing a colour or solidity on these points; and the absurdity of both the extremes is a demonstration of the truth and reality of this medium. The system of physical points, which is another medium, is too absurd to need a refutation. A real extension, such as a physical point is suppos'd to be, can never exist without parts, different from each other; and wherever objects are different, they are distinguishable and separable by the imagination. (*T*40)

Perceptual minima allow us to avoid the paradoxes of infinite divisibility and of mathematical points because, when added together, such minima are *perceived* to produce an extension. That indivisibles of perception combine to yield divisible extensions is, for Hume, an undeniable fact of *perceptual* space, and not only resolves the paradoxes, but shows this space to be wholly incommensurate with geometrical space.[30]

If "Ideas always represent the objects or impressions, from which they are deriv'd, and can never without a fiction represent or be apply'd to any other" (*T*37), how is it possible for the geometrical space we conceptualize to differ from the perceptual space we behold and imagine? That a fiction can account for the difference might at first seem unlikely. For, if perceptions "must necessarily appear in every particular what they are, and be what they appear" (*T*190), how can mathematicians possibly conceptualize space in a manner that departs from, much less conflicts with, perceptual geometry? Hume insisted that "our perceptions are our only objects" (*T*213) and "The perceptions of the mind are perfectly known" (*T*366); hence, one may well wonder how even so much as the fiction of mathematical space is possible. To understand how the two spaces may differ, we need first to know how they do not. Hume made war only on the *demonstrations* of geometry, not on its *definitions* (see *T*42). The latter derive directly from perceptual space and so have all the certainty of immediately sensible objects of consciousness: a point is a minimum of visual or tactile perception; a line (curvilinear or rectilinear) is a visual or tactile minimum in one dimension, but a complex of minima (i.e. divisible) in the other; and a plane is not a minimum in two of its dimensions; while space as such is divisible in every dimension.[31] Thus far, but *no further*, perception and geometry agree. They part ways as soon as geometers employ these definitions in the pursuit of their proper *métier*: the *comparison* of points, lines, and planes with an eye to relations like *equal to*, *greater than*, and *less than*. The problem arises from "the natural infirmity and unsteadiness both of our imagination and senses, when employ'd on such minute objects" (*T*42) as perceptual minima. The relation of equality offers a perfect example of the effects of this infirmity, and has momentous consequences for geometry:

> lines or surfaces are equal, when the number of points in each are equal; and ... as the proportion of the numbers varies, the proportion of the lines and surfaces is also vary'd. But tho' this answer be *just*, as well as obvious; yet I may affirm, that this standard of equality is entirely *useless*, and that it never is from such a comparison we determine objects to be equal or unequal with respect to each other. For as the points, which enter into the composition of any line or surface, whether perceiv'd by the sight or touch, are so minute and so confounded with each other, that 'tis utterly impossible for the mind to compute their number, such a computation will never afford us a standard, by which we may judge of proportions. No one will ever be able to determine by an exact numeration, that an inch has fewer points than a foot, or a foot fewer than an ell or any greater measure; for which reason we seldom or never consider this as the standard of equality or inequality. (*T*.45; see also *TApp*637, *TAbs*658, and *E*XII/ii.H166n.)

The only *true* standard for the equality of perceptions is that of equality of number of constituent minima; yet, owing to the infirmity of the senses and imagination, it is an utterly *useless* standard, be it for geometry or anything else. The geometer is obliged to rely on an approximate, purely comparative standard, which Hume terms the *general appearance*:

since equality is a relation, it is not, strictly speaking, a property in the figures themselves, but arises merely from the comparison, which the mind makes betwixt them. (*T*46)

'Tis evident, that the eye, or rather the mind is often able to determine the proportions of bodies, and pronounce them equal to, or greater or less than each other, without examining or comparing the number of their minute parts. Such judgments are not only common, but in many cases certain and infallible. (*T*47)

[W]e have no precise idea of equality and inequality, shorter and longer, more than of a right line or a curve; and consequently ... the one can never afford us a perfect standard for the other. An exact idea can never be built on such as are loose and undeterminate. The idea of a *plain surface* is as little susceptible of a precise standard as that of a right line; nor have we any other means of distinguishing such a surface, than its general appearance. (*T*50)

It is not that a standard based on the general appearance is invariably false, or even fallible, for in cases of gross disproportion no one can doubt its agreement with the true standard (see *T*47). Nevertheless, there are many cases where the disproportion is so slight that one simply cannot tell from the appearance whether or not there is equality. Owing to the ineliminable vagueness at the threshold of minimal perception, however, "'tis impossible for the mind to find this equality by proceeding *in infinitum* with these references to inferior quantities; 'tis evident, that at last we must fix some standard of equality different from an enumeration of the parts" (*T*46). The ideal of a true standard must therefore be renounced, and geometers, like the rest of us, must learn to make do with arbitrary standards of equality, fixed by convention (inches, feet, yards, etc.). That is, instead of an exact enumeration of simple, indivisible points (minima), they have no choice but to employ "a compass or common measure" (*T*51) in order to effect a more exact determination of equality.

The upshot is that any standard genuinely applicable to perceptions, and so useful to us, is inevitably arbitrary and inexact. A truly exact geometry would be possible only if our senses and imagination were as acute at the minimum of perception as they are away from it. Yet, the significant fact about such a geometry, from Hume's perspective, is that it would be nothing whatever like geometry as his contemporaries conceived it. For, not only in its *definitions*, but in its *axioms* as well, it would directly mirror the nature of perceptual space (for example, it would be a geometry of simple, indivisible points which, when combined, nevertheless yield a divisible, complex, expanse). Since all obscurity and vagueness regarding points would be eliminated, Hume's thesis that geometry is a science of perceptions *and nothing but* would become manifest to all. Minima are quite literally "in the figures themselves," and do not arise "merely from the comparison, which the mind makes betwixt them," i.e. from general appearances; *yet, precisely because they pertain to the perceptions themselves rather than our consciousness of them in imagination, no standard of equality based on minima could be presumed to have application beyond perceptions.* If, as Hume maintained, "Ideas always represent the objects or impressions, from which they are deriv'd, and can never without a fiction represent or be apply'd to any other" (*T*37), it follows, given a geometry based on a true (but, by hypothesis, *not* useless) standard, that not even the *fiction* of an objective (i.e. non-psychological) geometry could exist. Such a fiction is made possible only by the false-but-useful, arbitrary, convention-bound standards made necessary by the infirmity of our imagination and senses. For, precisely because these standards are rooted not in the constitution of the perceptions themselves, but merely in a conscious comparison made upon their general appearance, we are led to believe that, in employing them, the progress of our thought is not subject to the same limits as our perception. That is, the true standard, simply because it is not *used*, is supposed not to *apply*, and so we scoff at the notion that the perceptible minimum represents an absolute limit to division. In this manner, we arrive at an ideal standard of equality, less even than the perceptible minimum, and in relation to which the minimum is highly complex, *possibly even infinitely divisible.*

Before the slightest credence could be attached to the possibility of some such micro-standard, it would first have to be shown that we are capable of forming ideas less even than the idea of a minimum of perception (as an extra-linguistic criterion of significance). Since an idea less than the idea of a minimum is by definition impossible, Hume treated with the utmost scorn any pretence either to comprehend or to explain the complexity of a minimum of perception ("there is evidently a medium, *viz.* bestowing a colour or solidity on these points; and the absurdity of both the extremes is a demonstration of the truth and reality of this medium," *T*40). His view is exactly parallel to that he expressed regarding geometers' ideal of perfect figures: "In vain shou'd we have recourse to the common topic, and employ the supposition of a deity, whose omnipotence may enable him to form a perfect geometrical figure and describe a right line without any curve or inflexion. As the ultimate standard of these figures is deriv'd from nothing but the senses and imagination, 'tis absurd to talk of any perfection beyond what these faculties can judge of; since the true perfection of anything consists in its conformity to its standard" (*T*51). Similarly, it is absurd to suppose that a deity could find complexity in a simple, indivisible *sensible* point; for, as the *true* standard of geometry, and source of its key definitions, is the sensible point, even the geometry of a deity would be obliged to adhere to it.

Hume concedes that we are led by "a sound reason" (*T*48) to suppose that our senses "give us disproportion'd images of things, and represent as minute and uncompounded what is really great and compos'd of a vast number of parts" (*T*28). This can occur in either of two ways. (i) The vulgar, "carried, by a natural instinct or prepossession, to repose faith in their senses" (*E*XII/i.118), straightforwardly *identify* their visual and tactile sensations with physical objects (see *T*192ff.).[32] (ii) Philosophers, believing their sensations mere perceptions, reject this identification; nevertheless, being themselves subject to the same instincts as the vulgar, they make their reason accord with it by positing a *representational* isomorphism between sensations and physical objects (see *T*211ff.). Accordingly, minima of sensation are regarded, in the former case, as *themselves* complex physical points, and, in the latter, as complex (albeit indistinctly apprehended) *representations* of complex physical points; either way, they have been converted into complex objects fully conformable to the ideal of precise geometrical determination.

For Hume, it is no less illusory to identify minima with physical points or their representations than to posit the possibility of geometrical precision beyond the capacity of the senses and the imagination ("the supposition of a deity, whose omnipotence ... "). For this seeming gain comes only at the price of ceasing to regard sensations as *perceptions*. Since the only way to treat sensible minima as complex (as the fiction of perfectable geometry requires) is to disregard their *appearance* as simple and indivisible (plus their inseparability by imagination) and suppose them to *be* complex, this is tantamount to ceasing to regard sensations as perceptions at all and instead treating them as objects (perceptions "must necessarily appear in every particular what they are, and be what they appear," *T*190). Moreover, in so doing, we must likewise overlook the manifest disparity between the *appearances* of things and what our geometry tells us they *are* (the intersection of two lines *appears* to be an area when the angles are small; two things which *appear* equal to a third may yet be discernibly unequal to one another; a one-inch regular myriagon *appears* the same as a circle; etc.). How, despite the fact that "Our perceptions are our only objects" (*T*213) and we have not the least idea of anything other than perceptions, geometers are able to perform this remarkable feat of prestidigitation is, however, merely a part of the larger mystery of how human beings generally are able to convince themselves that they are aware of such things as physical objects in the first place. Its full explanation therefore cannot be given until we reach *Treatise* I/iv (in

Part III). Here, it suffices merely to note that the account in I/iv ties up with that of I/ii in three different ways. First, the fiction of a standard more exact than any of which the senses and imagination can furnish is central to Hume's explanation of why and how we attribute to objects a unity and coherence greater than can actually appear to the senses or be conceived in imagination (see *T*198 and *T*262). Second, the fiction of a time abstractum (analyzed on *T*65) is essential to his account of our ability to ascribe numerical identity to perceptions that in themselves are distinct and only qualitatively identical – be the awareness of them interrupted or not (see *T*200f.). Third and finally, he traced the tendency to treat interrupted identity as if it were perfect identity (see *T*202f.) to our propensity, when dealing with abstractions, to confound similar operations of the mind, and so too the resulting relations of ideas (see *T*60f.).

We may now return to the issue with which we began: the suitability of common language to give expression to a theory of ideas which purports to build the public world out of private mental experience. If this question were posed directly to Hume, he would probably have treated linguistic standards much as he did geometrical: just as minima are true-but-useless for the one, so too are they for the other; we thus must rely on arbitrary conventions derived from general appearances and common points of view (see section C above). Were our senses and imagination under no infirmity with regard to the clear conception of the least discernible constituents of complex perceptions, an ideal language might be developed in which one sort of name was assigned to minima of perception and another to the natural relations of perceptions in consciousness; we could then completely and unambiguously describe any given complex of perceptions merely by joining together the two sorts of names into a complex with a truth value, i.e. a proposition. But, since the deficiency of our faculties prevents us from using minima as a standard for language, Hume can have felt no temptation to either chase after the mirage of an ideal language or bewail and deride language for being what it actually is. His sentiments in this matter are therefore best captured in Berkeley's counsel that "in such things we ought to think with the learned, and speak with the vulgar ... A little reflection on what is here said will make it manifest that the common use of language would receive no manner of alteration or disturbance from the admission of our tenets" (*PHK* §51).

Nevertheless, it may be wondered whether the renunciation of exact standards in philosophy does not diminish or imperil Hume's philosophical methods and results. I think not. For, while linguistic standards are necessarily inexact, this seems to pose no insuperable difficulty except in those few areas of language where precision is at a premium. Geometry is such an area; but even here the application of a concept like "greater than" can often be infallibly determined from general appearances alone. In general, the absence of sharp boundaries between concepts resulting from our dependence on arbitrary, convention-bound standards is rarely a problem. One can almost always determine in an instant whether a thing is, say, an elephant or a rhinoceros, a taxi or a bus, a cup or a saucer, blue or brown, desirable or repellent, proud or envious, etc. Only very infrequently do we feel the want of sharp boundaries between concepts, and even more rarely do we actually take the trouble to find new criteria whereby to attain greater exactness. The ideal of perfect precision, which induces us to posit standards beyond those capable of being derived from the senses and imagination, can only arise where exactness has become an end in itself. But since, for Hume, the bounds of sense and imagination pose absolute limits to our thought, we can be reasonably certain that he would have regarded this ideal as simply one more fiction of imagination rooted in the natural propensities (and infirmities) of the mind.

In so far as Hume himself ventured after greater than ordinary precision in his own philosophy, it was almost always with a critical end in view and with a keen awareness that no standard can be extended beyond the senses and imagination ("'tis absurd to talk of any perfection beyond what these faculties can judge of; since the true perfection of any thing consists in its conformity to its standard," *T*51). This is true even in the case of our idea of a minimum of perception. Hume explained it by inviting us to put a spot of ink on paper and then retire to a distance where it is on the verge of disappearing from view. In asking us to regard the spot not as material ink on paper but as a perception in our visual field, he was doing no more than employing accepted norms of common language (i.e. talk of how it looks to *me*, how *I* see it – as found, say, in art criticism, optometric examinations, psychology experiments, etc.). Nor was it an obvious abuse of these standards when, following up on this, he proposed that we *imagine* such points of sensation as the units which define and fill visual and other perceptual spaces, so that the general appearances at which our attention is ordinarily directed might properly be described as *composed* of perceptible minima. The important thing is that he made no pretence to perfect the arbitrary, convention-bound standards of our common language of mental experience to the point where exact descriptions of general appearances *as* compounds of related minima become envisageable. For Hume, none of the standards of our language admit of an absolute perfection: however *useful* they may be, they remain, in the final analysis, *false*; and to imagine them extended indefinitely in the direction of greater precision, far from yielding a perfect language of mental experience able to do justice to the characteristics ("grammar") of perceptual fields, would merely deprive them of all usefulness. Hume therefore cannot be supposed to have fallen prey to the very ideal of precision he himself so trenchantly criticized (see chapter 1-C).

Let us assess Hume's philosophical methods and aspirations in the light of an example from the late writings of Wittgenstein:

> But one would like to say: "Human mental life can't be described at all; it is so uncommonly complicated and full of scarcely graspable experiences. In great part it is like a broth of coloured clouds, in which any shape is only a transition to other shapes, to other transitions. – Why, take just visual experience! Your gaze wanders almost incessantly, how could you describe it?" – And yet I do describe it! – "But that is only a quite crude description, it gives only the coarsest features of your experience." – But isn't this just what I *call* description of my experience? How then do I arrive at the concept of a kind of description that I cannot possibly give? ... There is no such thing as exactness in this language-game. (As, that is, there is no knight in draughts.)[33]

Is Hume a fit object for this criticism? One might well suppose that a philosopher who denied that vision, thought, and the other powers of the soul "remain unalterably the same, perhaps for one moment" (*T*253), could hardly be immune to it. Yet, we must be careful not to misunderstand the butt of Wittgenstein's criticism. It was not his purpose *here* either to affirm or deny that our perceptions constitute a flux, or that it is illegitimate to describe them so even in normal surroundings. His concern was rather to expose and neutralize any inclination to suppose that a less crude, possibly exact, description of human mental life is possible, even in principle. In other words, his target was the very same illusory ideal of precision in psychological description which Hume condemned in geometry and would almost certainly have extended to mental description generally. Hume's basic point is, therefore, akin to Wittgenstein's: "the true perfection of any thing consists in its conformity to its standard." And, since, by their very nature, the standards we employ in thinking and describing our perceptions do not admit of perfect exactness, there is nothing that may legitimately be *called* a description of mental experience that is also an *exact* description.

Admittedly, Hume based his denial of ideal precision on the infirmity of the senses and imagination, which implies that, in the absence of any such infirmity, an exact description of mental experience would be possible. Wittgenstein would certainly not have accepted that the impossibility of a perfect sensation language derives from some specifiable, factual lack (as the absence of wings prevents men from flying unaided). Yet, Hume did not mean quite this either. For him, the true-but-useless-standard of mental experience has no analogue in those we actually have and know how to apply: *in our present state*, we are as completely ignorant of how to utilize minima to describe complexes as we are of the aerodynamics of angelic flight. The two types of standard are so radically incommensurate that a perfect comprehension of the one would not enable us to determine even the first thing about the other. Thus, Hume's talk of a "true but useless" standard of perceptible minima, and his perceptual atomism as a whole, does not involve the issuance of worthless IOUs for a complete analysis of complexes into simples of the sort criticized by Wittgenstein.[34] On the contrary, he stated quite forthrightly that the infirmity of our senses and imagination "affects most of our reasonings on the present subject, and makes it almost impossible to answer in an intelligible manner, and in proper expressions, many questions which may arise concerning it" (*T*42).

There is a moral to this consideration of Hume's conception of language. Philosophical commentators often hold their subjects to standards of exactness and consistency in their use of language which are not only impossible in practice to meet (not if one wants to have readers), but which they themselves would not pretend to be able to satisfy. The application of such a standard to Hume could not be more unwarranted or unrewarding. A philosopher who precluded the possibility of exact standards in philosophical language aspires only to portray the truth, not compute it. It may be owing more to a clash of outlooks than any shortcomings of his own that Hume is so regularly accused of carelessness and inconsistency (for example, Passmore's likening him to "a philosophical puppy-dog, picking up and worrying one problem after another, always leaving his teeth-marks in it, but casting it aside when it threatened to become wearisome").[35] To those whose ideal of empiricism derives from the definiteness and rigor of the sciences, the attitudes, methodology, and objectives of Hume may seem too casual and haphazard to be persuasive. One can only hope that such judgments may be tempered by the recognition that his philosophy derives from a considered appreciation of the descriptive possibilities open to one, and that, much like Wittgenstein, it instilled in him a deep suspicion of the devotion to precision for its own sake.

To argue, as commonly happens, that Hume's theory of understanding is not about what it seems to be about, and then to complain or apologize for its deficiencies in respect of what it never claims to be – a philosophy of language, philosophical anthropology, philosophy of history, hermeneutics, etc. – is, to borrow Berkeley's analogy, just to raise a dust and then bemoan that one can no longer see. The common-life approach of Livingston, Baier, and others is one such example: by construing "common life" too specifically in terms of human life, it fails to be common enough. Bennett's linguistic approach is another: "When Hume speaks of 'ideas' his real topic is meaning and understanding ... His official equation of 'understanding' with 'having ideas,' since it dictates his wording of the theory and also affects details in his handling of it, cannot be neglected; but the theory ought not to be seen as primarily one about ideas."[36] Though it is the nature of interpretation to treat a philosophy as something other than it "seems," one should try to refrain from the pretension to know better than Hume himself what kind of theory he was advancing and how best to express it. If his express objective had been to explain the understanding of fully acculturated, language-reliant, modern human adults, then the appropriate standards would apply. But it is abundantly clear that his concern was with understanding "in a state of nature," prior to, and independently of, education or circumstance, and indifferent even to the species line. With this as the objective, a subjective psychologism needs no apologies; it is one of the few credible explanatory approaches available. To claim Hume as "one of our own" is, in my view, to misconstrue the nature of his project and ignore its distance from the culturally and linguistically oriented philosophy prevalent today. It requires immense effort on our part to suspend preconceptions and capture a sense of how infinitely supple and subtle an instrument the theory of ideas was in the hands of a Hume or a Kant, as well as to see past the psychologistic excesses of more recent practitioners like James or Russell. But not to do so is to open ourselves to the charge of lacking the flexibility and/or sympathy necessary to reckon with a philosophical standpoint markedly different from our own.

Part II

The cement of the universe

Thro' this whole book, there are great pretensions to new discoveries in philosophy; but if any thing can intitle the author to so glorious a name as that of an inventor, 'tis the use he makes of the principle of the association of ideas, which enters into most of his philosophy. Our imagination has a great authority over our ideas; and there are no ideas that are different from each other, which it cannot separate, and join, and compose into all the varieties of fiction. But notwithstanding the empire of the imagination, there is a secret tie or union among particular ideas, which causes the mind to conjoin them more frequently together, and makes the one, upon its appearance, introduce the other ... 'Twill be easy to conceive of what vast consequence these principles must be in the science of human nature, if we consider, that so far as regards the mind, these are the only links that bind the parts of the universe together, or connect us with any person or object exterior to ourselves ... they are really to us the cement of the universe, and all the operations of the mind must, in a great measure, depend on them. *TAbs*661f.

4 Beyond the senses

A. The role of cause and effect in Hume's theory of ideas

A philosopher's reliance on examples confronts the interpreter with the problem of determining what, and how much, of the object or situation portrayed is pertinent to his purpose, and what is extraneous, even vital to ignore. The point of an example can be distorted, obliterated, or even turned on its head if the focus is misplaced. A case in point is Hume's favorite example of causation, the collision of two billiard-balls.[1] While a graphic illustration of the impossibility of direct insight, unaided by experience, into causal connections, it is apt to lead one to believe that the proper vantage from which to regard Hume's account of causal relations is the physical world. In my view, nothing could be further from the truth. The most significant and distinctive function of causal relations in Hume's theory of understanding is discharged well before a world of minds and bodies is even possible. Failure to bracket out the physical character of billiard-balls or the mental content of sensations, reflexions, and thoughts is therefore likely to be the occasion of considerable misunderstanding.

Few, if any, interpreters of Hume share this view. They regard him as the philosopher of natural – that is, naïve – human understanding, access to which is simply a matter of letting come to mind what most readily does. In the case of causal relations, one thinks either of examples of the billiard-ball variety or such as concern the thinking, willing mind. What *never* occurs to one are causal relations between perceptions, "none of which contain any efficacy, nor seem to have *any* connexion with *any* other existence." (*T*248) Billiard-balls careen off one another; a person voluntarily moves a limb; but fleeting sensations and thoughts seem powerless to exert the least influence on, or be influenced by, anything else. Considered in isolation from minds and bodies, perceptions neither are nor appear to be agents or patients ("all our distinct perceptions are distinct existences, and ... the mind never perceives any real connexion among distinct existences," *TApp*636). They simply appear and vanish; their conception does not even entail reference to the mind (see *T*207, *T*233f., *T*244, and *T*252).[2] Yet, while a category mistake to ascribe cause and effect relations *directly* to perceptions, they are just as liable to being associated in relations of cause and effect by and for *imagination* as physical objects or states of mind are. Even if, in ordinary reasoning, causality tends to be confined to the spheres of mind and matter, this does not mean that *these* are the causal relations that most concerned Hume or played the most important role in his theory of understanding. So, in approaching his account of cause and effect, we should be chary of conventional assumptions and prepared for a theory quite different than we have become accustomed to expect.

Before proceeding to the specifics of the role of cause and effect in Hume's theory of understanding, let us look at some general reasons for believing that he did not conceive this relation as essentially, or even first and foremost, a physical or mental relation. There are at least three ways in which, for him, objective causal relations presuppose cause and effect relations between perceptions. (i) A precondition for acquiring an idea of the mind is causal relations among perceptions (see *T*261); only when these relations are in place can the imagination feel the smooth transition between them which it mistakes for identity. (ii) Since there is reason to believe that Hume regarded the idea of the self as a precondition for that of an external object (see discussion of *T*189ff. in chapter 7-A), they share the same precondition; and, in general, any identity that extends beyond memory and the senses is possible only given causal relations between perceptions (see *T*74). (iii) Only through their *ideas* can any two objects – be they will and deed or billiard-balls – be associated as cause and effect in imagination; yet, these ideas must *already* be associated with impressions as copies and originals if their customary connection is to have significance for us *vis à vis* the (verisimilar) realities present in sensation or reflexion, and this association is both causal and specifically between *perceptions as such* (see chapter 1-E). Together, (i)–(iii) suggest that the role of causal relations between perceptions in Hume's theory of understanding is *solely to prepare the way* for conception and belief in mind and body. If so, it could hardly be more misleading or less conducive to a correct and complete analysis of his account of causal relations to concentrate our attention on mental and/or physical paradigms.

So, what is the primary function of causal relations for Hume? To find the answer, we need only consider these relations in the same light he did – as one of the three basic idea-enlivening relations of perceptions:

when of two objects connected together by any of these relations, one is immediately present to the memory or senses, not only the mind is convey'd to its co-relative by means of the associating principle; but likewise conceives it with an additional force and vigour, by the united operation of that principle, and of the present impression. (*T*107)

Recalling that vivacity is verisimilitude (see chapter 1-B), this means that if two perceptions are associated as cause and effect, then the appearance of one or the other as an impression of sensation or reflexion will not only convey our thought to an idea associated with it, but will induce us to regard the idea as no less real than the impression (for example, in the inference from perceived smoke to unperceived fire, we fear incineration as much as asphyxiation). Indeed, according to Hume, the ability of causal relations to generate belief in the reality of the unperceived ("to raise up a simple idea to an equality with our impressions, and bestow on it a like influence on the passions," *T*119) vastly excels every other relation: "tho' I cannot altogether exclude the relations of resemblance and contiguity from operating on the fancy in this manner, 'tis observable that, when single, their influence is very feeble and uncertain. As the relation of cause and effect is requisite to persuade us of any real existence, so is this persuasion requisite to give force to these other relations" (*T*109). The special role of causal relations in Hume's account of human understanding rests on their unrivalled capacity to engender belief in the reality of the *unperceived*, such that, without them, nothing could bring us to believe in the reality of anything not present to our senses or memory (see *T*73f.).

No other habitual relations of ideas can fill this breech, including those which, like causal relations, involved no immediately discernible connection between their relata. Words are a case in point. Since no resemblance, contiguity, or other *perceptible* relation connects "Fido" to that with which it is associated, only custom based on experience (training) can conjoin them in imagination. But, since, unlike cause and effect, this association is not a natural relation, the sensible presence of "Fido" in speech or writing can serve at most to bring to mind an idea of the animal, not induce me to believe in its real, though unperceived, presence (yet even here Hume forswore dogmatism – see *T* 116f.).

Hume was quite explicit and unequivocal about what gives causal relations their unique importance:

the mind in its reasonings from causes or effects carries its view beyond those objects, which it sees or remembers. (*T*82)

All reasonings concerning matter of fact seem to be founded on the relation of *Cause and Effect*. By means of that relation alone we can go beyond the evidence of our memory and senses. (*E*IV/i.22)

[Without the] relation of cause and effect ... Inference and reasoning concerning the operations of nature would, from that moment, be at an end; and the memory and senses remain the only canals, by which the knowledge of any real existence could possibly have access to the mind. (*E*VIII/i.64)

[A]ll our evidence for any matter of fact, which lies beyond the testimony of sense or memory, is derived entirely from the relation of cause and effect. (*E*XII/ii.127)

The unique importance of causal relations to human understanding lies in their power to make us *believe* something really exists, or existed, that we presently are not sensing and may never have sensed in the past.

The most sustained and detailed exploration of the role of causal relations in expanding the scope of verisimilar reality beyond the memory and the senses is *Treatise* I/iii/§2, a crucial yet unaccountably undervalued text. There, Hume begins by distinguishing cause and effect relations from those discoverable immediately by consciousness:

All kinds of reasoning consist in nothing but a *comparison*, and a discovery of those relations, either constant or inconstant, which two or more objects bear to each other. This comparison we may make, either when both the objects are present to the senses, or when neither of them is present, or when only one. When both the objects are present to the senses along with the relation, we call *this* perception rather than reasoning; nor is there in this case any exercise of the thought, or any action, properly speaking, but a mere passive admission of the impressions thro' the organs of sensation. According to this way of thinking, we ought not to receive as reasoning any of the observations we may make concerning *identity*, and the *relations* of *time* and *place*; since in none of them the mind can go beyond what is immediately present to the senses, either to discover the real existence or the relations of objects. 'Tis only *causation*, which produces such a connexion, as to give us assurance from the existence or action of one object, that 'twas follow'd or preceded by any other existence or action; nor can the other two relations be ever made use of in reasoning, except so far as they either affect or are affected by it. (*T*73f.)

As products of the comparison of perceptions in imagination, all relations, natural and philosophical alike, would be restricted exclusively to the senses and memory were it not for the bridge constructed of causal relations to the reality beyond. For although causal relations are not requisite to *conceive* of their application beyond immediate consciousness, they are, according to Hume, indispensable if we are to *believe* them so to apply ("'Tis only causation, which produces such a connexion, as to give us *assurance*..."). For example, without the assistance of causal connections to link the perceptions of sense and memory to what is prior to, posterior to, absent from, or never encountered by, these faculties, our imaginations could never associate them in relations of contiguity or identity:

There is nothing in any objects to perswade us, that they are either always *remote* or always *contiguous*; and when from experience and observation we discover, that their relation in this particular is invariable, we always conclude there is some secret *cause*, which separates or unites them. The same reasoning extends to *identity*. We readily suppose an object may continue individually the same, tho' several times absent from and present to the senses; and ascribe to it an identity, notwithstanding the interruption of the perception, whenever we conclude, that if we had kept our eye or hand constantly upon it, it wou'd have convey'd an invariable and uninterrupted perception. But this conclusion beyond the impressions of our senses can be founded only on the connexion of *cause and effect*; nor can we otherwise have any security, that the object is not chang'd upon us, however much the new object may resemble that which was formerly present to the senses. Whenever we discover such a perfect resemblance, we consider, whether it be common in that species of objects; whether possibly or probably any cause cou'd operate in producing the change and resemblance; and according as we determine concerning these causes and effects, we form our judgment concerning the identity of the object.

We may *suppose* that certain objects are always remote or always contiguous; we can likewise *conceive* an object to continue the same though absent from the senses. But what can *persuade* us that these notions have anything whatever to do with the reality beyond our thoughts? According to Hume, nothing save a foundation in causal relations: they alone can forge connections transcending the immediate purview of consciousness *in which belief can be reposed.*

Although Hume does not state it explicitly, his view implies that no relation whatsoever can be believed to hold of a reality beyond the senses and memory except on the foundation of causal relations. For example, while we might *conceive* our perceptions to resemble what lies beyond the senses and memory in the absence of causal relations between them, we could never attain any *conviction* that this was so:

But tho' I cannot altogether exclude the relations of resemblance and contiguity from operating on the fancy in this manner, 'tis observable that, when single, their influence is very feeble and uncertain. As the relation of cause and effect is requisite to persuade us of any real existence, so is this persuasion requisite to give force to these other relations. (*T*109)

Relations of resemblance and contiguity can "assist that of cause and effect, and infix the related idea with more force in the imagination" (*T*109). But they do so only in so far as "the contiguous and resembling object be comprehended in [that] system of realities" (ibid.) connected by cause and effect:

'Tis this latter principle, which peoples the world, and brings us acquainted with such existences, as by their removal in time and place, lie beyond the reach of the senses and memory. By means of it I paint the universe in my imagination, and fix my attention on any part of it I please ... All this, and every thing else, which I believe, are nothing but ideas; tho' by their force and settled order, arising from custom and the relation of cause and effect, they distinguish themselves from the other ideas, which are merely the offspring of the imagination. (*T*108)

Only via causal relations conjoining perceptions with the unperceived reality beyond the senses and memory can we come to *believe* that the objects of the senses and memory resemble or stand contiguous with them.

It is not enough that perceptions actually *have* relations to that which lies beyond the immediate purview of consciousness: in order for them to become something more *for us* than mere appearances (i.e. be more than they appear and appear less than they really are), we must somehow be made *aware* of these relations and *believe* they actually exist. Yet, how can we possibly become conscious of a network of relations, and an entire universe of unperceived beings, when both the relations themselves and that with which they connect the impressions of sense and memory are, by definition, beyond our purview? As Hume well realized, short of resorting to traditional metaphysical fixes like intellectual intuition or innate ideas, this problem is intractable unless the "reality" in question is construed strictly in terms of vivacity/verisimilitude. For this at once affords the key to understanding (i) how we are able to become *aware* of a consciousness-transcending reality, (ii) precisely in *what* such an awareness *consists*, and (iii) under what circumstances we come actually to *believe* in its existence. The theory of association, especially as concerns cause and effect, is tailor-made for this purpose. Instead of having to invoke "a pure and intellectual view, of which the superior faculties of the soul are alone capable," Hume could explain belief in a consciousness-transcending reality entirely in terms of the *habitudes* engendered when perceptions are found to be *constantly conjoined* in temporal sequence, together with a natural propensity to regard any idea so related to a present or past impression as being *verisimilar* in nearly the same degree as impressions:

> Here we must not be contented with saying, that the vividness of the idea produces the belief: We must maintain that they are individually the same. The frequent repetition of any idea infixes it in the imagination; but cou'd never possibly of itself produce belief, if that act of the mind was, by the original constitution of our natures, annex'd only to a reasoning and comparison of ideas. (*T*116).

In this way, an idea is believed to represent a presently or previously existing reality (according to whether its associate is an impression or a memory) situated *outside* the immediate purview of consciousness. This is all Hume meant when he asserted that the causal relation is "the only one, that can be trac'd beyond our senses, and informs us of existences and objects, which we do not see or feel" (*T*74). What normally is taken for transcendence of immediacy is, in his view, nothing more than the enlivening of an idea *already* in our possession when an impression present to the senses or memory sufficiently resembles another previously associated with it to trigger the *experience-bred* habit. This is all the foundation requisite in order for other relations like identity, resemblance, and contiguity – which otherwise could never "be trac'd beyond our senses" – to yield *believable* (verisimilar) connections of perceptions with (verisimilar) realities beyond the purview of consciousness (external objects, mind, etc.).[3]

Hume's tendency to couple memory with the senses in explicating the role of causal relations is in one respect misleading. Memory, as explicated by him, is itself a causal relation; for, in order to regard an idea as the image of a past perception, it is essential to believe it to be existentially dependent on its original (see chapters 1-E and 2-B). Hence, with memory, causal relations have *already* extended the purview of consciousness beyond the perceptions immediately present to it. So why did Hume ignore memory when explicating the role of causal relations in opening our view to the unperceived beyond? The answer, I believe, is this: memory is confined to those realities that were once immediately present to consciousness; it cannot, by itself, extend the compass of reality beyond that delimited by the contents immediately present to one or another immediate consciousness. In other words, memory is incapable, by itself, of yielding a reality external to the self, and so is useless for overcoming the solipsism of immediate consciousness (memories, which arise when "Our impressions give rise to their correspondent ideas," are simply part of that "system of different perceptions or different existences ... link'd together by the relation of cause and effect" which constitute "the true idea of the human mind," *T*261). For Hume, the important causal relations are those between non-resembling perceptions (and here it cannot be stressed too strongly that the relations in questions are specifically between perceptions and not imagined mental or physical entities). Such relations extend the scope of *present* (and thereby also *past*) reality beyond the immediacy of consciousness by engendering belief in unperceived existents; things as yet unperceived, and perhaps never to be perceived, can by this means alone play a role in our thoughts and action. For example, having constantly seen fire precede the appearance of smoke, the sight of smoke billowing through the door not only conjures up an idea of fire, but makes us believe in its present existence in an unperceived space contigiuous to that present to our senses.

It would be difficult to exaggerate the importance of appreciating the role of causal relations for correctly comprehending Hume's (causal) explanation of the origin of the idea of cause by reference to experienced constant conjunction, and his analysis of its content. A case in point is Stroud's insistence that a people able to recognize constant conjunctions, but differing from us in never enlivening ideas brought to mind by associated impressions, would still be capable of "getting beliefs about the unobserved"; and that we, "the beneficiaries of an additional mental item," differ from them only in "the otherwise empty ritual of adding [the] unanalysable idea of necessary connection to some of our beliefs."[4] Hume's reply would likely have been that people, lacking the capacity to enliven an idea linked to an impression by a relation of constant conjunction, would be quite incapable of *believing* in the real existence (verisimilitude) of that represented by the idea (for example, upon the appearance of smoke, they might *think* fire, but not *believe* and *fear* it; they thus would take precautions only against asphyxiation, not incineration). If "belief arises only from causation, and ... we can draw no inference from one object to another, except they be connected by this relation" (*T*108f.), then the difference between causation (necessary connection) and constant conjunction can hardly be only an empty ritual! Indeed, since memory (belief in the dependence of present ideas on past perceptions from which they are derived) itself would be beyond these people's ken, constant conjunctions too would lack all significance for them. Their reality would thus not, quite literally, extend beyond their immediate senses.

Flew's criticism of Hume is another example of the misunderstanding that results from flouting Hume's distinction between the immediacy of the senses and memory, on the one hand, and the experience, founded on causal relations, which takes us beyond the senses and memory, on the other:

> consider the ... case of the philosophically scrupulous applicant, who responds to the advertisement of a farmer seeking to hire hands with experience of cows. In interview he, or she, has to admit that – despite having had both many dreams of cows and abundant cowish sense-data – he, or she, neither is nor ever will be in a position to know that there even are such things as cows. Such an applicant would be lucky simply to be dismissed from interview, without suffering any penalty for impertinence.[5]

In fact, anyone claiming to have *Humean* experience of cows would have exactly what the farmer wants: an unshakeable conviction that cows fall within a nexus of real objects outside, but causally connected with, the perceptions of his/her senses and memory plus a recognition that dreams of cows are no substitute for actual experience (i.e. verisimilar impressions and memories). This is why Hume laid such stress on the inference from impressions to ideas: our belief that the content of an idea is just as *real* as the impression with which it is associated is what first takes us beyond the confines of sense and memory. Even commentators as astute as Danford, who recognizes that Hume made causation the condition of all other relations, tend to overlook its importance.[6] Taking Hume to be a philosopher not of ideas, but of common life, Danford cannot acknowledge this as the first, crucial step from a private world of ideas to a public, objective world of bodies, persons, and social institutions. Yet, if no such step needs to be taken, what sense can we make of Hume's thesis? How could there even be such a thing as "common life" unless and until our purview extended beyond the senses and memory? Danford does not consider this problem, but it seems to me that the only way to make sense of Hume's procedure in *Treatise* I/iii, and in particular why he attached so much importance to the inference from the impression to the idea, is to recognize that he was, through and through, a subjective idealist. His vantage, as a philosopher, was that of immediate consciousness, and his problem was explaining how we are able to break out beyond its solipsistic precincts. Causal relations furnish the solution because they enable the mind to compose for itself, and believe in, a present reality outside its immediate purview; further, by linking impressions of the senses and memory to this reality, they pave the way for additional relations: of contiguity, resemblance, and, above all, identity (only then does the possibility of causal relations involving mental and/or physical entities arise).[7] Once we consent to view Hume's enterprise in this light, there is no difficulty comprehending why the inference from the impression to the idea was paramount for him.

What is true of perceptions is true likewise of consciousness itself: by extending its purview beyond the flux of perceptions which appear to it, causal relations bestow upon it a *being* over and above its *appearance*. For, simply by virtue of being able to believe itself in relation to a reality of broader compass than the flux of the senses and memory, consciousness can no longer regard these faculties as its sole and entire "window" on reality, and ceases to conceive itself exclusively in terms of them. Of course, until identity and other relations are factored in, this wider reality, too, can only be conceived as a flux:

> 'tis evident, that whenever we infer the continu'd existence of the objects of sense from their coherence, and the frequency of their union, 'tis in order to bestow on the objects a greater regularity than what is observed in our mere perceptions... But... the extending of custom and reasoning beyond the perceptions can never be the direct and natural effect of the constant repetition and connexion, but must arise from the cooperation of some other principles. (*T*198)

Nevertheless, the crucial step would already have been taken. The self is a network of perceptions of sense and memory: "Our impressions give rise to their correspondent ideas; and these in their turn produce other impressions. One thought chaces another, and draws after it a third, by which it is expell'd in its turn" (*T*261). Once causal relations between non-resembling perceptions link this network to a reality beyond, our purview expands to encompass the entire universe:

Of these impressions or ideas of the memory we form a kind of system, comprehending whatever we remember to have been present, either to our internal perception or senses; and every particular of that system, joined to the present impressions, we are pleas'd to call a *reality*. But the mind stops not here. For finding, that with this system of perceptions, there is another connected by custom, or if you will, by the relation of cause or effect, it proceeds to the consideration of their ideas; and as it feels that 'tis in a manner necessarily determin'd to view these particular ideas, and that the custom or relation, by which it is determin'd, admits not of the least change, it forms them into a new system, which it likewise dignifies with the title of *realities*. The first of these systems is the object of the memory and senses; the second of the judgment ... By means of [this latter principle] I paint the universe in my imagination, and fix my attention on any part of it I please. I form an idea of ROME, which I neither see nor remember; but which is connected with such impressions as I remember to have received from the conversation and books of travellers and historians. This idea of *Rome* I place in a certain situation on the idea of an object, which I call the globe ... I look backward and consider its first foundation; its several revolutions, successes, and misfortunes. All this, and every thing else, which I believe, are nothing but ideas. (*T*.108)

Once the foundation of causal relations is in place, identity and other relations can be established between perceptions lying beyond the senses and memory, and a world of matter and minds opens up before consciousness. Since the universe and everything in it are constituted of causal and other relations between the very same perceptions that comprise the system of the senses and memory, the contents of Hume's two systems are in fact identical, the sole and entire difference between them consisting in the standpoint of imagination, which views one as a system of perceptions (the "true idea of the human mind," *T*261), the other as a system of objects. The self of judgment (i.e. causal inference between non-resembling perceptions) thus contains within it the universe of matter and mind, which in turn contains the self of memory and the senses.

Here one cannot help but be struck by the close parallel between Hume's self of judgment and Kant's transcendental *I think* (also an I of judgment), which likewise contains the world within it ("The whole of the objects of intuition – the world – is merely within me (transcendental idealism)," *AA* 22, p. 97). Much as causal relations grounded in customary transitions of thought are for Hume the presupposition of all objective determination and the cement of the universe of human understanding, so Kant's principles of association, and most particularly cause and effect (i.e. the Second of the Three Analogies of Experience), realize the unity of discursive understanding (apperception, the *I think*) at the same time as they produce an all-encompassing unity of nature:

Our Analogies thus actually display the unity of nature in the interconnection of all appearances under certain exponents, which express nothing other than the relation of time (insofar as all existence is comprehended therein) to the unity of apperception which can only take place in synthesis according to rules. Together they therefore say: all appearances lie within one nature, and must lie therein, because without this a priori unity no unity of experience, and thence also no determination of objects therein, would be possible. (*CPR* A216/B263)

The intimate connection between the unity of intellectual consciousness and the systematic order of the universe in the philosophies of both Hume and Kant is so basic to the thought of each, and so unlike anything that came before, that it seems natural to link them together as representatives of a single philosophical conception. If Kant's transcendental philosophy differs in any fundamental way from Hume's psychology, it is owing solely to the former's transcendental idealism *vis à vis* space and time, and the "Copernican" transformation effected thereby. For, in consequence, Kant's self of judgment, together with the objective world contained within it, does not, as in Hume, presuppose, but rather is presupposed by the self of the senses and memory.[8]

B. The causal maxim

Treatise I/iii/§3 is devoted to the analysis of the "general maxim in philosophy, that *whatever begins to exist, must have a cause of existence*" (*T*78). Although fully in keeping with the work's internal logic, Hume came bitterly to regret publishing it. Not only did it prevent him from gaining a sympathetic hearing for his ideas, he was even made to suffer materially for his miscalculation: in the campaign to prevent his election to the Chair of Ethics and Pneumatic Philosophy at the University of Edinburgh in 1745, he was accused of holding "Principles leading to downright Atheism, by denying the Doctrine of Causes and Effects, where he maintains, that the Necessity of a Cause to every Beginning of Existence is not founded on any Arguments demonstrative or intuitive" (*LGFE*115).[9] In the *Enquiry Concerning Human Understanding*, published shortly after his failed attempt to gain entry into academia (1748, under its original title, *Philosophical Essays Concerning Human Understanding*), Hume excised this material, made mention of the maxim only very infrequently, and then merely in passing.[10] That this was not the result of a change in view is clear; for, while considerably toned down, the claim that the certainty of the maxim is neither demonstrative nor intuitive is no less evident in the *Enquiry* than the *Treatise*. Nevertheless, detractors like Beattie continued to exploit the easy target presented by *Treatise* I/iii/§3, and this no doubt was instrumental to Hume's eventual decision, on the eve of his death, to disown the *Treatise* as an authoritative statement of his views. Still, he was careful to make clear that its sin, in his eyes, lay not in its contents, but the manner of their presentation ("my want of success in publishing the *Treatise of Human Nature* had proceeded more from the manner than the matter," *ML*5; see also the 1777 edition *Enquiry* advertisement).

Hume's decision to begin with the general maxim and proceed to particular causal inferences in the *Treatise* was, in a variety of ways, a major strategic blunder. The reverse procedure (adopted in the *Enquiry* – see *E*IV/i.23ff.) would have given his views a far more moderate cast, and been in keeping with positions adopted by a number of previous philosophers (few of whom found themselves ridiculed or condemned for their views on causation). Among these philosophers, the most important for Hume were Malebranche and Berkeley.[11] The latter, especially, expressed many of the very ideas that have since come to be associated with Hume:

> All our ideas, sensations, or the things which we perceive, by whatever names they may be distinguished, are visibly inactive: there is nothing of power or agency included in them. So that one idea or thought cannot produce or make any alteration in another ... [W]hen we perceive certain ideas of Sense constantly followed by other ideas, and we know this is not our own doing, we forthwith attribute power and agency to the ideas themselves, and make one the cause of another, than which nothing can be more absurd and unintelligible. Thus, for example, having observed that when we perceive by sight a certain round luminous figure, we at the same time perceive by touch the idea or sensation called *heat*, we do from thence conclude the sun to be the cause of heat ... That food nourishes, sleep refreshes, and fire warms us; that to sow in the seed-time is the way to reap in the harvest; and in general that to obtain such or such ends, such or such means are conducive – all this we know, not by discovering any *necessary connexion* between our ideas, but only by the observation of the *settled laws* of nature. (*PHK* §§25, 32, 31)

Hume would have found nothing here in any way exceptionable. That Berkeley could espouse such views with regard to ideas of sensation, without once doubting that something we can never observe causes them, was because he never thought to question the warrant of the causal maxim itself. In taking its truth for granted and never hesitating to apply it beyond the reach of any possible experience, he treated it as a self-evident truth of reason. It was this assumption that Hume challenged in *Treatise* I/iii/§3; yet, by doing so in a full frontal assault at the outset of his discussion of causation, he set himself beyond the pale philosophically. For, in the wake of Malebranche and Berkeley, whatever residue of certainty and rationality our particular causal inferences retained was due solely to their foundation in the purportedly self-evident general causal maxim. That Hume was careful to entitle the section in which he denied it this status "Why a cause is always necessary," in order to stress that his question was not *whether*, but *why*, a cause is always necessary for every beginning of existence (see

*T*78), could not save him; for, to his readership, in supplanting rational certainty with natural certainty, he cannot but have seemed to be denying the only rationally credible evidence and validity left to causal inferences. Given this mindset, the fact that he meant only to question the generally presumed *nature* of its certainty and *extent* of its warrant – not the *fact* of its certainty or its validity *within* experience – was all too easily overlooked or discounted.

Hume's theory of natural relation and generality may have had a part in this miscalculation. For the sadder but wiser author of the *Enquiry* omitted the analysis of generality (save for *E*XII/ii.125n.) and began his discussion of causation by arguing against the intuitive certainty not of the general maxim, but of particular causal inferences (the imperceptibility of causal connections). By situating his discussion of causation in the *Treatise* after treating relation and abstraction, it would have seemed to Hume a simple, straightforward matter to show that the general maxim was neither intuitively nor demonstratively certain. For, like all general claims, such a status could be attributed to it only if particular instances of causal relation could be shown to have it:

here is an argument, which proves at once, that the foregoing proposition is neither intuitively nor demonstrably certain. We can never demonstrate the necessity of a cause to every new existence, or new modification of existence without shewing at the same time the impossibility there is, that any thing can ever begin to exist without some productive principle; and where the latter proposition cannot be prov'd, we must despair of ever being able to prove the former. (*T*79)

The decisive test of whether *every* new existence has a cause is, according to Hume, whether *any* thing can begin to exist without a cause. As I read him, this means that the status of the general maxim as an intuitive or demonstrable truth turns on proving the impossibility of any individual thing beginning to exist without a cause; if one can adduce even so much as a single instance in which one can imagine a beginning of existence in which no productive principle is involved, then it cannot be such a truth. Now, for reasons that will become clear shortly, instead of furnishing us with an actual instance, Hume chose simply to invoke the Berkeleian criterion of imaginability by which he distinguished perceptions from aspects:

Now that the latter proposition [i.e. that any thing can ever begin to exist without some productive principle] is utterly incapable of a demonstrative proof, we may satisfy ourselves by considering, that as all distinct ideas are separable from each other, and as the ideas of cause and effect are evidently distinct, 'twill be easy for us to conceive any object to be non-existent this moment, and existent the next, without conjoining to it the distinct idea of a cause or productive principle. The separation, therefore, of the idea of a cause from that of a beginning of existence, is plainly possible for the imagination; and consequently the actual separation of these objects is so far possible, that it implies no contradiction nor absurdity; and is therefore incapable of being refuted by any reasoning from mere ideas, without which 'tis impossible to demonstrate the necessity of a cause.

The gist of Hume's argument is as follows. (i) Since any individual cause is necessarily precedent to the beginning of the existence of its (no less individual) effect, cause and effect are, by definition, distinct existents. (ii) Since it is always possible to imagine distinct existents separately, it cannot be impossible to imagine the beginning of the existence of the effect independently of this or any other particular cause (for example, by supposing that it had no predecessor). (iii) This, however, proves only that there is no intuitive or demonstrable bond between any *individual* cause and *individual* effect (not that there is not *some* cause for *every* beginning of existence). For this reasoning to apply to the generalized thesis, it is necessary to import from Hume's account of generality the additional premise that our general ideas of "cause" and 'beginning to exist" are nothing more than habitudes of comparison directed exclusively upon individual ideas, so that, like any generalization, it is simply shorthand for particular habits of comparison.[12] With this factored in, the conclusion follows: (iv) since the two general ideas are separate and distinct, the general maxim can have neither intuitive nor demonstrable certainty.

Why does this argument seem unconvincing to so many? Hume himself pinpointed the reason when he said of the maxim, "'Tis supposed to be founded on intuition, and to be one of those maxims, which tho' they may be deny'd with the lips, 'tis impossible for men in their hearts really to doubt of" (*T*79). Even after considering his argument, or any of the others he provided, most of us remain skeptical of his claim that we can genuinely imagine a beginning of existence without a cause. Anscombe gave persuasive expression to these misgivings:

Hume is over-easy with his argument from imagination ... [H]e says "'twill be easy for us to conceive an object to be non-existent one moment, and existent the next, without conjoining to it the distinct idea of a cause." It is very easy to accept this. Till recently I have done so, I have thought nothing easier than to imagine an object non-existent one moment and existent the next. One can make a picture of it ... and of course one can do this without thinking of a cause. I criticized the suggestion that being able to imagine something-coming-into-existence-without-a-cause proved anything, or was proper material for an argument from imagination. I said that "something coming into existence without a cause" was a mere title one gave to one's mental picture of something – a rabbit, say, or a star – coming into existence. But I did not then notice that just the same is true of the description "something coming into existence" ... I am to try and imagine – really imagine, i.e. imagine the serious supposition, that some object has come into existence without any cause. Now what reason have I, on this supposition, to assign one time and place to this coming into existence rather than another? Can I just suppose some particular time and place without more ado? Not if what I am to propose to my imagination is that I am truly judging that this object came into existence. I need to envisage myself as having reason to say it came into existence at this time and place and not any other ... I have got to suppose the object to have been not existent anywhere one moment, existent in this place the next. How can I do that without supposing a cause which justifies me in judging that *that* was the time and place?[13]

Anscombe puts her finger on a problem which, in my view, "proceeded more from the manner than the matter" of Hume's reasoning. No one was more insistent than he that all beliefs regarding fixed places and times, physical objects, and the universe as a whole, entail causes (see *T*108); and, without "the customary transition from causes to effects, and from effects to causes ... human nature must immediately perish and go to ruin" (*T*225). But it is essential to recognize that, when Anscombe questions whether we can really imagine something to begin to exist without a cause, the "something" she has in mind is a physical object as ordinarily conceived. Beliefs relating to physical realities are precisely those Hume deemed to be founded on relations of cause and effect (see *T*.74). Their identity, situation in space and time, and every other facet of their immediacy-transcending objectivity depends on causal relations as that which alone can extend verisimilitude to ideas beyond the solipsistic confines of the senses and memory; causal connections are therefore presupposed in their very conception. So, within the confines of the world of judgment of *T*108, Hume would surely have concurred with Anscombe: while our inability immediately to perceive necessary connections means that no particular causal inference is immune from doubt, the general causal maxim could not be questioned short of doubting the very world itself together with everything in it (an "opinion ... peculiar to a few extravagant sceptics; who after all maintain'd that opinion in words only, and were never able to bring themselves sincerely to believe it,: *T*214; see also *T*187).

But the world of judgment is not the only one, according to Hume; there is also the world of the memory and senses, comprised of impressions, ideas, and their relations – resemblance, constant conjunction, and original/copy. Like the world of judgment, it is a product of the deepest, most basic propensities of human nature, and is invested with all the certitude of natural belief. In particular, its objects have exactly the same kind of, and as much, reality as those of the world of judgment founded on custom – vivacity/verisimilitude; so they too are believed really to exist. This is what Anscombe and so many others overlook when they doubt that any *existent* can be believed not to have a cause. The existents Hume had in mind are perceptions *considered as such*.

The first things we encounter in our conscious lives are perceptions; we then, according to our feeling of vivacity, divide them into impressions and ideas. Until this division occurs and something is believed really to exist, associative imagination remains dormant (for, as Hume conceived it, its role is to enliven ideas by associating them with what is *already* believed, viz. impressions). In other words, there is a point in our conscious lives before relation, and *a fortiori* necessary connection, can play any role in forming our beliefs. Hence, when we first invest sensations and reflexions with the verisimilitude of impressions, we believe them to exist without any belief whatsoever that there is a cause of their existence. And throughout our lives, there is a level of our consciousness in which this is always the case: perception, of which even an animal as lowly as an oyster may be supposed capable (see *ECHU* II/ix/§13 and *TApp*634). It is no use to complain that such experience is unknown in the world of judgment, in our dealings with physical objects, minds, or other products of associative imagination. For Hume would grant the point straightaway, but still insist "'twill be easy for us to conceive any object to be non-existent this moment, and existent the next, without conjoining to it the distinct idea of a cause or productive principle," namely, objects of the world of the senses.[14]

It is true that Hume never once cited an actual example of a beginning of existence without a cause. This was in all likelihood because no one was more keenly aware than he that, in the absence of causation, "Inference and reasoning concerning the operations of nature would, from that moment, be at an end; and the memory and senses remain the only canals, by which the knowledge of any real existence could possibly have access to the mind" (*E*VIII/i.64) That is, for him, the only alternative to reasoning in accordance with causation *is no reason at all* ("all reasonings concerning *matter of fact* are founded on the relation of cause and effect," *TAbs*649). The influence of abstract reasoning upon our beliefs and actions (see section C), reasoning in the conduct of life (*TAbs*650), belief in history (*TAbs*650), belief in a fixed and settled order of space and time (*T*108), belief in bodies (*T*74 and *T*195f.) and minds (*T*261), belief in any inference concerning matters of fact or real existence (*T*73f., *T*107, *E*IV/i.22), and even the status of ideas as representations (*T*5): all, in his view, hinge on this relation. To adduce an example of a beginning of existence without a cause, it would be necessary to renounce inference, experience, memory, speech, in short, everything needed for learning (connection of past with present, the relevance of the present to the future, etc.). Any pretence of judgment then, where mental life is but a random flux and jumble of perceptions, is a farce: we cannot make perceptions objects of reflection without employing associative imagination; yet, to do so, is necessarily to ignore them as they really are, and to "read" *through* them, as though characters on a page, something *else* which exists only in and for imagination (see chapter 2-A).

For similar reasons, we should not be unduly disturbed by Anscombe's tacit invocation of ordinary usage in urging us to "imagine – really imagine, i.e. imagine the serious supposition, that some object has come into existence without any cause." The danger here is exactly that pointed out earlier: thinking in terms of paradigms, those examples which come most readily to mind, rather than letting oneself be guided by the terms of Hume's theory. It should not be forgotten that he situated common language in the physical, interpersonal world, and so would not have been in the least surprised if, in ordinary usage, we found ourselves unable to attach any meaning to the phrase "an object come into existence without a cause." The important thing, for him, is that "the slightest philosophy ... teaches us, that nothing can ever be present to the mind but an image, or perception" (*E*XII/i.118); and since his own philosophy teaches that perceptions are prior to, and independent of, both minds and bodies, it follows that, in the portion of verisimilar reality of which "we are most intimately conscious," we not only may conceive, but *cannot but believe* that an object begins to exist without a cause.

Having addressed the difficulties posed by the *manner* of *Treatise* I/iii/§3, let us turn now to its *matter*. Kant, for whose own philosophical awakening Hume's critique of the general causal maxim was decisive, perhaps expressed it best:

Hume dwelt principally upon the law of causality and noted, quite rightly, that its truth, indeed even the objective validity of the concept of an efficient cause in general, was based on no insight, i.e. cognition a priori, and that therefore it is not this law's necessity but only a mere general utility in the course of experience, together with a subjective necessity arising from it which he calls custom, that constituted its sole authority. From the incapacity of our reason to make use of this law in a manner which transcends all experience (*einen über alle Erfahrung hinausgehenden Gebrauch*), he thus inferred the nullity of all pretensions of reason generally to advance beyond the empirical ... The unkind fate which has been metaphysics' lot to the present day decreed that Hume was to be understood by no one. One cannot, without feeling a certain pain, behold how entirely every one of his opponents – Reid, Oswald, Beattie, and lastly Priestley – missed the point of his endeavor (*Aufgabe*); they took for granted precisely what he questioned while demonstrating with vehemence, and often great presumption, what he never took into his head to doubt, and so misunderstood his hint at an improvement [of metaphysics] that all was left as before, as though nothing had happened. His was not the question, is the concept of cause correct, serviceable, and in respect of the whole of our knowledge of nature indispensable? About this Hume was never in doubt. His question was rather whether the concept can be thought through reason a priori, and in such a way as to have an inner truth independent of all experience, and thence a much extended usefulness, not confined to the objects of experience. Here was where Hume expected to make a new beginning. His concern was directed to the origin of this concept, not the indispensability of its use: if only that could be ascertained, the conditions of its use and the scope of its validity would already have been given.[15]

Kant's analysis is, in my view, correct in every regard. Reid, for instance, held that there are only three possible attitudes one can adopt towards the causal maxim: "either that it is an opinion for which we have no evidence, and which men have foolishly taken up without ground; or, *secondly*, That it is capable of direct proof by argument; or, *thirdly*, That it is self-evident, and needs no proof, but ought to be received as an axiom, which cannot, by reasonable men, be called in question."[16] In opting for the third, Reid failed to see that Hume's proposal was not the first, but a fourth he failed even to consider: the maxim, while supported by the evidence of our every experience and so indispensable to reason that to reject it is to reject reason itself, is only *subjectively* necessary. The supreme authority of the general principle, and the undoubted objective validity of the general concept of cause, derive not from any insight or reasoning a priori, and are in no sense *internal* to them, but arise solely from their *subjective indispensability* "in respect of the whole of our knowledge of nature" (the world of judgment of *T* 108). Their necessity and validity is apt to *seem* internal since they are the foundation of all reasoning beyond the senses and memory, and so the basis of belief in bodies, the mind, and even the representative character of thought. Yet, since this foundation is itself rooted in experience-bred customs and the natural propensity of imagination to enliven a mere thought when a perception associated with it by constant conjunction presents itself in sensation or reflexion, the applicability of both causal maxim and concept is bound up with the subjective necessity of imagination, *and limited thereby* ("the incapacity of our reason to make use of this law in a manner which transcends all experience").

Kant took issue with Hume's view that the maxim is founded on experience. But, instead of adopting any of Reid's three alternatives, he proposed a fifth, according to which the subjective necessity of imagination (association) is founded on an objective necessity of this same faculty (affinity).[17] The endeavor to articulate and establish this position involved some of the most intricate, arcane, and ingenious philosophizing ever. But Kant deemed it worth the effort since, after Hume had discredited the options enumerated by Reid, Hume's own was the only viable alternative remaining; and to espouse it "would be as much as to say that there is no metaphysics and can never be."[18] This, it seems to me, is precisely the message Hume meant to send in *Treatise* I/iii/§3: "Since it is not from knowledge or any scientific reasoning, that we derive the opinion of the necessity of a cause to every new production, that opinion must necessarily arise from observation and experience" (*T*82). If true, this would sound the death knell of traditional metaphysics. For, if the causal maxim and the general concept are rooted in the phenomenological feelings of imagination triggered by the observation of constant conjunctions, their application is necessarily restricted not just to perceptions *per se*, but to what perceptions are *in and for associative imagination*. From this it follows that the causal inferences characteristic of metaphysics, which neither are nor can be supported by experience and custom, are "nothing but sophistry and illusion" (*E*XII/iii.132).

For Kant to be able to refute Hume and so salvage causation from the wreck of dogmatic metaphysics, it was not enough to show that, without the a priori validity of the concept of cause as the basis of a principle governing the thought of any beginning of existence, objective experience would be impossible. For he knew quite well that Hume himself founded objective experience on causation ("the concept of cause ... [is] in respect of the whole of our knowledge of nature indispensable"). So, to re-establish an a priori basis for causal inference, Kant needed to show that, unless perceptions and their connection in imagination are determined a priori in accordance with the logical form of hypothetical judgment (from which he derives the category of cause), objective experience of the kind Hume supposes could never arise.[19]

Whether Hume would have found the Kantian alternative so compelling as to re-embrace metaphysics shall forever remain a mystery. For our purposes, the important point is that the only viable candidate as source of the idea of cause, in Hume's eyes, is experience. For this leaves only one legitimate question for the philosopher: "*how experience gives rise to such a principle*?" (*T*82). Precisely because it is framed in *causal* terms ("gives rise to"), and so calls for a *causal* explanation of the maxim, only empirical reason is capable of furnishing an answer. Yet, its obvious circularity, especially in the form Hume eventually gave it (the *production* of habits which *induce* imagination to recall a specific idea in preference to others and, if its associate is an impression, to *enliven* that idea), has tempted many to suppose that, in practice, whether wittingly or not, he treated the causal maxim as an a priori truth (Kemp Smith, Wright, G. Strawson, and, more or less tacitly, all commentators save a very few, for example, Winkler). Whatever its drawbacks, this proposal at least has the merit of eliminating the circularity of attributing causal powers to experience in order to explain the origin of the maxim; for, instead of being an affair of custom and experience, this causality would be an expression of innately determined, metaphysically real acts of the mind. Yet, its drawbacks are of such dimensions as to give one pause. It asks us to accept that Hume either overlooked or actually countenanced something manifestly inconsistent with one or another cardinal tenet of his philosophy. For any *idea* we might have of the *power* of experience to give rise to the maxim must, in that case, either not be copied from any impression at all or have its source in an immediately witnessable real power and efficacy. Either alternative renders the teaching of *Treatise* I/iii completely otiose.

Hume's follow-up to his question gives hope that a resolution might be found. For, after posing it, he informed his readers, without any further clarification or explanation, that it will "be more convenient to sink this question in the following, *Why we conclude, that such particular causes must necessarily have such particular effects, and why we form an inference from one to another*? 'Twill, perhaps, be found in the end, that the same answer will serve for both questions" (*T*82).

C. Why reason?

Hume did not fulfill his promise to return to the question of how experience gives rise to the causal maxim until *Treatise* I/iii/§14. In the interim, he picked up the analysis of particular causal inferences where Malebranche and Berkeley left it, and took it in strikingly new and fruitful directions. Several of its elements have already been explored, in varying degrees of detail, in the course of our examination of consciousness, vivacity, representation, and the relation of imagination to sense, memory, and understanding. In considering how these pieces fit together, it is important to keep in mind that, at the outset of his discussion of particular causal inferences (*Treatise* I/iii/§4), much of this material still lay ahead.

Hume's treatment of particular causal inferences begins with the remark that "without the authority either of the memory or senses," any chain of inferences from causes to effects or effects to causes would "be chimerical and without foundation. Every link of the chain wou'd in that case hang upon another; but there wou'd not be any thing fix'd to one end of it, capable of sustaining the whole; and consequently there wou'd be no belief nor evidence. And this actually is the case with all *hypothetical* arguments" (*T*83). For him, it is itself simply a matter of fact that we repose *belief* in causal inferences and treat them as *evidence* in matters of fact only if, at some point, they tie up with actual or remembered impressions (toward which all activity of associative imagination is directed – see chapter 2-A). Since their unrivalled ability to generate belief is the source of the importance of causal relations for the student of human nature, Hume quite naturally directed his sights at the inference from impressions of sense or memory to ideas associated with them as cause or as effect. In particular, he sought to explain: "*First*, The original impression. *Secondly*,

The transition to the idea of the connected cause or effect. *Thirdly*, The nature and qualities of that idea" (*T*84).

Regarding the original impression, Hume set out to establish "that the *belief* or *assent*, which always attends the memory and senses, is nothing but the vivacity of those perceptions they present; and that this alone distinguishes them from the imagination. To believe is in this case to feel an immediate impression of the senses, or a repetition of that impression in the memory" (*T*86). As interpreted in previous chapters, this simply means that human nature disposes our consciousness to regard sensations, reflexions, and any memories thereof as real (or once real) in the strongest possible manner. Our *belief* in the real existence of these perceptions and the *feeling* Hume titled "force and vivacity" (verisimilitude) which pertains to them are one and the same. The only alternative, in his view, is to suppose that belief is a distinct idea in its own right which the mind annexes to some of its perceptions in preference to others. Yet, before considering his reasons for rejecting it, we need briefly to examine a criticism that is sometimes raised about the dilemma itself: that it is false to the logic of "belief" and its cognates. This criticism is not so much mistaken as misconceived. As understood by Hume, belief is "that act of the mind, which renders realities more present to us than fictions, causes them to weigh more in the thought, and gives them a superior influence on the passions and imagination" (*TApp*629; see also *E*V/ii.40). This obviously does not correspond to the use of the word "belief" or the value attached to it in the daily commerce of language. Nor does it seem to have been Hume's concern that it should. His interest lay in the *psychology* of belief, and, though this could mean many things, in his case it precludes reference to linguistic usage along with all institutions, practices, behavior, capacities, etc., peculiar to acculturated humans. His focus was *natural belief* – the sort capable of manifesting itself as clearly and unmistakably in the judgments and passions of mute savages, simpletons, infants, and even animals as in fully socialized modern human adults. He no doubt would have objected to his critics that their linguistic "belief" is only a derivative of the natural variety, and of less concern to the philosopher since it cannot be esteemed the original source of our convictions regarding real existence, cause and effect, mind, or the external world:

> It seems evident, that men are carried, by a natural instinct or prepossession, to repose faith in their senses; and that, without any reasoning, or even almost before the use of reason, we always suppose an external universe, which depends not on our perception, but would exist, though we and every sensible creature were absent or annihilated. Even the animal creation are governed by a like opinion, and preserve this belief of external objects, in all their thoughts, designs, and actions. (*E*XII/i.118)

Nature must have provided some other principle, of more ready, and more general use and application; nor can an operation of such immense consequence in life, as that of inferring effects from causes, be trusted to the uncertain process of reasoning and argumentation. (*E*IX.84)

Such convictions are too important to survival for nature to have entrusted them to anything less certain than itself. They may no more be left to the vagaries of linguistic norms rooted in cultural history and peculiar societal circumstances than to the uncertainty of reasoning and argumentation. With no role for norms and conventions in explicating beliefs of an instinctive nature, Hume was therefore quite warranted in narrowing the range of possibilities to two: belief as an idea in its own right, capable of being annexed to others by imagination; or a feeling in the mind's contemplation of an idea or impression; there is no third alternative.

The reasoning behind Hume's rejection of the notion that natural belief is an idea in its own right consists of two distinct components. Although the first is only implicit in the argument as presented in *Treatise* I/iii/§7, both appear clearly in an appendix:

Either the belief is some new idea, such as that of *reality* or *existence*, which we join to the simple conception of an object, or it is merely a peculiar *feeling* or *sentiment*. That it is not a new idea, annex'd to the simple conception, may be evinc'd from these two arguments. *First*, We have no abstract idea of existence, distinguishable and separable from the idea of particular objects. 'Tis impossible, therefore that this idea of existence can be annex'd to the idea of any object, or form the difference betwixt a simple conception and belief. *Secondly*, The mind has the command over all its ideas, and can separate, unite, mix, and vary them, as it pleases; so that if belief consisted merely in a new idea, annex'd to the conception, it wou'd be in a man's power to believe what he pleas'd. We may, therefore, conclude, that belief consists merely in a certain feeling or sentiment; in something, that depends not on the will, but must arise from certain determinate causes and principles, of which we are not masters. (*TApp*623f.)

Hume here employs his criterion for distinguishing genuine ideas from mere aspects to show that there is no idea of existence distinct from the idea of the thing itself. It is absurd to suppose that the idea of existence might stand alone, or be the only perception present to a mind; but this is what we would have to admit if were we to suppose that belief is a distinct idea, rather than a mere aspect, since "every perception is distinguishable from another, and may be consider'd as separately existent" (*T*207). There is thus no real distinction between a perception and its conception or belief: "To reflect on any thing simply, and to reflect on it as existent, are nothing different from each other ... Any idea we please to form is the idea of a being; and the idea of a being is any idea we please to form ... since every object, that is presented, must necessarily be existent" (*T*66f.). But the difference is also not a distinction of reason, "founded on the different resemblances, which the same simple idea may have to several different ideas" (*T*67). This, presumably, is because vivacity admits of degrees, extending from mere conception (a "perfect idea") to conviction. So, to treat it as only distinct in reason from the perception concerned, and so as an aspect of it, would be to make vivacity as inseparably part of the perception as timbre is of a sensation of sound or color of a visual sensation; and it would thus be impossible for *that same* content to be believed at one point in time, and disbelieved at another. Here again, one is obliged to recognize that vivacity, for Hume, is a feeling in our consciousness of perceptions, not a feature of the perceptions themselves; hence, the perceptions are really distinct from vivacity, whereas the latter, as a mere intentional attitude toward perceptions, cannot exist, or be conceived, separately, in isolation. Thus, since existence is not a distinct idea conceivable or believable independently of conception or belief regarding some particular thing, it cannot be what distinguishes mere conception from belief, and, *a fortiori*, it cannot be a distinct idea which, when conjoined with any other idea, induces us to believe it.

Hume recognized that, even with existence eliminated, the mere fact that he could think of no other candidate for a distinct idea of belief cannot prove there is no such idea. So, to deprive this possibility of even a shadow of probability, he offered a second argument based on the freedom of imagination to rearrange ideas in whatever way it wills. If belief were a distinct idea, then anyone having the original impression of belief could, in imagination, freely annex the idea copied from it to any other, and so, by mere caprice, induce himself to believe even the wildest, most arbitrary fancy with the same fixity and steadfastness as he believes that the sun will rise in the morning (moreover, equally capriciously, he could choose to disbelieve the latter proposition as totally as he disbelieves that an ordinary billiard-ball, upon being struck by another, will transform itself into a wedding cake). From this, Hume concluded both that belief is no more a distinct perception in its own right than existence is, and moreover, like existence, it pertains solely to our *consciousness* of a perception rather than the *perception itself*. The difference between them is merely the degree of the feeling of verisimilitude that attends consciousness in its contemplation of perceptions: if the feeling is slight, then the perception is regarded merely as a *possible* existence (i.e. real only in idea); if present in a high enough degree, we view it as a *real* existence (real outside the idea).[20]

The second point requiring explanation in a causal inference from the impression to the idea is "The transition to the idea of the connected cause or effect." Since any perception, as such, satisfies the separability principle and so can exist separately from any other perception, Hume held that no transition from one perception to another is ever necessary. Yet, for this very reason, perceptions themselves are also powerless to determine the imagination to call up a specific idea in preference to any other. Since imagination is free each moment to shift its attention wheresoever it pleases, the transition we make in imagination from cause to effect cannot be "deriv'd merely from a survey of these particular objects, and from such a penetration into their essences as may discover the dependance of the one upon the other" (*T*86). Hume concluded that we must look to some other source than immediate perception in order to discover the cause of this transition.

That source, just as in the case of the general causal maxim, is experience: "'Tis therefore by EXPERIENCE only, that we infer the existence of one object from that of another" (*T*87). Hume illustrated this experience as follows: "we remember to have seen that species of object we call *flame*, and to have felt that species of sensation we call *heat*. We likewise call to mind their constant conjunction in all past instances. Without any farther ceremony, we call the one *cause* and the other *effect*, and infer the existence of the one from that of the other." One must be careful, however, to distinguish the *learning* of a causal relation from its employment in *reasoning*: "in all those instances, from which we learn the conjunction of particular causes and effects, both the causes and effects have been perceiv'd by the senses, and are remember'd: But in all cases, wherein we reason concerning them, there is only one perceiv'd or remember'd, and the other is supply'd in conformity to our past experience" (*T*87). When learning a relation of cause and effect, the perceptions and their spatial and temporal contiguity relations must be directly perceived and remembered; only when the custom becomes established can we reason from a directly perceived or remembered cause or effect to its *unperceived* associate. Since it is in the inference to the unperceived reality that the true importance of the relation consists (see section A above), Hume thenceforth restricted his attention to reasoning (from the impression to the inferred idea), and ignored the learning of causal relations.

Now, as it turns out, despite certain remarks early in his discussion suggestive of the contrary,[21] Hume deemed neither spatial nor temporal contiguity essential to causal reasoning. For, although very common, spatial contiguity is absent in the case of causal relations involving perceptions that, quite literally, exist nowhere (see *T*167 and *T*235f.); and, whereas the temporal *precedence* of the cause in respect of the effect is essential, *actual contiguity* may be lacking ("our distant perceptions influence each other, and [give] us a present concern for our past or future pains or pleasures," *T*261; see also *E*VII/i.52). So, aside from precedence, the only relation Hume regarded as essential to causal relations is *constant* *conjunction* (though even here exceptions are conceivable).[22] For, although he conceded that we sometimes infer a cause from an effect or vice versa after a single observation, he ascribed this to the presence of a sufficiently close analogy between the objects concerned and causal relations of a kind that *are* the effect of experienced constant conjunction to trigger the custom involved in the latter (see *T* 104f. and *T* 131). More generally, just as reasoning in a chain from causes or effects must ultimately terminate in some *impression* of the senses or memory in order to *persuade* us of any matter of fact, so a chain of such analogies must always terminate in a causal relation produced through *constant conjunction* in order to engender *belief* in their connection. So, either directly or indirectly, constant conjunction is a necessary condition for any and all belief in real existence founded on causal inference.[23]

Having established the primacy of constant conjunction, Hume's argument reaches its *nervus probandi*: the basis of our belief in the general uniformity of nature on which all our inferences from past conjunctions to present and future situations are founded. Hume is commonly faulted for surreptitiously relying on a deductive model of reason in what is ostensibly a matter of mere probable reasoning, a criticism that goes back at least to Peirce ("I show that all the old metaphysicians such as Hume support their skepticism by virtually assuming ... that the only kind of valid inference is deductive").[24] If correct, Hume's entire analysis of causal relations in terms of custom is cast in doubt; his treatment of probable reasoning therefore demands the closest scrutiny.

Hume begins with the following observation:

> It may be thought, that what we learn not from one object, we can never learn from a hundred, which are all of the same kind, and are perfectly resembling in every circumstance ... From the mere repetition of any past impression, even to infinity, there never will arise any new original idea, such as that of a necessary connexion; and the number of impressions has in this case no more effect than if we confin'd ourselves to one only. (*T* 88)

What possible difference can the repeated observation of a conjunction of two perceptions make? If no necessary connection could be discerned the first time, how could one be discovered by simply repeating the same observation? Were it not for the *fact*, amply attested by experience, that constant conjunction causes us to infer a causal connection between the objects conjoined, it seems thoroughly improbable that anyone would ever reason so. It seems a complete mystery that anyone should even conceive, much less repose faith in, an unperceived existent for the sole reason that there is something present in perception that resembles things that in the past had been found to be regularly conjoined with it. For a creature whose nature was quite unlike ours, such a procedure might seem ridiculous. Since it is none the less a fact of human nature, Hume set out to determine "Whether experience produces the idea by means of the understanding or by the imagination; whether we are determin'd by reason to make the transition, or by a certain association and relation of perceptions" (*T*88).

Focusing first on understanding, Hume claimed that "If reason determin'd us, it wou'd proceed upon that principle, *that instances, of which we have had no experience, must resemble those, of which we have had experience, and that the course of nature continues always uniformly the same*" (*T*89). If this principle were demonstrable by reason a priori, its opposite would have to be a contradiction. But it seems by no means impossible to imagine the truth of the proposition, "instances of which we have had no experience need not resemble those of which we have had experience, and the course of nature may not continue uniformly the same." Nor is there a contradiction in the principle that instances of which we have had no experience *never* resemble those of which we have had experience, and the course of nature *never* continues uniformly the same (so that were "all the scenes of nature ... continually shifted in such a manner that no two events bore any resemblance to each other, but every object was entirely new, without any similitude to whatever had been seen before ... The relation of cause and effect must be utterly unknown to mankind," *E*VIII/i.64; see also *TAbs*650f. and *E*IV/ii.30). Thus, if the uniformity principle has any support in reason at all, it cannot be deductive reason.

Probable reason fares no better than demonstrative since it is premised on the very principle it here is called upon to explain:

> We have said that all arguments concerning existence are founded on the relation of cause and effect; that our knowledge of that relation is derived entirely from experience; and that all our experimental conclusions proceed upon the supposition that the future will be conformable to the past. To endeavour, therefore, the proof of this last supposition by probable arguments, or arguments regarding existence, must be evidently going in a circle, and taking that for granted, which is the very point in question. (*E*IV/ii.30; see also *T*89f. and *TAbs*651)

On this basis, Hume concluded that it is solely from "custom operating upon the imagination, that we can draw any inference from the appearance of one [object] to the existence of another ... Thus all probable reasoning is nothing but a species of sensation" (*T*103).

Hume's reasoning has come in for severe criticism because, as Flew put it, "it is neither necessary nor correct to represent the form of all arguments from experience as a broken-backed syllogism, crippled for lack of a suitable middle term."[25] According to this reading, Hume's case against a rational basis for belief in the uniformity of nature is enfeebled by a conception of probable reason that is merely deductive reason in another guise. The probable arguments Hume invoked turn on *previously* established relations of cause and effect. He supposed that if these relations are to be capable of rationally upholding the uniformity principle, they must be presumed to hold true not only of the past, but of the *present* and *future* as well. Since the extension of the past to the present and future is precisely what is at issue, the probable arguments Hume adduced for the uniformity principle all suffer from exactly the same evidential gap he attributed to the principle itself: they outstrip their "premises" – remembered constant conjunctions. But does it follow that the premises fail *altogether* to support their premises? Of course not. Probable means just that: the conclusion does not follow of necessity, but it does nevertheless follow! Accordingly, it seems that Hume's argument overshot its target.

Stroud has proposed a line of defense. In his view, Hume's argument was directed not against deductive reasoning, but against a particular "self-conscious notion of reason" initiated by Descartes, according to which a "fully rational agent is not one who proceeds rationally only at the last step," but one whose beliefs are grounded in "something we could not fail to be reasonable in believing" (so that all and only beliefs of the latter sort may be deemed "*reasonable*"). Hume's concern was therefore with the reasonableness of the belief...

> that what one has experienced is good reason to believe what one does about the unobserved. And then Hume's question, which he thinks leads to scepticism, is how one can ever get a reasonable belief to that effect. If that question does in fact lead to scepticism, it is not because Hume implicitly assumes that all reasons must be deductively sufficient ... [A]n experienced constant conjunction between As and Bs, along with an observed A, is good reason to believe that a B will occur. But clearly this more complicated belief, when added to what was originally believed, still does not provide the person with a deductively sufficient set of premisses for the conclusion that a B will occur.
>
> If to the two premisses:
>
> (PE) All observed As have been followed by Bs.
>
> (PI) An A is observed now.
>
> we add the further statement:
>
> (R) PE and PI are reason to believe that a B will occur.
>
> we still do not have a deductively valid argument to the conclusion that a B will occur. If PE, PI, and R are all true, it is still possible for a B not to occur. There can be, and one can have, very good reason to believe what is in fact false.[26]

On Stroud's view, the gap between past experience and present beliefs is not a matter of "an arbitrary assumption about the deductive nature of all reasoning," but of a "man's having (higher-order) belief about the reasons for his (lower-order) beliefs."[27] However, this line of defense does not seem very promising (as Stroud himself avers). In the first place, it must not be overlooked that, in Hume's view, belief in the uniformity of nature extends to infants, inarticulate savages, and animals; hence, any probable reasoning that could be supposed to support it must be so simple and obvious as to be virtually indistinguishable from instinct. Higher-order beliefs seem not to meet this criterion. Secondly, while PE, PI and R do not imply that a B will occur, it does deductively follow that anyone who accepts the truth of these premises will *believe* that a B will occur. And this belief, not the actual occurrence of B, is precisely what is at issue: why do we believe (infer) that B will occur on the sole and entire basis of an experienced constant conjunction of As with Bs? Hence, the addition of R serves only to repair the syllogism's broken back, and so does nothing to clear Hume of the charge of having failed to distinguish probable reasoning from deductive. Thirdly, Stroud's claim seems to be that we adopt R not because R *itself* is found to be reasonable, but because we regard other beliefs as reasonable *because* we have adopted R; and, since R is our rule or standard for the reasonableness of any belief, it can make no sense to ask whether R itself is reasonable. It still, however, has to be explained how R becomes a standard in the first place. In other words, (i) what induces us to seek a rule like R in the first place, and assuming that we have the "reason" to do so, (ii) what induces us to adopt R in preference to any possible rivals? Stroud does not really address either issue. Had he done so, it does not seem unlikely that, in the end, the reasonableness of desiring rules like R and of preferring R to alternatives will be a matter of our learning from *past* experience, including the results of having *previously* operated in accordance with both R and other rules. But if so, we would find ourselves confronted once again by the same evidential gap Stroud sought to exclude: the absence of a standard of reasonability for believing that results obtained in the past have any significance *vis à vis* present and future happenings.[28]

The main shortcoming of Stroud's defense is even more evident in Flew's would-be cure for Hume's problem:

> The much talked of but more rarely formulated Principle of Induction, upon which all conclusions from experience are supposed somehow to depend, might be presented: not as the indispensable, hidden, and indefensible missing premise required to complete all inductive would be syllogisms; but as a rational rule of procedure to guide us in shaping always fallible expectations in which to approach the unknown ... The only questions which can arise about a rule qua rule are not ones about its truth but ones about its reasonableness and about the results of adopting and observing it. But insofar as this particular rule is the principle of all argument from experience, to follow it must be as paradigmatically reasonable as to try to learn from experience. To challenge its reasonableness is to challenge the paradigm.

In addition to presupposing, and so failing to explain, our *need* "to approach the unknown" (for Hume the native propensities of associative imagination explain both why we are driven to approach the unknown and how we satisfy our drive – see section A above), Flew asserts that we adopt a rational rule of procedure because of "the results of adopting and observing it." This, of course, begs the question, since the "results" to which Flew refers involve a reference to past experience. In order for them to matter to us later, we must *already* have adopted the principle that things observed in the past have a bearing of some kind on things we observe now and in the future, and, in particular, a version of the uniformity principle, say, *procedures that have been found to have results in the past are likely to have results now and in the future.* So, unless we simply take the uniformity principle as the *meaning* of "reasonable" (which again begs the question),[29] the supposition that we adopt rules like Stroud's R because *past* results matter for us *presently* simply presupposes the very uniformity probable reason is supposed to underpin. If, in order to avoid falling into the evidential gap thus exposed, we omit all references to past results, past utility, etc., what then is left? There seem to be only two alternatives: either something like Humean instinct induces us to adopt maxims like R, or R is simply a part of the language and social practice handed down to us by our ancestors. Either way Hume wins, since R is simply "there" for us – a *given* – and not the result of anything one could legitimately describe as "rational," 'reasonable," 'justified," etc. It leaves empirical reason no role to play either in our adopting a maxim like R or in our preferring it to rivals; the problem of why and how we bring past experience to bear on our reasoning regarding the present and the future is therefore left untouched.

Instead of snatching solutions out of thin air (or, rather, out of recent philosophical journalism), our best hope for finding an adequate response to the objection that Hume's rejection of empirical reason as a basis for the uniformity principle turns on an inappropriate deductive sufficiency model is to draw on the tenets of Hume's own philosophy. When we do this, it immediately becomes plain that, in order for the gap between past experience and beliefs concerning present and future occurrences to qualify as deductive insufficiency, it must be supposed that Hume *unconditionally* extended the authority of deductive reason beyond ideas and their relations to impressions (i.e. verisimilar reality). For, were this not the case, and, in particular, *did such an extension itself presuppose causal relations*, it would be impossible to maintain that the deficiency of probable reason with respect to the uniformity principle is *logical* in nature, and the objection would have to be dismissed as unfounded. And this is what we find. Hume, it will be remembered, distinguished two sorts of truth: *relations of ideas* and *matters of fact* (see chapter 1-E). Considerations of deductive sufficiency belong, with mathematics, in the first category of truth: "Propositions of this kind are discoverable by the mere operation of thought, without dependence on what is anywhere existent in the universe" (*E*IV/i.20); their necessity "lies only in the act of the understanding, by which we consider and compare these ideas" (*T*167). As expressions of necessities of thought, their truth consists solely in the impossibility of thinking otherwise (without altering the ideas concerned). As such, it is wholly a matter of our subjective capacity of thought, and cannot be presumed to extend beyond it. But here, as always for Hume, it is imperative not to fall prey to the temptation to "transfer the determination of the thought to external objects" (*T*168; see *E*VII/ii.60n.); for "What peculiar privilege has this little agitation of the brain which we call 'thought,' that we must thus make it the model of the whole universe?" (*D*II.19). Before truths regarding relations of ideas can be *believed* to apply to impressions of sensation and reflexion, ideas must have the status of *representatives* (copies) of impressions. However, for Hume, this status is not intrinsic to ideas: they acquire it only by means of *perceived* natural relations of resemblance, temporal precedence, and *remembered* constant conjunction; thus, the representative character of ideas derives from a causal connection with impressions (see chapter 1-E). Moreover, the thesis that *causal relations* are presupposed in order for truths concerning relations of ideas to have validity beyond *thought* (imagination) is fully in keeping with Hume's general claim that the only means whereby an idea can attain the status of a belief in real existence is by means of causal relations. This is just to say that our belief in the application of relations of ideas (i.e. what holds true in our thinking) to matters of fact (what is the case in sensation or reflexion) is founded on causal relations. Accordingly, the extension of truths based solely on the relation of ideas to impressions cannot be regarded as unconditioned.

Although this reasoning simply requires that we take Hume's theory of ideas as seriously as he did himself, some readers may find it too speculative. However, there is another regard in which the objective validity of logical relations of ideas depends on causal relations about which we can be quite confident: their application *beyond* the impressions of the senses and memory. For Hume made quite clear that it is only by virtue of the framework provided by causal relations that any other kind of relation can be supposed (i.e. *believed*) to hold of reality at large, not just that immediately present to us (see section A above). Without causal relations of this kind, then, even given the representative variety (copies and originals), we could never attribute to any mere relation of ideas a validity other than subjective (i.e. an application other than to the sensations, reflexions, and memories present to one's consciousness). In order for us to *believe* that the truths of logic and mathematics apply in all places and times and to all things in them, causal relations are therefore essential: "Abstract or demonstrative reasoning... never influences any of our actions, but only as it directs our judgment concerning causes and effects" (*T*414).

It might be objected that I have taken *T*414 out of context. Its subject matter is the influence of understanding on volition:

I believe it scarce will be asserted, that [demonstration, i.e. the abstract relations of our ideas] alone is ever the cause of any action. As it's proper province is the world of ideas, and as the will always places us in that of realities, demonstration and volition seem, upon that account, to be totally remov'd from each other. Mathematics, indeed, are useful in all mechanical operations, and arithmetic in almost every art and profession: But 'tis not of themselves they have any influence ... A merchant is desirous of knowing the sum total of his accounts with any person: Why? but that he may learn what sum will have the same *effects* in paying his debt, and going to market, as all the particular articles taken together. Abstract or demonstrative reasoning, therefore, never influences any of our actions, but only as it directs our judgment concerning causes and effects.

The link between relations of ideas and volition is *belief* ("that act of the mind, which renders realities more present to us than fictions, causes them to weigh more in the thought, and gives them a superior influence on the passions and imagination," *TApp*629); and belief, in so far as it bears on the world of judgment and action, is founded on cause and effect ("all reasonings concerning *matter of fact* are founded on the relation of cause and effect," *TAbs*649). This is why relations of logic and mathematics, like all relations, presuppose causal relations in order to have any application to the "real world." In their absence, laws of logic and mathematics, lacking any idea-enlivening power of their own, could not extend either beyond thought itself or beyond the senses and memory, and belief in the ordering of nature in conformity with the principles of logic and mathematics would be absent. Now, where there is as yet no deduction, there also can be no deductive gaps. If probable reasoning were the basis of the uniformity principle, it would necessarily be so outside and independently of any framework of deduction. Hume's case against the foundation of uniformity on probable reason must therefore be understood accordingly. (His insight that the objects of the senses are not essentially subject to the laws of logic and mathematics which govern our thought of such objects struck Kant as well, for whom time, as form of sensibility, is a sensuous condition for the application of logic to appearances, as early as 1770; and, in the *Critique of Pure Reason*, his query, how are synthetic a priori judgments possible?, becomes the question, how are appearances subject to mere logical forms a priori?)

Since causal inferences themselves presuppose the uniformity of nature, Hume concluded that this principle cannot have a rational basis. What it requires is a *psychological* grounding. Accordingly, the "gap" Hume set out to expose in *Treatise* I/iii/§6 should be understood in terms neither of deductive insufficiency nor evidential inadequacy, but of *psychological underdetermination*. There is nothing intrinsic to past experience, however uniform the operations of nature therein, that ordains (determines, intimates, etc.) that we shall assume a present or future uniformity in accord with it; it is up to human nature to make it so. Having such a nature, we cannot but assume it; it is not subject to choice, to contingent norms of rationality, to the vagaries of history, the possession of language, etc. In consequence, Hume's problem of induction arises only at the very most primitive level of consciousness, where the mind *originally* extends its purview beyond the senses and memory. The entire edifice of criticism and response built on the assumption that *his* problem is a generalized one is therefore without foundation: he would vehemently insist that causal relations, and the belief in the uniformity of nature based thereupon, are a constitutive element of one's conception and belief in material objects and minds (including one's own), so that the question simply cannot even arise, whether things of this kind – the realities of the system of judgment of *T* 108 – have a cause of their existence.[30]

As in all matters of fact, our thought is free to proceed however it will; that it tends not to do so is due solely to the "gentle force" of association to which imagination is subject. Were our associative psychology different, we might either ignore past experience altogether or respond to it quite differently. What seems "reasonable" or "credible" to one whose imagination is subject to certain principles of association, would inevitably seem arbitrary and pointless to one whose imagination was governed by other such principles. If reason were sufficient to bridge the gap between past and present experience and establish the uniformity principle, then the constitution of imagination would be a matter of complete indifference. Hume's arguments are designed to show that it is not: that reason by itself is powerless to resist, much less compel, an imagination whose natural propensities were contrary to the uniformity principle. Underlying this is the thesis that vivacity alone can influence the imagination, and that pure reason – lacking as it does the power to enliven ideas – can give credibility to nothing. Direction in these matters must therefore come from instinct, from human nature; only thus can the gap between past and present experience be closed:

Had ideas no more union in the fancy than objects seem to have to the understanding, we cou'd never draw any inference from causes to effects, nor repose belief in any matter of fact. The inference, therefore, depends solely on the union of ideas. (*T*92) We are determined by CUSTOM alone to suppose the future conformable to the past. (*TAbs*652)

And this leads directly to the conclusion which is emblematic of Hume's entire philosophy:

Thus, all probable reasoning is nothing but a species of sensation. 'Tis not solely in poetry and music, we must follow our taste and sentiment, but likewise in philosophy. When I am convinc'd of any principle, 'tis only an idea, which strikes more strongly upon me. When I give the preference to one set of arguments above another, I do nothing but decide from my feeling concerning the superiority of their influence. Objects have no discoverable connexion together; nor is it from any other principle but custom operating upon the imagination, that we can draw any inference from the appearance of one to the existence of another. (*T*103)[31]

5 Custom and necessity

A. Custom: the feeling of facility

Of the three factors involved in causal inferences – remembered constant conjunction, custom, and belief – the one on which we have yet to focus is custom. Customary association is the centerpiece of Hume's theory of causation, just as of so much else in his philosophy:

Now as we call every thing CUSTOM, which proceeds from a past repetition, without any new reasoning or conclusion, we may establish it as a certain truth, that all the belief which follows upon any present impression, is deriv'd solely from that origin. (*T*102)

It is its *belief*-engendering power, its capacity to *enliven* ideas, that accounts for the preeminence of custom in Hume's theory of association and distinguishes it from all previous such theories:

According to my system, all reasonings are nothing but the effects of custom; and custom has no influence, but by inlivening the imagination, and giving us a strong conception of any object. (*T*149) Custom has two *original* effects upon the mind, in bestowing a *facility* in the performance of any action or the conception of any object; and afterwards a *tendency or inclination* towards it; and from these we may account for all its other effects, however extraordinary. (*T*422)

One thing often overlooked about Humean custom, especially as it concerns causal inference, is that its effect upon the mind, from an introspective point of view, is *not*, as is usually assumed, a feeling of *determination*, of being *irresistibly compelled* to think something when presented with a perception associated with it (nor does a transition of thought contrary to custom involve a feeling of *resistance*). Hume was quite consistent in describing the phenomenological content of our awareness in the case of a customary transition of perceptions as a "*facility* in the performance of any action":

supposing that in all past experience we have found two objects to have been always conjoin'd together, 'tis evident, that upon the appearance of one of these objects in an impression, we must from custom make an easy transition to the idea of that object, which usually attends it; and by means of the present impressions and easy transition must conceive that idea in a stronger and more lively manner, than we do any loose floating image of the fancy. (*T*115f.)

Introspectively, a custom is (i) a transition of thought from one perception to another, (ii) a felt ease in that transition, and, if a transition from an impression to an idea, (iii) an enlivening of the idea. If the custom is imperfect because "you weaken either the union or resemblance, [then] you weaken the principle of transition, and of consequence that belief, which arises from it ... The diminution of the union, and of the resemblance ... diminishes the facility of the transition, and by that means weakens the evidence" (*T*142f.). While in esoteric regions like skepticism and metaphysical speculation, well beyond the limits of the attractive influence of custom,

the action of the mind becomes forc'd and unnatural, and the ideas faint and obscure; tho' the principles of judgment, and the ballancing of opposite causes be the same as at the very beginning; yet their influence on the imagination, and the vigour they add to, or diminish from the thought, is by no means equal. Where the mind reaches not its objects with easiness and facility, the same principles have not the same effect as in a more natural conception of the ideas; nor does the imagination feel a sensation, which holds any proportion with that which arises from common judgments and opinions. The attention is on the stretch: The posture of the mind is uneasy; and the spirits being diverted from their natural course, are not govern'd in their movements by the same laws, at least not in the same degree, as when they flow in their usual channel. (*T*185)

Texts like those above are sufficiently common and representative to permit one to conclude that Hume's phenomenology of custom has nothing to do with being compelled or resisted. For an action to become habitual is simply for it to become so easy to perform that we become insensible of even doing it. Whether it be tying one's shoe laces, using one's native tongue, signing one's name, singing a familiar tune, or anything whatever one feels "at home" doing ("*facility* in the performance of any action"), custom is responsible. It contrasts with the awkwardness and difficulty of expressing oneself in a foreign language, of learning a new piece on the piano, participating in an unfamiliar sport, etc. When something is customary, it becomes "second nature": we pass from one step to a determinate successor without hesitation or reflection, even in performing routines of great complexity and difficulty (gymnastics). We train ourselves to the point where something seems as if it were the *only* way to proceed, the only sequence of actions that feels "natural." We may be quite unconscious of employing a skill, and even have no memory of ever having become proficient in it (for example, learning how to walk or speak); nevertheless, without the practice or training requisite to acquire the custom, we could no more execute the action than fly by flapping our arms. Clearly, the introspective content of such an activity is not a feeling of being compelled, or powerlessness to resist; it is an easy, fluid transition; effortlessness, naturalness; the absence of hesitation or reflection.[1]

Quite understandably, Hume often spoke of habits as *determining* the mind. Regarded from an *experiential* (causal) rather than an *introspective* (phenomenological) point of view, this is exactly what they do: when things are constantly observed to be conjoined, the repeated observation inculcates a habit, and the mere presence of the one will convey the mind to the other ("the mind is *determin'd* by custom to consider its usual attendant," *T*156). But there can be no more egregious indifference to context in the interpretation of Hume than to attach an introspective import to this determination. This would be to ascribe to him the view that we are able directly to perceive, without any assistance from experience, the operation of causal determination in the mental sphere, and no claim could be more immediately or entirely antithetical to his position regarding cause and effect. Here, as always, it should be kept in mind that, for Hume, the nature and sources of our knowledge of mental activity (agency) are exactly the same as those of our knowledge of physical activity: experience and habit (see *T*249, *TApp*632, and *E*VII/i.51–53). Immediate consciousness knows nothing of determination or any other causal notion ("We never have any impression, that contains any power or efficacy," *T*161). It was precisely to offer an alternative to the view of certain of his predecessors, most notably Locke (see *ECHU* II/xxi/§5) and Berkeley (*PHK* §28), that we can immediately perceive causal efficacy, particularly in respect of the voluntary and the involuntary, that Hume traced this idea to the *feeling* of customary transition (as one element of the reflexive impression of necessity – see section E).

Some interpret the introspective aspect of custom as a *feeling* of being determined, rather than a *real* mental determination.[2] Yet, such a notion runs directly counter both to the phenomenon itself and to the vast majority of Hume's descriptions of it. The more habitual an activity, the easier and more natural it feels, and the less sensible we are of any effort in performing it; full-fledged custom, far from feeling like being in the grip of an irresistible force, "may operate on our mind in such an insensible manner as never to be taken notice of, and may even in some measure be unknown to us" (*T*103). Moreover, being a mere feeling, what justification could there be for denominating it – or any other feeling, for that matter – a feeling of *determination*? If experience alone is capable of supplying us with knowledge of causality (determination, compulsion, etc.), then there can be nothing introspectible about the feeling itself to justify applying this epithet to it: introspectively, a feeling of toothache in an upper molar has as much, and as little, claim to be denominated "determination" as it does. When one tries to imagine what this feeling might be, what comes most readily to mind is something akin to a muscle reflex (as when the doctor strikes one's knee), and this Hume would surely have treated just as he did animal *nisus*:

It may be pretended, that the resistance which we meet with in bodies, obliging us frequently to exert our force and call up all our power, this gives us the idea of force and power. It is this *nisus* or strong endeavour of which we are conscious, that is the original impression from which this idea is copied. But, *first*, we attribute power to a vast number of objects where we never can suppose this resistance or exertion of force to take place: to the Supreme Being, who never meets with any resistance; to the mind in its command over its ideas and limbs, in common thinking and motion, where the effect follows immediately upon the will, without any exertion or summoning up of force; to inanimate matter, which is not capable of this sentiment. *Secondly*, this sentiment of an endeavour to overcome resistance has no known connexion with any event: What follows it we know by experience, but could not know it a priori. It must, however, be confessed, that the animal *nisus*, which we experience, though it can afford no accurate precise idea of power, enters very much into that vulgar, inaccurate idea, which is formed of it. (*E*VII/i.52n.; see also *E*VII/ii.60n.)

B. Custom and the uniformity of nature

In addition to "bestowing a *facility* in the performance of any action or the conception of any object," custom is also responsible for there being "afterwards a *tendency or inclination* towards it." This latter feature, obviously, is *experiential* rather than *introspective* in nature: there can be no such thing as a one-time-only *tendency*; unlike feelings, tendencies require time, and frequent recurrence, to manifest themselves. It is also the less important effect of custom so far as the interpretation of Hume's views on causal inference are concerned. If we interpret the inference in terms of customary inclination, his contention that causal relations stem from customs is sure to seem strained and unconvincing. For it seems far more plausible to say that the perception of *X* inclines one to think *Y because* one has conjoined them in a relation of cause and effect than vice versa. Moreover, the phenomenological sense of "custom" is logically prior to the dispositional: were there no feeling of facility in the transition, there would then be nothing to *signal to consciousness* that the transition was the result of experience-bred custom rather than a mere arbitrary sequence. Without an immediately evident indication (feeling) in the thousandth transition from a perception *X* to another perception *Y* to differentiate it, as our own mental activity, from mere passive observation, the occurrence of an *idea* of the one upon the appearance of its associate as an *impression* would in no way be distinguished amidst the flux of perceptions, and so could not then be enlivened by imagination or recognized as an effect of custom *qua* mental disposition. Since this is just to say that custom would amount to no more than an observed regularity, it would have been of no use to Hume in accounting for the origin of the new, original idea of cause ("by this means we can never discover any new idea, and can only multiply, but not enlarge the objects of our mind," *T*88). This demand for an immediate, consciously discernible difference between transitions of thought actuated by custom, on the one hand, and mere successions of perceptions, on the other, is satisfied by the feeling of easy transition. Only via the phenomenological sense of "custom" can we understand why Hume found it plausible to assert that *X* and *Y* are related as cause and effect *because* there is a customary association between them, and, more importantly, how custom itself can constitute (part of) the reflexive impression source of the idea of necessary connection.

Custom, in either sense, is insufficient, by itself, to generate *belief* in any causal relation. This requires, in addition to the relations of constantly conjoined temporally distinct perceptions (henceforth, *constant precedence*), the presence of one of the customarily associated perceptions in the form of an impression in sensation, reflexion, or memory. There are thus three distinct facets of Hume's account of the impression-original of the idea of cause: (i) the experience (memory) of a *constant precedence* of perceptions; (ii) a *custom* characterized by a feeling of facility in the transition of consciousness from one of the perceptions related by constant precedence to the other; and when one of these perceptions is present as an *impression*, (iii) the power of custom to induce us not only to *think* of its associate but to *believe* that it represents something really existent ("belief is an act of the mind arising from custom," *T*114).

It is its power to generate belief under the prescribed circumstances that warranted Hume's assertion that what commonly passes under the name of "reason" is nothing more than custom, grounded in instinctive propensities of human nature (see *T*103, *T*179, *T*267, *T*437, and *T*583). The elucidation and development of the role of custom in probable reasoning is the principal concern of *Treatise* I/iii/§§8–13. In §8, having established to his satisfaction the *nature* of belief, Hume focused on its *causes*, stating that he "wou'd willingly establish it as a general maxim in the science of human nature, *that when any impression becomes present to us, it not only transports the mind to such ideas as are related to it, but likewise communicates to them a share of its force and vivacity*" (*T*98). His use of such language has been the occasion of some misunderstanding. For the notion of one perception (viz. the impression) *communicating* its vivacity to another (the idea) contradicts one of the cardinal tenets of his philosophy: that immediate consciousness infallibly informs us that perceptions are utterly inactive, without causal connection of any kind, and so, in respect both of their existence and their qualities, entirely independent of one another ("All ideas are deriv'd from, and represent impressions. We never have any impression, that contains any power or efficacy," *T*.161; "our distinct perceptions are distinct existences, and ... the mind never perceives any real connexion among distinct existences," *TApp*636). Even more misleadingly, Hume speaks as if perceptions *have* vivacity to give to others, and so makes it seem as if vivacity were a quality of *perceptions themselves*, rather than merely our *consciousness* of them (since vivacity is a feeling of belief in the real existence of what one observes, such language seems unavoidable). One should therefore be careful to regard his "general maxim in the science of human nature" as shorthand, not a description of the actual process of associating perceptions. Respecting the latter, he made quite plain that *custom* is the sole agency through which vivacity can be "communicated" from impressions to ideas; and, since perceptions obviously cannot be bearers of habits of mind, there can be no doubting that vivacity transfers, like vivacity itself, are wholly an affair of consciousness (i.e. idea-relating and -enlivening imagination, in accordance with propensities indigenous to human nature).

Custom owes its central position in Hume's account of causality in *Treatise* I/iii to his having clad it in the mantle of the uniformity principle, once borne by reason (see *TAbs*652 and *E*V/i.36). For while, on the face of it, our belief in the uniformity of nature seems more beholden to resemblance (of present to past conjunctions of perceptions) than causation, its foundation in custom proves the contrary. This is a crucial point, often overlooked. Resemblances are among those relations "discoverable at first sight, and fall more properly under the province of intuition and demonstration" (*T*70); they thus do not presuppose experience (repeated observation). This is not to deny that they give rise to customs in their own right (generality being the most significant example). Yet, only causal relations are capable of taking us beyond the senses and memory (see chapter 4-A); and, since belief in the uniformity of nature requires this extension of our purview, no custom founded on resemblance alone is capable of accounting for it. Only customs based on constant precedence and underpinning causal inferences can account for belief in the uniformity of nature; causal relations are therefore the very fabric of a uniform nature.

That the customs constitutive of individual causal relations are also, cumulatively, constitutive of the uniformity of nature is evident, too, in

Hume's consideration of an ostensible counterexample to his account of causal inferences in terms of custom:

'Tis certain, that not only in philosophy, but even in common life, we may attain the knowledge of a particular cause merely by one experiment, provided it be made with judgment, and after a careful removal of all foreign and superfluous circumstances. Now as after one experiment of this kind, the mind, upon the appearance either of the cause or the effect, can draw an inference concerning the existence of its correlative; and as a habit can never be acquir'd merely by one instance; it may be thought, that belief cannot in this case be esteem'd the effect of custom. But this difficulty will vanish, if we consider, that tho' we are here suppos'd to have had only one experiment of a particular effect, yet we have many millions to convince us of this principle; *that like objects, plac'd in like circumstances, will always produce like effects*; and as this principle has establish'd itself by a sufficient custom, it bestows an evidence and firmness on any opinion, to which it can be apply'd. The connexion of the ideas is not habitual after one experiment; but this connexion is comprehended under another principle, that is habitual; which brings us back to our hypothesis. (*T*105; see *E*IX.84n.)

It normally requires but one encounter to be convinced of the desirability of keeping a safe distance from skunks ever after. Against such seeming counterexamples to his theory, Hume contended that the inference could not have been made (i.e. the belief generated) were it not that one had already become convinced "by a sufficient custom" "that like objects, plac'd in like circumstances, will always produce like effects." Without this general maxim of uniformity, based on custom and the "millions" of experiments that ingrain it in us, it would never occur to us to believe that a like encounter with a skunk would have like results, and so we would fail to take any preventative action when next we espy one. Hence, only through custom can the need for experienced constant precedence be superseded, both in individual instances and in our belief in the general uniformity of nature.

The particular variety of custom operative in causal inferences based on a single observation merits closer scrutiny. Although, at first sight, one might suppose the principle "that like objects, plac'd in like circumstances, will always produce like effects" to be merely an instance of a more general uniformity of nature, this cannot be correct. Hume made quite clear that this is the most general principle experience-bred custom is capable of yielding – the ultimate outcome of the comparison of innumerable particular customs founded on constant precedence and issuing in relations of cause of effect; hence, were one to suppose the uniformity principle more general still, it then could not, contrary to his express assertion, be founded on custom. Accordingly, when Hume spoke of millions of experiments giving rise to a custom which in turn convinces us of the principle that like objects placed in like circumstances will always produce like effects, he is referring to *the uniformity of nature itself, not merely an instance of it* (see also *E*IX.84n., §1). When we utilize the uniformity principle in reasoning with regard to present and future phenomena we are therefore relying on a belief which is simply the cumulative product of previous customary causal inferences. Nor is this a conjuring trick, a raising oneself up by the bootstraps: since past causal beliefs are constitutive of the uniformity of nature, it is no wonder that unfamiliar things found to be precedent and contiguous are, *ceteris paribus*, presumed to be causally related – the wonder would be if we responded otherwise!

Each particular causal inference is a uniformity principle in miniature; the implication of uniformity with respect to all places and times is not accidental, but essential to the relation. Against this, Blackburn contends that "there is no contradiction in supposing that the powers and forces with which events are endowed at one time cease at another, nor in supposing that any secret nature of bodies upon which these powers and forces depend itself changes, bringing their change in its wake."[3] Since it is not events, but agents that are endowed with "powers and forces,' Blackburn's point seems to be this: uniformity is not essential to causal relations because, if the nature of the agent should change, it may gain or lose some of its powers and forces. But if, for the causal tie to be broken, the things themselves must change in *nature*, how could one still claim to be encountering the *same* things subsequently? Words like "nature" and "same" are notorious slippery in philosophical contexts. Nevertheless, it is no counterexample to uniformity to suppose that things which, with their *present* natures are endowed with certain powers and forces, might lose these powers and forces if their natures were *different*. A true counterexample would be a case of the very same thing, with the very same nature, at one time possessing, and at another time lacking, a certain power or force; but this clearly would be a contradiction! Even a rationalist philosopher, rather than deny the uniformity implicit in causal connections, would simply presume that he has either overlooked some difference between the cases or misapprehended the power itself (i.e. that something additional, as yet undetected, is involved in the causation). So, too, Hume: "the custom or relation, by which [the mind] is determin'd, admits not of the least change" (*T*108); "The objects [that cause and effect] presents are fixt and unalterable" (*T*110). The great attraction for him of tracing causal relations to custom was surely that habits, as such, determine present and future expectations. Of course, habits are not perfect: they may weaken or disappear altogether in the face of inconstant conjunction; or, if an idea is regularly conjoined with different perceptions, then Hume's account of probability will apply and proof be degraded to probability (see section D). But precisely because, as a habit weakens, so does the necessity of the connection founded on it, this only serves to confirm the correlation: the connection is a "must" only in so far as, and so long as, the habit remains an "always"; but once the "always" becomes a "mostly," the "must" becomes only a "likely." Thus, for Hume, each causal inference implies its own distinct uniformity: "The same cause always produces the same effect, and the same effect never arises but from the same cause" (*T* 173).

A more widespread misconception about Humean custom as the ground of uniformity is illustrated by Goodman's oft iterated critique:

> The real inadequacy of Hume's account lay not in his descriptive approach but in the imprecision of his description. Regularities in experience, according to him, give rise to habits of expectation; and thus it is predictions conforming to past regularities that are normal or valid. But Hume overlooks the fact that some regularities do and some do not establish such habits; that predictions based on some regularities are valid while predictions based on other regularities are not. Every word you have heard me say has occurred prior to the final sentence of this lecture; but that does not, I hope, create any expectation that every word you will hear me say will be prior to that sentence... We must somehow find a way of distinguishing lawlike hypotheses, to which our definition of confirmation applies, from accidental hypotheses, to which it does not.[4]

Goodman overlooks the fact that a regularity that neither gives rise to nor has any basis in custom cannot, in Humean theory, yield *belief* in any necesary connection (see chapter 2-D). No custom, no causal belief; and a custom is possible only if (i) *all* the associated perceptions are observed and (ii) observed *repeatedly*. Goodman's actions would yield a Humean-type causal inference in his (regularly attending) students only if he ended *every subsequent lecture* with the word he ended his lecture with that day, and if the word was noticeable enough to be observed. For only if a perception is *constantly* observed to be conjoined with another can the two become associated; but, if either or both are observed only once, then, despite any other kind of regularity that may pertain to them, they cannot give rise to a custom and so cannot be believed to be causally connected. Far from overlooking "the fact that some regularities do and some do not establish ... habits," Hume exploited it in his theory of causal relations to account for how, quite naturally and without requiring any training or guidance, we discriminate law-like regularity from accidental concomitance. Regularities which can never be translated into *experienced* constant conjunctions cannot generate habits, and therefore are quite rightly never made the basis of causal inference and belief. Furthermore, Hume was careful to make allowance for the fact that not just any habit will give rise to a causal inference: customarily conjoined perceptions have also to stand in a relation of temporal precedence, and generally spatial contiguity as well, before the imagination will associate them as cause and effect (this excludes the sort of custom underlying generality). It is difficult to see what more he could need, or accommodate, to account for how not only we, but also infants, animals, etc., are able to distinguish law-like from accidental hypotheses. Most importantly, custom provides the key to distinguishing accidental from genuine philosophical causal relations, even though neither generates a custom. For, while philosophical relations exert no *direct* influence on imagination and lack any *inherent* power to generate belief, they are nevertheless outgrowths of natural, custom-based causal relations, and so have a *borrowed* ability to enliven ideas, and thereby influence our thought and action. Thus, rootedness in custom suffices to distinguish philosophical causal relations from mere accidental hypotheses.[5]

C. Custom and the universality of the causal maxim

Having explained the uniformity of nature through experience-bred custom, one can begin to assemble – as Hume never quite managed to do himself – the pieces of his response to the query posed in *Treatise* I/iii/§3: how experience yields the general causal maxim of a *necessity* of a cause for *every* beginning of existence.[6] When examining the issue initially (chapter 4-B), we found that the required explanation has an appearance of (vicious?) circularity, in that it calls for a causal explanation – how experience gives rise to the causal maxim – which, being causal, must itself depend on experience, etc. The conception of custom which emerges from Hume's investigations of particular causal inferences in sections §§4–8 affords at least a partial way out of this circle. (i) It reveals that experience (i.e. the memory of constant precedence) is incapable, *by itself*, of accounting for causal reasoning and belief; only in so far as a custom is generated, and only by means of such a custom, can experience be deemed a source of causal inference. (ii) Custom is likewise the essential underpinning of all our general conclusions regarding nature, above all our belief in its uniformity ("that like objects, plac'd in like circumstances, will always produce like effects"). (iii) Although Hume never enunciated it, his commitment to a causal explanation of causal inference seems sufficient to warrant ascribing to him the view that the same "millions of experiments" that give rise to a belief in the uniformity of nature also serve to convince us – animals, infants, etc., too – of the causal relation holding between *experience itself* and success in the acquisition of causal insight. In other words, the experienced constant precedence of the former *vis à vis* the latter gradually and insensibly inculcates a *custom* of consulting experience whenever causal understanding is desired.[7] The procedures in accordance with which such consultation takes place – for example, the great disparity in technique between an experienced hunting dog and a nuclear physicist – is of no consequence here. From Hume's point of view, what ought really to command our attention is this: due to the powerlessness of experience *per se* to yield causal insight (in that the 1,000th repetition shows us nothing we could not have perceived the first time), the true efficacy of experimentation, unbeknownst both to the vulgar and to the scientist, is *to instill a new custom* (whether directly, by giving oneself an experience of constant precedence, or, if the number of experiments is insufficient, indirectly, through application of the uniformity principle and general laws, which are themselves supported by custom founded on constant precedence). In the absence of customs, causal beliefs, and so belief in the uniformity of nature as well, could never arise; hence, the real purpose in resorting to experimentation is an instinctive need for the guidance only custom can provide: this is the sole foundation for the "authority" of experience, and we have only to reflect on what it would be for human nature to give rise to different "principles which are permanent, irresistible, and universal" (*T*225) to free ourselves from the myth that scientific methods take us in the direction of objective, independent truth ("all the LOGIC I think proper to employ in my reasoning ... might have been supply'd by the natural principles of our understanding," *T*175).

The preceding should suffice to make clear that the circle, in which experience instills in us the custom of consulting experience for causal explanations which in turn disclose the efficacy of experience in obtaining causal insight, is not vicious. It should also, if Hume is as good as his word, permit us to understand how experience, supported by custom, gives rise to our incorrigible certainty with regard to the causal maxim ("'Twill, perhaps, be found in the end, that the same answer will serve for both questions," *T*82). The explanation of our belief that *whatever* begins to exist *must* have a cause of its existence may be divided into two parts: the explanation of our belief in the *universality* of the maxim, and of that in its *necessity*. Neither part of the task can be discharged by reference to the uniformity principle. For this, by itself, assures us only that such objects as have been found *in the past* constantly to produce certain effects "will always produce like effects" in the future; and this falls far short of a guarantee that *every* beginning of existence (thing or event), *regardless of whether constant precedence has been observed in the past or will be observed in the future*, has a cause. Further, the uniformity principle is compatible with anomalies, including miracles, since it merely implies that only those things – and those sufficiently analogous thereto – that have been found to be constantly conjoined in the past will continue uniformly; by contrast, the causal maxim excludes anomalies because it affirms that *whatever* begins to exist must have a cause. (Of course, even if it could be shown that experience, as the foundation of custom, suffices to account for our belief in the universality of the maxim, it would still remain to be determined how we become convinced of its *necessity*, that is, how "necessity" should be understood in reference to a principle bearing exclusively on matters of fact.)

The essential element in Hume's account of the universality of the maxim has already been considered: the status of causal relations as our sole and entire means of penetrating beyond the senses and memory, and hence the foundation of all other relations of real existence (identity, spatial and temporal contiguity, etc. – see *T*73f.). Its relevance to the present question is evident from Hume's division of reality on *T*108 into two distinct systems of realities, that of the memory and senses, and that of judgment. The realities comprising the latter are "connected by custom, or if you will, by the relation of cause and effect." However, while causal relations are of themselves sufficient to take us beyond the memory and senses, they are incapable, without the aid of relations like identity, of doing more than extending the subjective flux to include unperceived realities (see chapter 4-A). Hence, while the second system *may* incorporate objects external to, and independent of, the senses (i.e. the identity-based objects of *Treatise* I/iv/§2), distant times and locales like ancient Rome, etc., none of these is *essentially* part of it. This is important, for only by recognizing the primitive, constitutive role played by causal relations in Hume's theory of objectivity can we appreciate their *all-pervasiveness* in the system of realities based on custom, and so, too, the *universality* of the causal maxim: since everything in this system of realities is founded on, and to that extent constituted by, causal relations, whatever existent we situate there must *ipso facto* be believed to have a cause ("'Tis this latter principle, which peoples the world, and brings us acquainted with such existences, as by their removal in time and place, lie beyond the reach of the senses and memory. By means of it I paint the universe in my imagination.").

Although *T*108 also contains the gist of Hume's conception of the necessity of the causal maxim as well ("[the mind] feels 'tis in a manner necessarily determin'd to view these particular ideas, and that the custom or relation, by which it is determin'd, admits not of the least change"), its consideration properly belongs to the examination of Hume's account of the origin of the idea of necessary connection in *Treatise* I/iii/§14. So, limiting our attention to the universality of the maxim, we find several strands of his theory of understanding merge neatly into one: experience as the basis of custom; custom as the source of causal inference and the belief reposed therein; causal relations as constitutive of all reality beyond the memory and senses; belief in the general uniformity of nature as the collective outcome of particular causal inferences; the exploitation of experience to breed new customary causal inferences; and, finally, an unassailable certainty as to the truth of the causal maxim in respect of all possible objects of judgment ("one of those maxims, which tho' they may be deny'd with the lips, 'tis impossible for men in their hearts really to doubt of"). Any inference from one perception to another, whether philosophical or natural, involves associative imagination and, insofar as it leads to belief in the reality of an associated idea, causal relations (see *T*.109f.). That the maxim does not hold in respect of the realities of immediate consciousness does not impair its universality since they are prior to, and independent of, all *relation* of perceptions in *imagination* (i.e. they are never objects of understanding). Consciousness of sensations and reflexions as impressions is, it could be said, belief in their real existence unaccompanied by any belief in their having a cause of existence. Yet, such belief is far too primitive to count as a genuine counterexample to the causal maxim. This would require a full-fledged judgment, or relation of ideas, which also has the vivacity of belief; but such a belief is quite literally impossible given that the *T*108 system of verisimilar (i.e. believed) realities of judgment requires the foundation only verisimilar causal relations can supply (see chapter 4). Custom is therefore the basis not only of a uniform nature, but also of a *unified* one: *every* objective existent is joined with every other in a single system (nexus) of cause and effect relations.

D. Custom and imagination: images of reflexion

Naturalistic philosophies are particularly vulnerable to the passage of time. Theories representing themselves as scientific in a bygone age may seem like fables when viewed from the distance of centuries; and the more explicit and pervasive a philosopher's commitment to his scientific model, the more pronounced the impression of the mythical likely to result. The risk is perhaps greatest for philosophers like Hume who put their faith in the methodology, principles, and data of empirical psychology. This is one reason the *Enquiry* is sometimes preferred to the *Treatise*: although one searches in vain for major shifts in doctrine (or even their manner of exposition), it tends to be more persuasive than the *Treatise* if only on account of its brevity, and in particular the excision or paring down of much of Hume's "psycho-mechanics." Aside from *Treatise* II, the account of probability in I/iii/§§11–13 is usually regarded as a particularly egregious example of this pseudo-science (only one brief section is devoted to it in the *Enquiry*). Nevertheless, if for no other reason than that it sheds so much light on Hume's conception of the operation of custom in bringing forth beliefs regarding causal relations, no one seriously concerned to understand his philosophy can afford to neglect it.

In the sections preceding probability, Hume confined himself to customs and causal inferences arising from the *constant* precedence of perceptions. In practice, however, the experience of precedence is frequently inconstant – the same thing, seemingly under the same circumstances, is often found to produce, or be produced by, sometimes one thing, sometimes another, and sometimes none at all (for example, the same medicine, on one occasion, may make one better, on another, worse, and on yet another, do nothing at all). This posed Hume the following difficulty: if custom is understood as an enhanced feeling of facility in the transition of thought from one idea to another, then contrary outcomes ought to have the effect either (i) of creating distinct, mutually incompatible customs, (ii) or, if customs based on less frequently experienced outcomes are cancelled out, of yielding only a single, proportionately weaker custom. In the former case, our thought would be channelled in different directions simultaneously, either creating in us the expectation of distinct, mutually incompatible outcomes or – given that it is impossible to believe and disbelieve the same thing at the same time – leaving us in a state of hopeless vacillation, unable to settle on any determinate object of belief (for "belief, however faint, fixes itself on a determinate object," *T*140). In the latter case, the belief would be all-or-nothing in character. For it is the nature of custom to render the transition from a given perception *A* to another *B* easier than that to any other perception *X*; so, however weak the remaining custom might be, it would suffice to send our thought – and, consequently, our belief – *always* to B, to the exclusion of all the other (cancelled-out) outcomes. Neither alternative, however, is substantiated by the facts. For what actually happens in such cases, according to Hume, is that belief is parcelled out among the various outcomes in proportion to their empirical support, and full conviction is reposed in none. It was therefore clear to him that the account of belief in terms of custom delineated prior to *Treatise* I/iii/§11 faces a serious challenge when confronted with the facts of probability.

Realizing that custom by itself is insufficient to explain beliefs based on inconstant precedence, Hume posited a special operation of imagination whereby vivacity is distributed among the various outcomes in proportion to their frequency of occurrence:

When we transfer contrary experiments to the future, we can only repeat these contrary experiments with their particular proportions; which cou'd not produce assurance in any single event, upon which we reason, unless the fancy melted together all those images that concur, and extracted from them one single idea or image, which is intense and lively in proportion to the number of experiments from which it is deriv'd, and their superiority above their antagonists. Our past experience presents no determinate object; and as our belief, however faint, fixes itself on a determinate object, 'tis evident that the belief arises not merely from the transference of past to future, but from some operation of the *fancy* conjoin'd with it. This may lead us to conceive the manner, in which that faculty enters into all our reasonings. (*T*140)

Suppose that *X* has been found conjoined with *A*, *B*, and *C*, and that *A* has been conjoined with it more frequently than *B* and *B* more frequently than *C*. To cope with this situation, Hume supposes that the imagination, in a kind of prismatic act of reflexion, splits its past experiences of *X*s into distinct groups of conjunctions with *A*s, *B*s, and *C*s. Although this may strike many as a somewhat mechanical solution to the problem, it involves a special twist, possible only given Hume's conception of "imagination, or the vivacity of our ideas." The operation he ascribed to imagination is not one of heaping together the various memory images of *A*s, *B*s, and *C*s, and estimating (by, say, their general appearance) which of the three collections is largest. A memory of approximately how many times *A*, *B*, and *C* have followed *X* is indeed a precondition for this refractive act; but what actually gets fused together by it are the phenomenological feelings of vivacity appertaining to each:

The only manner then, in which the superior number of similar component parts in the one can exert its influence, and prevail above the inferior in the other, is by producing a stronger and more lively view of its object... Now as the view [probability and possibility] present is in both cases full and entire, and comprehends the object in all its parts, 'tis impossible that in this particular there can be any difference; nor is there any thing but a superior vivacity in the probability, arising from the concurrence of a superior number of views, which can distinguish these effects... It remains, therefore, as the only reasonable opinion, that these similar views run into each other, and unite their forces; so as to produce a stronger and clearer view, than what arises from any one alone. (*T*137f.; see also *E*VI.46)

The imagination keeps a running account of its experiences, adding a dram, as it were, of vivacity and facility to the relation upon each new encounter with the conjunction ("Each new experiment is as a new stroke of the pencil, which bestows an additional vivacity on the colours, without either multiplying or enlarging the figure," *T*135). There is no need to suppose it an exact account (which would be out of keeping with his preference for general appearances and false-but-useful standards); it need merely suffice to form what might be called an *image of reflexion.* Besides distinguishing it from the memory image *before* consciousness, this expression brings out the affinity between the imagination's feelings of vivacity/facility and impressions of reflexion (passions, affections, desires, emotions). For, like the latter, phenomenological feelings have the ability to mix as ideas do not:

Ideas never admit of a total union, but are endow'd with a kind of impenetrability, by which they exclude each other, and are capable of forming a compound by their conjunction, not by their mixture. On the other hand, impressions and passions are susceptible of an entire union; and like colours, may be blended so perfectly together, that each of them may lose itself, and contribute only to vary that uniform impression, which arises from the whole. Some of the most curious phænomena of the human mind are deriv'd from this property of the passions. (*T*366)

Images of reflexion are a *total union* of feelings of vivacity in the sense described. No amount of combination of ideas (memories and/or fancies) could yield such a union (it could at most give one a "final cut," as when, in the editing of a film, pieces from different takes are spliced together). Phenomenological feeling meets this requirement; belonging to the very fabric of consciousness, its only magnitude is intensive (i.e. consisting of no parts, it can vary only in degree). Given an imagination with the capacity to produce images of reflexion, we then have merely to *feel* the difference in vivacity correspondent with frequency of observation in order to bestow more belief on *A* than on *B*, more on *B* than on *C*, and, finally, more on *C* than on other states of affairs which have never been found to be conjoined with *X*. Likewise, a transition to *A* will feel easier than one to *B*, a transition to *B* easier than one to *C*, and a transition to *C* easier than one to perceptions with no connection at all to *X* (i.e. the feeling of facility too is refracted and distributed through the image of reflexion). Accordingly, a perception of *X* will bring to mind all of its associates, but belief will be apportioned according to the magnitude of the images of reflexion pertaining to *A*, *B*, and *C*. Hume's phenomenological conception of belief and custom is, therefore, not only able to cope with inconstant precedence, but is particularly well suited to the purpose.

It is important not to overlook Hume's claim that the capacity of imagination to "melt together" various images and "extract from them" a "single idea or image which is intense and lively in proportion to the number of experiments from which it is deriv'd," enables us "to conceive the manner, in which that faculty enters into all our reasonings" (*T*140). That images of reflexion enter into *all* our probable reasonings indicates that, even where the precedence relation is constant, custom alone is insufficient to give rise to beliefs regarding causal relations. Some such "melting together" (total union) of discrete images into a single, lively one seems necessary, for, even if *X* is always succeeded by *Y*, these pairings are apt to occur at widely scattered intervals in experience, and so depend on imagination – which "is not restrain'd to the same order and form with the original impressions" – not only to group them together, but *to form from* *them a single lively image of reflexion.* Thus, if there were ever any doubt, we see once again that the salient feature of Humean imagination is not the sheer conjoining of ideas, but their *enlivening.* Custom interested Hume not as blind habit or conditioned reflex, but as a form of conscious experience as rich and varied as our emotions, passions, and desires. The capacity of imagination to feel, as well as to separate and connect, the perceptions it experiences is, for him, nothing less than our capacity to be enlightened and transformed by experience, and so the original source of all understanding and reasoning. Relations of ideas gain, lose, or divide up facility and vivacity with each new experience, so that knowledge is as natural an effect of experience as bodily maturation.

E. Necessity and the idea of cause

Treatise I/iii/§14, "Of the Idea of Necessary Connexion," has probably attracted more attention than any other piece of philosophical writing in English. This is somewhat surprising since few are of the view that Hume's derivation of the idea from an internal impression of reflexion is even so much as tenable, much less persuasive. Moreover, the wide variety of interpretations that have been (and continue to be) offered, ranging from metaphysical realism to psychologism to unalloyed skepticism, suggests that even the basics of his position remain unclear. Yet, whether justly or not, philosophers as distinguished as Kant have declared Hume's analysis of necessary connection a watershed in philosophy for dealing a death-blow to traditional metaphysics. This reputation, together with the conflicting interpretations on which it is based, encourages a greater than ordinary degree of modesty on the part of anyone seeking a fresh approach to section §14. One must content oneself with offering one among many possible readings, and aspire to show only that it makes better sense of the text than others, not to settle matters once and for all. It is in this spirit that I would have my own be considered.

One thing that tends to be overlooked, but which seems to me of great significance, is that, in Hume's eyes, section §14 is not a new step in the argument of *Treatise* I/iii, but the conclusion and summation of everything precedent: "I doubt not but these consequences will at first sight be receiv'd without difficulty, as being evident deductions from principles, which we have already establish'd, and which we have often employ'd in our reasonings" (*T*156). The premises to which he refers are these: (i) since all ideas derive from impressions, if we have any genuine idea of necessary connection, it must be copied from some impression; (ii) no such impression is found in the appearance of the objects to which necessity is ordinarily ascribed, for the only relations immediately evident to the imagination are of contiguity in time and place ("the object we call cause *precedes* the other we call effect," *T*155); (iii) *experience* never reveals anything more than constant precedence; and (iv) *reflection* on past experience "only repeats the same objects; and therefore can never give rise to a new idea" (*T*155). Yet, (v) repetition is found by experience to produce customs, and thereby influences the imagination. (vi) The imagination fuses the repeated observations into an *image of reflexion*, so that upon the presence as an impression (in sense, reflexion, or memory) of one or more of a group of customarily associated perceptions, the ideas of the remainder will be *enlivened* – their real existence *believed* – to a degree proportionate with the constancy and number of times they have been found conjoined in the past. Thus it is that (vii) the repetition "produces a new impression, and by that means the idea" (*T*155).

The "new impression" experience produces is nothing but an amalgam of the *phenomenological* feelings of facility and vivacity characteristic of custom-bred causal inferences in which one of the associated perceptions is present as an impression:

> after a repetition of similar instances, the mind is carried by habit, upon the appearance of one event, to expect its usual attendant, and to believe that it will exist. This connexion, therefore, which we *feel* in the mind, this customary transition of the imagination from one object to its usual attendant, is the sentiment or impression from which we form the idea of power or necessary connexion. Nothing farther is in the case. (*E*VII/ii.59)

> [A]fter a frequent repetition, I find, that upon the appearance of one of the objects, the mind is *determin'd* by custom to consider its usual attendant, and to consider it in a stronger light upon account of its relation to the first object. 'Tis this impression, then, or *determination*, which affords me the idea of necessity. (*T*156)

> When any object is presented to us, it immediately conveys to the mind a lively idea of that object, which is usually found to attend it; and this determination of the mind forms the necessary connexion of these objects. (*T*169; see also *T*165 and *TAbs*655f.)

Such passages should suffice to make clear that Hume's impression of necessity is "Nothing farther" than a composite of the phenomenological feelings of facility and vivacity attendant upon inferences from an impression to an associated idea (concerning the non-introspectible import of "determination" see section A above).[8]

It is worth stressing, because its neglect so often leads to error, that the impression of necessary connection involves not one but two feelings: that of *facility* attendant upon a customary transition of thought and that of *vivacity* (when one of the associated perceptions is present as an impression). Only if this dual character is recognized can we appreciate why Hume thought his explanation of necessary connection so evidently plausible and compelling that he feared only that it might "seduce us unwarily into the conclusion, and make us imagine it contains nothing extraordinary, nor worthy of our curiosity" (*T*156). For it loses all semblance of plausibility as soon as the necessity impression is construed solely in terms of custom, as so many do (see below). While we may concede that custom determines our thought by conveying it from one thought to another associated with it, this alone cannot account for our *belief* in the real (verisimilar) existence of the other perception. Even if one of them is presently before the mind as an impression, the most custom can do is bring the other to mind, not induce us to believe it. This shows clearly that something else, over and above the custom-bred facility of transition from one thought to another, is necessary if Hume's candidate for the impression-original of the idea of necessary connection is to have the evident plausibility he attributed to it. This is where the originality of his conception of belief as vivacity/verisimilitude proves most fruitful: in the customary transition from impression to idea, the imagination not only finds ease, but also *enlivens* the idea; consequently, we believe in its real existence.

Vivacity/verisimilitude must be invested in the entire complex idea of the relation, not merely its distinct perception relata; otherwise, we still would have nothing that could plausibly be described as an impression of necessary connection or belief in the objectivity of causal relations. Hume's account can be seen to satisfy this requirement simply by regarding the customary transition in the appropriate manner: from the standpoint of the imagination that makes it. When, on the occasion of an impression *X*, it performs the easy, customary transition to the idea of *X*'s associate *Y*, the imagination can only believe in the real existence of *Y* if it also believes in the real existence of its *connection* with *X*. For what distinguishes causal relations from the other natural relations is that, unlike resemblance and contiguity, causal relations are not immediately perceptible and so depend entirely on experience-bred custom to effect the association ("Objects have no discoverable connexion together; nor is it from any other principle but custom operating upon the imagination, that we can draw any inference from the appearance of one to the existence of another," *T*103). Apart from custom (as manifested to consciousness by the feeling of facility), there is nothing whatever to connect *X* with *Y* in imagination; their association is wholly a matter of this feeling in the transition from the one to the other. So, if the transition of thought it characterizes were not believed to be just as real as the perceptions it *and nothing else* connects, then it would be impossible for us to believe that anything related *Y* to *X* at all. In other words, the fact that an impression like *X* and an idea like *Y* are related to one another by the imagination in spite of there being nothing in immediate perception to connect them cannot be explained otherwise than by a belief in (i.e. ascription of reality to) the customary transition itself ("this customary transition is ... the same with power and necessity; which are consequently qualities of perceptions, not of objects, and are internally felt by the soul, and not perceiv'd externally in bodies," *T*166). The customary transition of thought, as the beneficiary of the vivacity accumulated through experienced constant conjunction, is thus accorded objective verisimilitude as a relation of existential dependence binding together otherwise independent perceptions, whereupon the latter, in their turn, are thenceforth regarded as receptacles of causal agency and patience ("we suppose necessity and power to lie in the objects we consider, not in our mind, that considers them; notwithstanding it is not possible for us to form the most distant idea of that quality, when it is not taken for the determination of the mind, to pass from the idea of an object to that of its usual attendant," *T*167).

Hume's promise, that "'twill appear in the end, that the necessary connexion depends on the inference [from impression to idea], instead of the inference's depending on the necessary connexion" (*T*88), is here fulfilled. For it is in and through this inference alone that custom is transformed from a mere psychological fact about the observer to an objective fact about the observed. Belief – verisimilitude – is for the first time attached not merely to individual perceptions, but to their *relation* in imagination as well; and this first objectification of a relation – the belief in the real existence of what is, in fact, a mere transition of thought – sets the stage for all the rest: objective identity, space and time, quantity and quality, etc. It is in this sense that Hume deemed custom the presupposed foundation of the objective order of nature: customary transitions *objectified* as causal relations, causal relations simply *verisimilar* customs. The lawful order of nature is thereby divested of the mystery and wonder that have led so many to stray into metaphysics, for it is, quite literally, as familiar as familiarity itself: the practiced facility characteristic of such mundane arts as buttering bread or speaking one's native tongue. The ease characteristic of a customary routine is projected onto the objects customarily conjoined, so that each and every one becomes in effect a master of the arts of nature: the faultless, effortless, unreflecting executor of nature's laws. The inevitability characteristic of determinism becomes, for Hume, nothing more than objectified customary transitions of thought, a necessity comprised wholly of facility and vivacity (verisimilitude). And it is undoubtedly this that underwrites his conviction that the Newtonian mathematical system of the world could and should be traced to an origin in human understanding:

Even *Mathematics, Natural Philosophy, and Natural Religion,* are in some measure dependent on the science of MAN; since they lie under the cognizance of men, and are judged by their powers and faculties. 'Tis impossible to tell what changes and improvements we might make in these sciences were we thoroughly acquainted with the extent and force of human understanding, and cou'd explain the nature of the ideas we employ, and of the operations we perform in our reasonings ... There is no question of importance, whose decision is not compriz'd in the science of man; and there is none which can be decided with any certainty, before we become acquainted with that science. In pretending therefore to explain the principles of human nature, we in effect propose a compleat system of the sciences, built on a foundation almost entirely new, and the only one upon which they can stand with any security. (*T*xvf.)[9]

It should not be thought that I have forgotten Hume's warning not to "transfer the determination of the thought to external objects, and suppose any real intelligible connexion betwixt them; that being a quality, which can only belong to the mind that considers them" (*T*168; see *E*VII/ii.88n.). The reality attributed to connections between perceptions is, on my account, a purely phenomenological verisimilitude. It ascribes to perceptions neither the appearance nor the reality of absolute, intelligible connections (nor, *a fortiori*, the *unintelligible* connections Kemp Smith, Wright, and others suppose Hume to have affirmed – see section F). Only verisimilar – "felt" – reality attaches to customary transitions; it is simply one more application of Hume's conception of belief as vivacity/verisimilitude. This is precisely what Passmore overlooked when he criticized Hume for failing to live up to his (supposed) positivism by venturing to objectify causal relations at all:

We may ask how it happens, under these circumstances, that ... we are ever led to imagine that the necessity attaches to the relation between the cause and the effect, as distinct from the workings of our own mind. Hume's answer is that "the mind has a great propensity to spread itself on external objects, and to conjoin with them any internal impressions, which they occasion, and which always make their appearance at the same time that these objects discover themselves to the senses." (*T*167). This device ... is typical; Hume tries to operate with a bold sweeping associationist psychology, but has constantly to supplement it with subsidiary "propensities". There is a suspiciously *ad hoc* air about the supplementation; Hume is well aware of this fact, and is careful to insist that the same propensity can be observed in operation on other occasions. We cannot, therefore, rule it out of court as an "occult quality," as a mere name for our ignorance, which "explains" the transfer of necessity by affirming that we have a 'propensity' so to transfer it.[10]

Passmore's thesis is that Hume, supposedly faced with a conflict between his theory and the objectivity universally ascribed to causal relations, posited a propensity of mind whose sole *raison d'être* was to reconcile them. Such a propensity would indeed be *ad hoc*. But Hume never had any need of it. Passmore has simply overlooked the most distinctive feature of Hume's associationalist psychology and the source of virtually all its explanatory power: the power of imagination to engender belief, that is, the feeling in virtue of which an object (in idea) is regarded by consciousness as real (verisimilar). In the case of causal relations, customary transitions are the beneficiary of this feeling. There is nothing whatever *ad hoc* about Hume's objectification of these complex ideas as causal relations:

You ask me, If the idea of Cause & Effect is nothing but Vicinity, (you should have said constant Vicinity, or regular Conjunction), I would gladly know *whence is that farther Idea of Causation against which you argue*? The Question is pertinent; but I hope I have answer'd it. We feel, after the constant Conjunction, an easy Transition from one Idea to the other, or a Connexion in the Imagination. And as it is usual for us to transfer our own Feelings to the Objects on which they are dependent, we attach the internal Sentiment to the external Objects. If no single Instances of Cause & Effect appear to have any Connexion, but only repeated similar ones, you will find yourself oblig'd to have Recourse to this Theory. (*LI*.155f.)

The feelings of facility and vivacity that transform customary transitions of imagination into "real" causal relations between its objects are not only nothing new in the theory of *Treatise* I, they are the inevitable outcome of the theory of association and natural relations articulated at its outset.[11]

Hume offered two definitions of causal relations. The first, defining the natural relation, is a synthesis of the ideas of necessity, precedence, and contiguity: "A CAUSE is an object precedent and contiguous to another, and so united with it, that the idea of the one determines the mind to form the idea of the other, and the impression of the one to form a more lively idea of the other" (*T*170).[12] Hume's definition of *philosophical* cause and effect differs from that of the natural relation in that neither element of the necessity impression is involved: "An object precedent and contiguous to another, and where all the objects resembling the former are plac'd in like relations of precedency and contiguity to those objects" (*T*170). This omission has led many to believe that philosophical relations of cause and effect are independent of or even presupposed by natural.[13] But such an interpretation must be able to reckon with the total inability of comparisons not rooted in natural relations to engender belief and so exert influence on our thoughts and actions. Since this seems to me impossible, I can only conclude that Hume deemed philosophical relations of cause and effect to be parasitic on their natural counterparts, that is, they have no inherent power to enliven ideas (i.e. yield belief), and so by themselves can have no influence on us: "tho' causation be a *philosophical* relation ... yet 'tis only so far as it is a *natural* relation, and produces an union among our ideas, that we are able to reason upon it, or draw any inference from it"

(*T*94). Further evidence that this is so is Hume's insistence that the idea of necessity is essential to any relation of cause and effect whatsoever:

I dare be positive no one will ever endeavour to refute these reasonings otherwise than by altering my definitions, and assigning a different meaning to the terms of *cause, and effect, and necessity* ... According to my definitions, necessity makes an essential part of causation. (*T*407)

Let any one *define* a cause, without comprehending, as a part of the definition, a *necessary connexion* with its effect; and let him show distinctly the origin of the idea, expressed by the definition; and I shall readily give up the whole controversy. (*E*VIII/i.74)

Since the idea of necessity is as essential to the philosophical notion of cause as the natural, its origin matters; and since its source is an impression inextricably linked with customary transitions of thought,[14] it is impossible for necessity to attach to philosophical cause and effect unless rooted in, and thence posterior to, natural relations of cause and effect. Otherwise, philosophical causation, deprived of all support from custom, collapses into constant precedence (i.e. an amalgam of the natural relations of contiguity and resemblance); but, without a customary transition of thought, there is then no relation left to vivify and project onto the objects concerned, and nothing connects them any longer. It is therefore as an implicit reaffirmation of the dependence of causal relations on custom that we must understand Hume's claim that philosophical and natural necessity "are at bottom the same" (*E*VIII/ii.75).[15]

We are now in a position to comprehend the necessity of the general causal maxim, that whatever begins to exist *must* have a cause of its existence. Hume left no doubt that it is to be understood in terms entirely of feelings of facility and verisimilitude attaching to customary transitions:

We may now be able fully to overcome all that repugnance, which 'tis so natural for us to entertain against the foregoing reasoning, by which we endeavour'd to prove, that the necessity of a cause to every beginning of existence is not founded on any arguments either demonstrative or intuitive. Such an opinion will not appear strange after the foregoing definitions ... [Regarding cause and effect as a philosophical relation] we may easily conceive, that there is no absolute nor metaphysical necessity, that every beginning of existence shou'd be attended with such an object ... [As for the natural relation] we shall make still less difficulty of assenting to this opinion. Such an influence on the mind is in itself perfectly extraordinary and incomprehensible; nor can we be certain of its reality, but from experience and observation. (*T*172)

The process whereby custom is objectified into causal relations is a perfectly natural, instinctive affair, with no role whatsoever for rational insight or demonstration to play. Habits are formed through experienced constant precedence, while this experience is in turn an instinctive product of the natural associative propensities in virtue of which the imagination attaches significance to perceived resemblances and contiguity in space and time. Necessity, the added component requisite for custom to be objectified as cause and effect (and presupposed by philosophical relations of cause and effect), is merely the verisimilitude instinctively attached to customary transitions of thought, that is, an amalgam of feelings of facility and vivacity. Such an impression could no more originate in, or be anticipated by, pure reason than joy, pride, love, etc. But, in Hume's eyes, the important point is this: not only does their reflexive nature not impair the certainty of causal relations, but, given that their certainty must be so elemental that even infants and animals may be assured of it, a certainty identical with an instinctive feeling is exactly the sort they must have. The same is true of the necessity of the causal maxim. Hume would surely have argued that, if anything can render the maxim doubtful in our eyes, it is viewing it as a metaphysical principle, since this entails a reference to something of which we can never have the least conception nor ever actually bring ourselves to believe: the secret, unknowable nature of the unperceived ("we can never have reason to believe that any objects exists, of which we cannot form an idea," *T*172). The necessity of the maxim, like its universality, is a function of the accumulated customs of a lifetime, which together prevent us from believing that anything could come into existence (i.e. have verisimilitude) without a cause. So it, too, is restricted to the system of realities that are the object of judgment, each and every one of which – identical selves, bodies, substances, the whole of space and time, indeed the "force and settled order" of the entire universe – derives "from custom and the relation of cause and effect" (*T*108). Thus, in the world founded on custom, anything we believe to begin to exist we *ipso facto* believe *must* have a cause.

However, Hume's identification of the necessity impression with feelings of ease of transition and vivacity poses a problem, since he never elsewhere characterized these feelings as impressions. An impression is a perception and as such, by the separability principle, is capable of existing in consciousness on its own, distinct from every other. Yet, it is the very essence of Hume's theory of belief that vivacity be neither an independent perception which the imagination might then arbitrarily conjoin to any perception whatever nor something distinguishable from a perception only abstractly, as an aspect (see chapter 4-C). So, too, the feeling of ease characteristic of custom: it must be felt in the *transition* from one perception to another and so obviously cannot exist apart from them, as a distinct perception in isolation from all others. Since Hume's text is quite clear that the impression-original of necessity is composed solely and entirely of these feelings (see *T*156, *T*165, *T*169, *E*VII/ii.59 and *TAbs*655f.), we must either convict him of inconsistency or suppose him to have had in mind the entire complex consisting of (i) the impression, (ii) its idea associate, (iii) the consciousness of their succession, and (iv) the feelings characterizing this consciousness. Yet, it would be odd to characterize this whole as a reflexive impression; these impressions are in theory distinct from the ideas that cause them (in the manner recounted on *T*8), and so should, like any other genuine perception, admit of standing alone before consciousness.

It has often been pointed out that Hume's separability principle works ill for most passions, desires, and emotions. Can one desire without an object of desire? Is fear possible without an object? These undoubted impressions of reflexion seem not merely causally dependent on the idea of their object, but inseparable from it, and so evince the same intentionality found to characterize phenomenological feeling. If so, then much that Hume classed as perception ought not to have been so ranked if he meant scrupulously to apply his separability principle. However, it is clear that he himself did not see it this way. Volition, "the internal impression we feel and are conscious of, when we knowingly give rise to any new motion of our body, or new perceptions of our mind" (see *T*399), is a case and point. How can one *will* without willing *something*, and so how can willing be separated from the idea of the thing willed? Nevertheless, Hume deemed them separable, as is evident in a remark in which he contrasted his own theory of belief with volition, which serves as the model for the concept of belief he *rejects*: "belief, beside the simple conception, consists in some impression or feeling, distinguishable from the conception. It does not modify the conception, and render it more present and intense: It is only annex'd to it, after the same manner that *will* and *desire* are annex'd to particular conceptions of good and pleasure" (*TApp*625). So, for Hume, not only is the idea willed separate from the willing of it, but also the willing is separable from the idea willed; and so, presumably, for all impressions of reflexion.

The difficulty of our question is only marginally ameliorated by the following passage, in which Hume enunciated criteria for determining whether something is an impression of reflexion:

> These five sounds making their appearance in this particular manner, excite no emotion in the mind, nor produce an affection of any kind, which being observ'd by it can give rise to a new idea. For *that* is necessary to produce a new idea of reflection, nor can the mind, by revolving over a thousand times all its ideas of sensation, ever extract from them any new original idea, unless nature has so fram'd its faculties, that it feels some new original impression arise from such a contemplation. (*T*36f.)

Here five criteria for being an impression of reflexion are evident: (i) *original* (i.e. content underivable); (ii) *affective* (i.e. feeling, not action – even if, through experience, we have become accustomed to regard them as mental acts, for example, volition as elucidated on *E*VII/ii.51ff.); (iii) arise through *contemplation* of ideas; (iv) are *observable*; and (v) *a source* of new ideas. Other texts suggest that reflexions (vi) *have no parts*, yet, like other impressions, (vii) admit of *total union* (in the sense described on *T*366), (viii) possess *the utmost degree of force and vivacity*, and, finally, as perceptions, (ix) are *distinct* and *independent*. If we evaluate the feelings of facility and vivacity by these criteria, we find, surprisingly, that there is none they unqualifiedly fail to satisfy. This is obvious in the case of the first three. As for the fourth, it depends on how we interpret "observe": if construed to refer only to objects distinct from consciousness (i.e. perceptions), they fail; yet, if taken to mean any content which can be known (felt) immediately by consciousness, without resort to experience, then they are observables. The fifth seems straightforward: Hume's theory of relation requires that we be able to recall ideas not only of perceptions, but also of actions of the mind in contemplating them (for example, memory as described on *T*105f. and resemblance on *T*203). The sixth and seventh criteria they satisfy easily (see section D above). Since only perceptions are intentional objects and admit of being *regarded* as verisimilar, neither feeling can, by itself, satisfy the eighth criterion. However, as the *entire complex* consisting of the customary transition of thought along with the cause- and effect-perceptions (whose sole connection to one another is the transition) – that is, the complex idea of necessarily connected cause and effect – is objectifiable, these feelings attain a "real existence" of their own therein (i.e. they *are* the "necessary connection"); so, in this one exceptional instance, feelings proper to the consciousness of perceptions become indirect beneficiaries of the very verisimilitude they confer upon perceptions. As for the ninth criterion, matters are less clearcut than might be imagined: since these feelings pertain not to perceptions, but our consciousness thereof, their difference from the former is real, not a mere distinction of reason (for example, my belief in the reality of this table is no more an aspect of the table as sensed than the flavor of a cherry is an aspect of its visual impression). What this comparison shows is that reflexions and phenomenological feelings agree in so many respects that there is no clear line to be drawn between them. Particularly in the case of the necessity impression, where customary transition alone constitutes the relation (there being no basis for it in immediate perception, by contrast with contiguity or resemblance), Hume may have found it counter-productive or impossible to apply the separability principle with complete rigor on this one occasion.[16]

Granted that he did make an exception in the case of the necessity impression, the question then is whether it should be regarded as a major lapse fatal to his system or merely a misdemeanor? In light of the considerations above, I am inclined to the latter view. For the main requirements of Hume's account of necessary connection are to (i) derive the idea from *repeated experience* (i.e. the impression of reflexion in which "similar views run into each other, and unite their forces," *T*137f.), (ii) trace it to a source which sets its *non-rational* nature beyond all doubt, and (iii) explain why necessity is always believed to lie *in the objects* and not our thought. These goals he achieved by identifying its "impression"-original with the feelings of easy transition and vivacity/verisimilitude. In reasoning about, recalling, or imagining necessary connections, we are merely reproducing a reflexive image instinctively formed in imagination. This image consists entirely of feelings occasioned by previous observations, and is no more rational in nature than fear, desire, and other (authentic) reflexive impressions. Moreover, not only *may* it "spread itself on external objects" (*T*167), but, consisting as it does, in part, of vivacity/verisimilitude, the image could not do otherwise: its essential nature is intentional. However, since it is composed entirely of phenomenological feelings, it is also in principle impossible for the impression of necessity (or *a fortiori* any idea of it) to obtain (apply) independently of idea-relating and -enlivening imagination; its objectivity is thus strictly limited to objects of experience (memory and judgment). The failure of vivacity and facility to qualify as genuine perceptions is therefore no hindrance to fulfilling their role in Hume's philosophy: showing that the necessary connections in terms of which we think and reason must be traced to an original affection of the mind ("nature has so fram'd its faculties, that it feels some new original impression arise from ... contemplation," *T*37). It is thence, in my view, no more than a misdemeanor that Hume saw fit to denominate facility/vivacity an "impression of reflexion" on this single occasion.

As exhibited here, the complex idea of necessary connection is entirely *phenomenological*. Everything for which experience is requisite – viz. remembered constant precedence and custom *qua* inclination or propensity (rather than as a feeling)[17] – proves to be external to the idea, part of its causal explanation rather than of its content. Nothing actually constitutive of that idea needs to be, or even *can* be, given in experience (viz. the *feelings* of facility and vivacity characteristic of the transition from impression to idea plus the *perceived* temporal precedence of the cause-perception *vis à vis* the effect-perception). Its contents are one and all objects of immediate consciousness, immanent to associative imagination. Experience simply informs us of the circumstances under which we come by the idea of cause, and, being a causal explanation, *may itself be interpreted wholly pheno-*

menologically. This means that there is no contradiction in supposing that one might come into possession of the necessity impression without any memory of constant precedence, or "discover" a causal relation as early as the second moment of one's existence: one need but feel ease – without pretending to understand the cause of the feeling – in the transition from an impression to a succeeding idea in order to enliven the idea (i.e. regard it as real), and so objectify the transition that alone conjoins them.[18]

F. Was Hume a metaphysical realist about causes?

It is no surprise that Hume protested vehemently against being labelled a skeptic regarding causation. Anything rooted so deeply and firmly in human nature as to be impossible to disbelieve is as certain as anything *can* be ("none but a fool or madman will ever pretend to dispute the authority of experience, or to reject that great guide of human life," *E*IV/ii.31). He legitimately claimed only to have sought to explicate the certainty attaching to the common (vulgar) belief that causes are real, not to cast doubt on it (which, according to his own theory, is impossible). Having done so in terms solely of customary transitions of thought and feelings of vivacity, he rightly concluded that the affirmation of the objective reality of causal connections has no validity beyond the purview of human reflexion (idea-enlivening imagination). His quarrel was solely with those who, "led astray by a false philosophy," fail to heed the dependence of necessary connections on thought (= associative imagination), "transfer the determination of the thought to external objects, and suppose any real intelligible connexion betwixt them; that being a quality, which can only belong to the mind that considers them" (*T*168). By showing the concept of cause to be intrinsically bound up with human nature and experience, *Hume therefore deprived none but metaphysicians of its use*.

This implication was first recognized by Kant, who justly criticized Reid and others for "ever taking for granted that which [Hume] doubted, and demonstrating with zeal and often with impudence that which he never thought of doubting."[19] But, with the rise of the naturalist reading of Hume in this century, doubt has been cast on Kant's assessment. One form of it concerns the issue of whether, and if so to what extent, Hume is to be taken literally when he speaks of mental acts, the determination of the mind by custom, the ultimate causes of our perceptions, etc. Kemp Smith is one of many inclined to interpret these as causal relations that, for Hume, have real existence outside and independently of idea-enlivening imagination:

> the actual occurrence of causation, as a mode of union or connexion, is presupposed throughout ... Hume cannot have been unaware that his definition of causation as a natural relation would require a reference to causal efficacy in a mental form,

i.e. as a *determining* of the mind, and this in the dual form as associative connexion and a process of enlivening.[20]

The vulgar, however, certainly do not ascribe a reality to their mental acts that they withhold from collisions of billiard-balls and the like, while Hume himself, on entirely empirical grounds, insisted that mind/body causation and mind/mind causation be treated exactly like purely physical instances of the relation ("The effect is there distinguishable and separable from the cause, and cou'd not be foreseen without the experience of their constant conjunction," *T.App*632; see also *T*249 and *E*VII/i.51ff.). The causal explanation he offers of particular causal inferences and the general maxim is, as we have seen, thoroughly empirical in conception and execution. Phenomenologically, the acts of the mind it posits resolve entirely into feelings, with no implication at all of metaphysically real agency. Any other understanding of these acts, such as would imply immediate awareness of real causal efficacy, is so manifestly contrary to Hume's iterated insistence that consciousness finds nothing of the kind either within or without it, that it seems incredible that a serious commentator would imagine that Hume could consent to it. There must be more to it than this; so, on what, other than speculation, are views like Kemp Smith's based?

Kemp Smith claimed that unequivocal confirmation of Hume's commitment to metaphysical realism about causation can be found on *T*167ff. Since this opinion has been echoed by several recent commentators, it merits close scrutiny. The passage in question contains Hume's response to an objection he thinks likely to occur to his reader: "What! the efficacy of causes lie in the determination of the mind! As if causes did not operate entirely independent of the mind, and wou'd not continue their operation, even tho' there was no mind existent to contemplate them, or reason concerning them. Thought may well depend on causes for its operation, but not causes on thought. This is to reverse the order of nature" (*T*167). The ridicule with which Hume treats his shocked would-be objector would seem to bode ill for metaphysical realist interpreters. Aware of the challenge, Kempt Smith chose to meet it head on, claiming that "Hume's manner of following up this objection shows very clearly that he does not mean to deny the objective reality of material bodies or their mutual influence."[21] Consideration of the text, however, suggests otherwise. Hume's reply begins with an example borrowed from Locke (see *L*98.200f.):

the case is here much the same, as if a blind man shou'd pretend to find a great many absurdities in the supposition, that the colour of scarlet is not the same with the sound of a trumpet, nor light the same with solidity. If we really have no idea of a power or efficacy in any object, or of any real connexion betwixt causes and effects, 'twill be to little purpose to prove, that an efficacy is necessary in all operations. We do not understand our own meaning in talking so, but ignorantly confound our ideas, which are entirely distinct from each other.

Hume's meaning appears quite plain. The blind man's assertion that the color of scarlet resembles the sound of a trumpet is entirely empty because he lacks the ideas of color needed to perform the requisite comparison. So, too, philosophers who purport to inform themselves about metaphysically real causes and necessary connections: like the blind man, their imaginations are stultified by the want of the necessary data to compare and relate. It is just as absurd, Hume is claiming, to suppose that our ignorance of things of which we have no conception can be overcome by drawing on the perceptual resources at our disposal as for the blind man to believe that he can divine the quality of visual sensations from his auditory experience. No features of perceptions can be abstracted from them and supposed capable of characterizing anything else; for perceptible qualities are given not via abstraction (aspect-seeing), but by comparison with an eye to resemblances (see chapter 3-B). Hume's point is that once we recognize that our only concept of a necessary connection is drawn from a reflexive impression bound up with phenomenological imagination, any temptation to suppose causal relations do, or even *can*, exist beyond the purview of consciousness must be renounced: "We do not understand our own meaning in talking so."

It is on the sequel that the greatest interpretive violence is inflicted:

I am, indeed, ready to allow, that there may be several qualities both in material and immaterial objects, with which we are utterly unacquainted; and if we please to call these *power* or *efficacy*, 'twill be of little consequence to the world. But when, instead of meaning these unknown qualities, we make the terms power and efficacy signify something, of which we have a clear idea, and which is incompatible with those objects to which we apply it, obscurity and error begin to take place, and we are led astray by a false philosophy. This is the case, when we transfer the determinations of the thought to external objects, and suppose any real intelligible connexion betwixt them; that being a quality which can only belong to the mind that considers them.

As Wright reads this, "*Hume himself clearly assumes the existence of what is contradictory and meaningless according to our human ideas.* For he goes on ... to say that '*we are ... ignorant of the ultimate principle*' which combines cause and effect. One cannot be ignorant of that which cannot exist!"[22] Wright would have us construe the above as an assertion not only that there exist qualities of objects with which we are utterly unacquainted, but that these qualities correspond to the terms "power" and "efficacy." This reading twists Hume's assertion of our total ignorance of matters of which we have no idea into an assertion of the reality of what he deemed us to be ignorant. Although implausible in itself, it is made doubly so by Hume's addition of the phrase "'twill be of little consequence to the world" to his statement that we may, if it pleases us, call by the names "power" and "efficacy" those qualities of material and immaterial objects with which we are utterly unacquainted. To say "there is no irony here," as Strawson does, seems to me a clear case of special pleading.[23] Hume might just as well have said "yin" and "yang" or "snark" and "jabberwocky" as "power" and "efficacy": being used to designate qualities with which we are totally unacquainted, no harm can arise from any nomenclature, however whimsical. Passmore seems to me quite correct in saying that Hume's "main anxiety is to show that experience reveals to us no necessary connexion between cause and effect; if anyone likes to believe that such necessary connexions none the less exist, beyond the range of any possible experience, Hume will let him indulge his fancy."[24] We get into trouble only when we apply these terms uncritically to that with which we *are* acquainted – viz. our perceptions (whether as they actually appear or as we fictitiously imagine them, for example, as continued, distinct existents). Thus, after yielding this barren concession, we find him taking a firm stand against anyone who would attach a meaning to the "power" and "efficacy" of perceived objects (of which we *do* have clear ideas) exclusive of any reference to the determinations of thought (custom and vivacity): "when, instead of meaning these unknown qualities, we make the terms power and efficacy signify something, of which we have a clear idea, and which is incompatible with those objects to which we apply it, obscurity and error begin to take place, and we are led astray by a false philosophy."

To interpret Hume's talk of unknown qualities, ultimate principles, etc., other than as a means of asserting our total ignorance of such things seems to me to make nonsense of his views. For, in direct contradiction to his theory of belief, it means that one could believe something one cannot even think: "we can never have reason to believe that any object exists, of which we cannot form an idea" (*T*172; see also *T*140). Metaphysical realist interpreters defend their interpretation by invoking Hume's references to "operations of nature [that] are independent of our thought and reasoning" in the next paragraph:

> As to what may be said, that the operations of nature are independent of our thought and reasoning, I allow it; and accordingly have observ'd, that objects bear to each other the relations of contiguity and succession; that like objects may be observ'd in several instances to have like relations; and that all this is independent of, and antecedent to the operations of the understanding. But if we go any farther, and ascribe a power or necessary connexion to these objects; this is what we can never observe in them, but must draw the idea of it from what we internally feel in contemplating them.

However, the supposition that "operations of nature independent of our thought and reasoning" refers to the "unknown qualities" of the previous paragraph has no basis in the text. The reference is unmistakably to the relations of contiguity, precedence, and resemblance. These associative relations presuppose neither experience nor habit, and so are justly deemed "operations of nature independent of our thought and reasoning." Causal relations, by contrast, are never immediately perceptible: nothing save custom links cause to effect. Causal relations are consequently always inferential in character, and therefore emblematic of experimental reason (judgment, understanding). This emerges clearly in the following:

> All kinds of reasoning consist in nothing but a *comparison*... This comparison we may make, either when both the objects are present to the senses, or when neither of them is present, or when only one. When both the objects are present to the senses along with the relation, we call *this* perception rather than reasoning... According to this way of thinking, we ought not to receive as reasoning any of the observations we may make concerning *identity*, and the *relations* of *time* and *place*. (*T*73)

The only independence Hume ascribes to contiguity, resemblance, etc., is with respect to causal reasoning based on repeated experience and habit; they are perceived (i.e. immediately felt) by imagination. The last thing he would wish his reader to infer is that they are altogether independent of associative imagination and might retain their significance for us even if deprived of their ability to enliven ideas. This would indeed be something new, but it is quite clearly incompatible with the theory of association and natural relation elaborated in *Treatise* I.

As for the causal implications of Hume's talk of "operations," we should keep in mind his remark in the preceding paragraph that "If we have really no idea of a power or efficacy in any object... 'twill be of little use to prove, that an efficacy is necessary in all *operations*." If, as Kemp Smith and co. suppose, the reference is the same on both occasions, then "operation" becomes a synonym for "efficacy" or "agency" and the result is a tautology ("an efficacy is necessary in all efficacies"). But if it is not a synonym for "efficacy" or "agency" here, then the same must be true of "the operations of nature are independent." We must guard against being over-literal with Hume, especially when it comes to talk of *mental operations*. Instead, we should let ourselves be guided by those texts in which his express purpose was to determine the status of mental operations; and they leave no doubt that he regarded them as no less dependent on experience and custom than any other efficacity with which we are acquainted (*T*249, *TApp*632, and *E*VII/i.51–53). So long as we are careful not to read into *T*168 efficacies not explicitly affirmed, we shall have no difficulty accepting Hume's anti-metaphysical intent.

In view of Hume's express rejection of real intelligible connections between the objects of which we have clear ideas, Kemp Smith sought to salvage his interpretation by supposing him to have affirmed real *unintelligible* ones on *T*169. Yet, this overlooks the fact that, only three pages later, Hume declared that

> we can never have reason to believe that any object exists, of which we cannot form an idea. For as all our reasonings concerning existence are deriv'd from causation, and as all our reasonings concerning causation are deriv'd from the experienc'd conjunction of objects, not from any reasoning or reflexion, the same experience must give us a notion of these objects, and must remove all mystery from our conclusions. (*T*172; see also *T*94)

Hume could not allow that we can even so much as think, must less believe in the real existence, of unintelligible connections. If talk of such connections has any meaning at all, it can only be as a confession of ignorance: something we are wise to keep silent about. Hume repeatedly insisted that his theory's replacement of "reasoning or reflexion" with "experienc'd conjunction" serves to "remove all mystery from our conclusions." The whole tenor of his thought is indicative of a devotion to clarity and simplicity, and an abhorrence of all that is abstract, obscure, and metaphysical (see *T*72). It therefore is highly unlikely that Hume would have had truck with such patent metaphysical nonsense as "real unintelligible connections" (not to mention the "inconceivable suppositions" – beliefs without ideas – and relations without relatives of Wright, Strawson, and others).

The source of Kemp Smith's notion of unintelligible connections is *T*169, immediately subsequent to the passage concerning the independent operations of nature. But Hume's use of "unintelligible" here does not seem able to support the metaphysical burden Kemp Smith wishes to impose on it. Far from signifying anything so remote and abstract, it refers to the unintelligible *feeling* which is the original of our idea of necessary connection. A necessary connection disclosed by "insight into the internal structure or operating principle of objects" would count as intelligible. But "intelligible" is not the way one would describe a necessary connection that consists solely of "that new determination, which we feel to pass from the idea of the one to that of the other" and "is not known to us any other way than by experience." In other words, Hume is simply iterating his constant theme that the connection between cause and effect is not an intelligible object of rational insight, but, as a matter of animal instinct (habit, feeling), something unintelligible (as in: "the *necessary connexion* is not discover'd by a conclusion of the understanding, but merely a perception of the mind," *T*405f.). To twist his words at *T*169 into an affirmation of the existence of metaphysically real unintelligible connections between objects is a burden Hume's text will not support.

I have yet to encounter a single text in which Hume explicitly and unequivocally affirmed the existence of consciousness-independent causal relations, whether intelligible or not. On the contrary, his views regarding what, if anything, lies beyond and out of reach of our perceptions fall somewhere between total agnosticism ("we can never have reason to believe that any object exists, of which we cannot form an idea") and a prototype of meaning-skepticism ("We do not understand our meaning in talking so"). It is true that he sometimes spoke of ultimate or unknown causes, and one might wish to see this as taking their existence for granted. But it is indisputable that, in none of the passages concerned, was it Hume's purpose to take a position on the issue of whether there are causes independently of consciousness. At no point, in any of them, does he lay out the possible alternatives and defend some one against the others. In so far as he concerned himself with the issue at all, it was only to aver that it is not in "any way material to our present purpose ... [M]y intention never was to penetrate into the nature of bodies, or explain the secret causes of their operations" (*T*84 and *T*64). To draw any positive conclusions from such passages, one way or the other, seems to me unwarranted (just as we cannot regard his frequent use of "mind" and "body" in those sections of the *Treatise* and *Enquiry not* concerned with the question of their reality as evidence that he affirmed it absolutely and unconditionally). It certainly cannot be said to have been his purpose, in these texts, to issue blank checks for experience-transcending speculation about the unintelligible and the inconceivable, much less to bestow his imprimatur on causal relations beyond the legitimate limits of the only idea of necessary connections we have ("When we say we desire to know the ultimate and operating principle, as something, which resides in the external object, we either contradict ourselves, or talk without a meaning," *T*267). Such tolerance would be completely incompatible with his iterated assertion that ideas have no real or legitimate application except to those perceptions from which they are derived (for example, *T*37, *T*85, *T*161, *T*212, and *T*216); and where ideas are lacking, our words are empty.[25] Any supposition that Hume affirmed the existence of ultimate and unknowable causes, or even the meaningfulness of talk about them, plainly contradicts these and other clearly enunciated, firmly held principles of his philosophy, and should thence be treated with the utmost suspicion.[26]

Such caution is all the more advisable since there is a less drastic alternative ready to hand. Philosophers have always had great difficulty giving expression to the limits to knowledge without seeming to overstep them, and Hume was no exception. Nevertheless, having made his views on the meaning and use of "cause" and "necessary connection" quite plain in the appropriate places (i.e. texts like *Treatise* I/iii/§14, where nary a word about ultimate causes escaped his pen save in a derogatory import), his use of them to designate that "with which we are utterly unacquainted" for the purpose of emphasizing the extent of human ignorance was, on one side, an effective way to make his point, and, on the other, an infraction of the bounds of sense so venial as to be itself "of little consequence to the world." Talk of ultimate causes thus tends to figure in Hume's discussion when his purpose is to emphasize the extent of human ignorance:

> It has been observ'd already, that in no single instance the ultimate connexion of any objects is discoverable, either by our senses or reason, and that we can never penetrate so far into the essence and construction of bodies, as to perceive the principle, on which their mutual influence depends. (*T*400)

> [N]o philosopher, who is rational and modest, has ever pretended to assign the ultimate cause of any natural operation. (*E*IV/i.26)

> It must certainly be allowed, that nature has kept us at a great distance from all her secrets, and has afforded us only the knowledge of a few superficial qualities of objects; while she conceals from us those powers and principles on which the influence of these objects entirely depends. (*E*IV/ii.29; see also *E*IV/i.26)

Nothing could have been further from Hume's mind than either to affirm or positively characterize that of which he claimed to be entirely ignorant. His sole objective was to demarcate the limits of natural knowledge: "It is only experience, which teaches us the nature and bounds of cause and effect, and enables us to infer the existence of one object from that of another" (*E*XII/iii.132; see also *E*XI.113).

Many will not be convinced by my analysis, and I am ready to admit that I may one day be persuaded of my error. Still, I would hope to have shown that it is at the very least premature to declare, as Capaldi does in his review of recent Hume literature, "that it is impossible to read the words of Beauchamp and Rosenberg and of Strawson and ever again have serious doubts about whether Hume was sceptical about the reality of causation." Those reluctant to accept this newly revealed wisdom are written off as suffering from a want of "consideration of the historical context of Hume's argument."[27] How curious then that Hume's own contemporaries and every major thinker of the eighteenth and nineteenth centuries understood him in exactly the opposite way. Presumably, their judgment close at hand is outweighed by the (thinly supported) speculations of present-day scholars, at two centuries remove, about what Hume may or may not have read, what he may or may not have derived from his reading, and which historical precedents he may or may not have been concerned to echo or refute. Such scholarship is certainly not without value, especially when the reins of speculation are gripped sufficiently firmly. But to pretend that it establishes beyond questioning that Hume was a realist about causation, and that all the textual evidence mustered in support of an interpretation like mine is magically cancelled out thereby, is ludicrous. The issue, at the very least, remains open.

Part III

Vulgar fiction and philosophical fallacy

> As long as we confine our speculations to the appearances of objects to our senses, without entering into disquisitions concerning their real nature and operations, we are safe from all difficulties. *TApp*638

> Nothing is more dangerous to reason than the flights of the imagination, and nothing has been the occasion of more mistakes among philosophers. Men of bright fancies may in this respect be compar'd to those angels, whom the scripture represents as covering their eyes with their wings. *T*267

Sometimes it is prudent to depart from a philosopher's own order of exposition and follow a different path. The fourth part of *Treatise* I seems such a case. In it, the topics of skepticism and identity are closely intertwined; and, while this is fully in keeping with Hume's design, the true nature and structure of his theory of identity tend to be obscured as a result. The interests of clarity and comprehension are, in my view, better served by separating the two topics so as not to mirror, but to complement, Hume's own mode of exposition. It also puts one in a better position to reckon with a possibility that, to my knowledge, has been neglected by every previous interpreter: that personal identity, though the subject of *Treatise* I/iv/§6, is nevertheless premised in the account of the identity of bodies in iv/§2 and substances in iv/§§3–5. The evidence that this is so seems compelling. Many passages suggest it (see chapter 7-A); but their import only becomes clear upon examining Hume's account of the identity relation itself, and, in particular, appreciating the significance of Hume's espousal of Locke's internally directed account of succession and duration of existence. Certainly, in the case of Hume's discussion of material and immaterial substance in *Treatise* I/iv/§§3–5, there can be no doubt, since he prefaces it by informing the reader that he is "going upon that supposition," that is, that "there is both an external and internal world" (*T*218).

Hume's way of organizing his analysis of identity, which makes so little sense considered in isolation, finds its rationale in the overall plan of

Treatise I. The book concludes with the attribution to associative imagination of that which, at the outset (*Treatise* I/i/§§1–4), seemed rather to be its presupposition: "the true idea of the human mind," wherein "impressions give rise to their correspondent ideas; and these ideas in turn produce other impressions" (*T*261). Since this perfectly matches the system of mind comprised of the various causal relations between impressions and ideas outlined in *Treatise* I/i/§2, Hume's intention, in my view, was to conclude his analysis of human understanding by declaring his own theory of ideas – employed throughout *Treatise* I to explicate relation, abstraction, space and time, necessary connection, and identity – to be itself a mere fiction of associative "imagination, or the vivacity of our ideas" (*T*265). When the dragon thus swallows itself up from the tail, the stage is finally set for the skeptical denouement of *Treatise* I/iv/§7.

However well suited this design may be to the elaboration of Hume's skepticism, it rendered his discussion of the identity of body and mind less coherent and persuasive than it might have been. To help make good this want, I have organized my discussion of identity in accordance with what I take to be the proper sequence of topics: starting with the concept of identity itself and a discussion of Hume's conception of perception, I then examine Hume's account of personal identity in *Treatise* I/iv/§6. Chapter 7 opens with a consideration of the reasons for believing that Hume premised personal identity in his account of the identity of bodies; I turn next to bodily identity itself, then to Hume's critique of philosophical conceptions of body, and conclude with a brief survey of his debunking of ancient and modern notions of substance. Hume's skepticism will be reserved for the conclusion.

6 The true idea of the human mind

A. Perfect identity

When Hume speaks of *identity*, he means numerical identity – an object *numerically* the same with itself. Like any relation, identity entails *comparison* (see *T*13 and *T*73), and comparison is possible only given *numerically different* things to compare. Since numerical identity is impossible between the numerically different, this led Hume to situate the identity relation at a point (logically) posterior to the distinction between *unity* and *number*. Neither unity nor number is a relation, since they are presupposed by, not the result of, any comparison. Unity is the view of any object (perception), in so far as it is sufficient simply to convey an idea of it, but nothing more; it thus is as omnipresent an idea as that of existence ("That idea, conjoin'd with the idea of any object, makes no addition to it," *T*66f.; cf. *ECHU* II/vii/§7). Since such a view necessarily precedes any operation of imagination which would distinguish the object as *complex* or *simple* within itself or *relate* it to something else without, the term "itself" in the statement "the object is the same with itself" merely repeats (i.e. is identical in content with) "object." Number, on the other hand, is the concurrence of several views, and yields only *diversity*, but *not yet relation*; it is merely the *prerequisite* for the comparison or association by which diverse perceptions are separated or related in imagination. However, since the comparison and association essential for relation are possible only on the basis of diversity, number seems to open the way for all relations *except* identity. For how can there be identity between things *already recognized* as distinct in number? "After one object is suppos'd to exist, we must either suppose another also to exist; in which case we have the idea of number: Or we must suppose it not to exist; in which case the first object remains at unity" (*T*200). This, for Hume, was the paradox of identity; and to resolve it, he drew on his analysis of time in *Treatise* I/ii.

On the question of the *origin* of ideas of succession and duration, Hume concurred fully with Locke's view that motion (change) in the objects of the external senses is the source of neither (see *T*.35). Only if such motion is accompanied by a train of ideas in reflective understanding can succession, and so too duration (= the distance between any two points of a succession), be perceived. Conversely, if a succession of thoughts can be perceived internally, then, even if no change is witnessed through the outer senses, we could still acquire ideas of succession and duration:

'Tis evident to any one who will but observe what passes in his own Mind, that there is a train of *Ideas*, which constantly succeed one another in his Understanding, as long as he is awake. *Reflection* on these appearances of several *Ideas* one after another in our Minds, is that which furnishes us with the *Idea* of *Succession*: And the distance between any parts of that Succession, or between the appearance of any two *Ideas* in our Minds, is that we call *Duration*. (*ECHU* II/xiv/§3)

While accepting Locke's account of the origin of these ideas, Hume differed with him in respect of their *application*. Locke, the abstractionist, held that the necessity of an internally perceived succession of perceptions for the *acquisition* of these ideas in no way restricts their *employment* (see *ECHU* II/xiv/§5). Temporal predicates may be applied to things even in the absence of trains of thought, just as shape may be abstracted from visual or tactile sensation and supposed to be a quality of matter (see *ECHU* II/xv/§3). For Hume, by contrast, no idea has application to anything other than that from which it may be derived; and, since every idea is a copy of an antecedent perception, they cannot apply to anything but perceptions. Temporal ideas are no exceptions:

I know there are some who pretend, that the idea of duration is applicable in a proper sense to objects, which are perfectly unchangeable; and this I take to be the common opinion of philosophers as well as of the vulgar. But to be convinc'd of its falsehood we need but reflect on the foregoing conclusion, that the idea of duration is always deriv'd from a succession of changeable objects, and can never be convey'd to the mind by any thing stedfast and unchangeable. For it inevitably follows from thence, that since the idea of duration cannot be deriv'd from such an object, it can never in any propriety or exactness be apply'd to it, nor can any thing unchangeable be ever said to have duration. (*T*37)

Philosophers and vulgar alike suppose themselves to possess a distinct (distinguishable, separable) idea of the *manner* in which perceptions make their appearance in the mind, and so have no hesitation in applying their ideas of succession and duration even where no change is perceptible (unchanging substance, God the eternal, etc.). In Hume's view, however, abstract succession and duration are, like all abstractions, mere fictions. Our *individual* perceptions are perceived in relations of temporal contiguity, with *this* contiguity (between perceptions *A* and *B*) sufficiently like *that* (between perceptions *C* and *D*, *E* and *F*, etc.) to induce us to form *general* ideas of succession and duration, and so suppose ourselves conscious of a *continuous* flux of perceptions (see chapters 2-B, -C, and 3-

D). It need not *in fact* be continuous, but, since we could not *perceive* any pauses without an internally perceived train of thoughts by which to do so, the imagination would remain temporally insensible through such pauses and so be unaware of any interruptions in the flux (the imagination must be conscious, however faintly, of a transition from present perceptions to their successors before an interruption could be recognized). Such generalization Hume deemed perfectly legitimate, and an accurate description of the scene played out before the senses and memory. However, it must never be forgotten that the conception and belief in this "perpetual flux and movement" (*T*252) are wholly the product of comparisons made by imagination with an eye to natural relations of resemblance and cause and effect (see *T*259ff.), not of a special abstractive act (aspect seeing – see chapter 3-B). For this restricts the application of the ideas of succession and duration to the *perceived* succession of *perceptions* and *their* relation by contiguity in associative imagination. They can hold of no objects besides perceptions, and of these only in so far as they are *believed* in associative imagination to form a succession. So, unlike Locke, Hume restricted the ideas of succession and duration to "the objects or impressions, from which they are deriv'd."

Given that the ideas of succession and duration are none the less regularly applied to unchanging things by philosophers and vulgar alike, Hume offered the following explanation of how such a *fiction* is possible:

> But 'tho it be impossible to shew the impression, from which the idea of time without a changeable existence is deriv'd; yet we can easily point out those appearances, which make us fancy we have that idea. For we may observe, that there is a continual succession of perceptions in our mind; so that the idea of time being for ever present with us; when we consider a stedfast object at five-a-clock, and regard the same at six; we are apt to apply to it that idea in the same manner as if every moment were distinguish'd by a different position, or an alteration of the object. The first and second appearances of the object, being compar'd with the succession of our perceptions, seem equally remov'd as if the object had really chang'd. To which we may add, what experience shews us, that the object was susceptible of such a number of changes betwixt these appearances; as also that the unchangeable or rather fictitious duration has the same effect upon every quality, by encreasing or diminishing it, as that succession, which is obvious to the senses. From these three relations we are apt to confound our ideas, and imagine we can form the idea of a time and duration, without any change or succession. (*T*65)

This fiction of something able, *without itself changing*, "to participate of the changes of the co-existent objects, and in particular of that of our perceptions" (*T*201) was utilized by Hume to illustrate how the opposition between unity and number are overcome, and the idea of identity attained. However, his explication of the fiction is sketchy and in need of filling out. According to the traditional view of succession, a perduring, unchanging, passive mind simply receives an idea of succession; it is imprinted in it as if in wax. The conception of succession advanced by Locke and adopted by Hume requires that imagination (understanding for Locke) *set itself* in motion by a train of ideas, so that a truly passive mind necessarily would remain oblivious to succession; succession is thus not observed change, but *actual* change within imagination.[1] Moreover, since any pause in its train of thought would necessarily be imperceptible, this means that, until a fiction of identity permits the imagination to ignore its actual appearance to itself, it can never find within it anything steadfast or perduring, anything that remains quite the same even from one instant to the next. Hence, the Humean mind, when it perceives itself, necessarily finds a succession of distinct, instantaneous apprehensions (= "consciousness" in the plural) of the manifold contents concurrent in its various perceptual fields. One *is* succession, one does not merely *observe* it. The *Treatise* I/ii notion of a minimum of perception, as applied to the time-dimension, therefore holds of imagination itself, which, just like the perceptions that appear to it, is "interrupted, and perishing, and different at every different return" (*T*211).

Since the changes requisite for consciousness of succession are internal to imagination, the way is opened for the conjuring trick whereby the fleeting appearances of perceptions external to imagination are transformed into the appearance of a single, unchanging object. Being predisposed toward relating perceptions according to their (felt) resemblances, the imagination will tend to associate successive perceptions in accordance with the qualitative similarity they exhibit (i.e. resembling sequences will *naturally* claim its attention). Further, being free to conceive a myriad of different series of perceptions that *might* have occurred instead of a qualitative continuity it actually experiences, imagination is able to consider the latter "as if every moment were distinguish'd by a different position, or an alteration." Now, the representation of a succession of exactly resembling perceptions as a *qualitative continuity* by means of a comparison with a kaleidoscopic series of changes (of relative position and/or quality) that *might* have been is quite veridical: it involves no fiction, merely the power of imagination to juxtapose and compare ideas, believed or not. What is neither legitimate nor possible by means of such a comparison is the representation of a succession of exactly resembling perceptions as a *numerical identity*, as if there had been no succession at all, and its duration were changeless. While coherent from the standpoint of the traditional conception of succession, this supposition is self-contradictory from that of Hume. For, according to Hume, if the view of imagination really did continue unchanged, consciousness would be like a motion picture camera locked on "freeze frame," and we would no more be capable of perceiving a duration than a succession (the camera metaphor is, however, misleading because of Hume's restrictions on the application of temporal predicates; even the imagination cannot be represented as unchanging in the absence of actual trains of thought). But if we do perceive succession, then our view must be constantly changing. Imagination (consciousness) cannot endure unchanged from moment to moment; its view is not a single sustained one but rather the synthetic outcome of associating distinct, instantaneous apprehensions in accordance with the natural relation of contiguity. Instead of an unchanging view of an unchanging object, each successive instant is distinguished by a different view (i.e. a distinct consciousness) and distinct appearances (i.e. objects of consciousness). On this basis, Hume denied the possibility of an unchanging view of an unchanging object.[2]

Were it possible for imagination to conceive of the reality of perceptions in distinction from their appearance, then a non-fictitious notion of an unchanging object might yet be salvageable; for, while the appearance would still be fleeting, the reality might nevertheless be unchanging. However, "since all actions and sensations of the mind are known to us by consciousness, they must necessarily appear in every particular what they are, and be what they appear. Every thing that enters the mind, being in *reality* a perception, 'tis impossible any thing shou'd to *feeling* appear different" (*T*190). Since "all impressions are internal and perishing existences, *and appear as such*" (*T*194 – emphasis mine), we therefore must, according to Hume, believe that they really are as they appear. Actually, the supposition that a perception (i.e. object of consciousness) might, unlike its appearance, have a non-instantaneous existence is just a holdover from the traditional conception of succession. Being unable immediately to perceive the past, a perception can only be compared to other perceptions, all of which appear only fleetingly. So, to find a perception to be external to and independent of *them* cannot furnish an idea of a continuing existence. What imagination requires is a standard of comparison in relation to which being external and independent would imply continuing existence. But if "Our perceptions are our only objects" (*T*213), what other than consciousness itself could furnish such a standard? Hence, the idea of the continued existence of a perception is possible only if consciousness itself can be represented as a continued existence. But whereas this supposition posed no problem for most previous philosophers, Hume's Lockean conception of succession precludes it: there can be consciousness *of* succession only if and in so far as consciousness *itself* is changing and discontinuous; and, where consciousness of succession is lacking (i.e. on "freeze frame"), the absence of qualitative change, whether of consciousness itself or any perception before it, cannot be perceived as a changeless duration. Hence, the fiction of an unchanging object is possible only given a fiction of an unchanging consciousness, which, in turn, presupposes the identity fiction itself (see chapter 7-A).

Hume introduced the idea of identity by means of the fiction of an unchanging object which "almost universally takes place":

when we consider any two points of this time, we may place them in different lights: We may either survey them at the very same instant; in which case they give us the idea of number, both by themselves and by the object; which must be multiply'd, in order to be conceiv'd at once, as existent in these two different points of time: Or on the other hand, we may trace the succession of time by a like succession of ideas, and conceiving first one moment, along with the object then existent, imagine afterwards a change in the time without any *variation* or *interruption* in the object; in which case it gives us the idea of unity. Here then is an idea, which is a medium betwixt unity and number; or more properly speaking, is either of them, according to the view, in which we take it: And this idea we call that of identity. (*T*201)

Despite what one may be tempted to suppose, both viewpoints are necessary to acquiring the idea of identity. Adopting the first, we reproduce different portions of a temporal sequence simultaneously in imagination, whereupon it becomes inescapably evident that the objects at those times, howsoever alike qualitatively, are numerically distinct. Adopting the second, we obtain an idea of a plurality of non-successive times, but *not* – since no more than a single idea is ever present to us at any one of these times – of a plurality of *ideas*; we thus obtain only an idea of unity from the object in successively tracing these non-concurrent times. By running this viewpoint together with the first, from which we obtain the idea of a plurality (requisite for relation) by multiply conceiving the same object, we arrive at the complex idea of identity:

By this means we make a difference, betwixt the idea meant by the word, *object*, and that meant by *itself*, without going the length of number, and at the same time without restraining ourselves to a strict and absolute unity.

Thus the principle of individuation is nothing but the *invariableness* and *uninterruptedness* of any object, thro' a suppos'd variation of time, by which the mind can trace it in the different periods of its existence, without any break of the view, and without being oblig'd to form the idea of multiplicity or number.

Since the two viewpoints remain incompatible, the imagination is obliged to engage in a kind of juggling act to arrive at the idea of identity.[3] It shifts sequentially, literally within the blink of an eye,[4] between unity and number, until it fancies that the object it conceives is neither one nor many during a succession; and this fictitious neither/nor is what we call "identity."[5]

Hume's analysis of the identity fiction is probably best conceived of as a thought experiment designed to present the idea in its pure form, stripped of all imaginary accretions and isolated from its natural surroundings – much as a biologist extracts tissue from an organism, slices it so thinly that light can pass through it, stains it, and examines it under a microscope. But a proper understanding of identity relations, as the common possession of infants and animals no less than fully acculturated adults, requires that they be investigated in a state of nature. For only thus can we discover the propensities and feelings of associative imagination which give rise to this fiction and infuse it with the life-blood of belief.[6]

To comprehend the phenomenological engine driving identity relation, we need first to examine the case of *perfect identity*, so named because Hume viewed it as the archetype of all identities. Its analysis is prefaced with a general remark crucial to the entire doctrine of identity in *Treatise* I/iv:

> Of all relations, that of resemblance is in this respect the most efficacious; and that because it not only causes an association of ideas, but also of dispositions, and makes us conceive the one idea by an act or operation of the mind, similar to that by which we conceive the other. This circumstance I have observ'd to be of great moment; and we may establish for a general rule, that whatever ideas place the mind in the same disposition or in similar ones are apt to be confounded. The mind readily passes from one to the other, and perceives not the change without a strict attention, of which, generally speaking, 'tis wholly incapable. (*T*203)

As in his subsequent consideration of imperfect identity (i.e. interrupted and/or discontinuous identity, as of mind, body, or substance), Hume's focus in his examination of perfect identity is less on the objects (perceptions) we contemplate than on "that action of the imagination, by which we consider the uninterrupted and invariable object" (*T*254):

> we must ... examine the disposition of the mind in viewing any object which preserves a perfect identity ... When we fix our thought on any object, and suppose it to continue the same for some time; 'tis evident we suppose the change to lie only in the time, and never exert ourselves to produce any new image or idea of the object. The faculties of the mind repose themselves in a manner, and take no more exercise, than what is necessary to continue that idea, of which we were formerly possest, and which subsists without variation or interruption. The passage from one moment to another is scarce felt, and distinguishes not itself by a different perception or idea, which may require a different direction of the spirits. (*T*203)

By contrast with a train of perceptions "which may require a different direction of the spirits, in order to its conception," the mere repetition of the same idea is an operation so easy and smooth that "The passage from one moment to another is scarce felt." The disposition of imagination dovetails perfectly with the identity fiction: not only is it the same idea repeated at each successive moment that we contemplate, but the contemplation, too, feels so steady and smooth that the imagination is hardly aware of even acting. Were our natures different and we found nothing so difficult as to repeat the same idea successively, then, qualitative identity notwithstanding, our imaginations would never be inclined to identify successively repeated ideas. Once it is recognized that the imagination, not the idea it contemplates, is the true focus of identity relations, the next thing one notices are the subtle qualifications Hume was careful to weave into his description of perfect identity: the repetition, though "*scarce* felt," is still felt; the faculties of the mind, while taking "no *more* exercise, than ... necessary to continue the idea," are none the less exercised; and though we do not "exert ourselves to produce any *new* image or idea of the object," we still exert ourselves to reproduce the *same* one. For if the imagination were literally passive (i.e. in "freeze frame"), it would not perceive a train of ideas, and so would be oblivious of any succession. Succession is an associative relation, not something given; the perceptions must be related by imagination in order for succession to be perceived. So, however faintly, the imagination must remain conscious of ("feel") itself as successively acting to reproduce the same idea if it is to conceive the succession it perceives as an identity. Otherwise, Hume's subsequent account of imperfect identity would be a non-starter: if the imagination were unconscious of acting successively to repeat the same idea, it could not find its disposition in perfect identity to resemble that in acting successively to relate *different* ideas in a *uniform* manner, and so would never confound successively contemplating the same *relation* of ideas (as imperfect identity) with successively contemplating the same *idea*.[7]

There is an important difference between perfect and imperfect identity. Since there is nothing in the former "which may require a different direction of the spirits," the imagination finds it easier and more natural to regard its own contemplation of the object as constant, and so no less invariable and uninterrupted, than the contemplated object itself. So long as the contemplated and the contemplating continue thus in tandem, their harmony uninterrupted and unaltered, their identities remain merged. Only when interruption and/or variation destroy the harmony and sunder their unity do consciousness and its object take on their own distinct, imperfect identities. Why, and how, identity continues despite the destruction of perfect identity will emerge in due course.

B. "The perceptions of the mind are perfectly known"

Before proceeding to Hume's account of imperfect identity, it will be helpful briefly to analyze his concept of perceptions. These, after all, are the ostensible subject-matter of his philosophy, as he indicates in the opening line of *Treatise* I: "All the perceptions of the human mind resolve themselves into two kinds, which I shall call IMPRESSIONS and IDEAS" (*T*1). However, if this leads one to expect that Hume will offer an extended account of the nature and causes of perceptions, then one will be sorely disappointed. Nothing of the kind is forthcoming. Apart from scattered asides and parentheses, Hume restricted himself entirely to what he deemed "the subject of the present treatise": "how [impressions and ideas] stand with regard to their existence, and which of impressions and ideas are causes and which effects" (*T*4). But however much the difference and relations between impressions and ideas may occupy center stage in his philosophy, it is nevertheless vital to understand the one regard in which they agree: as "perceptions of the human mind."

The prevailing opinion among specialists in Hume's philosophy is that there is little to be gained by an examination of his views on perceptions. It is felt, not entirely without warrant, that his treatment of the subject, apart from nomenclature, differs in no significant respects from those of his predecessors, especially Locke and Berkeley; so, while a discussion of perceptions may furnish the reader with useful background, the true interest and originality of his philosophy must be sought elsewhere.[8] But is it really credible that one so scrupulous and exacting as Hume – a thinker who never hesitated to depart from tradition on the most fundamental and far-reaching philosophical questions – should have uncritically adopted the most basic notion in his philosophical lexicon? In my view, while the *conception itself* may have been taken "off the rack," and quite intentionally so, the *use* Hume made of it cannot by any measure be deemed orthodox or unremarkable. His technique seems to me strikingly similar to Kant's in the case of imagination: taking his definition directly from the philosophical textbooks of the time as if to allay suspicions of chicanery, Kant, while always faithfully adhering to it, totally transformed its meaning (imagination becoming transcendental and, in that guise, the creator of space, time, and, with guidance from the categories, nature itself).[9] Hume seems to have appropriated the standard notion of perception for a similar strategic purpose. For it is evident that he eventually made a comparably radical break with tradition simply from the fact that, in his system, perception is more fundamental than mind itself ("mind" being a fiction of associative imagination compounded from pre-imaginatively given perceptions); this indicates a profound transformation of meaning his interpreter is under an obligation to understand.

Just how profound becomes clear when we consider the way Hume's conception of perception brings together the notion of *perfect knowledge* of an object with that of the *presence* of an object to consciousness (either as *conceivable* by it or capable of becoming *actually present* to it):

The only existences, of which we are certain, are perceptions, which being immediately present to us by consciousness, command our strongest assent, and are the first foundation of all our conclusions. (*T*212) The perceptions of the mind are perfectly known. (*T*366)

No beings are ever present to the mind but perceptions. (*T*212) Our perceptions are our only objects. (*T*213) We can never conceive any thing but perceptions. (*T*216) It has been observ'd, that nothing is ever present to the mind but its perceptions; and that all the actions of seeing, hearing, judging, loving, hating, and thinking, fall under this denomination. The mind can never exert itself in any action, which we may not comprehend under the term of *perception*.(*T*456) The mind never has anything present to it but the perceptions. (*E*XII/i.119)

At first sight, the notions of "perfect knowledge" and "object present to the mind" seem quite distinct and, in some ways, even incompatible. To say that perceptions are perfectly known implies that, in "being immediately present to us by consciousness," they are *always* and *fully* present to us (if they were ever wholly or in part absent, they would *to that extent* be unknown, and so only imperfectly known). This precludes their having a past, a future, a concealed interior, and everything else implying transcendence of the threshold of immediate consciousness. By contrast, the notion that any and every object present to the mind is a perception is at least compatible with perceptions being *sometimes* and/or *partially* absent from immediate consciousness (like the walls I see or the pen I hold); indeed, it may well be imagined that nothing else could justify distinguishing between an object of consciousness and consciousness itself in the first place.

Understanding Hume's conception of perception requires that one discover how the gap between his two characterizations of perception can be closed. There seem to be only two ways in which this might be done: either by freeing perfect knowledge of a thing from the condition that it be always and fully present to us immediately in consciousness; or by somehow precluding the possibility of an object becoming present to the mind that is not, *ipso facto*, perfectly known. That Hume opted for the latter alternative seems clear. One of the cardinal tenets of his philosophy is the restriction of *knowledge* to that "which can be accounted for from the qualities of the objects, as they appear to us; or which we cou'd foresee without the help of our memory and experience" (*T*70); everything else is merely probable (even if it lies beyond our capacity to doubt, for example, proofs – see *T*124).[10] Since a full and perfect acquaintance with something not transparent to immediate consciousness would obviously depend on memory and experience, it is clear that he would never have modified his conception of perfect knowledge to permit even the briefest absence of the object (impression or idea) from consciousness.[11] Thus, Hume's only alternative was to find grounds for precluding the possibility of objects immediately present to the mind that are not, *ipso facto*, perfectly known.

It was here that Hume made his first significant departure from the views of his predecessors: a substantial whittling down of the traditional conception of "being immediately present to us by consciousness." In this connection, it is useful to consider the following text, which is the closest he ever came to laying down adequate criteria for perception:

every impression, external and internal, passions, affections, sensations, pains and pleasures, are originally on the same footing; and ... whatever other differences we may observe among them, they appear, all of them, in their true colours, as impressions or perceptions. And indeed, if we consider the matter aright, 'tis scarce possible it shou'd be otherwise, nor is it conceivable that our senses shou'd be more capable of deceiving us in the situation and relations, than in the nature of our impressions. For since all actions and sensations of the mind are known to us by consciousness, they must necessarily appear in every particular what they are, and be what they appear. Every thing that enters the mind, being in *reality* a perception, 'tis impossible any thing shou'd to *feeling* appear different. This were to suppose, that even where we are most intimately conscious, we might be mistaken. (*T*190)[12]

The touchstone of a Humean perception is that everything it is, it also appears to be, *and* everything it appears to be, it also is. Since the reason he gives is that perceptions "are known to us by consciousness," it seems quite clear that perfect knowledge of an object requires that it be *given* right in consciousness itself, its *literal* immediate presence.

What is it that is given? The answer is paramount to the interpretation of Hume: *extraordinarily little*; indeed, *so* little that it represents a decisive shift from what any previous philosopher had supposed to be pre-imaginatively given in sense. For Hume's predecessors, perceptions were thought to be dependent on and/or representative of external objects and/or the faculty-endowed mind; for Hume, neither is true. This emerges most clearly in his discussion of whether the senses are capable of furnishing ideas of continued, distinct (i.e. independent, external) existents. After contending that the senses speak against continuity and neither for nor against distinctness, he asks whether the senses can convey to us the idea of distinct existences "by a kind of fallacy and illusion":

Upon this head we may observe, that all sensations are felt by the mind, such as they really are, and that when we doubt, whether they present themselves as distinct objects, or as mere impressions, the difficulty is not concerning their nature, but concerning their relations and situation. Now if the senses presented our impressions as external to, and independent of ourselves, both the objects and ourselves must be obvious to our senses, otherwise they cou'd not be compar'd by these faculties. The difficulty, then is how far we are *ourselves* the objects of our senses. (*T*189)

Suddenly, quite unexpectedly, Hume's problem has become "how far we are *ourselves* the objects of our senses."[13] The notion that the senses present impressions as external to and independent of ourselves presupposes that the self, too, be an object of the senses. Since we shall examine this claim in greater detail in chapter 7-A, it will suffice here to remark that his reasoning almost certainly derives from the account of duration he adapted from Locke: "For whilst we are thinking, or whilst we receive successively several ideas in our minds, we know that we do exist; and so we call the existence, or the continuation of the existence of ourselves, or anything else, commensurate to the succession of any ideas in our minds, the duration of ourselves, or any such other thing co-existent with our thinking" (*ECHU* II/xiv/§3). Since for Locke, as for Hume after him, our notions of succession and duration derive not from motions outside us, but from the train of perceptions within ("They are the successive perceptions only, that constitute the mind," *T*253), it is only in relation to the succession and duration *within* that the succession and duration of anything *without* can be comprehended. Since the only entity whose duration of existence is *directly* given in this manner is one's own, it can only be by comparison with the self that the duration (continuation of existence) of anything else can be comprehended.[14] So, for Hume, only if there were *immediate* self-perception could objects of the senses be – or, at least, by some "fallacy and illusion," be supposed to be[15] – continued and distinct rather than mere perceptions (whose reality and appearance correspond). Conversely, if, for want of immediate sensory self-consciousness, even the possibility of such an illusion is precluded, then, *on the basis of the senses alone*, it would be impossible, by Hume's reckoning, even so much as to suppose their objects distinct (independent and external). For one cannot be said to suppose what one cannot even conceive; and if the condition for the conception of such an object cannot be met (viz. immediate self-consciousness), then we really *could not, even if we would*, consider a genuine (or illusory) object of the senses to be anything other than a *perception* in the strict Humean sense (appearance = reality).

As is well known, Hume did not deem the self an object of the senses:

> For my part, when I enter most intimately into what I call *myself*, I always stumble on some particular perception or other, of heat or cold, light or shade, love or hatred, pain or pleasure. I never can catch *myself* at any time without a perception, and never can observe any thing but the perception. (*T*252) [I]dentity is nothing really belonging to these different perceptions, and unitying them together; but is merely a quality, which we attribute to them, because of the union of their ideas in the imagination, when we reflect upon them. (*T*260)

Hume thus deemed it "absurd ... to imagine the senses can ever distinguish betwixt ourselves and external objects" (*T*190). But as this means that it is impossible even to conceive an immediate object of consciousness as external and independent, then, since continued existence entails externality and independence (see *T*188), *it must likewise be impossible to suppose it sometimes or partly absent from the immediate presence of consciousness.* Further, since, according to Hume, "the true idea of the human mind" is founded on causal relations, and thence on custom (see *T*261), it is only in and for (idea-relating and -enlivening) imagination that perceptions count as internal and dependent *vis à vis* the mind. The senses, by contrast, are not in the business of relating different perceptions, and so are ignorant of the customary connections whereby "Our impressions give rise to their correspondent ideas; and these ideas in their turn produce other impressions" (*T*261). Hence, perceptions, as pre-imaginatively given, *exhibit* relation to neither body nor mind; and, since "they must necessarily appear in every particular what they are, and be what they appear," there is infallible certainty (i.e. supreme vivacity) in immediate consciousness that they *have* no such relations either.

The parenthesis in the preceding sentence is meant to suggest that the being of perceptions which is "perfectly known" by consciousness should not be understood ontologically, but phenomenologically, not as an intrinsic reality, but only a verisimilar reality felt by consciousness. To say that perceptions are what they appear to be can only mean, in view of Hume's theory of belief, that immediate consciousness *feels* them really to be all and only what is met with in (the nature, situation, and relations in) their appearance. Not being in the business of associating perceptions or comparing them for the purpose of making inferences, the senses are incapable of delivering any other verdict. Of course, since the senses do not judge, one might question whether they issue any verdicts at all. However, once we understand Hume's conception of belief rightly (as feeling of reality rather than propositional attitude), and recognize he had but one conception of it, then there can be no denying that the senses are responsible for verdicts on the reality of the objects immediately present to them, or that these beliefs weigh in our thoughts and actions just as surely as do those of associative imagination. *These, like all other verdicts about perceptions, must be construed as claims about their verisimilar reality, not their "absolute", or "ontological reality", regarding which Hume was necessarily agnostic (for want of any ideas to enliven).*

If we approach Hume with the assumption that his notion of perception is a borrowed one, we are sure to interpret it ontologically and see in some of his language confirmation of this. Yet, we have only to compare Hume's treatment of perception to that of a philosopher whose position really was ontological to discover that there are strong textual grounds to question such an assumption. Berkeley, for example, defined "idea" in much the same way that Hume defined "perception;" however, not only did he deny that we can imagine an idea to exist separately from consciousness, he deemed this impossibility to be among those "truths ... so near and obvious to the mind that a man need only open his eyes to see them" (*PHK* §6):

> That neither our thoughts, nor passions, nor ideas formed by the imagination, exist without the mind is what everybody will allow. And to me it seems no less evident that the various sensations or ideas imprinted on the Sense, however blended or combined together (that is, whatever objects they compose), cannot exist otherwise than in a mind perceiving them. I think an intuitive knowledge may be obtained of this, by any one that shall attend to what is meant by the term *exist* when applied to sensible things ... Their *esse* is *percipi*; nor is it possible they should have any existence out of the minds or thinking things which perceive them. (*PHK* §3)

For Berkeley, consciousness is for all intents and purposes an *aspect* of ideas themselves (sensations, reflexions, and thoughts), for he deemed it self-evident that we lack the power *really* to separate them in *imagination* (see *PHK* §5). Since the *esse* is *percipi* thesis implies that Humean vivacity, though a feeling proper to consciousness, is, for that very reason, an inseparable element of their *percipi* – i.e. a feature of the perceptions themselves – Hume could not have remained neutral on this point (for example, it would render it impossible for the same content to be, at one time believed, and, at another, disbelieved).

Before reviewing the evidence for beliving that Hume rejected *esse* is *percipi*, it will be helpful to focus the issue more sharply. If *esse* is *percipi* were to be construed simply as the thesis that perceptions are dependent existents, and so presuppose a mind-*substratum* in which to *inhere*, there would be no difficulty in determining Hume's position on the matter: he made quite clear that, in his view, there is no immediate evidence (intuition, self-evidence) that perceptions are in any sense dependent existents, whether it be on one another or on any manner of non-perception substrate (see *T*234, *T*244, and *T*252). Setting aside the issue of whether or not *esse* is *percipi* meant this to Berkeley, let us construe the thesis in intentional terms: not only is consciousness dependent on there being some perception immediately present before it, but perceptions themselves can be conceived to exist only in relation to some consciousness. If true, then consciousness and its immediate object would differ only by a distinction of reason; if not, the perception would be *really* distinct from the consciousness, that is, capable of existing without relation to any consciousness whatsoever. The difference may be illustrated as follows. Since I am unable to imagine a timbre existing without having *some* pitch or other, the difference between them is only abstract; by contrast, since I can quite well imagine the sound of a violin being emitted from a (visually apprehended) tuba, the aural and visual sensations are separable, distinguishable, and so really distinct. But whereas, in a sensation of sound, one can discriminate aspects like pitch and timbre (plus innumerable others for which we lack names), nowhere does one find in it the further aspect of *consciousness* of it (nor, *a fortiori*, in any idea-copy taken from the sound). Otherwise, it would be impossible to forget a past act of perceiving and remember only its object, and so mistakenly believe oneself to be imagining when one is in fact remembering or vice versa (see analysis of *T*105f. in chapter 2-B). However, if the two are not aspects of an unsunderable unity when represented in the past, why should things be any different when they are represented in the present? Why should we believe it impossible to *imagine* a sound occurring separately from any hearing of it (and, *a fortiori*, any feeling of vivacity accompanying that hearing)? All it requires is a capacity to separate in imagination (rather than merely verbally) what is perceived not only from *oneself*, the *person* perceiving, but from the *apprehending* of it. What exactly does this mean? If consciousness were itself a perception, there would be no problem in the matter since Hume regarded all perceptions as distinct and independent of one another.[16] If it is not, matters seem even simpler. For if consciousness is not a perception, this means it is not an idea; and what could be simpler for imagination than to separate its ideas from something that is not an idea? If we suppose that it can be conceived via its phenomenological contents, this still poses no problem for the imagination: while it cannot separate the timbre from the pitch of an aural image, quite clearly it can – and, according to the Humean theory of belief, must – be able to separate from it the feeling of vivacity in virtue of which it is regarded either as a present existent (inferred from the impression of an associate) rather than a hypothetical, or as a memory rather than a fancy (the theory requires that any idea be capable of being believed at one time, disbelieved at another, without ceasing to be the same idea; and this would be impossible if the phenomenological feelings of consciousness were aspects of ideas). So, from Hume's perspective, the fact that I am unable to imagine a perception occurring independently of consciousness (because imagination itself is a species of consciousness) shows nothing at all about perceptions – neither that they are dependent on consciousness nor that they are distinguishable from it only by reason (abstractly). Of course, it also proves nothing to the contrary; the only thing this may really be said to show is our inability to imagine consciousness in the absence of all perceptual data. Hume's proper position is, again, ontological agnosticism; for the standard of distinctness he employed elsewhere – separability in imagination – is useless to settle this question, and no other is available to use in its place. But if this be so, then we can at least be certain that he would not have endorsed Berkeley's assertion that it is a "manifest repugnancy" (*PHK* §23) to suppose consciously apprehended objects to be able to exist unperceived.[17]

Evidence that Hume held that the concomitance of perceptions with consciousness is, so far as we can know, only a relation of invariant concurrence, not analytic entailment, is found in the following:

what we call a *mind*, is nothing but a heap or collection of different perceptions, united together by certain relations, and suppos'd, tho' falsely, to be endow'd with a perfect simplicity and identity. Now as every perception is distinguishable from another, and may be consider'd as separately existent, it evidently follows, that there is no absurdity in separating any particular perception from the mind; that is, in breaking off all its relations, with that connected mass of perceptions which constitute a thinking being. (*T*207)

[S]ince all our perceptions are different from each other, and from every thing else in the universe, they are also distinct and separable, and may be consider'd as separately existent, and may exist separately, and have no need of any thing else to support their existence. They are, therefore, substances, as far as [the definition "something which may exist by itself"] explains a substance... Inhesion in something is suppos'd to be requisite to support the existence of our perceptions. Nothing appears requisite to support the existence of a perception. We have, therefore, no idea of inhesion. (*T*233f.)

If nothing else, passages like these make clear that Hume regarded the absolute independence and isolation of perceptions "from every thing else in the universe" as being at least conceivable (if not believable). Since there is no evidence anywhere in his writings that he was inclined to make an exception of their relation to consciousness, it would be difficult to imagine a more definite, albeit implicit, rejection of the *esse* is *percipi* thesis. He may well have granted that consciousness without an object is impossible. But he surely would have denied that there is any immediate, intuitive connection tying perceptions to consciousness which prevents us, other than via abstraction, from imagining a perception in a state of total detachment not only from all other perceptions, but from consciousness as well.

Humean perceptions owe their appellation not so much to their (contingent) relation to consciousness, much less a supposed inherence in a mind-substrate, but to their *appearance* as "interrupted, and perishing, and different at every different return" (*T*211). For Hume did undeniably espouse a *phenomenological* form of the *esse* is *percipi* thesis in so far as "our perceptions are our only objects" (*T*213) and "must necessarily appear in every particular what they are, and be what they appear" (*T*190 – with "being" construed as vivacity/verisimilitude). But it would be mistaken to attach an *ontological* import to it and infer that, apart from their appearance to and being for consciousness, there is nothing about perceptions (and consciousness) that is unknown to us. Hume emphasized nothing so much as "the weakness and narrow limits of human reason and capacity" (*E*VII/ii.59). This idea is bound up with the possibility that there may be much that lies beyond our capacity to conceive, and the last thing he would have wished to do is foreclose this possibility by denying that perceptions may *be* more than they *appear* to be *even if it should be impossible for us to conceive this "something more."* Since what fails to appear to us we cannot conceive, and since what we cannot conceive we cannot believe (see *T*172), this "something more" can in no way concern or influence us, whether in ordinary life or in philosophy. It is in relation to life and soundly (= empirically) based philosophical opinion that the reality and appearance of perceptions (i.e. that of which we *do* have clear ideas) are, for consciousness unblinkered by imagination, one and the same. The application of the principle that perceptions are what they appear to be and vice versa, like everything else in his philosophy, is restricted to that which we *can* conceive (imagine) our perceptions as being; and to pretend to be able to do more with it than this would contradict the very foundations of his empiricism. The absence from the *appearance* of perceptions of everything associative imagination conditions us to believe is true of them, and their *being* as "interrupted, and perishing, and different at every different return," is known by immediate consciousness, and carries the full imprimatur and irresistible authority of natural belief (vivacity). In particular, it enables us positively to affirm that, whether or not perceptions relate to anything we *cannot* conceive, they are *not* dependent on the bodies or to the minds we *can*, and the only "reality" that can pertain to them, or to the creatures of our imagination, is that of vivacity/verisimilitude (admittedly, the verdicts of imagination likewise possess the authority of natural belief, and so contradict those of the senses – see conclusion). So, while remaining sufficiently respectful of the limits of knowledge to reign up before the barrier of human ignorance (as so many of his ontologically committed predecessors had conspiculously failed to do), Hume was still able to define a conception of perception robust enough in its idealism to serve the most skeptical philosophical ends.

Considerations like these lead me to believe that Hume almost certainly would have denied that it is within our power to determine what sort of entity perceptions are: physical, mental, or anything else. Unlike Berkeley's "idea," Hume's "perception" was ontologically neutral (not to be confounded with being a neutral monist; I take him to have been agnostic regarding the entire question of entity – physical, mental, neutral, etc.). This is not to say that every time he used the word, irrespective of context, it carried an ontologically neutral sense; but on those occasions he employed it to give definitive expression to his own views, it has no positive meaning as an ontological category. Nor did he need to take a position on the question of what perceptions are: his interest in them was entirely epistemological, or, more properly, psychological, and so restricted to their status as data (both appearance and phenomenological feeling) of consciousness – i.e. that from which all relation of ideas in imagination takes its start.[18]

Hume was not the first to maintain that much of what is commonly thought to be the given of sense is in fact the doing of imagination and understanding (though, for him uniquely, the latter signifies merely "the general and more establish'd properties of the imagination," *T*267). Yet, his predecessors seem never to have considered the possibility that there could be so radical a break between sense and imagination that the ideas and principles proper to the latter lack even *possible* extra-imaginative validity. This, however, is precisely what follows from Hume's analysis of causality, identity, substance, and even reality itself in terms of phenomenological content (feelings in imagination). Perceptions, in themselves, are neither causes nor effects, variable nor invariable, subsistent nor inherent, real (verisimilar) nor fictitious, and so, for all intents and purposes, are completely indeterminate; only in and for consciousness (especially imagination) are these complex ideas possible at all and applicable to perceptions.

Apparent conflicts among Hume's characterizations of perceptions can be resolved by attending to their context – whether the standpoint adopted is that of imagination or immediate appearance. One such conflict concerns the independence of perceptions. Sometimes Hume described them as dependent:

> philosophy informs us, that every thing which appears to the mind, is nothing but a perception, and is interrupted, and dependent on the mind. (*T*193) [T]he doctrine of the independent existence of our sensible perceptions is contrary to the plainest experience. (*T*210) 'Twill first be proper to observe a few of those experiments which convince us, that ... our sensible perceptions are not possest of any distinct or independent existence. (*T*210f.) [A] little reflection destroys [the conclusion that our sensible perceptions have ... a continu'd and uninterrupted existence], by shewing that they have a dependent one. (*T*214)

The dependence of perceptions is threefold: on the *mind*; on *one other* (see *T*7f. and *T*261); and, as in the following, on the *external objects* that occasion them:

> We may observe, that 'tis universally allow'd by philosophers, and is besides pretty obvious of itself, that nothing is ever really present with the mind but its perceptions or impressions and ideas, and that external objects become known to us only by those perceptions they occasion. To hate, to love, to think, to feel, to see; all this is nothing but to perceive. (*T*67)

Since existential dependence implies *necessary* connection, one may be sure that Hume would have treated it as a species of natural or philosophical cause and effect relation and analyzed it accordingly (for example, *T*212). Central to any such analysis is that immediate consciousness (sense perception) of a causal relation is impossible: one cannot simply read off, on first acquaintance (or, for that matter, any number of presentations), whether and what causal powers and connections anything has (for example, *T*73, 139, 155ff., 223, 246, 632, and 636). It takes *experience* of the *constant conjunction* of one thing with another, until, *eventually*, a customary association between their ideas is forged in the mind and the objects are believed to be related as cause and effect. It is *constant experience* too that informs us that observed constant conjunction leads the mind to associate perceptions in relations of existential dependence. Hume's assertions that perceptions are dependent existents should therefore be construed as experiential and phenomenological in character, with no application to perceptions themselves prior to, and independently of, their association in imagination.

If, on the basis of experience-bred customs, the dependent character of perceptions is beyond doubt (i.e. verisimilar to a degree approaching impressions), Hume made equally clear that immediate consciousness gives us just as strong an assurance of their non-dependent status with respect to mind, external objects, and one another:

> there is no absurdity in separating any particular perception from the mind; that is, in breaking off all its relations, with that connected mass of perceptions, which constitute a thinking being. (*T*207)

> [A]s no beings are ever present to the mind but perceptions; it follows that we may observe a conjunction or a relation of cause and effect between different perceptions, but can never observe it between perceptions and objects. 'Tis impossible, therefore that from the existence or any of the qualities of the former we can ever form any conclusion concerning the existence of the latter, or ever satisfy our reason in this particular. (*T*212)

> All these are different, and distinguishable, and separable from each other, and may be separately consider'd, and may exist separately, and have no need of any thing to support their existence. (*T*252)

Where constant conjunction is unobservable, or where appearances before consciousness alone are considered (i.e. the enlivening effects of custom on consciousness are bracketed out), perceptions give not the slightest evidence of a need for anything to support their existence; the only necessary connections ascribable to them are purely imaginary. Strictly speaking, however, this is not really an assertion of their *independence* either since, in a framework not founded on custom (see *T*108), neither dependence nor independence can be attributed to them. For just as the denial that they are effects does not imply that they are *self*-caused (see *T*80f.), their not being dependent does not make them independent (i.e. *self*-subsistent – see *T*189f.). The effect of Hume's denial of dependence is rather to have "loosen'd all our particular perceptions" (*TApp*636), thereby precluding even the *possibility* of their being anything other than they appear (for example, representations of unperceived existents). Nor could things have been otherwise given that the self, external objects, and all manner of relation are absent from the immediate purview of consciousness.

C. The fictitious mind

Having considered perfect identity and perception, let us now proceed to examine Hume's treatment of imperfect identities. These extend across a spectrum ranging from the ever varying, never interrupted[19] identity of the mind to the never varying, forever interrupted[20] identity of substances, with the identity of physical objects, organisms, and such human creations as ships, churches, commonwealths, etc., falling somewhere in-between. Since the identity of the mind (self, person)[21] presupposes only perfect identity, and is itself presupposed by all other imperfect identities (see chapter 7-A), it is the natural starting point from which to comprehend Hume's theory of imperfect identity. The failure to realize this, and the consequent misapprehension of the background against which Hume supposed the idea of the mind to emerge, has been a source of considerable confusion and error in regard to his views on imperfect identity generally. For his account of personal identity is sure to be interpreted very differently depending on whether one supposes it to be set in the external world of continued, distinct existents or the internal world made up only of a flux of perceptions. Since it completely neglects the external world ("They are the successive perceptions only, that constitute the mind," *T*252f.; see also *T*261 and *T*635f.), many who believe this to have been its intended or implied setting have been perplexed, and attribute his failure to draw on the resources it provides (in particular, the possibilities of identification for a mind associated with a body) to an uncritical commitment to the theory of ideas and the poor state of philosophy at the time. For, as they see it, the problem of personal identity Hume was attempting to solve requires one to explain, *within the framework of the external world*, how minds are picked out from amongst physical objects, organisms, artifacts, etc.; how to recognize something as the same mind and not another; the distinction of an I from a thou; the possibility of self-ascriptions; etc.[22] Since Hume can hardly be said to have confronted any of these issues head on, and, in so far as he may have done so at all, only in a manner that wholly ignores the external world and the body, it is little wonder that his account of personal identity tends to be regarded as a splendid example of how *not* to handle this problem.[23]

To see Hume's problem with new eyes we have only to take seriously the possibility that his anti-abstractionist version of the Lockean conception of succession and duration led him to regard the identity of the mind as not only prior to, but a precondition for, all other imperfect identities (bodies, other minds, and substances). This may not correspond to *our* conception of the problem, and some may think it sufficient reason to dismiss the whole endeavor. Nevertheless, if one were to be convinced that, for Hume, the self is not a relative notion (to other things, other selves) but an absolute one, which, as such, is the essential prerequisite for advancing from consciousness of a flux of perceptions (the *T*108 world of the senses and memory) to consciousness of the external world as known to the vulgar and scientists alike (the *T*108 world of judgment which, through custom, is *developed out of* the world of senses and memory), it would have to be conceded that the standards by which his theory has hitherto been judged are inapplicable. Since in that case *his* problem of personal identity would proscribe reliance on any of the resources of the external world (the body, other persons, social security numbers, etc.), his drawing on them would be an occasion for criticism, not praise. So, in elucidating Hume's theory of personal identity, let our working assumption be that his problem is as I have suggested, while postponing detailed consideration of the evidence until chapter 7.

Two points should be kept in mind as we examine Hume's theory of personal identity. First, his quarry was not the metaphysical reality of persons, but the source of the idea. For, even if our successive perceptions did belong to a subject existing in some absolute (i.e. non-verisimilar) sense, this would not by itself suffice to guarantee the ability to conceive its identity, much less believe it. It is not enough merely to "be" an identical subject of perceptions if one cannot then acquire an idea of its identity and believe in it. Hume's brief was human understanding; his only concern was to discover the origin of our believed ideas and their contents. Since the idea of the self turns out to be irreducibly phenomenological, it is useless for the purpose of conceiving an absolute, metaphsyically real subject; so, on this matter too, he was surely agnostic. Second, one must keep in mind Hume's philosophical touchstone: an account of the origin of the idea should involve nothing that would set the idea beyond the grasp of infants and animals. For that reason, his criteria for selfhood had necessarily to be very loose and geared towards a most primitive level of consciousness (more primitive than awareness of external objects). This means, for example, that it does not premise the ability to comprehend or apply words like "I" or "my;" one need only be able to recognize a memory as such (a copy of a past perception), connect fear with the idea of an approaching predator, etc., to be able to form one's perceptions into the system of causally related existents that makes possible personal identity. Accordingly, amnesia, aphasia, and other types of disfunction, often adduced in the literature in connection with problems of personal identity, have at most a marginal bearing on Hume's problem, since it would take almost the total destruction of all causal relations between successive perceptions to cut down the number and regularity of smooth transitions of imagination to a point where they would cease to afford an idea of identity (i.e. ideas no longer connected as copies to impressions, reflexions no longer connected to ideas of sensation, etc. – consciousness reduced nearly to a *tabula rasa*).[24]

Hume distinguished "betwixt personal identity, as it regards our thought or imagination, and as it regards our passions or the concern we take in ourselves. The first is our present subject; and to explain it perfectly we must take the matter pretty deep" (*T*253). Although he left the basis of this distinction unclear, I think we are fairly safe in inferring that the self of the passions is the self of ordinary consciousness: an embodied self among other embodied selves in the external world. By contrast, the self of "thought or imagination" is the condition for the representation of all other imperfect identities (bodies, other minds, substances), and so "takes the matter pretty deep," down all the way to the least familiar (as both pre-objective and -subjective) of contexts: that of the perceptual flux. This does not mean that there are different selves in Hume's philosophy. Personal identity first arises through the ascription of identity to a succession of uniform relations of ideas the contemplating of which the imagination mistakes for perfect identity. The "true idea of the human mind" produced by imagination is "a system of different perceptions or different existences, which are link'd together by the relation of cause and effect, and mutually produce, destroy, influence, and modify each other" (*T*261). Only when *successive* causally related perceptions are thus united in identity can the influence of *distant* perceptions on present thought or action be ascribed to the same person, and the self of the passions emerge: "our identity with regard to the passions serves to corroborate that with regard to the imagination, by the making our distant perceptions influence each other, and by giving us a present concern for our past or future pains or pleasures" (*T*261). The imagination yields the idea of self that then, in the context of the external world, becomes our passionate concern.[25]

Hume's first thesis regarding personal identity is that the idea of a single, enduring, yet variable mind cannot be copied from any impression:

If any impression gives rise to the idea of self, that impression must continue invariably the same, thro' the whole course of our lives; since self is suppos'd to exist after that manner. But there is no impression constant and invariable. Pain and pleasure, grief and joy, passions and sensations succeed each other, and never all exist at the same time. It cannot, therefore, be from any of these impressions, or from any other, that the idea of self is deriv'd; and consequently there is no such idea. (*T*251)

Having excluded an impression origin of the idea of self, Hume next examines and rejects the rationalist supposition that mind is necessary to support the existence of particular perceptions:

All these [perceptions] are different, and distinguishable, and separable from each other, and may be separately consider'd, and may exist separately, and have no need of any thing to support their existence. After what manner, therefore do they belong to self; and how are they connected with it? For my part, when I enter most intimately into what I call *myself*, I always stumble on some particular perception or other, of heat or cold, light or shade, love or hatred, pain or pleasure ... And were all my perceptions remov'd by death, and cou'd I neither think, nor feel, nor see, nor love, nor hate after the dissolution of my body, I shou'd be entirely annihilated, nor do I conceive what is farther requisite to make me a perfect non-entity. If any one upon serious and unprejudic'd reflexion, thinks he has a different notion of *himself*, I must confess I can reason no longer with him.

Perceptions stand in no need of support: the manner in which they "belong to" and are "connected with" the self is not a species of dependence. On the contrary, since "They are the successive perceptions only, that constitute the mind," the dependence runs the other way:

But setting aside some metaphysicians of this kind, I may venture to affirm of the rest of mankind, that they are nothing but a bundle or collection of different perceptions, which succeed each other with an inconceivable rapidity, and are in a perpetual flux and movement. Our eyes cannot turn in their sockets without varying our perceptions. Our thought is still more variable than our sight; and all our other senses and faculties contribute to this change; nor is there any single power of the soul, which remains unalterably the same, perhaps for one moment. The mind is a kind of theatre, where several perceptions successively make their appearance; pass, re-pass, glide away, and mingle in an infinite variety of postures and situations. There is properly no *simplicity* in it at one time, nor *identity* in different; whatever natural propension we may have to imagine that simplicity and identity. The comparison of the theatre must not mislead us. They are the successive perceptions only, that constitute the mind; nor have we the most distant notion of the place, where these scenes are represented, or of the materials, of which it is compos'd. (*T*252f.; see also *T*207, *TApp*634f., and *D*IV.28f.)[26]

A bare succession of perceptions, without relations conjoining them, is insufficient to account for the idea of the self. Hume therefore set out in search of the relational support requisite to yield it. Since his explanatory procedure adheres closely to the general pattern of dealing with imperfect identity established in *Treatise* I/iv/§2, we shall here restrict ourselves to those aspects of his account that apply specifically to personal identity and postpone the remainder until chapter 7-B. However, before considering them, there is another issue arising in this connection that has a prior claim on our attention: the relation of Hume's associationalist account of "the true idea of the human mind" on *T*259ff. to the conception of mind delineated in *Treatise* I/i and employed in all his subsequent explanations of the nature and origins of ideas.

Treatise I/i/§1 investigates the distinctions and relations among "the perceptions of the human mind" (*T*1). Hume collected his results into the following sketch of the workings of the mind:

> An impression first strikes upon the senses, and makes us perceive heat or cold, thirst or hunger, pleasure or pain of some kind or other. Of this impression there is a copy taken by the mind, which remains after the impression ceases; and this we call an idea. This idea of pleasure or pain, when it returns upon the soul, produces the new impressions of desire and aversion, hope and fear, which may properly be called impressions of reflexion, because derived from it. These again are copied by the memory and imagination, and become ideas; which perhaps in their turn give rise to other impressions and ideas. So that the impressions of reflexion are only antecedent to their correspondent ideas; but posterior to those of sensation, and deriv'd from them ... And as the impressions of reflexion, *viz.* passions, desires, and emotions, which principally deserve our attention, arise mostly from ideas, 'twill be necessary to reverse that method, which at first sight seems most natural; and in order to explain the nature and principles of the human mind, give a particular account of ideas, before we proceed to impressions. (*T*8)

As portrayed here, the mind consists of various perceptions standing in causal relation to one another. Should these relations be understood as real or imaginary? When Hume laid down this scheme he had yet to discuss association, much less develop an account of causal relations. Then, when he did finally examine causal relations in *Treatise* I/iii, not only did he never subject those holding between impressions and ideas to scrutiny, his explanation presupposed them throughout. Since Hume appears to take them for granted, many interpreters have concluded that they fall outside the scope of the *Treatise* I/iii account and so should be construed realistically, not phenomenologically. Some recognize that, in *Treatise* I/i/§1, Hume's approach is empiricist, so that impressions and ideas are linked in causal relations only because they are found to be constantly conjoined (see *T*4f.). Nevertheless, in the absence of explicit evidence to the contrary, they believe it the soundest interpretive course to exempt these relations from the subjectivist, phenomenological limits imposed on causal relations in *Treatise* I/iii (those who believe that philosophical cause and effect is free of such limitation are not so circumspect and often assert outright that Hume's scheme of mind is to be understood realistically).

But is there in fact inadequate textual evidence to the contrary? It is true, that, save for a few suggestive remarks (especially Hume's "subtility" on *T*169), there is nothing unambiguous on this score in *Treatise* I/iii. But might not Hume have seen fit to postpone applying the results of *Treatise* I/iii until he was ready to take up the issue of our idea of the mind? Since he never tells us outright that this was his intention, we cannot be wholly certain. Nevertheless, a comparison between the account of "the true idea of the human mind" on *T*259ff. with that of *Treatise* I/i yields sufficient evidence, in my view, to leave little doubt that this was the case.

It is not difficult to see that the independent, distinct *existence* of perceptions would be an indispensable premise in any reasoning designed to show that the causal relations posited in *Treatise* I/i between perceptions have only verisimilar reality, in and for associative imagination. This premise was not elaborated and examined until *Treatise* I/iv (where nearly all of his remarks on the nature of perceptions are to be found – see section B above), and so was not available to be invoked either in *Treatise* I/i or *Treatise* I/iii. This shows, at the very least, that Hume was not ready to apply the *Treatise* I/iii account to perceptions specifically as such until well into *Treatise* I/iv. It thus should come as no surprise to find him invoking it in iv/§6 for the express purpose of discrediting a realist account of the mind:

'Tis evident, that the identity, which we attribute to the human mind, however perfect we may imagine it to be, is not able to run the several different perceptions into one, and make them lose their characters of distinction and difference, which are essential to them. 'Tis still true, that every distinct perception, which enters into the composition of the mind, is a distinct existence, and is different, and distinguishable, and separable from every other perception, either contemporary or successive. But, as notwithstanding this distinction and separability, we suppose the whole train of perceptions to be united by identity, a question naturally arises concerning this relation of identity: whether it be something that really binds our several perceptions together, or only associates their ideas in the imagination. That is, in other words, whether in pronouncing concerning the identity of a person, we observe some real bond among his perceptions, or only feel one among the ideas we form of them.[27] This question we might easily decide, if we wou'd recollect what had been already prov'd at large, that the understanding never observes any real connexion among objects, and that even the union of cause and effect, when strictly examin'd, resolves itself into a customary association of ideas. For from thence it evidently follows, that identity is nothing really belonging to these different perceptions, and uniting them together; but is merely a quality, which we attribute to them, because of the union of their ideas in the imagination, when we reflect upon them. (*T*259f.)

There can be no doubt: here, for the first time, Hume explicitly applies the *Treatise* I/iii account of causal relations to the relations connecting the perceptions of the mind *specifically as such*. His purpose, of course, is to explain personal identity. But, bearing in mind that the system of causal relations between perceptions is not itself personal identity, but only its presupposition (viz. a sequence of repeated *relations* of ideas the contemplating of which can *then* be confounded by imagination with the feeling, in perfect identity, of contemplating a sequence of repeated *ideas*), Hume's point bears immediately on the nature of the necessary connections between perceptions and only indirectly on the identity they make possible.

The idealistic import of Hume's application of the *Treatise* I/iii account to causal relations between perceptions with respect to the ostensibly real causal connections of *Treatise* I/i does not emerge until he enters into the details of the associationalist basis of personal identity:

Now the only qualities, which can give ideas an union in the imagination, are these three relations above-mention'd. These are the uniting principles in the ideal world, and without them every distinct object is separable by the mind, and may be separately consider'd, and appears not to have any more connexion with any other object, than if disjoin'd by the greatest difference and remoteness. 'Tis, therefore, on some one of these three relations of resemblance, contiguity and causation, that identity depends; and as the very essence of these relations consists in their producing an easy transition of ideas; it follows, that our notions of personal identity, proceed entirely from the smooth and uninterrupted progress of the thought along a train of connected ideas, according to the principles above explain'd. (*T*260)

Bypassing spatial contiguity on the ground of its irrelevance to the identity of a non-extended entity,[28] Hume focused first on resemblance. As Locke's prior example proves, it is a promising candidate. Hume chose to illustrate this by a thought experiment: supposing we might gaze upon the successive perceptions in the breast of another[29] who remembers "a considerable part of past perceptions," we would find that

nothing cou'd more contribute to the bestowing a relation on this succession amidst all its variations. For what is memory but a faculty, by which we raise up the images of past perceptions? And as an image necessarily resembles its object, must not the frequent placing of these resembling perceptions in the chain of thought, convey the imagination more easily from one link to another, and make the whole seem like the continuance of one object? In this particular, then, the memory not only discovers the identity, but also contributes to its production, by producing the relation of resemblance among the perceptions. (*T*260f.)

Since personal identity requires a relation capable of linking different varieties of perceptions – sensations and reflexions with thoughts so as to "make the whole seem like the continuance of one object" – it is no surprise that Hume deemed the association of ideas with impressions by resemblance an important source of this idea: hardly any other relation – including other species of resemblance – can rival the virtual omnipresence of memory in subjective experience.[30] But even more striking is the remarkable similarity of this text to Hume's observation at the outset of the *Treatise* regarding

> the great resemblance betwixt our impressions and ideas in every other particular, except their degree of force and vivacity. The one seem to be in a manner the reflexion of the other; so that all the perceptions of the mind are double, and appear both as impressions and ideas. When I shut my eyes and think of my chamber, the ideas I form are exact representations of the impressions I felt; nor is there any circumstance of the one, which is not to be found in the other. In running over my other perceptions, I find still the same resemblance and representation. Ideas and impressions appear always to correspond to each other. (*T*2f.)

Here Hume is clearly thinking of memory. He stresses the close resemblance of the memory image to the perception it copies, and the universality of this correspondence (in general appearance if not exact detail) in our mental life. One finds in this text the very continuity and unity imparted to "all the perceptions of the mind" that prompted Hume to invoke memory-resemblance to help explain the idea of personal identity. Can there be any doubt that he is talking about the same thing? Yet, there is also a crucial difference between the two texts. In *Treatise* I/i/§1, memory-resemblance is taken as given, and, barring rare hints to the contrary (for example, *T*105f. – see chapter 2-B), Hume simply premised it throughout *Treatise* I, even in his theory of relation. In *Treatise* I/iv/§6, however, memory-resemblance is expressly situated in the *ideal world* of associative imagination: rather than part of the *explanation* of ideas, "the faculty, by which we raise up the images of past perceptions" is here ascribed to "the uniting principles of the ideal world," "the very essence" of which "consists in their producing an easy transition of ideas." Any lingering doubts should disappear when, a few pages later, in reference to "that succession of perceptions, which constitutes our self or person," Hume states that "Without this quality, by which the mind enlivens some ideas beyond others ... those lively images, with which the memory presents us, [could never] be receiv'd as true pictures of past perceptions. The memory ... [is] founded on the imagination, or the vivacity of our ideas," *T*265). We are therefore on solid ground in thinking that Hume meant for us, or at the very least would invite us, to connect *Treatise* I/i and *T*259ff., and refer what is said to be true of the mind in the second to mental life as outlined in the first.

But by far the most compelling evidence that the idea of mind discussed in *Treatise* I/iv/§6 is identical with that of *Treatise* I/i is Hume's description of the role of causal relations in personal identity:

> As to *causation*; we may observe, that the true idea of the human mind, is to consider it as a system of different perceptions or different existences, which are link'd together by the relation of cause and effect, and mutually produce, destroy, influence, and modify each other. Our impressions give rise to their correspondent ideas; and these in turn produce other impressions. One thought chaces another, and draws after it a third, by which it is expell'd in its turn. In this respect, I cannot compare the soul more properly to any thing than to a republic or commonwealth, in which the several members are united by reciprocal ties of government and subordination, and give rise to other persons, who propagate the same republic in the incessant changes of its parts. And as the same individual republic may not only change its members, but also its laws and constitutions, in like manner the same person may vary his character and disposition, as well as his impressions and ideas, without losing his identity. Whatever changes he endures, his several parts are still connected by the relation of causation. And in this view our identity with regard to the passions serves to corroborate that with regard to the imagination, by the making our distant perceptions influence each other, and by giving us a present concern for our past or future pains or pleasures ... In this view, therefore, memory does not so much *produce* as *discover* personal identity, by shewing us the relation of cause and effect among our different perceptions. (*T*261f.)

Although Hume's express purpose here is to trace the idea of the human mind to the smooth transition of imagination made possible by the systematic recurrence of causal relations among perceptions, its unstated thesis – probably because to him it seemed to go without saying – is that the system of causal relations among perceptions originally sketched in *Treatise* I/i/§2 is strictly associative in character, a matter simply of "producing an easy transition of ideas" (*T*260) in "imagination, or the vivacity of our ideas" (*T*265). The correlations are almost too obvious to require comment: "Our impressions give rise to their correspondent ideas" corresponds to "Of this impression there is a copy taken by the mind"; "these ideas in their turn produce other impressions" to "the impressions of reflexion are only antecedent to their correspondent ideas; but posterior to those of sensation, and deriv'd from them"; and "One thought chaces another, and draws after it a third, by which it is expell'd in its turn" to "These again are copied by the memory and imagination, and become ideas; which perhaps in their turn give rise to other impressions and ideas." Yet, as with memory, there is one crucial difference between the two texts: *T*261 treats each of these causal relations as creatures of associative imagination, a matter entirely of the "easy transition of ideas" and "the vivacity of our ideas." No one can deny that Hume could not consistently maintain what he does on *T*261 unless he were willing to apply its associationalism to *Treatise* I/i/§2 as well. But I shall go further, discard the subjunctive, and aver that he declared his intent to do precisely this when, with regard to causal relations among perceptions, he stated that "This question we might easily decide, if we wou'd recollect what has been already prov'd at large, that the understanding never observes any real connexion among objects, and that even the union of cause and effect, when strictly examin'd, resolves itself into a customary association of ideas" (*T*259f.). The import of this claim is not that personal identity has to be understood in terms of cause and effect relations, for nothing would prevent us from obtaining the very same idea of the mind from a system of perceptions connected by *real* relations of cause and effect. Rather, it is an application of what had been proved about causal relations generally to the system of causally related perceptions which yields the idea of the mind; it affirms that these relations, too, are one and all customary transitions of thought characterized by feelings of vivacity and facility. So, of what then is "the true idea of the human mind" the truth if not the account of mind given in *Treatise* I/i/§2? Short of saying in so many words that the mind of *Treatise* I/iv/§6 is the same as that of *Treatise* I/i, I do not see what more we could reasonably ask in order to accept that this is how Hume would have us interpret him; the evidence for equating them is, in my view, so compelling that the burden of proof must lie on those who would deny it.

Granted that the mind of *Treatise* I/i/§2 and *Treatise* I/iv/§6 are one and the same, it is not difficult to see why Hume saved personal identity for the end of *Treatise* I. The application of the *Treatise* I/iii account of causal relations to the *Treatise* I/i/§2 scheme of perceptions arranged in a hierarchy of causal relations implies that perceptions are independent both of one another and of any substrate, and their causal relations are merely ideal (verisimilar) and imaginary (easy transition). This raises questions like: in what are our successive perceptions all united so that they can be associated and what agency is responsible for this associating?[31] These are natural and inevitable questions, but, from Hume's perspective, entirely meaningless. His position is clear. These queries express a demand for causes where no observations, no constant experience, and thence no customs are possible. We must therefore remain silent; the limits on our powers of reason do not permit us even to ask these questions, much less answer them. We can, if we like, pretend to penetrate these "infinite obscurities" (*T*232), and "run into the notion of a *soul*, and *self*, and *substance*" (*T*254). But such efforts are futile:

> We have no perfect idea of any thing but of a perception. A substance is entirely different from a perception. We have, therefore, no idea of a substance. Inhesion in something is suppos'd to be requisite to support the existence of our perceptions.

Nothing appears requisite to support the existence of a perception. We have, therefore, no idea of inhesion. (*T*234)

The import of this and passages like it (for example, *T*207) is that Hume did not hesitate to jettison the supposition of a mind in contexts bearing on *perceptions as such*. Explanation in terms of necessary connections – be it cause/effect, substance/accident, or what have you – is no longer possible when one traces perceptions back to the point before they have been associated in relations of cause and effect and form "that connected mass of perceptions which constitute a thinking being." Yet, to concede that such inferences are no longer possible is, in matters of fact, tantamount to saying there can be no explanation at all ("Inference and reasoning concerning the operations of nature would, from that moment, be at an end," *E*VIII/i.64). If we try to go further, our words outrun our ideas; we grope, invent principles whose meaning we do not understand, and to no purpose but to blind ourselves with our own smoke and mirrors. Recognition of the limits of causal explanation

not only cuts off all hope of ever attaining satisfaction, but even prevents our very wishes; since it appears, that when we say we desire to know the ultimate and operating principle, as something, which resides in the external object, we either contradict ourselves, or talk without a meaning. (*T*267)

So, too, consciousness itself: we have no alternative but to resist the urge to speculation and accept that the ultimate support and operating principles of the successive perceptions which furnish the "raw material" to associative imagination are veiled in impenetrable obscurity. In posing questions which ask for unobservable causes, capable neither of furnishing an easy transition of thought nor the vivacity (belief) possible only in the presence of an impression, "we either contradict ourselves, or talk without a meaning." Hume's solution of the problem of personal identity in terms of "imagination, or the vivacity of our ideas," brought his examination of human understanding to a jarring halt: further penetration into the facts is impossible within the bounds of his phenomenological empiricism.[32] For him, the only task remaining was a final skeptical taking stock before pressing on to the passions and morality.

Hume's "true idea of the human mind" has a fourfold basis in phenomenological feeling: memory-resemblances; causal relations between distinct perceptions (i.e. the belief that a customary transition of thought is a real connection of the objects/perceptions); the scarce felt passage from moment to moment essential to the fiction of perfect identity; and the myriad phenomenological cross-currents that yield the illusion of an imperfect identity (see chapter 7-B). To say this is to say that it is a fiction of the vulgar. But this, for Hume, is not to denigrate it, as his assertion about the equally vulgar fiction of the imperfect identity of body makes clear: "We may well ask, *What causes induce us to believe in the existence of body*? but 'tis in vain to ask, *Whether there be body or not*? That is a point, which we must take for granted in all our reasoning" (*T* 187). If this is true of body, it is surely so of mind: since the resemblances and causal relations utilized in Hume's account of the origin of the idea of mind are the simplest and most primitive of all, the idea of mind presupposes nothing not well within the power of infants and animals.[33] So, the only limitation its phenomenological character places on the idea of mind is to render it useless for any *metaphysical* employment. And is this not exactly what Hume wished? The mind on which his theory of understanding is predicated does not need to be established with a priori, much less metaphysical, certainty ("any hypothesis, that pretends to discover the ultimate original qualities of human nature, ought at first to be rejected as presumptuous and chimerical ... the only solid foundation we can give to [the science of man] must be laid on experience and observation," *T* xv-xvi). We would cross the line dividing vulgar fiction from philosophical fallacy were we to suppose the mind (in any sense we are able to conceive it) to have a reality over and above the sheer verisimilitude of its conception and to be capable of existing independently of the phenomenological feelings of imagination. All the certainty possible or necessary for the idea of mind is afforded by empirical understanding. The observation and memory of the constant precedence of perceptions, together with the verisimilitude attaching to their customary association, yields continuous confirmation of the reality of our self or person and a constant flow of information as to its nature and workings. Since Hume can hardly be supposed to have required more than this to equip himself for the task of explaining the understanding and passions in a strictly causal, experiential, non-metaphysical manner, he cannot be held to account for failing to pursue his inquiries further.

Let us turn finally to the identity aspect of Hume's account. He claimed that "our notions of personal identity, proceed entirely from the smooth and uninterrupted progress of the thought along a train of connected ideas," that is, "a system of different perceptions ... link'd together by the relation of cause and effect." Central to this account is the thesis that the idea of a *system* of different perceptions and the idea of an *identical object* are quite naturally and inevitably confounded:

That action of the imagination, by which we consider the uninterrupted and invariable object, and that by which we reflect on the succession of related objects, are almost the same to the feeling, nor is there much more effort of thought requir'd in the latter case than in the former. The relation facilitates the transition of the mind from one object to another, and renders its passage as smooth as if it contemplated one continu'd object. This resemblance is the cause of the confusion and mistake, and makes us substitute the notion of identity, instead of that of related objects. However at one instant we may consider the related succession as variable or interrupted, we are sure the next to ascribe to it a perfect identity, and regard it as invariable and uninterrupted. Our propensity to this mistake is so great from the resemblance above-mention'd, that we fall into it before we are aware; and tho' we incessantly correct ourselves by reflexion, and return to a more accurate method of thinking, yet we cannot long sustain our philosophy, or take off this biass from the imagination. Our last resource is to yield to it, and boldly assert that these different related objects are in effect the same, however interrupted and variable. (*T*253f.)

There being no resemblance between the *idea* of a perfect identity and the *idea* of a system of causally related successive perceptions, there can be no propensity to mistake them; yet, the *action of imagination in considering* them *feels* so similar, according to Hume, that the difference in appearance is readily overlooked (see also *T*202ff.). In a case of perfect identity, the imagination has only successively to repeat the conception of one and the same *idea* in order to engender the fiction of a single uninterrupted, invariable object (see section A). In the case of a system of distinct yet exactly resembling perceptions linked together by relations of resemblance and cause and effect, the imagination successively repeats the conception of the same *relations* of ideas. The contemplation of resemblances between impressions and ideas, and of the production of ideas of sense from sense impressions, of impressions of reflexion from ideas of sense, etc., feels to imagination no less unvarying and uninterrupted than the mere continuation of the same idea in perfect identity: here too "the passage from one moment to another is scarce felt," involves "no more exercise, than what is necessary to continue that idea," and "distinguishes not itself by a different perception or idea, which may require a different direction of the spirits, in order to its conception"; it thus *feels* to us almost exactly as if we were contemplating something invariable and uninterrupted. This close resemblance in *feeling* between the two kinds of contemplation leads us to confound the one with the other, and ascribe an identity to the system of causal relations despite its manifest variability.

Of course, although successively contemplating the same *idea* and successively contemplating the same *relations* of ideas may *feel* the same to imagination, Hume readily conceded that the vast difference in the *appearances* before us – the perfect identity comprised of the repetition of a single, never varying idea, and the imperfect identity consisting of different, kaleidoscopically varying ideas – cannot escape notice. This prevents us from doing what is our wont in perfect identity: restricting the succession to the time, while attributing a single enduring existence to the object contemplated. We are accordingly obliged to situate the identity of a system of perceptions interlinked by cause and effect elsewhere than in the perceptions themselves. A natural assumption is that the imagination transfers the succession to the objects (perceptions) in order to ascribe an invariable identity to the *contemplating consciousness itself.* But although Hume did conceive of personal identity in terms of consciousness ("personal identity *arises* from consciousness; and consciousness is nothing but a reflected thought or perception," *TApp*635), he did not deem consciousness the bearer of the identity. It is impossible for identity to be shifted from the succession of related perceptions to the consciousness which relates them, because an invariable consciousness would be incapable of *perceiving* their succession. On Hume's Lockean view of time, we would remain oblivious to a succession distinct from consciousness "unless that motion produces a constant train of successive ideas" (*ECHU* II/xiv/§6); but since to perceive the latter is to perceive consciousness continually varying, it is not identity, but its opposite that results. Moreover, Hume, again following Locke, sharply distinguished the question of the identity of person (mind), constituted by "the successive perceptions only" (*T*253), from the identity of an invariant immaterial substance in which perceptions inhere.[34] To treat consciousness as the bearer of the identity, and so as something invariant successively modified by different perception-states, is, however, to render it indistinguishable from an immaterial substrate of perceptions; hence, such a supposition is the surest way to conflate the two questions.

So what (who) is the bearer of the identity of the system of successive perceptions related by resemblance and connected by cause and effect? Hume's answer is that, "in common life ... these ideas of self and person are never very fix'd nor determinate" (*T*189f.). As all that differentiates the system of causally related perceptions from the identical mind is the feeling of smooth transition we obtain when contemplating it (which we confound with the feeling of contemplating a perfect identity), there is nothing else but this system itself to invest with personal identity. The identity is *felt*, but only variation *appears*; there simply is nothing there to which to attach the identity. Still, our feeling is genuine enough, and quite sufficient for the belief: "Our propensity to this mistake is so great from the resemblance above-mention'd" that "Our last resource is to yield to it, and boldly assert that these different related objects are in effect the same, however ... variable." For the common run of mankind (and animal-kind), this is quite enough: seldom are we in doubt of our identity. But this does not satisfy all of us: "In order to justify to ourselves this absurdity, we often feign some new and unintelligible principle, that connects the objects together, and prevents their interruption or variation ... and run into the notion of a *soul*, and *self*, and *substance*, to disguise the variation." Even "where we do not give rise to such a fiction, our propensity to confound identity with relation is so great, that we are apt to imagine something unknown and mysterious, connecting the parts, beside their relation ... And even when this does not take place, we still feel a propensity to confound these ideas; tho' we are not able fully to satisfy ourselves in that particular, nor find any thing invariable and ... to justify our notion of identity" (*T*254). Although the ascription of identity to a system of perceptions confounds the expectations of invariability and uninterruptedness instilled in us by the perfect identity prototype, the propensity to do so is too great to be deflected by such qualms.[35]

Hume analyzed the simplicity of the mind much as he did its identity. Though "There is properly no *simplicity* in it at one time, nor *identity* in different," there is none the less a "natural propension ... to imagine that simplicity and identity" (*T*253). The propensity is essentially the same in the one case as in the other:

> What I have said concerning the first origin and uncertainty of our notion of identity, as apply'd to the human mind, may be extended with little or no variation to that of *simplicity*. An object, whose different co-existent parts are bound together by a close relation, operates upon the imagination after much the same manner as one perfectly simple and indivisible, and requires not a much greater stretch of thought in order to its conception. From this similarity of operation we attribute a simplicity to it, and feign a principle of union as the support of this simplicity, and the center of all the different parts and qualities of the object. (*T*263; see *T*221)

The mind, at any given moment, consists of a bundle of perceptions tied together by relations of resemblance and causality. The uniformity of these relations makes the contemplation of this bundle feel so much like the contemplation of a perfectly simple identical object (like Hume's spot of ink on a piece of paper) as to outweigh the evident complexity of its appearance. So, while we cannot fail to note the complexity, our imaginations conspire to make us believe in some underlying "principle of union as the support of this simplicity, and the center of all the different parts and qualities of the object."[36]

Many perceptions are regarded as external and independent of the mind:

> there are three different kinds of impressions convey'd by the senses. The first are those of the figure, bulk, motion and solidity of bodies. The second those of colours, tastes, smells, sounds, heat and cold. The third are the pains and pleasures, that arise from the application of objects to our bodies, as by the cutting of our flesh with steel, and such like. Both philosophers and the vulgar suppose the first to have a distinct continu'd existence. The vulgar only regard the second as on the same footing. Both philosophers and the vulgar, again, esteem the third to be merely perceptions; and consequently interrupted and dependent beings. (*T*192)

The question arises whether perceptions, once believed to be distinct (= external and independent) from the mind, are still counted among "the successive perceptions ... that constitute the mind." The answer seems to be yes. There are here two equally natural and irresistible beliefs competing: the first, the conviction, based on experience and habit, that certain of our perceptions are continued, distinct existents; and the second, the certainty, based on immediate consciousness, that "all impressions are internal and perishing existences and appear as such" (*T* 194). The latter is compatible with the beliefs of associative imagination only in so far as we are inhabitants of the world of the senses and memory, wherein "Our impressions give rise to their correspondent ideas; and these ideas in their turn produce other impressions"; the former will not let us accept anything less than the world of judgment, which situates some of these same perceptions in an external world of bodies and other minds.[37] Clearly, our acquisition of an idea and belief in personal identity takes place entirely within the standpoint of the first world; and since it precedes and makes possible the world of judgment (see chapters 4-A and 7-A), there can be no doubt that the same impressions we subsequently identify with objects external to the mind are originally felt to be internal to it (for "they appear as such"). This does not cancel or mitigate the subsequent belief ("Nature has not left this to [our] choice," *T* 187); but neither does the latter belief erase the first (which is rooted no less deeply in human nature). We believe *all* our sensations to belong to the system of perceptions that constitute our mind (self or person), despite simultaneously believing *some* of them to be objects distinct from, and independent of, the mind. Though manifestly inconsistent, the viewpoints of the two worlds are so different, and so difficult to unite in imagination, as never in practice to cause us any trouble (see conclusion).[38]

7 From mind to body

So far we have found ample reason to believe that the identity of mind is independent of that of body. (i) Hume's account of personal identity involves a succession of uniform relations of resemblance and cause and effect the contemplation of which the imagination confounds with perfect identity; external objects are at no point presupposed. (ii) Since the system of perceptions defined in *Treatise* I/i/§2 is premised in the account of external objects and substances in *Treatise* I/iv/§§2–5, the equation of the former with the mind of *Treatise* I/iv/§6 suggests that the latter can be known independently of body. (iii) Hume's claim on *T*73f. that causal relations are presupposed in order for identity to apply beyond the memory and the senses means that bodily identity would remain unknowable in their absence; by contrast, there is no need to advance beyond the perceptions of memory and senses for the discovery of personal identity (see *T*260ff.). Nevertheless, nothing prior to *Treatise* I/iv/§2, "Of scepticism with regard to the senses," permits one to draw the stronger conclusion that the identity of mind is *premised* by that of body. But in that section one finds texts strongly suggesting that Hume did espouse this view. If so, it would have profound implications for how Hume's account of bodily identity should be understood and evaluated. However, since, to my knowledge, no interpreter has even so much as considered the possibility that personal identity may be premised in Hume's account of bodily identity, we must seek to determine whether, and if so why, he found it necessary to do so, before proceeding to the account itself.

A. The mind as condition for continued, distinct existents

In a well-known passage that has been exploited for any number of conflicting purposes, Hume declared it to be impossible for him or anyone sincerely to doubt the existence of bodies. The most the skeptic can claim is that this belief is neither founded on, nor defensible by, reason:

the sceptic ... must assent to the principle concerning the existence of body, tho' he cannot pretend by any arguments of philosophy to maintain its veracity. Nature has not left this to his choice, and has doubtless esteem'd it an affair of too great importance to be trusted to our uncertain reasonings and speculations. We may well ask, *What causes induce us to believe in the existence of body*? but 'tis in vain to ask, *Whether there be body or not*? That is a point, which we must take for granted in all our reasonings. (*T*187)

As was the case concerning cause and effect in *Treatise* I/iii, Hume's concern was not whether body exists, but the causes and nature of our idea and our certainty regarding it. In embarking on this inquiry, he found it useful to distinguish two facets of our belief in body: the belief that objects *continue* to exist even when absent from our senses, and the belief that their existence is *distinct* from the mind and its perceptions (i.e. "their *external* position as well as the *independence* of their existence and operation," *T*188). This was not to deny that, logically, continuity and distinctness are so "intimately connected together" that "the decision of the one question decides the other" (*T*188). Nevertheless, epistemically, "the opinion of the *continu'd* existence of body ... is prior to that of its *distinct* existence, and produces that latter principle" (*T*199; also *T*210). Since the origin of our beliefs, and the sequence of their acquisition, was Hume's central concern, he deemed it necessary to "carry along with us this distinction, and ... consider whether it be the *senses, reason*, or the *imagination*, that produces the opinion of a *continu'd* or of a *distinct* existence" (*T*188).[1]

Hume excludes the senses as a source of the idea of a continued existence straightaway. Continuity is the existence of "objects, after they no longer appear to the senses" (*T*188); so, for the senses to be the source of this idea we would have to suppose "that the senses continue to operate, even after they have ceas'd all manner of operation ... [which] is a contradiction in terms." On the contrary, the senses attest, with the full vivacity of natural belief, to the *discontinued* existence of the objects which appear to them ("all impressions are internal and perishing existences, and appear as such," *T*194).

As for the distinct existence of objects, the senses are incapable of giving us any idea at all, one way or the other. To yield an idea of distinct existence, the senses would have to "present their impressions either as images and representations, or as these very distinct and external existences" (*T*189). However, since only by means of "some inference of the reason or imagination" can we advance beyond the perceptions immediately present to us by consciousness (see *T*73f.), the senses by themselves can "never give us the least intimation of any thing beyond" (*T*189). Similarly, even though an impression of the senses may be denominated indifferently either "object" or "perception," it is still only a single existence (the imagination is incapable of separating its datum into two objects, an image and something external which it represents; so, by the *T*18 separability principle, they cannot *be* distinct existents).

Before concluding definitively that the senses are not the source of the idea of distinct existence, Hume examined the possibility that they "convey the impressions as those very existences, by a kind of fallacy and illusion" (*T*189).[2] This turns out to be the very view Hume ascribes to the vulgar (see *T*192 and *T*202), but through an illusion of imagination, not the senses. He offered two reasons to support his contention that the senses are incapable of spawning such an illusion. The first is that "All sensations are felt by the mind, such as they really are" (*T*189), and this is as true of their relations and situations as of their nature (see *T*190). Since the senses are incapable of deceiving us about their objects, the absence of any *appearance* of externality and independence implies the absence of the *reality* (i.e. verisimilitude) as well.[3]

However, it is the other reason Hume gave for denying that the senses yield an illusion of distinct existence that concerns us here: "if the senses presented our impressions as external to, and independent of ourselves, both the objects and ourselves must be obvious to our senses, otherwise they cou'd not be compar'd by these faculties. The difficulty, then, is how far we are *ourselves* the objects of our senses" (*T*189). This sudden shift to the question of personal identity has already been remarked (see chapter 6-B). It occurs in the context of a question not about whether the senses present their objects as *images* of distinct existents, but whether they present *these objects themselves* (impressions) as distinct existents. Hume's claim is that the only way they could do so is if, along with the impressions, they also yielded an idea of the mind ("the uniting principle, which constitutes a person," *T*189); and he makes quite clear that it is the mind as such, not the body or mind-body union, that is required for this comparison (see *T*191). More significantly, his reason for advancing this thesis suggests that it holds true *regardless* of whether the senses yield this idea veridically or by some fallacy and illusion: "[the senses] must be able to compare the object with ourselves; and even in that case they do not, nor is it possible they shou'd, deceive us" (*T*192). Hume's reason is of such a nature as to prompt one to ask *whether his thesis should* (*or even can*) *be confined to the senses as such, or whether it can* (*or must*) *be extended to the imagination as well.* For, if Hume thought a comparison with the mind necessary for sense impressions to be regarded as independently real and external, it seems evident that this should be so *irrespective* of the faculty of consciousness – the senses, reason, or imagination – doing the regarding. What could there possibly be, peculiar to the senses, that could restrict the demand for such a comparison to them? I cannot think of anything, and there is no indication that Hume thought so either. Since he never

expressly stated that the presupposition of personal identity is only in effect if it is the senses that are the source of our ideas of continued, distinct existences, it seems much more plausible that, on *T*189ff., he was simply applying a more general thesis to the specific case of the senses – a thesis he alas neglected ever to state explicitly in its full generality.

Before we can be confident in this conclusion, we must first answer two questions: (i) why, in the absence of any idea of the self, there can be no idea of distinct existence; and (ii) how, given an idea of the self, that idea becomes possible. To answer the first question, we need to consider what is lacking in the scene before consciousness prior to the advent of the self. Strictly speaking, it is only this: the identity-like feeling the imagination derives "from the smooth and uninterrupted progress of the thought along a train of connected ideas" (*T*260). Expunge this feeling, whereby alone the "system of different perceptions ... link'd together by the relation of cause and effect" (*T*261) is confounded with perfect identity, and that system would be quite incapable of furnishing an idea of mind (person, self); that is, nothing more than the elimination of the feeling is required to render self-consciousness impossible. But is that really all? Since a *difficult* and *interrupted* progress of thought implies the absence not only of uniform relations, but also of association itself ("the very essence of these relations consists in their producing an easy transition of ideas," *T*260), eliminating this feeling would mean doing away with the resemblances constitutive of memory, the causal relations between impression-originals and idea-copies, as well as the causal relations between ideas of sensation and impressions of reflexion (at best, these relations would be weak, and never more than slight probabilities – see chapter 5-D). By unravelling the fabric of mind, the "fixt and unalterable" (*T*110) order akin to a "commonwealth, in which the several members are united by the reciprocal ties of government and subordination" (*T*261), would give way to a kaleidoscopic flux so chaotic that understanding, properly so called, could never emerge, and, *a fortiori*, would preclude any possibility of conceiving, much less believing, sense impressions to be independent, external existents. In other words, in view of the phenomenological nature of perfect identity, the absence of the feeling characteristic of the smooth passage of thought along a sequence of uniformly *related* ideas would prevent the imagination from confounding such sequences with perfect identity, and so eradicate *all* imperfect identity, including that of distinct, continued existents (this feeling gives imagination that "biass" which alone can induce it to overlook the appearance before our senses and "boldly assert that these different related objects are in effect the same, however interrupted and variable," *T*254). Since the uniform relations of ideas necessary to give us this feeling are precisely those comprising the

"system of different perceptions" that constitute "the true idea of the human mind," we therefore must *first* feel the smooth transitions from which the idea of ourselves is derived in order *subsequently* to acquire any ideas of distinct existents.

This brings us to the second question posed above: how, *given* the idea of the self, ideas of external, independent existents then become possible. It is not difficult to discern the answer, at least as it would likely have appeared to Hume. Since externality and independence are clearly relative notions, an object of the senses can only be external and independent with respect to something else (let it not be forgotten that Hume's discussion pertains to the vulgar view and that the "impressions ... are these very distinct and external existences," *T*189). Hence, how we understand externality and independence depends entirely on the *standard of distinctness* we employ. For example, if our standard were a single, fleeting perception, then anything external to and independent of *it* could qualify only as a distinct perception itself. Similarly, if our standard were a perfect identity, then anything judged to be external and independent with respect to it could qualify at most as another perfect identity. The only standard of comparison adequate for obtaining an idea of a genuinely distinct (external and independent) existence is something satisfying all of the following conditions: (i) it must have a duration, i.e. its existence must encompass a perceived succession of perceptions; (ii) it must preserve its identity through any and all variations of perceptions; (iii) it thence cannot itself be a perception or a perfect identity; yet, (iv) since our only objects are our perceptions, its existence must be constituted exclusively and completely by the successive perceptions themselves (i.e. its existence is neither external nor independent of perceptions, and so cannot continue if their succession be interrupted).[4] An object of the senses judged to be distinct from a thing satisfying all of these requirements would be *external* to the successive perceptions (since they are constitutive of the existence of that from which it is held to be distinct) as well as *independent* of them (since its own existence is not constituted by them). In other words, the successive perceptions *qua* perceptions (internal, perishing existents) must *first* be referred to a single, identical existent, which is conceived as constituted solely and entirely of them (not as anything more – not as, say, an immaterial subsistence in which perceptions inhere): only *then* is there a something relative to which being external and independent yields precisely the sense of "distinctness" necessary to the conception of body. Obviously, only the mind, as Hume defined it, can satisfy all these conditions ("They are the successive perceptions only, that constitute the mind," *T*253); and equally clearly, anything whose own existence is determined by comparison with it would "have an existence DISTINCT from the mind and

perception" (*T*188), and thence obviously could not be *internal* to, or *dependent* on, that mind. Without this standard of comparison, it would be impossible, by any other conceivable standard, to regard the impressions immediately present to our senses (even those characterized by constancy and coherence) as distinct existents – as the vulgar single existence view requires (see *T*192 and *T*202). It therefore follows that "the true idea of the human mind" (*T*261) is presupposed by such an existence, *regardless of whether the idea of it is derived from the senses, the imagination, or the understanding.*[5]

It may be wondered whether and how the mind's duration can be determined without resorting to yet another standard of comparison, and so *ad infinitum.* The answer lies in Hume's Lockean account of the origin of our ideas of succession and duration. This theory privileges reflection (= Humean imagination) over sensation (the appearances of perceptions). Its thesis is that we could never acquire an idea of succession if the change in our sense impressions were not accompanied by a change in consciousness itself in the apprehension of them (" unless that motion produces a constant train of successive ideas," *ECHU* II/xiv/§6). Hence, it is not what is present *before* consciousness, but *consciousness itself* that matters: only in so far as the perceptions are *perceived* to succeed can there be any idea of succession. Given such a view, it follows that we *could* not, even if we *would*, look beyond the succession of perceptions that constitutes the mind for a standard by which to become aware of our own (or anything else's) duration of existence. Our idea of duration of existence just *is* the idea of our identical self; and it is only by reference to it, as a standard of comparison, that duration of existence can be attributed to anything else ("whilst we are thinking, or whilst we receive successively several ideas in our minds, *we know that we do exist*; and so we call the existence, or the continuation of the existence of ourselves, *or anything else, commensurate to the succession of any ideas in our minds*, the duration of ourselves, or any such other thing *co-existent with our thinking*," *ECHU* II/xiv/§3 – emphasis mine). Hume's account of personal identity, however, includes some refinements on that of Locke. Locke held that the idea of the duration of our existence requires only memory (retention of the perceived succession of perceptions), whereas Hume believed that a succession of perceptions by itself is sufficient to yield at most the idea of a perfect identity, not that of an ever-varying identical mind; and perfect identities are an inadequate standard for recognition of distinct existents. Hume's account requires, in addition, that the successive perceptions be uniformly related by ties of causation, so as to form a genuine *system* of perceptions (the mind, construed as "bundle" or "heap," is still a "*connected* mass of perceptions," *T*207); only thus can the identity continue regardless of the flux and variation of our perceptions or gaps in memory (see chapter 2-B), and so furnish us with the standard essential for acquiring ideas of external, independent existents.

Once it is granted that Hume's standard of comparison for *distinct* existence is the mind, then it is not difficult to see why he thought that distinct existence entails *continued* existence, or why he thought the latter precedes the former. Since continued existence is the supposition that certain impressions of the senses continue in existence even after they have ceased to appear to the *senses*, comparison with a perduring (hence, *already* identified) *faculty-endowed mind* is essential to its conception. But the mind itself, however, may be characterized only as continued (through variation), not as distinct: being itself the standard of distinctness, there is nothing *as yet* in relation to which it can be assigned that determination. This means that anything represented in relation to this standard is *immediately* determined as continued in its own existence (i.e. coexistent with the mind, hence continued through absences from the senses), and only as a *consequence* of this is determined as distinct in the sense definitive of an external object. Since the act of comparison with the mind and the act constitutive of continued existence are immediately one and the same, "'Tis the opinion of a continu'd existence, which first takes place, and without much study or reflection draws the other along with it, wherever the mind follows its first and most natural tendency" (*T*210).

B. Bodies as vulgarly conceived

Having excluded the senses as the source of our opinion of continued or distinct existents, Hume next considers reason. As might be expected, it fares no better. He observes that the very suggestion is prima facie implausible, for it obviously is not by demonstrative or probable argument "that children, peasants, and the greatest part of mankind are induc'd to attribute objects to some impressions, and deny them to others" (*T*193; see also *E*XII/i.118). If reason is any guide in the matter, its verdict must be contrary to vulgar opinion: "philosophy informs us, that every thing, which appears to the mind, is nothing but a perception, and is interrupted, and dependent on the mind; whereas the vulgar confound perceptions and objects, and attribute a distinct continu'd existence to the very things they feel or see. This sentiment, then, as it is entirely unreasonable, must proceed from some other faculty than the understanding" (*T*193). Experience also teaches that perceptions are dependent on external objects, where the "experience" appealed to consists of experiments in which causal inference plays a central role (see, for example, *T*210f., *T*226, and *T*230f.). Philosophers' denial of the vulgar single existence view is *reasonable* precisely because it is founded on causal inference, i.e. custom, this being, for Hume, emblematic of empirical rationality (see Part II). The vulgar, too, are not unaware of the testimony of reason (everyone has pressed an eyeball and seen double), yet have no difficulty unholding contradictory beliefs (imagination finds more difficulty opposing them than neglecting their opposition – see conclusion). Moreover, because the vulgar view *identifies* external object and sensation, the possibility of relating them as cause and effect is precluded. Causal inference requires that there be two distinct items experienced in constant conjunction so that a transition of thought from one to the other is possible (this the vulgar can do in the case of pleasure and pain since these are associated as effects of those impressions which are identified with external existents). Since everything Hume classed as empirical reasoning is a matter of causal inference (i.e. tracing or hypothesizing lineages of existential dependence), it is impossible for the vulgar view to arise through reasoning. Moreover, "Even after we distinguish our perceptions from our objects, 'twill appear presently [*T*212 and *T*216], that we are still incapable of reasoning from the existence of one to that of the other: So that upon the whole our reason neither does, nor is it possible it ever shou'd, upon any supposition, give us an assurance of the continu'd and distinct existence of body" (*T*193).

Having disposed of both the senses and reason, Hume concludes that the opinion "of the continu'd and distinct existence of body ... must be entirely owing to the IMAGINATION" (*T*193). To understand how this belief can prevail despite the fact that "all impressions are internal and perishing existences, and appear as such," it must first be recognized that it "does not extend to all of them," and so "must arise from certain qualities peculiar to some impressions" (*T*194). Neither the *involuntariness* of impressions nor their superior *force and violence* can be the qualities responsible, since both pains and passions can operate with as great ferocity as, and no less involuntarily than, those impressions considered to be continued distinct existents. Instead, Hume traces the opinion to the qualities *constancy* and *coherence*. Constancy is the steadfast order and manner of appearance characteristic mainly of visual and tactile impressions, which seem undisturbed "upon account of any interruption in my seeing or perceiving them" (*T*195). Coherence comes into play once constancy is subverted by change: variation is coherent which conforms to regular determinate causal sequences, such that certain positions or qualities are found never to succeed one another without certain others being interposed (i.e. change according to predictable patterns). Pains and passions fall far short of the constancy and coherence manifested in sensations of mountains, rivers, and other visual and/or tactile phenomena; hence, when the former are absent from our perception, "on no occasion is it necessary to suppose, that they have existed and operated, when they were not perceiv'd, in order to preserve the same dependance and connexion, of which we have had experience" (*T*195). By contrast, visual and tactile objects are observed to continue so steadily and to operate in ways so predictable that to suppose them to be anihilated the moment we close our eyes goes against the grain of our regularity-loving imaginations; when absent from our senses, they "require a continu'd existence, or otherwise lose, in a great measure, the regularity of their operation" (*T*195f.). For these and allied reasons, Hume felt confident that these two qualities furnish all that is requisite "to support so vast an edifice, as is that of the continu'd existence of all external bodies" (*T*199).

To have any hope of correctly comprehending Hume's analysis of the belief in body it is essential to understand just what the vulgar, or *single existence view*, in fact is. Much of the effort of explication and criticism will be wasted either if we suppose him to have attributed to the vulgar an "ontologically neutral" position (where objects have no distinction from perceptions) or if we take him to have denied that a good many lay people, as well as scientists and philosophers, regard their constant, coherent impressions as merely *effects*, or *images*, of objects and not as "these very distinct and external existences" (*T*189).[6] The principal relevant text is the following:

> That I may avoid all ambiguity and confusion on this head, I shall observe, that I here account for the opinions and belief of the vulgar with regard to the existence of body; and therefore must entirely conform myself to their manner of thinking and of expressing themselves. Now we have already observ'd [on *T*192], that however philosophers may distinguish betwixt the objects and perceptions of the senses; which they suppose co-existent and resembling; yet this is a distinction, which is not comprehended by the generality of mankind, who as they perceive only one being, can never assent to the opinion of a double existence and representation. Those very sensations, which enter by the eye or ear are with them the true objects, nor can they readily conceive that this pen or paper, which is immediately perceiv'd, represents another, which is different from, but resembling it. In order, therefore, to accommodate myself to their notions, I shall at first suppose [until *T*210]; that there is only a single existence, which I shall call indifferently *object* or *perception*, according as it shall seem best to suit my purpose, understanding by both of them what any common man means by a hat, or shoe, or stone, or any other impression, convey'd to him by his senses. (*T*202)

If, in Hume's eyes, the vulgar regard many of their impressions of sensation as identical with "these very distinct and external existences," he can hardly be said to have deemed them ontologically neutral! The vulgar are as ontologically committed as it is possible to be: their pains and pleasures, along with their reflexions and thoughts, are regarded as mere internal dependent existents (which is what *they* mean by "perception in the mind"), while the rest of their sense impressions they take to *be* distinct, continued existents (see *T*192). Is Hume's view warranted? It seems to me that a doubt can only arise if one equates Hume's "vulgar" with the "lay person" or "common man." Pears, for example, claims that "one of [Hume's] most important errors occurs right at the beginning, when he assumes that the plain man's belief does not presuppose any distinction between his impressions and physical objects. This enables him to represent 'the opinion of double existence' as the extravagant speculation of philosophers."[7] But Hume made quite plain who the vulgar are: "children, peasants, and the greatest part of mankind" (*T*193); "Even the animal creation are governed by a like opinion, and preserve this belief of external objects, in all their thoughts, designs, and actions" (*E*XII/i.118). Now, it may well be true that many, perhaps (to be very charitable) most, contemporary lay people may, at some point in their lives, have learned that ordinary physical objects are not "really" colored and such like, but only "appear" so owing to the constitution of our sense organs and brain. But can the same be said of an illiterate peasant in an eighteenth-century Highland glen? Stone Age tribesmen? Two-year olds? Dogs, horses, tigers? If we understand "the vulgar opinion" as Hume would have us do, it is clear that he was quite correct in maintaining that the vulgar do not believe their sense impressions (save pain and pleasure) to be mere *perceptions*, and so only *effects* or *representations* of true external objects, never immediately present to them. The natural belief of higher animals including man, is that these sensations are the very external objects themselves. It is *this* belief in external objects, instilled in us by nature long before education exerts any influence, and retained until the last cogent moment of our existence, that Hume sought to explain in his wonted psycho-phenomenological manner.

Likewise, Hume was quite warranted in claiming that we have no further to look than ourselves for examples of this vulgar belief. Instinct resumes full control over us, and reality ceases to consist of hadrons and leptons or ideas and impressions, directly when we step from our laboratories, lecterns, and word-processors. Reality is the ladder on which I am precariously perched as I paint the ceiling a very real shade of blue; and the car I see careening down the street directly at me I immediately, without further ado, believe to be the physical reality itself, and do not for a moment regard as the mere effect or image in me of something not immediately perceptible ("even philosophers themselves, for the greatest part of their lives, take their perceptions to be their only objects, and suppose that the very being, which is intimately present to the mind, is the real body or material existence," *T*206). I do not have to be taught to believe this, and require no evidence or convincing. It is of a piece with what I have believed since my earliest days, quite naturally and inevitably (given human nature). This belief had first claim on Hume's attention because he quite plausibly deemed it the support on which everything else we believe about the external universe ultimately rests; for it is such that, upon its removal, all the wild speculations of philosophers and scientists would be impotent to bring us to believe, at least with anything approaching the certainty we now have, in the reality of continued, distinct existents (see section C).

Hume divided his investigation of the vulgar belief in body into four stages: identity as such; why identity comes to be attributed to our interrupted perceptions on account of resemblance relations (= imperfect identity); the propensity to unite these illusorily identified, interrupted perceptions in a continued existent (= body); and how the propensity gives verisimilitude to the conception. The principle of identity has already been examined (chapter 6-A), and enough has been said regarding the confusion by imagination of the feeling of contemplating a succession of uniformly *related* ideas with the feeling in successively contemplating the same *idea* to require here only a brief addendum. The imperfect identity of body differs from that of mind by virtue of being invariable (constant) and interrupted rather than variable and uninterrupted.[8] Otherwise, the two are, for all intents and purposes, the same: in each case, uniform relations of ideas are confounded with perfect identity not because of any resemblance on the side of the *ideas* (where variation or interruption cannot help but be noticed), but because there is such similarity of feeling in their *contemplation* that "The mind readily passes from one to the other, and perceives not the change without a strict attention, of which, generally speaking, 'tis wholly incapable" (*T*203). In particular, the constancy of certain impressions (i.e. their uniform resemblance relations, despite interruptions) is so great as easily to dupe us into believing we are confronted by a genuine identity: "An easy transition or passage of the imagination, along the ideas of these different and interrupted perceptions, is almost the same disposition of mind with that in which we consider one constant and uninterrupted perception. 'Tis therefore very natural for us to mistake the one for the other" (*T*204).

The fiction of continued existence, the third part of Hume's system, is the result of the attempt by imagination to reconcile its *feeling* of contemplating a perfectly identical object with the interruption in its *appearance* to the senses. According to Hume, it is simply a fact of human nature that a discord of this kind gives rise to a "perplexity" and "sensible unease" (*T*205); in consequence, the mind "will naturally seek relief from the uneasiness" occasioned by the "opposition betwixt the notion of the identity of resembling perceptions, and the interruption of their appearance" (*T*206). This discomfort can be removed only by eliminating the identity or the interruption. Hume rules out the former since, like the opposition, it is *the imagination itself* that feels this identity; that is, it can no more help feeling the smooth, identity-like passage of thought occasioned by the resembling perceptions than it can help feeling the unease occasioned by its conflict with the interrupted appearance. It must therefore eliminate the interruption.

To explain how this is possible, Hume invokes his account of personal identity and, in particular, the posteriority of mind relative to perceptions (see chapter 6-B). Since the mind is merely "a heap or collection of different perceptions, united together by certain relations," perceptions cannot possibly be inseparable from it. For just as each perception can be separated in imagination from every other, nothing prevents the imagination from "breaking off all its relations, with that connected mass of perceptions, which constitute a thinking being" (*T*207). Since distinctness *from a mind* is specifically the sort necessary for the conception of a distinct, continued existent (only continuity and distinctness relative to a mind can yield this idea – see section A above), to say this is just to say that the imagination has it within its power to form a conception of such an existent. The uneasiness occasioned by the contradiction between interrupted appearance and felt identity furnishes the inducement for the imagination to exercise this power; and the constancy and coherence of some of our sense impressions make them the obvious (i.e. natural) choice to have the interruption in their appearance eliminated. So, on the principle that "Whatever strikes in with the natural propensities, and either externally forwards their satisfaction, or internally concurs with their movements, is sure to give a sensible pleasure" (*T*205), the imagination, naturally and unthinkingly, does precisely this.[9]

How, then, is the interruption eliminated? An interruption destroys perfect identity by introducing a new content which requires "a different direction of the spirits, in order to its conception" (*T*203). The variation in perception caused by the interruption does not, however, bring the continued existence of the *consciousness* side of perfect identity to an end, since the imagination still finds a uniformity of *relations* of ideas so similar to repeating the same idea successively that it confounds it with perfect identity (see chapter 6-C). This imperfect identity is the mind (self, person), and the idea of it enables the imagination to view the successive perceptions that constitute it in either of two ways: in accordance with the separability principle as prior to it (as on *T*207); or as posterior to it in that the identity of the mind-bundle, once conceived, is then *believed* by imagination to preexist each new impression and continue in existence after it has ceased (i.e. identity is retained despite variation). In this way, the imagination is free not only to regard its perceptions as distinct from the mind-bundle, but also to regard the mind-bundle as an existent in its own right, distinct from any of its perceptions. Herein lies the key to Hume's solution to the problem of the identity of bodies. Unless correlated to the mind, the imagination would have nothing in relation to which it could distinguish the *existence* of a perception from its *appearance*, and so would have no alternative but to accede to the verdict of the senses that an interruption in the appearance of a perception terminates its existence. In order to conceive a perception to be able to continue in existence beyond the cessation of its appearance, the imagination must somehow distinguish the *existence* of a perception from its *appearance*. This requires it to conceive of appearance as a *relation* into which a perception may enter, but which in no way compromises its existential independence; and the way this is done is by conceiving of appearance as the relation of perceptions to a mind-bundle. For the mind itself is *already* conceived to have an existence independent of its appearance: we believe it to retain its identity despite the kaleidoscopic flux of appearances (variations and interruptions of appearance are no more than incidents in the life of the mind). Accordingly, *something whose distinct (external, independent) existence is conceived by correlating it with the mind (as coexistents) and yet external to, and independent of, the mind can be conceived freely to enter into and emerge from appearing relations with it, with no implications at all regarding its existence* (something Locke too grasped – see *ECHU* II/xiv/§3, cited in section A). This is the point of Hume's argument on *T*207f.: the crucial, but easily overlooked, premise is the determining of perceptions as distinct in relation to the mind-bundle which enables the imagination to conceive of appearing as a relation between perceptions and a mind. For then, finding "no absurdity in separating any particular perception from the mind; that is, in breaking off all its relations, with that connected mass of perceptions, which constitute a thinking being," the imagination can conceive any of its perceptions as existentially prior to, and independent of, its appearing-relation to this mass. "The same continu'd and uninterrupted Being may, therefore, be sometimes present to the mind, and sometimes absent from it, without any real or essential change in the Being itself. An interrupted appearance to the senses implies not necessarily an interruption in the existence" (*T*207f.).

The preceding is true of any perception: the imagination always has the *option* of distinguishing an interruption in the appearance of a perception from its existence. It chooses not to exercise it in the case of ideas, impressions of reflexion, pains and pleasures, and, to a certain extent, impressions of sensation other than vision and touch. But visual and tactile sensations exhibit a sufficient degree of constancy and coherence to induce the imagination to ascribe to them a *continued* existence; so, in their case only, it conceives existence to be *distinct* from appearance and ascribes any interruption in the latter simply to the severing of their *appearing relation* to the mind-bundle. If it causes anyone consternation to apply the name "perception" to such an existent, Hume is happy to accommodate him by replacing it with "object" or "being," which, "standing for the very same thing," "renders not this separation from a mind absurd and contradictory" (*T*207). Either way, the identity is a total fiction from the ground up. First, the imagination is only able to feign the existence of body by conceiving certain of its impressions as external to, and independent of, a mind, and this it can do only because the mind is likewise its own invention (a product of "uniting principles in the ideal world ... the very essence [of which] consists in their producing an easy transition of ideas," *T*260). Second, the imagination performs a kind of confidence trick in so far as it illicitly extends the genuine independence pertaining to perceptions *vis à vis* other perceptions (including bundles thereof), to the same perceptions regarded as distinct, continued existents. For our only *actual* idea of their distinctness *vis à vis* the mind demands that the latter be conceived as a mere "heap or collection of different perceptions, united together by certain relations"; otherwise, experience takes over and, *ceteris paribus* (i.e. aside from the fiction of continued existence), we naturally (vulgarly) believe all our perceptions to be "interrupted and dependent beings" (*T*192; see also *T*193 and T210f.). However, in order to conceive of (some of) these same perceptions as continued, distinct existents, the mind must be conceived differently; in particular, it must be fictitiously assumed to have an identity that renders it indifferent to the comings and goings of perceptions, and so to be something *over and above* the aggregate (bundle) of individual perceptions and their relations. This "equivocation" makes the distinctness of bodies, and the continued existence that goes with it, a sham. Third, like the mind, the body is not truly an identity at all, but something the imagination confounds with identity because its feeling in contemplating a succession of uniformly *related* ideas is not sensibly different from that in contemplating the same *idea* successively repeated. Fourth, and finally, identity itself results from running together distinct and incompatible notions, unity and number, and fictitiously supposing them to combine to yield something new.[10] Nevertheless, we can now see why, for Hume, the identity of body is inconceivable except on the presupposition of that of mind, and that only the identity of mind can enable us to conceive the sort of externality and independence requisite for acquiring the vulgar idea of body. Moreover, just as Hume's rejection of abstraction implies that duration cannot be conceived independently of a succession of thoughts, so the concept of an external independent existent has no validity except in relation to mind (and so to the related bundle of successive perceptions that constitute it).[11]

Hume recognized that his account would remain incomplete if he could not explain why belief is reposed in the fiction of continued existence. Since his reasoning in this matter is somewhat difficult to penetrate, we will do well to apply it first to the simpler case of perfect identity. Here the imagination is obliged to reckon with the conflict between its *repetition* of the idea of the object from moment to moment (without which there could be no perception of change in the time) and its belief in an *invariable and uninterrupted* existence. The question is why the imagination reposes belief in an identity in preference to the perceived plurality (viz. the numerical repetition of qualitatively identical ideas). The solution would appear to lie in the role of *memory* in the identity fiction. Memory here serves a dual function: the *source* of the awareness of perceptions sheerly as a succession (i.e. bare retention as such) and the *condition* of the awareness that successive perceptions both resemble one another and are causally related as original and copy. Since belief in real existence could not be reposed in a bare succession of ideas were the ideas not *causally* linked to impressions, and thereby enabled to partake of a vivacity approaching that of the latter (see chapter 2-B and -C), only the second, idea-enlivening facet of memory can concern us here. The fiction of perfect identity, and the conviction that goes with it, must therefore be so construed that the "scarce felt" repetition of the same idea (memory) induces us to relate our successive memories as copies, or representations, to *a single*, *identical* original. For, so long as we regard our ideas as different not only *qua* perceptions, but *qua* representations, we cannot but *believe* that we are confronted by a multiplicity of different impression originals.[12] What tips the scales of belief towards unity and away from multiplicity is the vivacity of the memory-representatives with which the perfect identity fiction is concerned: the fusion of memories into the fiction of a single, enduring existence simply means that the imagination "melts together" the vivacity of a succession of memories to form a single extremely vivid image of reflexion (see chapter 5-D). Since vivacity/verisimilitude *is* belief (see, for example, *T*116), its concentration in a single object of representation is belief in that object's real existence. In other words, production of the identity fiction at the same time concentrates all the belief that would otherwise be divided up among different remembered impressions – had the passage of thought been *strongly* felt and *new* directions of the spirits been unavoidable – in the conception of one invariable and uninterrupted existent. The fiction is effectively self-confirming: since a propensity to run a series of memories into one is, *ipso facto*, to form an image of reflexion, it is at the same time a propensity to vivify, and so believe in, the identity;

hencc, no imagination that has the propensity could withhold belief from its result. Nor is the propensity in any sense rational, even in Hume's attenuated sense of "reason" as custom: it amounts to nothing more than the natural tendency of imagination to find pleasure in whatever affords it a smooth, unobstructed passage of thought. It is therefore sheer serendipity (i.e. human nature) that the perfect identity fiction is the smoothest path for imagination when confronted by a succession of qualitatively identical memory-representatives, for this alone makes it more natural for it to concentrate their vivacity in the image of a single, unchanging object rather than disperse it among several distinct ones.

Hume's reasoning regarding belief in imperfect identities is quite similar. For, while the circumstances motivating imagination are different in the two cases,[13] the propensity to unite successive, qualitatively identical memory-representatives in a single enduring object is the same. The only difference between the two cases that matters – the interruptions in the appearance of the object – poses no serious obstacle for imagination. For here, too, the fiction is self-confirming: given that the natural inclination of imagination is to suppose that temporally separated, qualitatively identical memories represent (are copies of) one and the same enduring existence, this fictional identity inevitably becomes the repository (as image of reflexion) of all the vivacity contained in these representatives, and thus is *believed*. Since this is just to say that the time span from the earliest memory to the most recent is believed to encompass a single enduring existence, we have a corresponding natural inclination to doubt that interruptions in its *appearance* constitute interruptions of its *existence*. For, once the image of reflexion reaches the point of conviction in the identity, it is far more soothing for imagination to extend the vivacity of its memory representatives to the intervals where memory is absent than not to do so; consequently, the continued (i.e. unsensed, unremembered) existence is accorded the same vivacity as the remembered intervals, and the whole span is believed to be united by a single, invariable and uninterrupted existence.

Once belief in continued existence is understood, there is little difficulty explaining belief in either distinct existence or variable identity (coherence). If a thing is accorded continued existence, then its existence must be *independent* of our perceiving it; and if its existence is independent of the senses, it can hardly be deemed *internal* to the mind. Since independent, external existence is just Hume's definition of distinct existence, he was justified in asserting that "the opinion of the *continu'd* existence of body ... is prior to that of its *distinct* existence, and produces that latter principle" (*T* 199). But how can we still regard something as the same object if there is any variation during an interruption in its perception? Hume's answer is that identity can be preserved through change if the variations exhibit *coherence*, that is, a regular causal dependence on one another. Past experience leads us to associate events in *chains* of causal relations: *Z* is found to occur only if preceded by *Y*, *Y* only if preceded by *X*, *X* by *W*, etc. Thus, if I am witness first to *W* and then, after an interruption, *Z*, I can only reconcile this with my past experience by supposing *X* and *Y* to have existed unperceived by my senses (this, after all, was for Hume the *raison d'être* of causal relations: they extend verisimilar reality beyond the senses and memory – see chapter 4-A). But if, in addition, *Z*, *Y*, *X*, *W*, etc., (i) resemble more closely those perceptions nearer to them in the sequence than those farther, and (ii) all share the same or similar relations of contiguity and causation to perceptions outside the sequence, the passage of thought from one to the next is apt to feel so smooth and easy to imagination that it will be inclined to confound it with the contemplation of a single, invariable and uninterrupted object ("The smooth and uninterrupted progress of the thought, being alike in both cases, readily deceives the mind, and makes us ascribe an identity to the changeable succession of connected qualities," *T*220). Coherence so great as to induce the imagination to mistake the continuation of a like *relation* of ideas for the continuation of the same *idea* suffices to preserve an identity through almost any amount of variation. Hence, though *Z* may have no resemblance to *P*, if the transitions from *Y* to *X*, *X* to *W*, ..., and *Q* to *P*, are sufficiently smooth, the imagination will join *Z* with *P*, together with the intervening states, in a relation of (imperfect) identity. Furthermore, if these transitions are invested with the authority of experience and custom, then, even if none save *Z* and *P* are perceived, it will still be inclined to unite them by identity. Thus does our belief in a continued, distinct existence of an object survive even great variation (the beeswax in Descartes' Second Meditation is a good example; yet, Hume undermines Descartes' argument by eliminating the need for a distinct faculty of intellect over and above associative imagination).

C. Philosophical fallacies of double existence

Although Hume chose to entitle the section in which he placed his account of identity "Scepticism with regard to the senses," one meets little in the way of skepticism until its final pages, where the focus shifts from the vulgar to the philosophical notion of body. Philosophy (which, in Hume's sense, includes what we call "science") is here synonymous with reason; and, since reason, in matters of fact, means *causal* reasoning, skepticism regarding the vulgar notion of body is grounded in causal inference. Hume stated on two previous occasions that causality speaks against the belief in continued, distinct existence: first in dealing with reason (*T*193) and then with imagination (*T*197). Nevertheless, only upon concluding his account of the vulgar belief in body did he marshall it in the service of philosophical skepticism.

It was quite natural for Hume to set his sights on the vulgar belief that constant, coherent perceptions are *causally independent* of the senses (as he forewarned on *T*191). Earlier, having found that the senses cannot support the vulgar belief that certain sensations are independent of our sense organs and their nature, he proceeded to show how the imagination can produce it through experience and observation. But then, having done so, he doffs his vulgar habit, dons philosopher's raiment, and proceeds to maintain that experience contradicts this belief:

> When we press one eye with a finger, we immediately perceive all the objects to become double, and one half of them to be remov'd from their common and natural position. But as we do not attribute a continu'd existence to both these perceptions, and as they are both of the same nature, we clearly perceive, that all our perceptions are dependent on our organs, and the disposition of our nerves and animal spirits. This opinion is confirm'd by the seeming encrease and diminution of objects, according to their distance; by the apparent alterations in their figure; by the changes in their colour and other qualities from our sickness and distempers; and by an infinite number of other experiments of the same kind; from all which we learn, that our sensible perceptions are not possest of any distinct or independent existence. (*T*210f.)

The dependence here in question is dependence on the *body*, not the mind. Clearly, it suited Hume's purpose to advance the most modest kind of philosophical argument ("philosophical" only in the eighteenth-century sense, when natural sciences were apt to be so denominated). Optical and physiological considerations of this sort, along with the mutual entailment between continued and distinct existence, seemed to him quite sufficient to prove to any *reasonable* person – anyone willing to defer to the verdict of *experience* (= *custom*, *causal* explanation) – that the vulgar opinion is false ("our sensible perceptions are not possest of any distinct or independent existence").

Reasons for asserting dependence on the *mind* are advanced on *T*226, *T*230f., and *T*372ff. In the *Enquiry*, the two steps are collapsed (see *E*XII/i.118). The more careful reasoning is that of the *Treatise*: the only thing Hume needed to establish in order to refute the vulgar belief in the independence of external objects (= constant/coherent impressions) is their dependence on an observer, where it is left indeterminate whether the observer is a body, a mind/body, or a mind. In fact, Hume was far more careful in these matters than sometimes is supposed, and certainly more so than Locke or Berkeley:

Were I not afraid of appearing too philosophical, I should remind my reader of that famous doctrine, supposed to be fully proved in modern times, "That tastes and colours, and all other sensible qualities, lie not in the bodies, but merely in the senses." The case is the same with beauty and deformity, virtue and vice. This doctrine, however, takes off no more from the reality of the latter qualities, than from that of the former; nor need it give any umbrage either to critics or moralists. Though colours were allowed to lie only in the eye, would dyers or painters ever be less regarded or esteemed? There is a sufficient uniformity in the senses and feelings of mankind, to make all these qualities the objects of art and reasoning, and to have the greatest influence on life and manners. And as it is certain, that the discovery above-mentioned in natural philosophy, makes no alteration on action and conduct; why should a like discovery in moral philosophy make any alteration? (*EMPL*XVIII.166n.)

Hume's arguments against vulgar belief rest not on idealism, but on common experience of the organs of sense buttressed by natural science. He makes no pretence that this suffices also to refute the philosophical view; his aim is simply to establish the falsity of the opinion of the vulgar with pretensions as modest as possible (i.e. innocent of philosophical complications because restricted to the physical). Yet, this reasoning, too, is founded on imagination: not only because, in asserting *dependence*, it presupposes the idea of cause, but also, by setting up the sense organs and brain for the same treatment as other objects of sight and touch, it sets all impressions and ideas on a par and converts the dependence into one on *mind* (as a system of causally linked perceptions and as that which precedes and makes possible the idea of an external object). Scientific reasoning also depends on imagination for its distinctions of reason between primary and secondary qualities – differences that, according to Hume, resolve into habitudes of comparison with an eye to resemblances. Nor is this all: since mind itself is nothing but a connected heap of perceptions, the true stopping point of philosophical reason is the flux of perceptions prior to their relation in imagination – which undoubtedly is why it is the *starting*-point of the *Treatise*.

Other philosophers did not venture so far. Nevertheless, as persons who purport to be guided by reason, the experience-based arguments against the vulgar opinion oblige them to find an alternative satisfactory to reason. Accordingly, "they change their system, and distinguish ... betwixt perceptions and objects, of which the former are suppos'd to be interrupted, and perishing, and different at every different return; the latter to be uninterrupted, and to preserve a continu'd existence and identity" (*T*211). Hume christened this the *double existence view* and proceeded forthwith to dash any hopes we might be tempted to place in it. Double existence is a mere "palliative remedy," with "no primary recommendation, either to reason or the imagination" (*T*211); and, since "the philosophical system acquires all its influence on the imagination from the vulgar one" (*T*213), its persuasive power is wholly parasitic on the vulgar view. Of course, the "reason" to which it has no recommendation is again *causal imagination*, and Hume's case to this effect derives directly from his earlier analysis of causal relations:

> The only conclusion we can draw from the existence of one thing to that of another, is by means of the relation of cause and effect, which shews, that there is a connexion betwixt them, and that the existence of one is dependent on that of the other. The idea of this relation is deriv'd from past experience, by which we find, that two beings are constantly conjoin'd together, and are always present at once to the mind. But as no beings are ever present to the mind but perceptions; it follows that we may observe a conjunction or a relation of cause and effect between different perceptions, but can never observe it between perceptions and objects. 'Tis impossible, therefore, that from the existence or any of the qualities of the former, we can ever form any conclusions concerning the existence [or qualities] of the latter, or ever satisfy our reason in this particular. (*T*212; bracketed insert from *T*216)

A causal inference is a transition of thought from one perception to another; where there is no perception, there can be no transition to it, no customary determination of the imagination, no conjunction of ideas, nor anything at all that might feel to imagination like a relation of ideas. Since the thesis that sense impressions are the effects of *imperceptible* objects violates precisely this requirement, it expresses an impossibility – a relation lacking a relative – and so is empty. Even if it were not, with no idea of the unperceived object for imagination to enliven, how could it ever be believed really to exist? The double existence view is neither conceivable nor believable by custom-governed imagination; nor, given its "abstractedness and difficulty" (*T*213), can it be supposed to be rooted in non-causal forms of imaginative association either. So how do philosophers convince themselves of it? Its acceptance requires one to believe that the table he touches, the people he sees gathered around him, the wine he rolls across his tongue, and the money in his wallet the waiter expects him to hand over afterwards are all mere perceptions, no more external to, and independent of, his mind than the pleasantness of the flavor, the thoughts running through his head, or his feeling of well-being. This certainly does not come easily to the imagination; it is unnatural, strained, difficult. But then he is reassured to learn that the real imperceptible objects which cause the perceptions are characterized by the same qualities of constancy and coherence vulgarly supposed to be found in sense impressions themselves. It thus "pleases our reason, in allowing, that our dependent perceptions are interrupted and different; and at the same time is agreeable to the imagination, in attributing a continu'd existence to something else, which we call *objects*" (*T*215). The surprising result of Hume's analysis is that "the philosophical system acquires all its influence on the imagination from the vulgar one" (*T*213).

The vulgar opinion derives directly from human nature: "[it] has taken such deep root in the imagination, that 'tis impossible ever to eradicate it, nor will any strain'd metaphysical conviction of the dependence of our perceptions be sufficient for that purpose" (*T*214). Hume will grant that, while philosophical (including physiological) reflections remain fresh in our minds, they create a certain resistance to our natural inclinations. At such times, our imaginations seek relief from the discomfort of being drawn in different directions at once, and cast about for some conciliating hypothesis to restore harmony. This, in Hume's day, was more than likely to be double existence (in our own time too, though some contemporary philosophers are more inclined to find solace in the sanctity of ordinary language):[14]

> by which means we can humour our reason for a moment, when it becomes troublesome and sollicitous; and yet upon its least negligence or inattention, can return to our vulgar and natural notions. Accordingly, we find, that philosophers neglect not this advantage; but immediately upon leaving their closets, mingle with the rest of mankind in those exploded opinions, that our perceptions are our only objects, and continue identically and uninterruptedly the same in all their interrupted appearances. (*T*216)

Nevertheless, all is in vain: this "monstrous offspring of two principles, which are contrary to each other" (*T*215), is subject to "all the difficulties of the vulgar system, with some others, that are peculiar to itself" (*T*211). For, besides being parasitic on the vulgar single existence view for both the conception and the belief in continued, distinct existences, it

> is over-and-above loaded with this absurdity, that it at once denies and establishes the vulgar supposition. Philosophers deny our resembling perceptions to be identically the same, and uninterrupted; and yet have so great a propensity to believe them such, that they arbitrarily invent a new set of perceptions, to which they attribute these qualities. I say, a new set of perceptions: For we may well suppose in general, but 'tis impossible for us distinctly to conceive, objects to be in their nature any thing but exactly the same with perceptions. What then can we look for from this confusion of groundless and extraordinary opinions but error and falshood? And how can we justify to ourselves any belief we repose in them? (*T*218)

Consciously or not, philosophers realize that to have a causal relation it is necessary to have ideas of both terms in the relation. Since the sole things of which we have ideas are our own perceptions, the only way they can regard their impressions as effects of imperceptible objects is by tacitly equating objects with their perceptions so as to have some idea of them (they would have their cake and eat it too). Intellectual honesty ought to bring them to admit that they lack any idea of such objects and so cannot even conceive, much less believe, that our perceptions are causally related to them. In that case, one who would refrain from transforming objects into a second set of perceptions (by not extending to them the qualities and relations of sense impressions) might still "suppose in general" (*T*218) their existence. But this concession is as barren, of as "little consequence to the world," as that made in *Treatise* I/iii to those who "please to call *power* or *efficacy*" those qualities "with which we are utterly unacquainted" (*T*168). Moreover, Hume claimed to "have already shewn its absurdity" (*T*188). For to suppose objects absolutely incommensurate with perceptions is to say we have no idea of them whatsoever. No idea means that no transition from perceptions to objects in thought is possible, and thence no relation of any kind, causal or otherwise; and with nothing to which sense impressions may send idea-enlivening imagination, it is as impossible to believe in such objects as to conceive of them (at least the double existence view, with its second set of perceptions, furnishes the imagination ideas it might enliven). Hume left no doubt as to his low opinion of the inconceivable supposition theory: "Bereave matter of all its intelligible qualities, both primary and secondary, you in a manner annihilate it, and leave only a certain unknown, inexplicable *something*, as the cause of our perceptions; a notion so imperfect, that no sceptic will think it worth while to contend against it" (*E*XII/i.123).

Many commentators, most persuasively Wilson, nevertheless maintain that Hume was a partisan of the philosophical system against the vulgar:

> Hume's argument is one which assumes the existence of sense organs, nerves, animal spirits, etc. that is, to put it briefly, *it accepts realism* ... Hume's argument is from such phenomena as the appearance of double images when the eye is pressed in a certain way. But its concern is not to establish subjectivism or scepticism; rather, it is to establish something about the *causal status* of sensed impressions. Moreover, Hume clearly takes it to be a *sound causal inference*. Indeed, the sceptical reading of Hume must also take it to be a sound causal inference ... The point is that reasoning *within* the system of the vulgar will lead one *outside* that system to another, contrary, system ... What the system of the philosophers does better than that of the vulgar is introduce greater coherence among the sensed impressions ... The two systems disagree in the predications they make ... and it is the system of the philosophers that yields the better predictions, and thereby introduces greater coherence.[15]

Wilson's interpretation depends crucially on the sentence which follows the paragraph retailing the experiments (for example, eyeball pressing) Hume supposes to prove "that our sensible perceptions are not possest of any distinct of independent existence":

> The natural consquence of this reasoning shou'd be, that our perceptions have no more a continu'd than an independent existence; and indeed philosophers have so far run into this opinion, that they change their system, and distinguish, (as we shall do for the future) betwixt perceptions and objects, of which the former are suppos'd to be interrupted, and perishing, and different at every different return; the latter to be uninterrupted, and to preserve a continu'd existence and identity. (*T*211)

Wilson is not dissuaded from taking this as an affirmation of the view of philosphers by Hume's remark that "however philosophical this system may be esteem'd, I assert that 'tis only a palliative remedy and contains all the difficulties of the vulgar system, with some others, that are peculiar to itself" (see also *T*214). One must admit the sentence is hardly pellucid. As I read it, Hume and the philosophers agree that perceptions are neither independent nor external. But there the agreement ends: he will no more have truck with their inference to *imperceptible* causes of perceptions than with their supposition that these causes have continued existence and identity. Note first that Hume calls his proofs that impressions are not independent or external *experiments*. This is because they are purely observational. For example, nothing imperceptible, present or implied, enters into the conjunction of the tactile *impression* of a pressure on the eyeball with the doubling of one's visual impression in a relation of cause and effect. Nerves, animal spirits, etc., are likewise known only as sense impressions (any "unknown" causes mentioned in such contexts, for example, a theorized enzyme catalyst, are conceived – i.e. imagined – from materials scavenged from data previously collected from sensation and reflexion, and so still count as observables). Is this realism? Not at all:

> our own body evidently belongs to us; and as several impressions appear exterior to the body, we suppose them also exterior to ourselves... But to prevent this inference, we need only weigh [the following consideration]... That, properly speaking, 'tis not our body we perceive, when we regard our limbs and members, but certain impressions, which enter by the senses; so that the ascribing a real and corporeal existence to these impressions, or to their objects, is an act of the mind as difficult to explain, as that which we examine at present. (*T*190f.)

When, by eyeball pressing and such like, one discovers that impressions one vulgarly supposes to be distinct, continued existents *vis à vis* certain other impressions (= one's own body) are in fact not so, the *proper inference* is that the former are dependent on the latter in the same (vulgar) sense pains and pleasures are (see *T*192); it furnishes no warrant whatsoever for an inference to *imperceptible* causes. Hume's rejection of the systems of philosophers on the ground "that they arbitrarily invent a new set of perceptions" (*T*218) applies as much to their observationally insupportable inference to a set of imperceptible causes as to their supposition that these causes remain "identically the same, and uninterrupted"; it is the notion of double existence *as such* that he considers a "Confusion of groundless and extraordinary opinions" from which we can expect nothing "but error and falshood." Wilson too recognizes that Hume deemed it "impossible ... from the existence or any of the qualities of [perceptions], we can ever form any conclusion concerning the existence [or qualities – *T*216] of [objects], or ever satisfy our reason in this particular" (*T*212). But, once we further acknowledge that Hume undermined the vulgar fictions of external objects by relying solely on experience-based causal inferences of the very same kind familiar to the family dog, we can see that Wilson has no basis for his claim "that reasoning *within* the system of the vulgar will lead one *outside* that system to another." The opinion which bears the imprimatur of reason (causal inference) is not that of philosophers – it can never be reasonable, in Hume's sense, to infer a cause where no conjunction of perceptions can be observed and no customary transition of ideas is possible – but one as vulgar as the belief in the external, independent existence of constant, coherent impressions it contradicts. Nothing besides impressions and their experience-based, associative relations are involved; nor can we ever, in this or any manner, reason our way *outside* the sphere of perceptions. The conflict is therefore between two equally natural (vulgar) and irresistible beliefs, in which incompatible relations are ascribed to the same impressions:

> tho' these two operations be equally natural and necessary in the human mind, yet in some circumstances they are directly contrary, nor is it possible for us to reason justly and regularly from causes and effects, and at the same time believe the continu'd existence of matter. (*T*266)[16]

I even cannot agree with Wilson that Hume would endorse the view that "the system of the philosophers ... yields the better predictions, and thereby introduces greater coherence." For on which system do we rely in all the judgments of daily life, whose predictive powers therein are matchless, and whose seamless coherence gives our lives their very shape? Even in the laboratory or classroom, we rely on the vulgar system in manipulating pen and paper, walking to and fro, shifting a chair, exchanging views over E-mail, etc. Far from suspending belief in the vulgar system while engaged in philosophy or science, we might more aptly be said to suspend our non-belief in the philosophical (actually, the physical sciences are "philosophical" not because of any commitment to double existence, but because of their heavy reliance on philosophical rather than natural relations).[17] The vulgar view has human nature on its side: our propensity to believe our constant, coherent sense impressions to be continued, distinct existents is far too strong to be countered by the pressing of an eyeball or neurobiological considerations, much less the relative ideas and other speculative fancies of metaphysicians. We thus cannot doubt it even if we would: "Nature has not left this to [our] choice, and has doubtless esteem'd it an affair of too great importance to be trusted to our uncertain reasonings and speculations" (*T*187; see also *E*XII/i.118).[18]

D. The identity of substances

Another species of continued, distinct existent that concerned Hume was substance. Unlike bodies which, whether vulgarly or philosophically conceived, admit of (coherent) change, substances are supposed to be simple and invariable. Since nothing of the kind is actually met with in perception (save simple perceptions themselves), substantial identity is the antipode to personal: invariable but permanently interrupted (i.e. imperceptible). Having already discredited the notion of substance early in the *Treatise*, Hume's concern in I/iv/§§3–5 was simply to identify the quirks of human nature that lend credibility to this supposition in the eyes of its non-vulgar exponents (philosophers, theologians). It gains a foothold through the coherence of changes in an identical object, which "deceives the mind, and makes us ascribe an identity to the changeable succession of connected qualities" (*T*220). Discomfited by the supposition of identity in the presence of change, the more reflective imagination, unlike the vulgar, seeks to rationalize it away, and "In order to reconcile which contradiction the imagination is apt to feign something unknown and invisible, which it supposes to continue the same under all these variations; and this unintelligible something it calls a *substance, or original and first matter*" (*T*220). It also cannot rest easy in ascribing simplicity to an object that manifestly consists of many parts and qualities (albeit bound together by so close and strong a relation that its contemplation feels the same as the contemplation of something really simple and indivisible). The reflective imagination will therefore "feign an unknown something, or *original* substance and matter, as a principle of union or cohesion among these qualities, and as what may give the compound object a title to be call'd one thing, notwithstanding its diversity and composition" (*T*221). Though these words are without any meaning, "it naturally happens, that after the frequent use of terms, which are wholly insignificant and unintelligible, we fancy them ... to have a secret meaning, which we might discover by reflection ... By this means these philosophers set themselves at ease, and arrive at last, by an illusion, at the same indifference, which the people attain by their stupidity, and true philosophers by their moderate scepticism" (*T*224; see also *T*72).

Modern philosophers pretend to be able to reclaim substances from their fallen state by dispensing with the occult notions of their ancient forebears and (i) relying solely on clear and distinct ideas, and (ii) reasoning strictly in accordance with "the solid, permanent, and consistent principles of the imagination" (*T*226). Hume attacked this pretense at what he considered its weakest point: the distinction between primary and secondary qualities. Though he agreed with the moderns' belief that "many of our impressions have no external model or archetype" (*T*227; see also *E*XII/i.119), he denied their claims that some at least do. To demonstrate this, he took his cue from Berkeley (see *PHK* §10) and simply held them to their word: if "colours, sounds, tastes, and smells be merely perceptions, nothing we can conceive is possest of a real, continu'd, and independent existence; not even motion extension and solidity, which are the primary qualities chiefly insisted on" (*T*228). That is, if all the visual, tactile, and other sensible properties of bodies are excluded, how can we continue to imagine motion, extension, or solidity? Only if humans had a real capacity of abstraction (instead of mere habitudes of resemblance) could the supposition that there are insensible, unimaginable entities characterized by primary qualities even be *conceived*, let alone *confirmed*. But, once we concede there is no such capacity, we must conclude that primary qualities are every bit as internal and dependent as secondary; and so, for the same reasons the latter are supposed not to resemble anything in the nature of substances, we are obliged to acknowledge that the former, too, can teach us nothing of their nature ("We have no perfect idea of any thing but of a perception. A substance is entirely different from a perception. We have, therefore, no idea of a substance," *T*234). Thus, modern philosophy finds itself trapped in the following predicament:

> there is a direct and total opposition betwixt our reason and our senses; or more properly speaking, betwixt those conclusions we form from cause and effect, and those that persuade us of the continu'd and independent existence of body. When we reason from cause and effect, we conclude, that neither colour, sound, taste, nor smell have a continu'd and independent existence. When we exclude these sensible qualities there remains nothing in the universe, which has such an existence. (*T*231)

Having dispatched the thesis that substances *resemble* the perceptions they are supposed to cause, Hume concluded his analysis of substance with the philosophical view that perceptions *inhere* in a substance, whether material or immaterial. Turning first to the substance of the mind (i.e. the supposed soul-substrate underlying both personal identity and the system of related successive perceptions that constitutes it), he argued that our idea of this is no clearer than that we have of the substance underlying body. Had we an impression of the soul, it could not represent it otherwise than by resembling it; yet, "how can an impression resemble a substance, since, according to this philosophy, it is not a substance, and has none of the peculiar qualities or characteristics of a substance?" (*T*233). Even if this difficulty is ignored, we would still be at a loss to say *which* impression it resembles: "Is it an impression of sensation or of reflection? Is it pleasant, or painful, or indifferent? Does it attend us at all times, or does it only return at intervals? If at intervals, at what times principally does it return, and by what causes is it produc'd?" (*T*233). If, to avoid the challenge to produce an impression corresponding to the idea of the soul, we were to resort to the vacuous definition that "a substance is *something which may exist by itself*," then, since each and every one of our perceptions would satisfy this definition, the only possible conclusion is that they stand in need of nothing to support their existence:

> since all our perceptions are different from each other, and from every thing else in the universe, they are also distinct and separable, and may be consider'd as separately existent, and may exist separately, and have no need of any thing else to support their existence. They are, therefore, substances, as far as this definition explains a substance. (*T*233; see *T*244 and *T*252)

Hume then scrutinizes the dualist thesis that "Thought ... and extension are qualities wholly incompatible, and never can incorporate together into one subject" (*T*235). While it may do nothing to bring clarity to our notion of the *substance* of the mind, it does at least imply that no modification of a soul (i.e. perceptions) can be a modification of a material substance, and that mind (consciousness) can therefore exist even in the absence of body (just as there can be body in the absence of mind). Yet, in Hume's view, the dualist thesis collapses if the only idea of necessary connection on which it can draw is that derived from customary associations founded on constant precedence. For our only idea of cause is that of a customary transition founded on constant precedence; hence, if, sensations lacking extension, reflexions, or thoughts are found to enter into relations of constant precedence with extended sensations, then causal relations between them not only are possible, but will command our belief as well:

> If you pretend ... to prove *a priori*, that such a position of bodies can never cause thought; because turn it which way you will, 'tis nothing but a position of bodies; you must by the same course of reasoning conclude, that it can never produce motion; since there is no more apparent connexion in the one case than in the other. But as this latter conclusion is contrary to evident experience, and as 'tis possible we may have a like experience in the operations of the mind, and may perceive a constant conjunction of thought and motion; you reason too hastily, when from the mere consideration of the ideas, you conclude that 'tis impossible motion can ever produce thought, or a different position of parts give rise to a different passion or reflexion. Nay 'tis not only possible we may have such an experience, but 'tis certain we have it; since every one may perceive, that the different dispositions of his body change his thoughts and sentiments ... [W]e find

> by comparing their ideas, that thought and motion are different from each other, and by experience, that they are constantly united; which being all the circumstances, that enter into the idea of cause and effect, when apply'd to the operations of matter, we may certainly conclude, that motion may be, and actually is, the cause of thought and perception. (*T*247f.)

Since the division of substance into material and immaterial is predicated on the supposed impossibility of any non-supernatural causal connection between them, it thus is quite groundless. And "What is unknown, we must be contented to leave so" (*T*232).

Conclusion
The Cartesian nightmare come true

> No conclusions can be more agreeable to scepticism than such as make discoveries concerning the weakness and narrow limits of human reason and capacity. *E*VII/ii.59

> This sceptical doubt, both with respect to reason and the senses, is a malady, which can never be radically cur'd, but must return upon us every moment, however we may chace it away, and sometimes may seem entirely free from it. *T*218

> Errors in religion are dangerous; those in philosophy only ridiculous. *T*272

In the concluding section of *An Enquiry Concerning Human Understanding* – "Of the Academical or Sceptical Philosophy" – Hume offered the following description of Cartesian skepticism:

> There is a species of scepticism, *antecedent* to all study and philosophy, which is much inculcated by Des Cartes and others, as a sovereign preservative against error and precipitate judgment. It recommends an universal doubt, not only of all our former opinions and principles, but also of our very faculties; of whose veracity, say they, we must assure ourselves, by a chain of reasoning, deduced from some original principle, which cannot possibly be fallacious or deceitful. But neither is there any such original principle, which has a prerogative above others, that are self-evident and convincing: or if there were, could we advance a step beyond it, but by the use of those very faculties, of which we are supposed to be already diffident. (*E*XII/i.116)

Cartesian doubt, as Hume understood it, has at its focal point human nature itself ("our very faculties"). Its prime concern is not to adduce possible grounds for doubting this or that proposition, or class of propositions, but rather, in a single stroke, to put all knowledge in doubt by questioning the soundness of the instrument whereby it is attained, viz. the human mind. If through "fate or chance or a continuous chain of events, or by some other means,"[1] this instrument were defective, or even inimical to apprehending things truly, then precisely that which our understanding apprehended most clearly and distinctly, and seemed to us most indubitable, would, *ipso facto*, be false.

Whether this depiction of Cartesian skepticism is accurate may be doubted,[2] but it does seem to have been the way Hume thought it should be understood; and, since he saw fit to define his own skepticism, as consequent, in contrast to Descartes' antecedent variety, his view of it calls for close examination. It is a uniquely hellish vision of Cartesian doubt: instead of tormenting us from without, the malicious demon lies *within* us – indeed *is* us, our very being. Even the fact that it is quite beyond our power to believe, or even seriously entertain, the possibility that our natures are so rotten as to tend invariably towards error and away from truth merely enhances the horror. For it means that not only is escape from our predicament impossible, but our flawed natures, bent as they are on falsehood and self-deception, render us so incurably complacent that we are prevented even from *seeking* a way out (i.e. lacking the capacity to believe this of ourselves, we are powerless not to persist in "our former opinions and principles"). And, while Descartes himself relied on God to restore confidence in our native ability to distinguish truth from falsehood, Hume thought it futile to invoke a *deus ex machina* "by the use of those very faculties, of which we are supposed to be already diffident."[3]

Hume raised the spectre of a human nature tending naturally towards error only to dash it to pieces. He would have no truck with extreme forms of skepticism regarding human nature, whether antecedent to, or consequent upon, scientific inquiry. Yet, though his moderation was genuine, its warrant must be carefully scrutinized if we are not to misconstrue or exaggerate it. Above all, we must not assume, simply because a skepticism is denominated "mitigated" (*E*XII/iii.129ff.), that it is milquetoast. In my view, no interpretation of Hume's skepticism can be credited which would have us suppose that, upon surveying the results of his study of human knowledge, he suddenly grew timorous and desired to "mitigate" the skeptical implications of his analyses of causality, identity, real existence, and space and time by either backpedalling or willfully blinding himself to their consequences. The proper procedure for Hume's interpreter is not, as many seem to believe, to make the rest of his philosophy answer to whatever one supposes "mitigated" to mean, but to try to understand how skeptical moderation can be conceived in the aftermath of his analysis of human understanding.

The scene of that aftermath, as Kant and others have averred, is one of utter devastation, equal to the worst Cartesian nightmare.[4] For example, Hume's examination of identity, with its many references to the infallibility of immediate consciousness, seems to lead to the conclusion not merely that our belief in body *may* be false, but that it most *certainly* is. For, if it is inconceivable "that our senses shou'd be more capable of deceiving us in the situation and relations, than in the nature of our impressions" (*T*190), it follows that we not only *can* but *do* know – and know *infallibly* – that the objects immediately present to consciousness are *not* the continued, distinct existents our imaginations represent them to be. This is not to deny that their continued, distinct existence "is a point, which we must take for granted in all our reasonings," and even the skeptic "must assent to the principle concerning the existence of body" since "Nature has not left this to his choice, and has doubtless esteem'd it an affair of too great importance to be trusted to our uncertain reasonings and speculations" (*T*187). Yet, since the true situation and relations of our perceptions are at the same time always immediately before us, we cannot help observing, and so believing, that this irresistible natural belief is nevertheless a mere "fallacy and illusion" (*T*189). So, too, everything else human nature compels us to believe which, according to Hume, rests solely on "the imagination, or the vivacity of our ideas" (*T*265): our particular causal inferences, the general causal maxim, natural kinds, the mind, space and time, and even the application of demonstrative reason. In all these cases, it is not simply that we can *conceive the possibility* that our natural beliefs are fictitious, but that we *know* them to *be* so. For what interpreters seem almost invariably to overlook in their analyses of Hume's skeptical theses is that each involves a clash between two kinds of *equally natural and irresistible belief*: one founded on the senses (immediate consciousness) and the other on imagination (relation, association).[5] As with belief founded on imagination, "the *belief* or *assent*, which always attends the ... senses, is nothing but the vivacity of those perceptions they present" (*T*86). Since vivacity, according to Hume, is merely a feeling rooted in human nature like any other, this means that the certainty attaching to immediate consciousness itself – the infallibility of the awareness whereby the natural beliefs of imagination are disclosed to be one and all mere natural illusions – is entirely a function of human nature, and so likewise a hostage to it. Accordingly, our natures condemn us, without possibility of reprieve, to know the falsehood of that which we are powerless to disbelieve; and what is this if not the Cartesian nightmare come true?

The position I ascribe to Hume should not be mistaken for a negative dogmatism (i.e. denial of reality to bodies, causes, etc.). It is a genuine skepticism, defined by the clash of natural, equally irresistible beliefs. Its foundation stone is the thesis that all belief, including that founded on immediate consciousness, is vivacity (verisimilitude), and all vivacity belief, including that of impressions. For, if we take Hume at his word, the sheer factual presence of perceptions before consciousness is inadequate to yield belief, infallible or otherwise, without an accompanying feeling of vivacity: this feeling alone induces us to regard sensations and reflexions as real existents in the highest degree (= impressions), while only owing to its weakness do we treat thoughts (the effects of association aside) as mere conceptions (= ideas). Yet, Hume scholars, if they think about it at all, simply assume that Hume either failed to see any need to account for belief founded on immediate consciousness or conceived of it differently from belief founded on imagination. I have contended that this is not the case (see chapters 1-B and -E, 2-A, 4-C, and 6-B), and hope at least to have put the ball in the other court. Without their assumption that belief founded on immediate consciousness is somehow "unnatural" and "merely philosophical," the (snowballing) trend in Hume scholarship to downgrade the skepticism, or virtually discard it altogether, would be a non-starter. For it could not be sustained were it acknowledged that what conflicts with natural beliefs of imagination are not mere conceptual possibilities, but other, equally imperative, natural beliefs founded on immediate consciousness prior to, and independently of, the relating and enlivening of ideas in imagination.

In my view, there is in Hume a kind of natural dialectic no less irresolvable than that attributed to reason by Kant. The infallibility of immediate consciousness consists of nothing but the phenomenological feeling of vivacity, in an irresistibly high degree. No matter how much the imagination may enliven ideas in accordance with our native associative propensities, it is quite impossible for it to override or obliterate the conviction naturally reposed in the verdicts of immediate consciousness. A myth "the given" may be, but not for Hume: far from treating these verdicts as byproducts of philosophical reflection, he gives every indication of having deemed them evident to everyone at some (perhaps oyster-like) level of perception; the philosopher then merely articulates their consequences. In particular, I think Hume would deny that anyone is altogether unaware, even if he never reasons out the consequences, (i) that belief (vivacity) is neither a perception nor a quality of perceptions (i.e. the objects of consciousness), but a feeling in our consciousness of them, a primitive prototype of intentional attitudes; (ii) that all our perceptions are distinct, independent existents (i.e. no ties of existential dependence bind them); (iii) that perceptions consist of temporal, visual, etc., minima; (iv) that a thought remains merely a thought, whatever it may be made out to be in imagination (i.e. believed *thoughts* do not, for that reason, become *sensations* or *reflexions*, even if, as in the madman, they can assume the full vivacity of *impressions*); and (v) that however much vivacity custom may lend to an idea, no idea can elicit quite the degree of belief in real existence as an impression (they only "approach an impression in force and vivacity," *T*119). Since these and other verdicts of immediate consciousness carry the same authority of natural belief as the opinions of associative imagination, natural belief is not the safe haven from conflict interpreters of a naturalist bent suppose. Quite the contrary, Hume's naturalism is the very seed from which the extreme skepticism of the Cartesian nightmare springs.[6]

To concede that Hume's philosophy involves a natural dialectic between the senses and imagination is not to admit that he himself saw it that way. In the view of many, the philosophical reflection which artificially sets one belief beside the other (to generate actual contradictions of the form P & ~ P) is precisely the sort that seemed to him "so cold, and strain'd, and ridiculous, that I cannot find in my heart to enter into them any farther ... I must yield to the current of nature, in submitting to my senses and understanding; and in this blind submission I shew most perfectly my sceptical disposition and principles" (*T*269). When the heat in the philosophical kitchen becomes too intense, the remedy is "to live, and talk, and act like other people in the common affairs of life" (*T*269). Yet, if this proves anything at all, it is only that the natural tendency of our intellects is not towards truth, as Descartes supposed, but our own ease and comfort. More importantly, far from being endorsed by Hume, he deemed this desire for solace in society nothing more than "the sentiments of my spleen and indolence" (*T*270). Inclinations to ease and comfort are counter-balanced by the equally natural impulses of curiosity: "'tis almost impossible for the mind of man to rest, like those of beasts, in that narrow circle of objects, which are the subject of daily conversation and action" (*T*271). This is simply another way of saying that philosophical speculation is as natural and satisfying an activity for human beings as dining, gaming, and conversation. For, "Where reason is lively, and mixes itself with some propensity, it ought to be assented to" (*T*270); to deny it and rest forever at the level of given appearances and customs, as Pyrrhonists prescribe, is no less contrary to human nature than the endeavor to conduct one's life in accordance with the principles of the most extreme solipsistic idealism. Accordingly, while there is, and can be, no *resolution* to conflicts in which both sides are rooted in human nature and have an equally imperative claim to our assent, our natures likewise prevent us from entirely overlooking or forgetting their existence. They cannot be escaped.

When Hume advocated a mitigated skepticism, I believe it was never his intention to water down in the slightest, much less turn his back upon, the radical skeptical consequences of his analysis of human understanding (i.e. the natural illusions and antinomies it exposes). Skepticism of the garden variety (sober mistrust of improbable claims, avoid fanaticism, etc.) is fine for the greater part of mankind who, not given to sustained philosophical inquiry, lack any clear, articulate recognition that their natures impel them into the embrace of wholly contradictory, equally unrenouncable beliefs. But for more reflective individuals, and above all for readers of the

Treatise, this simply will not do. Once having tasted the apple – i.e. once contradictory conjunctions of natural beliefs have been formed and the genie is out of the bottle – things can never be quite the same again. The skepticism which slowly engulfs the reader of the first book of the *Treatise* is not a product of wild dreams or intoxicated visions (and in that sense is no nightmare) but of cold, hard reflections emblematic of reason at its soberest and most vigilant: reason determined at all costs to remain true to sound, wakeful experience and to be guided exclusively by "principles which are permanent, irresistable, and universal" (*T*225). These twin resolves reflect reasoning at its most natural, in closest conformity with the bases of human nature itself; but precisely because this is so, Hume's despair when observation and the permanent principles of human reasoning are found to conflict is all the more understandable. I cannot believe that his intent was that this result be ignored or discounted. The true import of his counsel that we mitigate our skepticism, as I see it, is that, while ever remaining cognizant of the illusory, antinomial character of our natural beliefs, we retain our composure and be content to let nature take its course, never refusing "any innocent satisfaction, which offers itself, upon account of... our doubts and scruples" (*T*273).

This advice is simply an adaptation for philosophers of what, for Hume, all men are obliged to do anyway. Hume did not, in my view, describe vulgar beliefs as fictions because they fail to live up to some arcane notion of verification or rigor; he did so because they wear their absurdity on their face, and no one's imagination is so blinkered as to escape the testimony of the senses or so complacent as to be entirely comfortable in disregarding it. Belief in the continued existence of body is a case in point. While we can never "take off this biass from the imagination" in favor of continuity, we can also neither fail to notice its own evident absurdity nor its conflict with the verdicts of our senses. The more reflective among us may seek "to justify ourselves this absurdity" through "the notion of a *soul*, and *self*, and *substance*," or simply by imagining "something unknown and mysterious, connecting the parts." But "*even when this does not take place*, we still feel a propensity to confound these ideas, tho' we are not able fully to satisfy ourselves in that particular, nor find any thing invariable and uninterrupted to justify our notion of identity" (*T*254f. – emphasis mine). It would be a gross misunderstanding to object that this misrepresents the situation of ordinary people who never scruple to justify their ideas of identity before employing them. The need for justification arises in a wholly natural manner and is felt by all. For, in addition to reposing the firmest possible belief in the products of imagination, we have no less strong a belief in the immediate evidence of consciousness, which, according to Hume, runs directly counter to the opinion of a continued existence (see *T*188f.). Perpetually confronted with such conflicting evidence, even the least philosophical person cannot help being troubled, albeit inarticulately and without contemplating the consequences, by the absence of a justification for belief in continued existence; and, while our imaginations are amply equipped to fashion illusions to deal with the ensuing discomfort, we must accept that, in the end, they can only tame, not resolve or conceal, conflicts between natural beliefs ("This sceptical doubt, both with respect to reason and the senses, is a malady, which can never be radically cur'd, but must return upon us every moment, however we may chace it away, and sometimes may seem entirely free from it," *T*218).

It is important to recognize that the Cartesian nightmare does not arise simply from the thesis that imagination plays an essential role in the representations of identical objects and causal relations. This origin does not preclude the existence of objects external to this faculty which correspond to these ideas. As traditionally conceived, it is "the faculty of compounding, transposing, augmenting, or diminishing the material afforded us by the senses and experience" (*E*II.13); its involvement in the production of a representation is thus quite compatible with its truth, that is, its correspondence to something existing outside and independently of imagination. However, in adopting this conception, Hume extended it in an entirely unprecedented direction, asserting that imagination not only separates and combines, but *enlivens* ideas as well, and thereby is the basis of many of our most firmly held beliefs ("The memory, senses, and understanding are, therefore, all of them founded on the imagination, or the vivacity of our ideas," *T*265). Moreover, while not the first to attribute association to imagination or to note the feeling of practiced facility characteristic of customary transitions of thought, Hume broke dramatically with precedent by maintaining that this feeling, together with vivacity, constitutes the reflexive impression from which we derive all of our ideas of necessary connection ("this customary transition is ... the same with power and necessity; which are consequently qualities of perceptions, not of objects, and are internally felt by the soul, and not perceiv'd externally in bodies," *T*166); and since "necessity makes an essential part of causation" (*T*407), these feelings are nothing less than the foundation of all our causal inferences, and so all probable reason (see chapter 5-E). Phenomenological feelings are essential not merely to our *belief* in causal relations but to the very *idea* of the relation itself.[7] The same is true of the idea of perfect identity (see *T*200–203) and all the other identities into which it enters: the feelings of vivacity and smooth transitions of thought play a constitutive role in the formation of "the true idea of the human mind" (*T*261), ideas of bodies, substances, organisms, artifacts, institutions, etc. But if true that, for Hume, imaginative feeling is constitutive of everything that enters into objective conception (agency, power, necessary connection, externality, self-subsistence,[8] etc.), it follows that any idea incorporating into its content *feelings* immanent to the *consciousness* of perceptions in imagination (rather than to these *perceptions* themselves) can have neither sense nor significance outside and independently of imagination; that is, anything "corresponding" to such an idea can have reality only in and for "the imagination, or the vivacity of our ideas."

The conflicts among natural beliefs dealt with so far all concern the senses and imagination. However, there seems to be an instance of the Cartesian nightmare even within the precincts of the senses themselves, in respect of the division of perceptions into impressions and ideas (Hume also identified natural conflicts internal to imagination: see *T*231 and *T*266). Here the imagination can have no involvement, for there is as yet no question of the *relation* (combination or separation) of distinct perceptions, nor *a fortiori* of the enlivening of *ideas* through association. Hume made quite clear that this division of perceptions rests solely on a difference in force and vivacity, and so is strictly a matter of immediate consciousness (see chapter 1-A). But this does not mean that vivacity is a quality found in the sensations and reflexions before us. Vivacity here, as in all cases, is simply a feeling, or natural attitude of assent (= belief in real existence), which we have in apprehending sensations and reflexions, but lack when conscious of mere thoughts; it thus pertains not to the perceptions themselves but to our *consciousness* of them (see chapter 1-B). However, if superior vivacity is merely an attitude immanent to the *consciousness* contemplating perceptions, then there is nothing in the actual appearance of thoughts that makes them in any way less "real" than sensations and reflexions, and these latter therefore enjoy no intrinsic advantage over them. In so far as the mere *presence* of perceptions before consciousness is concerned, all are on a par: thoughts are no less "there" than sensations, are perceived just as truly as reflexions, and nothing intrinsic to one sort of perception either privileges or handicaps it in respect of the others. It is solely the native propensity of human consciousness to regard sensations and reflexions with the strongest possible feeling of vivacity that marks them off from thoughts as impressions, realities of maximum verisimilitude; and it is only because our natures do not favor their images in thought with as much of this feeling that they are found to lack verisimilitude (were it not for idea-enlivening imagination, they would never in the least concern us). There thence arises a conflict within the sphere of immediate consciousness itself between what actually *appears* before us and what we immediately *feel* in contemplating it; and, while the former necessarily lacks the force of a genuinely natural belief (since it is considered apart from feelings of vivacity), the absence of any intrinsic mark of reality to demarcate sensations and reflexions from thoughts is at least unsettling to the philosopher who discovers it.

This and the other conflicts we have been considering are all of the same type: a comparison between a consciousness of perceptions informed by certain phenomenological feelings and a consciousness stripped of some or all of these feelings. Since Hume maintained that "Our perceptions are our only objects" (*T*213) and perceptions "must necessarily appear in every particular what they are, and be what they appear" (*T*190), it follows that, for him, the less we allow such feelings to muddle our apprehension of the reality actually before us, the truer our picture of it will be. His skepticism therefore has exactly the same foundation as his naturalistic analysis of human understanding: a pre-imaginative, privileged viewpoint which, by disclosing what it is we *really* are aware of (the given, the successive data, "immediately present to us by consciousness"), permits us to investigate the psychology underpinning natural beliefs (i.e. the causal efficacy and the external objects to which we *believe* ourselves witnesses). The Cartesian nightmare develops directly out of, and is the inevitable consequence of, a naturalism predicated on the ability to poke through the curtain of natural belief and descry, with eyes unblinkered by natural sentiment, the actuality there before us (while stitching up this curtain, as Kant recognized, is a prerequisite for the "refutation of idealism").[9]

Pre-phenomenological consciousness is not itself a skeptical attitude. Skepticism, in all its myriad forms, is a rational proceeding, whose principal concern is reason itself. Skeptics seek "to destroy *reason* by argument and ratiocination" (*E*XII/ii.124). They pit one kind of reasoning against another in order to expose limits and deficiencies: vulgar reason vs. philosophical; reasoning from "principles which are permanent, irresistible, and universal" vs. reasoning from "principles, which are changeable, weak, and irregular" (*T*225); reason as a sovereign capacity subject only to the will vs. the same as "a faculty, which nature has antecedently implanted in the mind, and render'd unavoidable" (*T*183); etc.[10] By contrast, pre-phenomenological consciousness is not a form of reason at all: it judges nothing, takes no positions, and adopts no attitudes (not even the most primitive of all, whereby perceptions are divided into impressions and ideas). Since reason can formulate no position in its name, it furnishes no grist for the skeptic's mill. Nevertheless, it is anything but irrelevant to the skeptic's concerns. Being unencrusted with feelings of vivacity and smooth transition, its position is that of the *object* towards which all intentional attitudes (natural beliefs) are directed, the *presence* with which all other forms of consciousness must be compared. It is unmoved and unmoving, a state of complete indifference, of utter *objectivity*.

Oppositions of the sort on which the skeptic thrives involve reasoning of the most refined, metaphysical variety. Yet, as Hume was no less aware, the same is true of the naturalist who warns us not to engage in an unwinnable combat with human nature. For claims such as that "Nature, by an absolute and uncontroulable necessity has determin'd us to judge as well as to breathe and feel" (*T*183), that all probable reasoning is but "a species of sensation," and that "'Tis not solely in poetry and music, we must follow our taste and sentiment, but likewise in philosophy" (*T*103), are "built on ... reasoning, which will be allow'd to be sufficiently refin'd and metaphysical" (*T*268). Contrary to what many commentators seem to think, in declaring reason a mere instinct in our souls, Hume did not, even in a mitigated way, espouse the Pyrrhonists' counsel to submit oneself to the dictates of vulgar belief. No one was more keenly aware than he that "you expresly contradict yourself" if you seek thereby to "cut off entirely all science and philosophy" since it takes nothing less than all the "refin'd and metaphysical" (*T*268) reasoning of the whole first book of the *Treatise* to arrive at this conclusion! The unavoidability of reliance on the most sophisticated and elaborate argumentation in order to comprehend that even "philosophical decisions are nothing but the reflections of common life methodized and corrected" (*E*XII/iii.130) shows how Hume could be unreservedly robust in his idealism and, at the same time, a defender of the reasonings of common life against the pretensions of metaphysics. Indeed, as I understand him, the lesson he would have us learn from his example is that nothing is better suited to teach us that all reasoning is vulgar than a skeptical philosophy founded on distinctions as recondite as that between pre- and post-phenomenological consciousness, impression and idea, the world of the senses and memory and the world of custom, etc.

It might still be urged against the present interpretation that conflicts such as that between pre- and post-phenomenological consciousness fail the one test that really counts for Hume's philosophy: relevance to common life. Pre- and post-phenomenological consciousness do not conflict in common life. On the contrary, each is the natural *complement* of the other: in the former, we become aware of sensations, reflexions, and thoughts; in the latter, we feel a vivacity (belief in reality) when apprehending sensations and reflexions we do not when contemplating our thoughts, from which results the division of perceptions into impressions and ideas. This, in turn, enables the imagination to associate ideas with impressions, through relations of resemblance and causation, as copies and originals, thereby conveying to the former a measure of the vivacity enjoyed by the latter. With vivacity attaching to ideas, the remainder of

Hume's account of vulgar consciousness develops as naturally as does a seedling into a mature plant: by acquiring habits of comparison, general representation is attained; through custom, verisimilar reality is extended beyond the senses and memory (see *T*73f.); through the identity fiction, perfectly identical unchanging objects are conceived and believed (see *T*203); through natural resemblance, the feeling in imagination of contemplating a succession of *like-related* ideas is confounded with that of repeatedly contemplating the same *idea*, thereby yielding ideas of imperfect identities like the mind and physical objects and an incorrigible belief in an external universe in which we dwell with other human beings. Each of these phases of consciousness naturally dovetails into the next, the two meshing together to make possible yet another, so that the germ of full-fledged human understanding may already be said to be present in pre-associative awareness. So, to try, when doing philosophy, to separate and oppose what is naturally complementary, is to oppose the grain of human nature; it inevitably seems "cold, and strain'd, and ridiculous." Pre-phenomenological consciousness is pre-adapted, by human nature, to *harmonize* with – not *correspond* to – post-vivacity, as are: pre-*representative* consciousness and that for which ideas are copies of impressions; pre-*experiential* consciousness and that informed by custom; pre-*identity* consciousness and that for which reality consists entirely of unchanging objects and their properties and relations. For Hume, human understanding is very much a self-constituting organism, the final outcome of a kind of epigenesis.[11] And, since the seedling is therefore in no sense the blueprint – the preformed homunculus – of the mature human understanding, one may well argue that we do violence to Hume's naturalistic psychology when we read skeptical implications into its beginnings, and so in effect intellectualize the essentially non-intellectual.

Such considerations cannot, however, entirely exorcise the Cartesian demon within us. When adopting the skeptical view, "The attention is on the stretch: The posture of the mind is uneasy; and its spirits being diverted from their natural course, are not govern'd in their movements by the same laws, at least not to the same degree, as when they flow in their usual channel" (*T*185). The vulgar understanding "saves itself from this total scepticism only by means of that singular and seemingly trivial property of the fancy, by which we enter with difficulty into remote views of things" (*T*268). The philosopher, however, braves these obstacles and, by extending vulgar understanding (= "the general and more establish'd properties of the imagination," *T*267) beyond the familiar landmarks of common life, is rewarded with a degree of insight into human understanding – its nature and workings – that otherwise exceeds our reach. Philosophical reasoning, it cannot be emphasized too strongly, is as natural as any other: it exploits exactly the same natural proclivities, is just as causal and observational, as ordinary inferences like that from the odor of smoke to belief in an unseen fire. Taking them to their limits, however, exacts a price: the sobering recognition that it is reason's nature, the very price of its possession, perpetually to fall victim to illusions and irresolvable conflicts – and, seeing this to be so, to be powerless to prevent it.[12] And a final irony: human nature deprives the philosopher of even the satisfaction of a tragic or despairing end: "Most fortunately it happens, that since reason is incapable of dispelling these clouds, nature herself suffices to that purpose, and cures me of this philosophical melancholy and delirium, either by relaxing this bent of mind, or by some avocation, and lively impression of my senses, which obliterate all these chimeras" (*T*269).

If philosophers, too, sometimes succumb to bright fancies, like "those angels, whom the scripture represents as covering their eyes with their wings" (*T*267), a good dose of the "gross earthy mixture" of "honest gentlemen" will cool their "warm imagination" and preserve them from "hypotheses embrac'd merely for being specious and agreeable" (*T*272). We are always at risk of this when, in the throes of "the most elaborate philosophical researches," we are "positive and certain in *particular points*, according to the light, in which we survey them in any *particular instant*" (*T*273); at such times, "we are apt not only to forget our scepticism, but even our modesty too" (*T*274). To check his own susceptibility to such excesses, Hume entered "a *caveat* against any objections, which may be offer'd on that head," avowing "that [certain and positive] expressions were extorted from me by the present view of the object, and imply no dogmatical spirit, nor conceited idea of my own judgment, which are sentiments that I am sensible can become no body, and a sceptic still less than any other" (*T*274). As dogmatism is never more unbecoming than in one who professes himself a skeptic, Hume was severer toward Pyrrhonism than any other species of philosophical excess ("he must acknowledge, if he will acknowledge anything, that all human life must perish, were his principles universally and steadily to prevail," *E*XII/ii.128). Human nature is such that only "a more *mitigated* scepticism or *academical* philosophy ... may be both durable and useful" (*E*XII/iii.129). For it can inspire the learned "with more modesty and reserve, and diminish their fond opinion of themselves, and their prejudice against their antagonists," while "the illiterate may reflect on the disposition of the learned, who, amidst all the advantages of study and reflection, are commonly still diffident in their determinations." Apprised of "the natural powers of the human mind," they need only "compare them with their objects" to ascertain what are, and are not, "proper subjects of science and enquiry;" and armed with the recognition that "we cannot give a satisfactory reason, why we believe, after a thousand experiments, that a stone will fall, or fire burn," philosophers will never more "be tempted to go beyond common life" (*E*XII/iii.130). Everything however depends on having the courage to press our reasonings forward to their remotest consequences, never succumbing to the temptation to avoid uncomfortable truths in the science of human nature by forsaking empirical reason and having recourse to abstract metaphysics or obscurantist fideism.

But, if *Treatise* I concludes with reason locked in self-destructive yet inescapable combat with itself, should Hume not have laid down his pen then and there? I think not; this seems to me precisely the result Hume needed in order to press his inquiries forward into the spheres of the passions and morality. For the latter require that "the combat of passion and of reason" be brought to an end, so that the latter may fulfill its proper task: "Reason is, and ought only to be the slave of the passions, and can never pretend to any other office than to serve and obey them" (*T*415). Reason had to be humbled, but not, as with the Pyrrhonists, humiliated. A balance of sorts is achieved at the end of *Treatise* I due to the simple fact that we are unable to mourn for our reasons. For, just as the aforementioned "singular and seemingly trivial property of the fancy" (*T*268) saves us from skeptical despair in the cases of reason (*T*185) and the senses (*T*217), so, too, are we spared here by the difficulty "by which we enter ... into remote views of things, and are not able to accompany them with so sensible an impression, as we do those, which are more easy and natural." The possession of contradictory beliefs can pose a problem for us only if they are brought into actual opposition, within a single purview. Yet, no attitudes or modes of awareness are less suitable to be so combined than those of immediate consciousness and imagination: the point of view of the one is a world of disparate, instantaneous perceptions in perpetual flux, while that of the other is a world of dynamically interconnected, enduring objects. On the contrary, the imagination juggles these views with the same practiced virtuosity and insensibility to contradiction with which it runs together unity and number to yield the fiction of identity (see chapter 6-A). Were it to try to examine itself while at the same keeping up pretences, it would be as the juggler who, the moment he attempts to scrutinize his art during performance, forthwith drops all his balls. Nothing less than the disciplined skill of a psychologist of Hume's order can subdue the imagination to the point where it can discern, however imperfectly and fallibly ("The phænomenon may be real, tho' my explication be chimerical," *T*60), the secrets of its own juggling act. The rest of us, while at some level aware that perceptions and objects are one and the same existents, lack the skill and fortitude to arrest our imaginations in their habitual courses, force them into ways of regarding to which they are naturally resistant, and confront our Humean predicament. Were our natures different, this might be performed with ease, whereupon we would all of us forthwith succumb to irremediable skeptical despair. We are rescued from this fate thanks only to having the nature we do, one that dampens the capacity of such conflicts to make a strong, enduring impression, and so removes their sting. This, above all, the philosopher must recognize; for then, when confronted by the "manifold contradictions and imperfections in human reason," he will not be led to question his methods and results by the fact that something seemingly so grave and dire as the falsity of reason is far less burdensome to him than the travails of daily life (an overdue mortgage), much less matters of life and death (a knife held to one's throat). Trivial suggestions of the fancy draw us back from the skeptical abyss, and they alone; and by acknowledging this, we will not be tempted to turn our backs on philosophical reason in favor of a quasi-fideistic naturalism. For where our natures spare us the need for succor, there is no excuse in seeking it. This, in my opinion is the position of Hume: a "mitigated skepticism" not in respect of its undisguisably nightmarish content, but of our naturally moderate reaction to it.

Accordingly, far from being incompatible, philosophical modesty and the affirmation of unbridgeable gaps separating our beliefs from their objects (= perceptions) go hand in hand. Only thus, I believe, can we comprehend how an apostle of "modesty and reserve" could at the same time couch his final skeptical prescription to us in the incendiary language of the zealot:

> When we run over libraries, persuaded of these principles, what havoc must we make? If we take in our hand any volume; of divinity or school metaphysics, for instance; let us ask, *Does it contain any abstract reasoning concerning quantity or number*? No. *Does it contain any experimental reasoning concerning matter of fact and existence*? No. Commit it then to the flames: for it can contain nothing but sophistry and illusion. (*E*XII/iii.132)

Notes

INTRODUCTION

[1] Annette Baier reads this passage differently: "Which option gives us a false reason, and which gives us no reason at all? I take it that the reason subverted by its own unrestrained and reflexive application is ultimately 'no reason at all,' whereas the false reason is the prophetically Kantian understanding which uses forbidden reasoning to arrive at the very prohibition, which thinks beyond the limits of the understanding to discern those limits. It is false to itself – it expressly and manifestly disobeys its own ruling" (*A Progress of Sentiments. Reflections on Hume's* Treatise, Cambridge: Harvard University Press, 1991, p. 14). Yet, it is clear in the text that "false reason" signifies the "General maxim, that no refin'd or elaborate reasoning is ever to be receiv'd" derived from the "trivial property of the fancy;" so, far from being anything like Kantian self-prohibiting understanding, it is rather Hume's own, decidedly un-Kantian conception of a trivial property of our nature which "breaks the force of all sceptical arguments in time, and keeps them from having any considerable influence on the understanding" (*T*187 – the passage to which Hume himself refers on *T*267). The issue as Hume framed it has to do with the limits of *belief*, not conception: human nature prevents us from giving credence to any argument that runs counter to it. Our reason is as inseparable from the whole of human nature (passions, feelings of vivacity, etc.) as the heart from the body; it is no more capable of sustaining itself when detached from it (as "pure reason") than is a detached heart, for pure reason (like the negative dogmatism of certain skeptics) is then severed from that whereby alone belief can be engendered. Reason is thus said to be "false" because its power to command assent depends wholly on feeling and other putatively non-rational elements of our nature, apart from which it is "no reason at all."

[2] See Kant's Preface to *Prolegomena to Any Future Metaphysics*, *AA* 3, pp. 257–61. A century later, T. H. Green stated that Hume "showed knowledge to be impossible" (*Works of T. H. Green*, Volume I, London: Longmans, Green, and Co., 1885, Vol. I, §3).

[3] Kemp Smith was not of course alone: one thinks also of Laird, Maund, and Hendel.

[4] Norman Kemp Smith, *The Philosophy of David Hume*, London: Macmillan and Co., 1941, pp. 129ff., 102, and 135; see also p. 401.

[5] See chapters 1 note 47, and 7-C. I do not doubt that many of these interpreters

would question my characterization of their view; however, the stress they place on "secret connexions" and such like seems to me overtly metaphysically realist, contrasting with Kemp Smith's normative naturalism.

[6] There is undeniably great diversity within the naturalizing school, e.g. those who situate Hume's naturalism in the subjectivist framework of empiricist theory of ideas (Stroud, Fogelin, Pears), as against those who situate it within the sphere of "common life" (Livingston, Baier, Costa).

[7] In the eyes of some interpreters, Hume shifted his ground so frequently and randomly that there are no fixed points to be found, e.g. Passmore's characterization of him as "a philosophical puppy-dog, picking up and worrying one problem after another, always leaving his teeth-marks in it, but casting it aside when it threatened to become wearisome." (*Hume's Intentions*, third edition, London: Duckworth, 1980, pp. 87f.).

[8] *David Hume*, p. 211.

[9] Ibid., p. 210.

[10] Kemp Smith's denial of a univocal sense to "vivacity" is premised on a supposed distinction between "infallibility" and "belief," e.g.: "when [Hume] came ... to distinguish between perceptions, which as the *immediate* objects of consciousness are *infallibly* known, and the objects which are objects only of *belief*, not of immediate consciousness." He simply did not consider that infallibility is nothing more than irresistible belief, and thus has the very same basis as our irresistible natural convictions that bodies exist or that there are real causes: all alike are matters purely of vivacity, and thence of feeling, not insight. See chapter 1.

[11] *David Hume*, pp. 11f. and 9f. See also John P. Wright, "Hume's Rejection of the Theory of Ideas," *History of Philosophy*, 8: 2, April, 1991, pp. 154f.

[12] *David Hume*, p. 209. This was an echo of Maund – see chapter 3 note 7.

[13] The authorship of the *Abstract* continues to be debated (see e.g. John Nelson, "The Authorship of the *Abstract* Revisited," *Hume Studies*, 17: 1, April, 1991). I concur with Paul Nidditch's view that Hume's approval of its contents is a virtual certainty, and his authorship "overwhelmingly likely" (Textual Notes, p. 667 of the *Treatise* edition used in this work). One item of evidence which I have yet to see brought forth is the close structural resemblance between the *Abstract* and early editions of the *Enquiry*. For not only is the greatest part of each consecrated to cause and effect, but, more significantly, both seem to single out the same bits of *Treatise* I (the main exception being Hume's silence regarding personal identity in the *Enquiry*): e.g. the true-but-useless standard of equality, general appearances, liberty and necessity, the basis of belief in witnesses and history, and a comparison of association with literature.

[14] *David Hume*, p. 388.

[15] Ibid., p. 387.

[16] Ibid., pp. 73ff. The citation from Hume's second *Enquiry*, Appendix 1 (246) actually concerns taste, not association.

[17] The single exception seems to be the association of resembling impressions (see *T*283): the imagination only associates ideas, not impressions.

[18] There is no text in which the so-called "Hutchesonian conception of belief" is more prominent than *TApp*628f.; yet, this remark is appended to a passage the

subject of which is belief as "determin'd by... custom or a principle of association" (*T*97).

19 Husserl viewed Hume as a forerunner of phenomenology: "This Humean psychology [the first systematic attempt at a science of the pure givens of consciousness], I would say, is an attempt at a pure egology ... Hume's *Treatise* is the first project of a pure phenomenology" (*Die Krisis der europeaische Wissenschaften und die tranzendentale Phänomenologie*, in *Husserliana*, Haag: Martinus Nijhoff, Vol. 1, pp. 156f.). On belief in particular there is an even greater affinity with William James (see chapter 1-B).

20 Perhaps the finest recent study of the uses of "skepticism" common in the eighteenth century and how they do or do not apply to Hume is D. F. Norton's *David Hume: Common-Sense Moralist, Sceptical Metaphysician* (Princeton University Press, 1982). I shall not repeat the essentials of the case he presented so admirably.

21 Hume uses the term "reflexion" for "passions, desires, and emotions" (*T*8); it has nothing to do with reflection in the intellectual sense (thoughtfulness, contemplation, deliberate as distinct from impulsive action, etc.). To remain cognizant of the difference, I have opted to employ "reflexion" as the counterpart to "sensation," and "reflection" to indicate discursive activity. Hume himself used both spellings indifferently.

22 The experiential nature of the relation of ideas to impressions as copies to their originals is evident on *T*4f. (the reference to constant conjunction as the source of this information suggests that Hume was self-consciously following the theory he would spell out only in *Treatise* I/iii). Since even resemblance is lacking between ideas of sense and impressions of reflexion, one cannot doubt that, for Hume, discovery of this relation, too, is impossible by means solely of immediate consciousness.

23 Neither entails the other: e.g. experience teaches us the *conditions* – viz. relations of constant conjunction – under which the phenomenological feelings *constitutive* of the perception of necessary connection arise; thus, since constant conjunction forms no part of the impression of reflexion which furnishes the content of our idea of necessary connection, the falsehood of this "story of origins" (i.e. the absence of any consciousness of constant conjunction) would not imply the impossibility of having the idea of causality. This distinction does not, however, correspond to Hume's two definitions of cause (see *T*170). In my terminology, *both* the natural and the philosophical definitions are experiential: the former despite *also* incorporating phenomenological components, the latter despite excluding custom (as indicated earlier, I take the view that philosophical relations are parasitic on natural, so that, in the absence of the natural, custom-based relation, constant conjunctions would not signify necessary connections, and so would not constitute causal relations – see chapter 5-E).

24 Despite the fact that Hume was known to have sent a copy of the *Treatise* to Berkeley and so surely would have made a close study of his philosophy beforehand, it was claimed by some commentators that Hume's knowledge of Berkeley was entirely second-hand. Since the discovery of a letter proving the contrary, it is maintained instead that Berkeley was only a minor influence. For a fuller discussion of Hume's relation to Berkeley, see Michael Ayers, "Berkeley and Hume: A Question of Influence" in *Philosophy in History*, Rorty,

Schneewind, Skinner, editors, Cambridge University Press, 1984; and Raynor, "Hume and Berkeley's *Three Dialogues*" (*Oxford Studies in Modern Philosophy*, M. A. Stewart, editor, Oxford University Press, Volume 1).

25 Thus, "The full explication of this principle [of association] and all its consequences would lead us into reasonings too profound and too copious for these Essays" (*E*III.H39).

26 Quoted from "My own Life" in the Hendel edition of the *Enquiry*.

27 James King's review of Baier's *A Progress of Sentiments*, in *Bulletin of the Hume Society*, Fall, 1991.

28 This Baier overlooks when she claims that "membership in a linguistic community, itself one of several such communities whose languages 'nearly correspond' to each other, is essential for the sort of mental activity that [Hume] is analyzing in Part I of Book One, indeed in the whole of the *Treatise*. Only in Part IV of Book One, when scepticism and solipsism are worked through, is there any experiment made of separating the thinker from the normal human world" (*Progress*, p. 32). Hume regarded it as the touchstone of any theory of human understanding, and particularly his own account in part iii of causation in terms of customary association, that it also be applicable to higher animals (see *T*176ff.). See also Terence Penelhum, "The Self of Book 1 and the Selves of Book 2," *Hume Studies*, 18: 2, November, 1992.

1 IMPRESSIONS AND IDEAS

1 That impressions *in general* resemble and precede their corresponding ideas *in general* does require experience to discover: "I consider the order of their *first appearance*; and find by constant experience, that the simple impressions always take the precedence of their correspondent ideas, but never appear in the contrary order" (*T*5). See also Daniel Flage, *Hume's Theory of Mind*, London: Routledge, 1990, pp. 22ff.; and Baier, *Progress*, p. 74.

2 See Kemp Smith, *David Hume*, pp. 210f.; John Laird, *Hume's Philosophy of Human Nature*, pp. 27ff. and 109ff.; Barry Stroud, *Hume*, London: Routledge and Kegan Paul, 1977, pp. 27ff., and Flage, *Hume's Mind*, pp. 168ff. Below, both in the main text and in notes, their views will be considered.

3 However, Hume made quite clear that one thing impressions are *not* is, as Don Ross would have it, "*impacts*, the shock of which resonates and produces disturbances throughout the system" ("Hume, Resemblance and the Foundations of Psychology," *History of Philosophy Quarterly*, 8: 4, October, 1991, p. 346): "By the term of impression I would not be understood to express the manner, in which our lively perceptions are produced in the soul, but merely the perceptions themselves" (*T*2n.).

4 Donald Livingston takes a view of this kind: "The force and vivacity of a perception is internal to it and can be discerned only through a distinction of reason" (*Hume's Philosophy of Common Life*, Chicago University Press, 1984, p. 57). See also Stanley Tweyman, "Some Reflections on Hume on Existence," *Hume Studies*, 18:2, November, 1992, pp. 142f.

5 E.g. impressions precede their resembling ideas; impressions are original, ideas derived; impressions can be mixed, while ideas exclude one another.

[6] Livingston holds that Hume's notion of "perception" is not a philosophical notion at all: "The opening pages of the *Treatise* tell us very little about perceptions and nothing that requires us to view them as sense data or private mental images ... Having given a virtually vacuous definition of 'perceptions,' Hume disarms questions the reader may have by pointing out that by 'impression,' 'idea,' 'force and liveliness,' he means what we all in common life mean by the difference between feeling and thinking ... Hume is bringing to the discussion of the *Treatise*, on the very first page, the vulgar consciousness of things as having an original authority to monitor and discipline philosophical explications of concepts ... where experience is conceived not as something arrived at introspectively as in the egocentric tradition but publicly 'as they appear in the common course of the world, by man's behavior in company, in affairs, and in their pleasures' (*T*xix)" (*Common Life*, pp. 44–45; see also Janet Broughton, "What Does the Scientist of Man Observe?," *Hume Studies*, 18:1, November, 1992, pp. 160f.). Yet, the introspective purport of Hume's assertion that "Every one *of himself* will readily perceive the difference betwixt feeling and thinking" and "must be conscious *in his own breast*" at *T*2 seems unmistakable: to construe this call to *perceive* in *one's own breast* as a call to *renounce* introspection seems a perverse construction indeed. One should also note Hume's reference shortly before to "the degrees of force and liveliness, with which they *strike upon the mind*, and make their way into *our thought or consciousness*" (emphasis mine): this is hardly the language one uses to describe what cannot be "arrived at introspectively ... but publicly." Nor should it be overlooked that Hume explicitly associated his procedure with that of Locke (whose terminology alone he criticizes, and not in the name of ordinary language but in order to denominate something "for which there is no particular name either in *English* or any other language, that I know of"). From its opening sentence, the *Treatise* is anything but ego-neutral: "the perceptions *of the human mind*" (*T*1). Such validity as Livingston's criticism of the "egocentric," phenomenalistic reading of Hume may have, it owes to the fact that, at the level of immediate consciousness, there can be no ego, no subjectivity, nothing over and above the flux of perceptions itself, and so no "private mental images": but this is only because the self, for Hume, is a *product* of the causal relation of perceptions in imagination (see *T*261), and so perceptions have no real "owner" or substance in which to inhere (see *T*207). And this is of course a notion of perception even more remote from the ordinary than those of Descartes, Locke, and Berkeley (see chapters 6-B and -C).

[7] See also *TAbs*654 [Hume describing himself in the 3rd person]: "He seems sensible, that 'tis impossible by words to describe this feeling, which every one must be conscious of in his own breast. He calls it sometimes a *stronger* conception, sometimes a more *lively*, a more *vivid*, a *firmer*, or a more *intense* conception. And indeed, whatever name we may give to this feeling, which constitutes belief, our author thinks it evident, that it has a more forcible effect on the mind than fiction and mere conception;" see also *T*106 and *E*V/ii.40. Needless to say, Hume never abandoned the "force and vivacity" locution – it recurs frequently in the *Enquiry*.

[8] See also *T*112: "He feels a more sensible pleasure from its magnificence; which

is a proof of a more lively idea: And he confounds his judgment with sensation; which is another proof of it." Here, quite clearly, the difference between impression and idea remains inviolate despite the fact that, owing to the extraordinary vivacity of the idea, judgment is confounded with sensation. One could also mention the impressions Hume describes as so calm as to be well-nigh insensible (see *T*417–18).

9 There are passages in *Treatise* I that seem to anticipate Hume's doctrine of sympathy, e.g. *T*224: "There is a very remarkable inclination in human nature, to bestow on external objects the same emotions, which it observes in itself; and to find every where those ideas, which are most present to it."

10 In an appendix to *T*123 published with *Treatise* Book III, Hume considers the case of poetry: "We may observe the same effect of poetry in a lesser degree; and this is common both to poetry and madness, that the vivacity they bestow on the ideas is not deriv' from the particular situations or connexions of the objects of these ideas, but from the present temper and disposition of the person." However, as distinct from madness, when gripped by a "poetical enthusiasm," there is only "the mere phantom of belief or persuasion."

11 Curiously, in the corresponding passage in the appendix to the *Treatise* (*TApp*629), the italicized phrase is missing. That he felt he could sharpen his meaning by adding to "or what is taken for such" serves to confirm the interpretation of vivacity as verisimilitude.

12 Hume's expression for an idea devoid of vivacity on *T*8 (though it is used in a different sense on *T*234).

13 The vivacity of belief "plainly makes no addition to our precedent ideas," it "can only change the *manner* of our conceiving them" (*T*96).

14 Careful attention should be paid to the terms in which Hume spelled out what, in his view, are the only two possible positions regarding belief: "belief is some new idea, such as that of *reality* or *existence*, which we join to the simple conception of an object, or it is merely a peculiar *feeling* or *sentiment*" (*TApp*623). In either case, it is clear that, for him, "belief" means "reality" or "existence"; and there is every reason to suppose the same to be true of impressions.

15 *Principles of Psychology*, V. 2, p. 283 (emphasis mine).

16 *Collected Papers*, Vol. VII (1913 *Theory of Knowledge* manuscript), p. 140f.

17 Even Wittgenstein seems to have recognized that there is a use of "belief" of the kind exploited by Hume (however, unlike Hume's sense, Wittgenstein's is not merely manifested in behavior, but rooted in it): "Imagine an observer who, as it were automatically, says what he is observing. Of course he hears himself talk, but, so to speak, he takes no notice of that. He sees that the enemy is approaching and reports it, describes it, but like a machine. What would that be like? Well, he does not act according to his observation. Of him, one might say that he speaks what he sees, but that he does not *believe* it. It does not, so to speak, get inside him" (*Remarks on the Philosophy of Psychology*, Vol. I, §813). This is an appropriate occasion to remark that, on Hume's conception of belief, it does not seem possible for the paradox Wittgenstein ascribed to Moore to arise (see *Philosophical Investigations*, Pt. II/x). The paradox can be illustrated by the statement "This room is on fire and I don't believe it": although not a logical contradiction, it is nevertheless nonsensical, and so needs

to be excluded by any account of the logic of belief. Now, in a Humean framework, the first part of the statement is only possible if there are *impressions* of a fire (otherwise, it would be but the memory or fantasy of a fire); however, the vivacity that makes them impressions also renders it impossible to disbelieve in the real existence of the fire (since belief *is* vivacity). This, it should be noted, is not a *logical* impossibility; for we might have been so constituted that our sensations were not felt as impressions, but as perfect ideas: in that case, although having sensations of approaching flames and searing heat, we would *not* believe a fire was present. Thus, it is only because human nature is the way it is that the paradox is prevented from arising in our case.

18 The need for it, if not the distinction itself, is clearly foreshadowed in Locke: "I ask any one, Whether he be not invincibly conscious to himself of a different Perception, when he looks on the Sun by day, and thinks on it by night; when he actually tastes Wormwood, or smells a Rose, or only thinks on that Savour, or Odour? We as plainly find the difference there is between any *Idea* revived in our Minds by our own Memory, and actually coming into our Minds by our Senses, as we do between any two distinct *Ideas*" (*ECHU* IV/ii/§14). Since he seems to be referring to the differences noticed *in the perceptions themselves* ("conscious to himself of a *different perception*"), I am inclined to think that his point concerns the first axis. More probably, Locke simply failed to distinguish qualitative differences observed in the perceptions themselves from felt differences in our consciousness of them; this may have been the motive behind Hume's criticism of Locke's terminology on *T*2n.

19 Only the variability of vivacity *vis à vis* the perception itself is wholly independent; the perception can vary only slightly without ceasing to be (qualitatively) the same (cf. "A particular shade of colour may acquire a new degree of liveliness or brightness without any other variation. But when you produce any other variation, 'tis no longer the same shade or colour," *T*96).

20 Hume described memory as "somewhat intermediate betwixt an impression and an idea;" (*T*8) but he never, to my knowledge, referred to any perception as intermediate between thought and sensation.

21 According to Flage, "Hume's attempt to distinguish impressions from ideas on the basis of the greater force and vivacity of an impression *vis-à-vis* its corresponding idea failed, since he was quite willing to acknowledge that there are cases in which the force and vivacity of an impression and idea are indistinguishable" (*Hume's Mind*, p. 168). But this does not follow if, as I maintain, Hume categorized perceptions along two axes (impression/belief/conception and sensation/reflexion/thought). The mere fact that, in cases of mental dysfunction (e.g. madness or sinking into unconsciousness), a thought can take on the status of an impression while remaining a thought, or a sensation that of an idea while remaining a sensation, hardly counts as a "failure." On the contrary, in my view, it serves to highlight the independent variability that gives Hume's categorization of perceptions its strength. Laird too seems to be mistaking a silk purse for a sow's ear when he asserts, on the ground that "dreamers do normally accept dream-manifestations as 'realities' *during their dreams*," that "if dream-manifestations are mere 'ideas', Hume's theory falls ... [T]he reason why we all learn to dismiss dream-memories so very promptly from waking life, is largely, if not principally, their lack of

interconnexion, *inter se* and with waking life, rather than any lack of apparently intrinsic 'reality'" (*Human Nature*, p. 114f.). Hume, as I interpret him, could reply that a sufficient criterion by which to distinguish dreaming from wakeful experience is the directly discernible phenomenological difference between sensations and thought-images. In this connection, Laird neglects to mention that, during sleep, not only are our faculties not in their normal working order (i.e. sleep is a state of dysfunction akin to that of passing into a coma, in which sensations and reflexions lose their feeling of "reality"), but there are no sensations with which to compare and contrast thought-images; it is thence not surprising that ideas of sensation, as the most vivid perceptions before the sleeping mind, are apt to be regarded as real by default (there being no sensations whose reality can cast a shadow over them). Of course, if by "reality" Laird meant specifically *physical reality*, then one would have to take into account the qualities of constancy and coherence (see *T*194ff.); but such reality would not be possible in the first place if there were not some immediately perceptible feature in our consciousness of perceptions that leads us to regard sensations and reflexions as real (i.e. impressions) in a way that thought-images (even memories) of them can never be.

22 We must not be too literal in accepting "the great resemblance betwixt our impressions and ideas in every other particular, except their degree of force and vivacity" (*T*2).

23 This, and the citations to follow, are from *The Concept of Mind*, pp. 249–50.

24 So, too, Livingston's view that, for Hume, "all ideas are propositional ... To say a simple idea exactly represents a simple impression is to say that both have the same propositional and intentional content" (*Common Life*, pp. 56–57).

25 On any other interpretation of vivacity, it seems to me that one would be obliged to say, as Stroud does (after Ryle), that, although "it is certainly a matter of common experience that there is some difference between believing what you read and taking it as fiction ... it is clear that Hume has not captured it here [*T*97f.]. What he says is almost completely untrue in every respect, and he must have known that as well as anyone. Does a person knowingly reading fiction have a 'less lively conception' of the incidents described than one who takes what he reads as true? Does he fail to 'form a notion' of the 'features, air, and person' of the characters described? This looks like a clear case of Hume's denying the obvious under the pressure of what he thinks his philosophical theory requires. But he feels he has no alternative. And although in the Appendix to the *Treatise* (pp. 628–9) he expresses great dissatisfaction with that part of his theory of belief, he finds nothing satisfactory to put in its place" (*Hume*, pp. 71f.). Actually, Hume expresses dissatisfaction not with the theory ("I think I understand the subject perfectly") but only the expressive means available to him. It is also going too far to ascribe to Hume the view that we *fail* to form a notion of the features, etc., of a fictional personage: his claim was simply that we form "a more faint and languid conception of these particulars." Now, whether or not one thinks Hume guilty of overstatement, it does not strike me as at all implausible that, as he says, when one believes a personage to be fictitious, the impetus to imagine details omitted from the narration is weakened, and some of the satisfaction in doing so is lost; nor is it as easy to enter into the emotions and concerns of a person we know to be wholly the

whim of a writer. Stroud might have been more cautious had he recalled the behavior of listeners to Orson Welles' radio production of *The War of the Worlds*: those who believed what they were hearing was really happening thought and behaved very differently than those who took it to be a mere radio drama.

26 One can easily imagine losing the ability to see colors other than yellow; but if one can see yellow, it is difficult to think that one would be unable to see more than one shade of it and impossible to think one could not see more than one degree of "liveliness or brightness" of the same shade. The same holds for the difference in vivacity between impressions and ideas and that between convictions and fictions: one might be conscious only of impressions or only of ideas, and so be entirely unable to conceive the other (see my analysis of the dreaming case in note 21 above); but could one be conscious of both and still be unable to conceive a greater or lesser degree of certainty with respect to one and the same idea? I think not.

27 Flage treats vivacity as an impression of reflexion: "at the phenomenal level, impressions are to be distinguished from ideas, not on the basis of any of their inherent characteristics, but on the basis of the impressions of reflection that are 'annexed' to them, that is, as impressions of reflection 'force and vivacity' function fundamentally as the basis for the differentiation of cognitive states" (*Hume's Mind*, p. 182). This view may seem similar to my own, but is not, in fact, the same. Flage considers only two possibilities: either vivacity is separable from the perception to which it is "annexed" (an unfortunate term since it connotes association) only by a distinction of reason or, like other impressions, it is a distinct perception in its own right. The latter clearly is a nonstarter: this would permit the imagination to attach or separate vivacity to or from any other perception at whim, and, since vivacity is just belief, this would commit Hume to a view of belief he firmly rejected (see e.g. *TApp*623ff.). However, the former fares little better. If vivacity is separable from a perception only by a distinction of reason, then, according to how one interprets such distinctions, it must either be treated as part of its content (i.e. an aspect of the perception itself) or as the product of an association by resemblance. In the second case, the problem of separating and combining a distinct perception of belief re-emerges. In the first case, since a change in vivacity, like any change in aspect, would then imply a distinction of perceptions, this would render it impossible for one and the same perceptual content to be believed at one time and disbelieved at another. Vivacity is analogous to the brightness of shade of color: just as a change in brightness does not imply a change of shade, so, too, a change in vivacity must not imply a change in perception. But the analogy is not perfect. In particular, we must not suppose that simply because a change in brightness does not imply a change of *shade* that it also does not imply a change of *perception*. For since one obviously can separate in imagination two color perceptions differing solely – but greatly – in brightness, they must be counted as distinct perceptions by Hume's separability principle of *T*18 (see section C, especially note 32 below). Hence, two axes of description are essential if vivacity is to perform the role in which Hume cast it: as a feature of our *consciousness* of a perception, able to vary independently, it ceases to be an aspect of the perception itself; yet, since consciousness is intentional and cannot

exist without any object to perceive, vivacity lacks the full independence of a genuine perception.

28 It falls directly out of Hume's conception of a perception as that which is everything it appears to be and appears to be just what it is (see *T*190). See chapter 6-B.

29 There is another way in which the principle that separability in imagination implies real distinctness might be thought to argue against a literal construal of the sympathy doctrine. The latter supposes that an idea of an emotion is *succeeded* by an impression of it; and, since successive perceptions are necessarily distinct perceptions (i.e. they can be separated in imagination by supposing one to occur and the other not), the separability principle implies that the idea and the impression must be distinct perceptions. But this argument cannot work. Instead of being directed towards the identity of the *content* of the perceptions (emotion and thought of the emotion), it relates only to the question of their *numerical* identity. Numerical identity is not here at issue; for Hume would never think of denying that the perfect idea of a thing at one time and the same idea believed at another time are numerically different. For him, they are nevertheless *qualitatively* identical, the same thought-*content*. The issue here is whether the content of the idea of an emotion and that of the impression of the emotion are qualitatively the same; and the answer I offer is no: a thought and a reflexion are qualitatively discernible quite independently of their difference in vivacity.

30 E.g. Stroud, *Hume*, p. 20f.

31 The portion of the sentence between the dashes has no counterpart in Locke (who treated, e.g., extension and color as distinct simple ideas even though neither can be imagined separately from the other). In truth, Locke's criterion of simplicity tended to waver. In the case of the distinction between simple and complex substances or modes, simplicity signifies non-compositedness. But, as applied to ideas in *ECHU* II, the simple seems to differ from the complex as the pre-intellectualized given (the raw material of perception) contrasts with products of intellection (only much later does he actually say that a simple idea is "an *Idea*, which has no composition at all," *ECHU* III/iv/§7). Where Locke went wrong in the eyes of Berkeley and Hume was in his willingness to count mere abstracta among the raw material of perception (see note 33 below). As Fred Wilson has remarked, Hume's criterion of simplicity almost certainly derives from Berkeley's criterion of distinctness based on separability in imagination ("Hume on the Abstract Idea of Existence," *Hume Studies*, 17: 2, November, 1991, p. 168; see citation of *PHK* Intro. §10 and Pt. I §5 in chapter 3-B).

32 According to William Williams, "one may wish to charge Hume with confusing identity with indistinguishability, arguing that whereas the first is transitive, the second is not. Thus, shades A and B and B and C may not be distinguishable one from the other, whereas A and C are. B, so the argument would go, is then a different shade, but, contra Hume, one for which there is no distinct impression or idea" ("Is Hume's Shade of Blue a Red Herring?" *Synthese*, 92, 1992, p. 97n.2). In my view, Hume would almost certainly have explained this and related phenomena in terms of the weakness and infirmity of imagination: if it had greater acuity, we would have no difficulty discriminating B from A or

C. What I feel certain he would not have done is what Williams suggests: treat the difference as a distinction of reason (in the form of a relative idea of B). Shades of color, far from being mere aspects, are, for Hume, "really different from each other" (*T*5f.); for any one shade can exist in the mind in the absence of any other. And this brings me to the heart of my disagreement with Williams: "if simple ideas are derived from simple impressions, the simplicity he has in mind is qualitative, not spatial or temporal ... By a distinction of reason we can differentiate their color (say) from their punctiformity, though we cannot conceive of that color or the punctiformity standing by itself. The color is qualitatively simple; the minimum sensible, spatially simple, but qualitatively complex" (p. 84f.). In my view, it was precisely to avoid falling into the morass of abstraction characteristic of Locke's criteria of simplicity that Hume, following Berkeley, wished only to debunk the notion that simple ideas might be abstracta (see note 39). Moreover, Hume explicated distinctions of reason as habits of associative resemblance, thereby eliminating abstractive mental operations (aspect-seeing) from his psychology (see chapter 3-B); there thus is nothing in the least "simple" about distinctions of reason (i.e. like all relations founded on custom, they are complex ideas). Admittedly, when discussing the missing shade, Hume seems to treat qualities as simple ideas; yet, if one bears in mind that he regarded different shades as different perceptions, it does not follow that the quality itself (whether as mere distinction of reason or as a patch in the visual field) is the simple idea, rather than some spatial and temporal minima imaginable in it (as is confirmed by an analogy with touch: "The impressions of touch are simple impressions, except when consider'd with regard to their extension," *T*230f.). Simple is initially distinguished from complex as that which admits "of no distinction or separation ... into parts" (*T*2), which is true only of "perfectly simple and indivisible" (*T*27) minima.

33 Certainly a better understanding than Locke, who saw no problem in treating solidity as a distinct idea even though it could never appear separately from extension: "It is true solidity cannot exist without extension, but neither can scarlet ... this hinders not but that they are distinct ideas. Many ideas require others as necessary to their existence or conception which yet are very distinct ideas" (*ECHU* II/xiii/§11). Locke's confusion is even more evident in the case of the idea of power, which initially he classifies as simple (II/vii/§8), then says "includes some kind of relation" (II/xxi/§3), and finally confesses "are truly complex *Ideas*" (II/xxiii/§7). For Hume (assuming that the specific shade of color characterizing a non-extended *minimum visibile* cannot be discerned), extension and scarlet are merely different *aspects* of one and the same simple perception, i.e. mere distinctions of reason, explicable in terms of relations of resemblance (hence, for Hume, "abstract idea" is an oxymoron – as abstract and so unable to exist on its own, it cannot be a perception, and thus not an idea). Locke's admission of aspects as full-fledged ideas (or, in Humean parlance, perceptions) plunged the notion of a simple idea into a morass of confusion, which both Berkeley and Hume concerned themselves to rectify.

34 Reginald Savage complains that "it cannot be sensibly established that the objects of our everyday experience are constituted by atomic sense data in the way that the atomists' material extended objects are supposedly composed of atoms" ("Hume's Missing Shade of Blue," *History of Philosophy Quarterly*, 9:

2, 1992, p. 203). Yet, it is not on the senses but imagination that Hume bases the *generality* of his claim that perceptions are either simple or compounded of the simple (as all generality is a function of imagination and its customs – see chapter 3-B). Imagination is the faculty of compounding and separating ideas, as it is likewise that of associating them. It is both from the perspective and on the basis of this faculty that the general principles of Hume's theory of ideas are advanced (e.g. copy/original, resemblance, custom, et al); thus, it is the *imagination* that "reaches a *minimum*, and may raise up to itself an idea, of which it cannot conceive any sub-division" (*T*27) and *imagination* that is charged "to bring [a sense impression] into its component parts" with the aim of conceiving it "as a single point" (*T*42). Humean simplicity is purely psychological, not an a priori theoretical construct as Savage supposes; and this, I believe, undercuts his criticism of Hume's missing shade of blue (which, incidentally, a person supplies "from his own *imagination*," *T*6), premised as it is on the a priori, non-associative nature of the copy/original relation (see p. 204).

35 Ross, too, draws attention to this problem – see "Psychology," p. 350. He also recognizes what he calls the *functionalist* aspect of resemblances, that is, their dependence on the imagination and what it feels in contemplating perceptions (p. 352). However, he does not bring us any nearer than this to understanding how Hume could have dealt with the problem.

36 Hume held that qualitative identity persists even over variation in "liveliness or brightness" (*T*96). Presumably, he would not have extended the identity to incongruent counterparts or visual sensations that differed only in apparent size. For, while he would grant that we can often be fooled into treating things as resembling that are in fact not (e.g. if there were a series of transformations linking them so gradual that "The passage from one moment to another is scarce felt, and distinguishes not itself by a different perception or idea, which may require a different direction of the spirits," *T*203), the fiction of imagination this requires – of which we cannot but, at some level, be conscious ("all impressions are internal and perishing existences and *appear as such*," *T*194 – emphasis mine) – exposes them as only aspect-resemblances.

37 This exception is the only case of non-imaginative association; whether this means that it is independent of (pre-imaginative) consciousness altogether is unclear but seems unlikely.

38 Hume made this observation for the purposes of explaining (perfect) identity (see chapter 6-A); however, its interest is not confined to this matter.

39 What Hume has left us less well equipped to explain is how a *simple* impression and *simple* idea can ever be felt to resemble. For, where perceptions are simple, what detail is there for the mind to delineate? But in that case how can it find their contemplation resembling in the face of the qualitative disparity in their appearances? There seem to be two responses open to Hume. The first is to grant that a mind which had no complex perceptions at all would be unable to associate sensations/reflexions with thought in relations of resemblance; however, since in humans perceptions always arrive in manifolds, and the apprehension of a manifold always involves the apprehension of a form or order (succession or juxtaposition), the feeling in imagination when it reproduces this organization in thought is sufficiently similar to that present in

apprehending it in sensation or reflexion for it to associate them. The second possible response depends on the thesis "that no object is presented to the senses, no image form'd in the fancy, but what is accompany'd with some emotion or movement of the spirits proportion'd to it ... [A]n impression, secretly attends every idea" (*T*373 and *T*375); for this allows us to suppose that even if a simple impression were encountered by itself (i.e. without being part of a complex), a simple idea might still be found to resemble it if the accompanying emotions that secretly attend them were felt to resemble.

40 Hume's claim only makes sense if construed epistemologically, in terms of the theory of ideas, and on a basis of complete ontological agnosticism: given that perceptions are what they appear to be and appear what they are, the fact that no necessary connection ever *manifests* itself between them allows us to infer that they *have* none (see chapter 6-B).

41 It should be remarked that it is one thing for a perception to play the role of a *criterion* for the meaningfulness of words, quite another to *identify* perceptions with meanings. In my opinion, there is no basis for attributing the latter view to Hume (see chapter 3-C).

42 *David Hume*, p. 21. John Losee too seems to take this view: "the Copy Principle is ineffective as a criterion of demarcation ... because it is inconsistent to maintain both that all simple ideas copy impressions and that some simple ideas do not copy impressions" ("Hume's Demarcation Project," *Hume Studies*, 17: 2, April, 1992, p. 53).

43 *Hume*, p. 34.

44 Bearing in mind that the relation of an idea to an impression as copy to original is a causal relation (i.e. the existence of the former depends on the latter and is related to it by virtue of a custom founded on constant precedence), Hume's defense of his analysis of the causal maxim (viz. that whatever begins to exist must have a cause of existence) applies equally to the present case: "Now, it being the [*Treatise's*] Author's Purpose, in the Pages cited in the Specimen, to examine the Grounds of that Proposition; he used the Freedom of disputing the common Opinion, that it was founded on *demonstrative* or *intuitive Certainty*; but asserts, that it is supported by *moral Evidence*, and is followed by a Conviction of the same Kind with these Truths, *That all Men must die*, and that *the Sun will rise To-morrow*. Is this any Thing like denying the Truth of that Proposition, which indeed *a Man must have lost all common Sense to doubt of*?" (*LGFE*118). Williams dismisses this point as "irrelevant to the question" ("Is Hume's Shade of Blue a Red Herring?" p. 98n.6). One may doubt that he has grasped it, however, when he further claims that the missing shade of blue is the mere tip of the iceberg of a "general and systematic" exception to the copy/original principle. For this seems to me like inferring from the *possibility* that tomorrow the earth could be destroyed by a collision with an asteroid or some other unanticipated cataclysm that we are *actually* in some kind of mortal danger. Williams himself admits that the missing shade is a mere "thought experiment" which can only be implemented with great difficulty (p. 97n.2). Nor do I believe him justified in maintaining that the missing shade is a red herring because Hume's "real concern is whether words express clear ideas – not how we acquire the ideas expressed" (p. 92). For he bases this claim on a passage (*E*II.17) in which a term is said to have meaning only if it expresses an

idea; but the reason Hume gives for saying that the idea establishes the meaning of the term is that the idea is copied from an impression; hence, the facts relating to the acquisition of the idea turn out to be the prime determinant of meaning.

45 If Hume's maxim is to be considered vulnerable at all, it has to be in the entirely different regard of the dialectic of natural belief discussed in the introduction: that our *natural beliefs* might in fact all be *natural illusions* – i.e. that the very things we cannot but believe to be true we may know, by immediate consciousness, to be false.

46 Volition (an impression) might be supposed to be an exception: constant conjunction with ideas leads to its association with various ideas. But this is a different *causal* relation, not to be confused with that involved in the second variety of truth (between a *representative* and what it represents, a copy and its original); in particular, causal relations in general, and that between volitions and thoughts in particular, imply no *resemblance* between cause and effect.

47 Wright's failure to appreciate the empirical, causal nature of representation is responsible for what, in my view, is a misreading of Hume's definition of adequacy at *T*29 ("Whenever ideas are adequate representations of objects, the relations, contradictions and agreements of the ideas are all applicable to the objects; and this we may in general observe to be the foundation of all human knowledge"). For his attempt to paint Hume a realist depends in great part on transforming this claim about the representational adequacy of ideas *vis à vis* their objects (viz. impressions) into a quite different claim regarding their adequacy to *external*, *even imperceptible*, *consciousness-independent* objects (see *Sceptical Realism*, Minneapolis: University of Minnesota Press, 1983, pp. 88ff.; also "Hume's Rejection of the Theory of Ideas," pp. 157f.). This surely was not Hume's meaning: the only "object" an idea can meaningfully be said to *represent* is the exactly resembling impression of which it is a copy. The context of *T*29 also speaks against Wright's reading since it has nothing whatever to do with what, if anything, lies beyond the purview of consciousness (whose only objects are perceptions): Hume's sole concern was to analyze our *ideas* of space and time in terms of *original data of perception*, i.e. *impressions*. So, although Wright is quite correct that "Hume ties his conception of human knowledge to that of *adequate representation*," he failed to see (or at least made no credible case for disputing) that this is entirely a matter of how, and how well, ideas – as a matter of readily discernible *empirical fact* – represent impressions, and has nothing to do with the representation of things lying beyond impressions (which cannot be given to consciousness empirically or otherwise). Since, by Wright's own admission, Hume denied that we have any *ideas* of such things, there cannot even be a question of adequacy here: where we have no idea at all, there is nothing to correspond to or agree with the object. This, however, did not deter Wright and others who share his view, since they hold that, for Hume, while we have no ideas of anything beyond our perceptions, we nevertheless have a "relative idea" or "inconceivable supposition" of them (Galen Strawson follows him in *The Secret Connexion*: *Causation, Realism, and David Hume*, Oxford University Press 1989, pp. 52ff., as does Flage, *Hume's Mind*, pp. 44ff.; also Costa, Craig, and Broughton). The principal evidence for this view is the following: "as every idea is deriv'd from a preceding perception, 'tis

impossible our idea of a perception, and that of an object or external existence can ever represent what are specifically different from each other. Whatever difference we may suppose betwixt them, 'tis still incomprehensible to us; and we are oblig'd ... to conceive an external object merely as a relation without a relative ... [W]e may suppose, but never can conceive a specific difference betwixt an object and impression" (*T*241; see also *T*218). But there are at least four reasons not to attribute such a notion to Hume. (1) The remark concerning inconceivable suppositions comes from Hume's discussion of Spinoza's "infamous" philosophy. Since the express purpose of this discussion was to render all doctrines of unknowable causes and substrates "odious" (*T*242), any suggestion that he was indulging in his own form of Spinozism seems incompatible with that intention (on Hume's use of "supposition" see Kenneth Winkler, "The New Hume," *Philosophical Review*, 100: 4, October, 1991, Cornell University Press, pp. 560f.). (2) Hume is supposed to have affirmed the notion of a relative idea on *T*68, and reaffirmed it in *Treatise* I/iv/§5. But it should not be overlooked that, on *T*68, when Hume said "of this more fully hereafter," he referred his reader not to *Treatise* I/iv/§5, but to *Treatise* I/iv/§2, where the sole reference to the notion of relative ideas is a claim to "have already shewn its absurdity" (*T*188). (3) Since on *T*188 Hume refers us only to the text in which relative ideas are introduced but does not mention them explicitly, Wilson suggests that the absurdity does not extend to them (see "Hume's Critical Realism: A Reply to Livingston," *Journal of the History of Philosophy*, 29: 2, April, 1991, p. 294). This I deny, but it obliges one to specify how anything prior to *T*188 could be supposed to show their absurdity. Most likely it is a consequence of the analysis of cause and effect in *Treatise* iii (Wilson places great weight on *T*68, where Hume introduces and does not disown relative ideas; but since Hume had yet to analyze causal relations, it seems only natural that, if that analysis provides the reason for rejecting them, he should postpone doing so until after it had been completed). Relative ideas are causal relations in which one of the relatives is unobservable and so not present in any idea (e.g. the imperceptible cause of sense impressions). But, without any idea, there can neither be a transition of thought to it nor an observable conjunction (constant or otherwise) of it with any perception, and, *a fortiori*, no custom associating it with any perception. A causal relation without a relative is an oxymoron: no relation – causal or any other kind – is conceivable for Hume where there can be neither a transition of thought nor a conjunction of perceptions ("Bereave matter of all its intelligible qualities, both primary and secondary, you in a manner annihilate it, and leave only a certain unknown, inexplicable *something*, as the cause of our perceptions; a notion so imperfect, that no sceptic will think it worth while to contend against it," *E*XII/i.123). (4) Moreover, since "we can never have reason to believe that any object exists, of which we cannot form an idea" (*T*172; also: "belief, however faint, fixes itself on a determinate object," *T*140), it follows that *anything totally inconceivable cannot be at all believable*. Belief, for Hume, is not a distinct perception, but simply our feeling in regarding it; and to suppose belief to be possible in the absence of any perception at all (idea, conception), as these interpreters do, is to make nonsense of his doctrine (and, since the motive they ascribe to him for embracing inconceivable suppositions is to defend the natural beliefs against the onslaughts of skepticism, they could not be farther from their mark). See chapters 5-F and 7-C.

2 IMAGINATION AND THE VIVACITY OF IDEAS

1 Volitions, etc., are simply perceptions like any other (see e.g. *TApp*632f.). Hume regarded the imagination as active only in the ordinary *experiential* sense (in which moving billiard-balls are believed to be active) – see note 9 below and chapter 5-E.

2 Each perception is a distinct, independent existence; even the connection of ideas to impressions as copies to originals presupposes a natural relation of resemblance and experience of the constant precedence of impressions *vis à vis* the correspondent ideas.

3 This follows if one takes Hume at his word that even memory is founded on imagination (see *T*105f. and *T*265 – both texts are discussed below).

4 Hume distinguished two senses of existence – see chapter 3 note 15.

5 What of the case of remembered thoughts? The past thought has to be *felt* to be connected to my present remembrance by a causal relation (as copy to original); and, since the idea of cause derives from an impression, there is, in this case too, an impression which, as the focal point of reality, governs the imagination.

6 But these shifts are not *in spite*, but *because*, of Hume's adherence to a few basic principles such as that of separability, that ideas are copied from impressions, and that no existential ties bind one perception to another independently of imagination. Not surprisingly, Broughton finds *T*85 "hard to understand" ("What Does the Scientist of Man Observe?," p. 167n.12) when she contends that there is no indication that Hume abandoned the fixity of order criterion in favor of vivacity (and she entirely overlooks *T*105 when, on p. 160, she asserts that Hume's views on memory have nothing to do with Locke's – see discussion below and note 10).

7 There are, however, exceptions: education can bring the imagination to "conceive [ideas] in so full a light, that they may operate upon the mind in the same manner with those, which the senses, memory or reason present to us." But, as he goes on to say, this occurs only in so far as they are "built almost on the same foundation of custom and repetition as our reasonings from causes and effects" (*T*117).

8 Kemp Smith claimed that "'imagination' in the special sense [as belief] does not reappear in the *Enquiry Concerning Human Understanding*. Such usage is there, indeed, quite explicitly disavowed" (*David Hume*, p. 461f.). This is mistaken. In the very passage cited in evidence, he deleted the following: "Whenever any object is presented to the memory or senses, it immediately, by the force of custom, carries the imagination to conceive that object, which is usually conjoined to it; and this conception is attended with a feeling or sentiment, different from the loose reveries of the fancy" (*E*V/ii.39). Also: "The concurrence of these several views or glimpses imprints the idea more strongly on the imagination; gives it superior force and vigour; renders its influence on the passions and affections more sensible; and in a word, begets that reliance or security, which constitutes the nature of belief and opinion" (*E*VI.46). Other

examples abound (there is even one in which the imagination of animals is credited with the power to conceive ideas "in that particular manner, which we denominate *belief*," *E*IX.84), but it is unnecessary to belabor the point that, just as in the *Treatise*, there are two distinct senses of "imagination" at work in the *Enquiry*.

9 I concur with Wilson that "There is for Hume no such thing as a faculty. There is rather only settled dispositions or regularities. But Hume does not need Aristotelian faculties. The settled dispositions or regularities explain all that needs to be explained" ("Hume's Theory of Mental Activity," *McGill Hume Studies*, D. Norton, N. Capaldi, and W. Robison, editors, San Diego: Austin Hill Press, 1979, p. 115). However, his notion that the mind monitors its own activities (p. 118) requires the caveat that actions of the mind, insofar as they are construed not simply as ways of regarding, but also as causal agents, are known only via experience and habit (see *TApp*632f. and *E*VII/i.51ff.).

10 The twofold character of memory also seems to have furnished Locke a solution to the problem of personal identity in *ECHU* II/xxvii: awareness of one's identity over time is simply a matter of recollecting one's perceiving along with the contents perceived. Remembrance of acts of reflexion and personal identity are, for Locke, one and the same (see e.g. xxvii/§13; cf. *TApp*635).

11 As always with Hume, there are exceptions that prove the rule, e.g. the liar example on *T*86. Oliver Johnson objects to Hume's allowing it: "this cannot be, because the only thing that makes an idea the kind of idea it is, either of memory or imagination, is its relative force or vivacity. A weakened memory-idea cannot be *taken for* an imagination-idea for the simple reason that it now *is* an imagination-idea ... [and] an imagination-idea that acquires force and vivacity cannot *pass for* or *counterfeit* a memory-idea because it now *is* a memory-idea" ("'Lively' Memory and 'Past' Memory," *Hume Studies*, 13:2, November, 1987, p. 345). Had he been confronted with this objection, Hume would probably have conceded that it is not entirely unwarranted, but noted (as is in fact the case) that very few of us are such pathological liars that the vivacity of the lie becomes so strong as really to be indistinguishable from the memory (as in the case of poetry – see *T*123 and *TApp*630). And even in those cases where the lie actually is believed, he would probably say that the liar still retains *enough* awareness of the the act of fabricating his story and/or is aware of not recollecting a perception of what he recounts to remain aware that his belief is not a memory (for Hume never claimed that the only believed ideas are memories: ideas causally associated with impressions are believed, as are certain things drummed into us by repetition, i.e. education, as on *T*117 – including the sort of "self-education" involved in the frequent repetition of a lie). Strangely, Johnson overlooks *T*105f. and so fails to recognize the twofold character of a memory (i.e. idea of object observed and of action of observing) that allows Hume this way out.

12 Stroud takes Hume to task for claiming that we can "tell by inspection of the mind that for every simple idea there is a corresponding simple impression, and vice versa ... This of course makes the outrageously unacceptable assumption, which Hume relies on throughout, that our impressions can somehow 'remain' in the mind after they have been 'had', so that we can then notice their similarities with their 'corresponding' ideas. He seems to be engaging ... in the

fiction that all (or a sizeable number) of our past perceptions can be 'present' to us, or at least that they remain available for inspection. But on the theory of ideas, strictly speaking, we can make no sense of this alleged possibility" (*Hume*, pp. 28, 35, and 252 n.5). It is not merely that Stroud is wrong – that Hume made no such assumption (himself affirming that it is "impossible to recal the past impressions, in order to compare them with our present ideas," *T*85) – but, more importantly, he failed to see that Hume offered a very sophisticated, coherent phenomenological treatment of memory (Livingston, who would use this absurdity to show that Hume was not a theorist of ideas at all, also neglected *T*105f. – see *Common Life*, pp. 92ff.).

13 For example, although Hume often denominated memories "impressions" on account of the degree of conviction attaching to them (see *T*86, *T*89, and *T*209), it would be wholly unwarranted to infer that he wavered regarding their true status as ideas.

14 Hume's question on *T*105f. specifically concerns an inference from the *existence* of one thing to the *existence* of another distinct from it (viz. from the believed *existence* of the present idea to a belief in the *existence* of its impression-original). As such, for him, it can be only an inference from cause to effect or from effect to cause (and the context, especially of the paragraph immediately preceding, leaves no doubt that a relation of cause and effect is at issue). Thus, it must be seen against the background of habitual, natural associations of ideas and their correspondent impressions as causes and effect – exactly as recounted on *T*4f. (see chapter 1-F).

15 Memory is therefore more than a mere storehouse of ideas copied from past impressions. When Hume asserted that memory is founded on the imagination it seems clear that he did not have in mind retentive memory (i.e. memory in the sense of a storehouse): "'tis also necessary we shou'd preserve the idea of their colour or tangibility in order to comprehend them by our imagination ... Upon the removal of the ideas of these sensible qualities, they are utterly annihilated to the thought or imagination" (*T*38f.).

16 In addition, on *T*265 memory, like the other functions of the mind referred to imagination, is depicted as dependent on experience and habit, i.e. cause and effect.

17 If it is thought remarkable that imagination should be able to do all this every instant of our lives without our once noticing, we should again think back to Locke – see section A above.

18 This seems to have been Hobbes' view: it was by construing imagination as "decaying sense" (*Leviathan*, Pt., I, Harmondsworth: Penguin Books, Ltd., 1968, chapter 2) that he assimilated memory with it (however, on such a conception, it would seem more accurate to say that he subordinated imagination to memory).

19 Descartes (letter to Arnauld, 4 June 1648), Locke (*ECHU* II/vii/§9), and Berkeley (*PHK* §98) are only the most famous of Hume's forebears to credit our awareness of succession to sense and retention.

20 See, e.g., James, *Principles of Psychology*, New York, Henry Holt, 1890, Vol. I, and Russell, *Collected Papers*, Vol. VII (1913 *Theory of Knowledge* manuscript), chapter 6.

21 There may be an introspectively ineliminable phenomenon of the kind to which

exponents of the specious present refer; yet, alternative explanations seem possible. For example, rather than having to espouse the hard-to-swallow notion of immediate awareness of distinct, non-simultaneous perceptions (i.e. immediate perception of a past time), the phenomenon might be something akin to the reverberation of a piano string after being struck by the hammer: a penumbral reverberative quality of present perceptions, akin to visual blurring, would be itself a present perception and not entail conscious access to any past time; and its appearance would have just the aspect to tempt one to *describe* it as present awareness of a content of the immediately preceding instant.

22 For these reasons: (i) Since the non-simultaneity of the perceptions in the specious present implies the distinctness of these perceptions, it also implies the distinctness of the *consciousness* apprehending them (by the *T*18 separability principle). But, since the specious present entails a single, indivisible consciousness, it implies the sort of simplicity and individuality *over a distinguishable time* that Hume's theory of personal identity, and of identity generally, precludes (see chapter 6). (ii) To treat succession as an immediate datum of sense is to regard a relation – temporal contiguity – as a full-fledged object of consciousness, and so to set it on a par with sensations, reflexions, and thoughts; but objectifying relations would create havoc for Hume (see criticism of Kemp Smith in introduction).

23 According to Wilbanks, "Clearly, the most important notion in his general conception of this faculty [reason] is that of comparison; and it is the latter which distinguishes it from the imagination" (*Hume's Theory of Imagination*, p. 79). But what other than imagination can be supposed to perform comparisons? Imagination is consciousness in so far as it can freely unite, separate, etc., ideas; what is it then if not the faculty of comparison? What distinguishes philosophical relations from natural is that, in the case of the former, the imagination is freed from the "gentle force," the "attraction in the mental world," that prevails in the case of the latter. Of philosophical resemblance, for example, Hume remarked: "When a quality becomes very general, and is common to a great many individuals, it leads not the mind directly to any one of them; but by presenting at once too great a choice, does thereby prevent the *imagination* from fixing on any single object" (*T*14). Admittedly, there is one occasion where Hume described as *reasoning* comparison with an eye to discovering relations (*T*73), but he had in mind the relation of cause and effect which he had long since been ascribed to imagination (see *T*11). Reason, like understanding (see *T*96n.), should be understood as simply "the general and more establish'd properties of the imagination" (*T*267).

24 Modes, lacking even the natural associative basis in contiguity and causation of substances, are wholly makeshift contrivances; their foundation is not human nature but human purpose.

3 WORDS AND MEASURES

1 See for example Richard Aaron's *John Locke*: "Berkeley attacked a theory of abstract ideas which, I believe, Locke never held" (Oxford University Press, 1971, p. 197). Although I am in agreement with Aaron, my analysis is somewhat different.

[2] In a letter to Lord Stillingfleet, Locke wrote: "he must think very oddly, who takes the general name of any idea to be the general idea itself: it is a mere mark or sign of it, without doubt, and nothing else." "You again accuse the way of ideas, to make common nature no more than a common name. That my Lord is not my way by ideas." (cited in Aaron, p. 199n.2)

[3] "*General and Universal*, belong not to the real existence of Things; but *are the Inventions and Creatures of the Understanding*, made by it for its own use ... universality belongs not to things themselves which are all of them particular in their existence, even those words which in their significations are general" (*ECHU* III/iii/§11). "[A general idea] is something imperfect, that cannot exist" (*ECHU* IV/vii/§9).

[4] Berkeley's citation in *PHK* Intro. §13 begins with the second sentence. I have omitted a portion at the end as well as Berkeley's italicization of "all and none" and "inconsistent."

[5] Berkeley here contradicts *PHK* §1, in which operations of the mind are classed among ideas.

[6] *David Hume*, pp. 263 and 260.

[7] "[E]ven when he appears to be asserting that all accusatives [i.e. perceptions] are impressions or images he is also discussing relations and abstract ideas ... The chief defect of Hume's view is that he says that apprehension of the abstract idea is apprehension of a particular image and a custom, and does not explain, though his discussion assumes it throughout, that the custom can only be accounted for by reference to the concept" (*Hume's Theory of Knowledge*, cited by Kemp Smith on p. 267 and p. 267n.4.)

[8] Like Kemp Smith, Russell saw no difference between relations and universals: "Berkeley and Hume ... did not recognize that they were reducing qualities to relations, but thought they were getting rid of 'abstract ideas' altogether. You can perfectly well do in that way a formal reduction of predicates to relations. If you think it is worth while you can proceed in exactly the same way with dyadic relations, which you can reduce to triadic" (*The Philosophy of Logical Atomism*, La Salle: Open Court Publishing, 1985, p. 68). There is a close analogy between the question we are exploring and the dispute over whether the objects of Wittgenstein's *Tractatus Logico-Philosophicus* include relations and properties as well as objects. There is considerable direct evidence that he did so, e.g. a diary entry, dated 16 6 15, in which Wittgenstein wrote that "Relations and properties, etc. are objects too" (*Notebooks* 1914–1916, G. H. von Wright and G. E. M. Anscombe, editors, University of Chicago Press, 1979, second edition, p. 61; see also Desmond Lee's notes, p. 120 and esp. TS 220, pp. 86–87, cited by Hilmy in *The Later Wittgenstein*, Oxford: Basil Blackwell, 1987, pp. 256f.). Most commentators hold that Wittgenstein cannot have meant to count universals as objects (e.g. Anscombe, Copi, Pitcher, Ishiguro, Carruthers); others insist that he should be taken at his word that relations are objects (Black, J. and M. Hintikka, and Hilmy). I take the latter view, not only for textual reasons, but because it seems to me essential to grasping the significance of Wittgenstein's *Grundgedanke* (4.0312), the denial that logical constants are representatives, that it be seen against the background of the affirmation that symbols for relations and concepts *are* representatives; hence, concepts and relations stand on the same level of *singular* reality as that

which they relate or qualify (i.e. Wittgenstein did not, like Hume, subjectivize relations). Still, in a sense, both sides are correct: in setting relations and properties on a par with objects, Wittgenstein was not making *singulars* of *universals*; rather, not unlike Hume and Kant before him, he recognized that a property or relation is not a universal until it (i.e. its representative) *functions* as a *conceptus communis* – i.e. something bound up with propositional thought.

9 John Tienson regards repetition, or indefinite repeatability, as tantamount to "objective cases of things being alike or of the same kind" ("Resemblance and General Terms," *Philosophical Studies*,1989, p. 106n.2). However, if we imagine a mind like Hume's oyster, and "suppose it to have only one perception" (*TApp*634), it would know nothing but repetition; yet, I doubt very much whether it could properly be said to have a *general* idea. What I find most questionable in Tienson's analysis is his conclusion "that for Hume relations are real and objective" (p. 93). By overlooking texts like *T*46 ("a relation ... is not, strictly speaking, a property in the figures themselves, but arises merely from the comparison, which the mind makes betwixt them") and *T*203 (discussed in chapter 1-D), he never once considers the possibility that Hume would not countenance an explanation of our psychological habitudes of comparison with an eye to resemblances in terms of objective resemblances (which he calls "skinny universals," i.e. "perfectly determinate qualities," p. 92): qualitative identity between perceptions is not sufficient for resemblance; there must also be a feeling in the associative imagination that considers the perceptions.

10 See too Wilson: "Hume's positive account of abstract ideas depends upon his associationist psychology" ("Hume on the Abstract Idea of Existence," *Hume Studies*, 17: 2, November, 1991, p. 171). This recognition however seems incompatible with Wilson's claim that Hume affirmed relative ideas (inconceivable causes of perceptions). He justifies it by asserting that "Failure to sense these particulars does not falsify the causal principle, owing to the presence of the existential quantifier" ("Is Hume a Sceptic with Regard to the Senses?," *Journal of the History of Philosophy*, 27: 1, January, 1989, p. 58). But *what* are we then supposed to be thinking? A relative idea is *at best* an abstraction (something resembling a perception in some aspect, e.g. shape, but not otherwise, e.g., because it is made not of sensation but of matter), at worst inconceivable, and so unbelievable (see chapters 1 note 47, and 7-C, especially note 15). If the generality (the existential quantification) resolves into an association, there must be ideas to associate. But, since, in a merely relative idea, the relative is not a distinct perception in its own right, there not only can be no association, but also no relation of any kind. A relation requires a transition from *one perception* to *another*; an observed *conjunction* requires ideas of at least two conjuncts; but, in the absence of distinct perceptions to relate, there can be no relation. On the other hand, if quantification cannot be resolved into ideas or their relations, then, so far as Hume would be concerned, it must, like all generality irreducible to associative psychology, be purely linguistic; hence, while possibly a useful device for studying language, quantificational analysis can have no place in an associationalist psychology of ideas instinctively related in imagination. See also chapter 6 note 6.

11 "Whatever we can imagine, is possible" (*T*250).

[12] Without denying the importance of highly general, philosophical (i.e. non-natural) causal relations to science and philosophy, it seems to me importantly wrong to suppose, as Beauchamp and Rosenberg do, that "the truth of singular causal statements depends on the truth of law statements (instead of the reverse) ... [i.e. that Hume denied] the primacy of individual causal sequences in understanding causal relations" (see *Hume and the Problem of Causality*, Oxford University Press, 1981, pp. 80f.). To put philosophical relations before natural (as they do when they emphasize constant conjunction), or even to set them on a par, is, in my view, a paradigmatic instance of putting the cart before the horse: the whole (empiricist) impulse of Hume's theory of relation is to explain philosophical relations in terms of natural, and reduce everything that passes under the name "reason" in matters of fact to instinctive propensities of association. Until the habit is formed and the association fixed, *there is no philosophical causal relation*, only a constant conjunction (which *itself* is grounded in natural relations of resemblance and contiguity – see chapter 2-D); philosophical causal relations are merely an extension of natural causal relations, dealing solely with *aspects* of the latter. Useful they may be for understanding natural causal relations retrospectively; but they must never be proffered or advertised as an *autonomous* foundation for such relations or an *independent* standpoint from which to view them (see Part II). If nothing else, it should not be forgotten that Hume deemed it a virtue (indeed a touchstone) of his account of causation that it applies also to the reason of animals: this alone suffices to show that, for Hume, causal relations presuppose neither law statements nor, in general, the forms and uses of language.

[13] Berkeley too stressed this point – see *PHK* Intro. §19. According to Putnam, one "simply *evinces* his pain by saying 'I am in pain' – he does not first reflect on it (or heed it, or note it, etc.) and then consciously describe it. (Note that this simple possibility of uttering the 'proposition' 'I am in pain' without first performing any mental 'act of judgment' was overlooked by traditional epistemologists from Hume to Russell!)" ("Minds and Machines," p. 368, in *Philosophical Papers*, Vol. 2). Putnam however neglects the custom which "renders us, in great measure, insensible" (*T*25) of performing mental acts. Experience and habit render such activity so routine as to be automatic; but precisely because it presupposes experience and habit it is more aptly described as judgment than perception. This is an iterated theme in Hume (e.g. *T*103f., *T*133, *T*203f., *T*305, and *T*373), probably deriving from Locke (see *ECHU* II/ix/§§8–10). The insensible character of customs, together with the difficulty of correctly describing them ("'tis very difficult to talk of the operations of the mind with perfect propriety and exactness; because common language has seldom made any very nice distinctions among them," *T*105), need to be taken into account in inquiry regarding the mental/physical "facts" behind generality. As Chomsky has observed in reference to the Kripkenstein skeptic (in *Wittgenstein on Rules and Private Language*, Cambridge MA: Harvard University Press, 1982), "If we say that Jones is obeying a rule 'privately,' and hence that he is obeying a rule, nothing follows at all about whether he thinks that he is obeying the rule ... We must avoid the temptation to assume some notion of 'accessibility to consciousness' with regard to mental states and their contents ... What [Kripke's skeptic] has shown is that the facts concerning

Jones's past behavior and conscious mental states are not sufficient to establish that Jones is following the rule R, but it does not follow that 'there can be no facts about him in virtue of which he accords with his intentions or not,' that is, in virtue of which he can be said to follow the rule R ... It does not provide justification ... But it does not follow that we must accept the skeptical conclusion that there is no fact as to whether Jones means plus or quus" (*Knowledge of Language*: *Its Nature*, *Origin*, *and Use*, New York: Greenwood Press, 1986, pp. 229f. and 239f.).

[14] See discussion of *PHK* Intro. §16 in section A above.

[15] One seeming exception is the abstract idea of existence: as existence is supposed by Hume to be an aspect of every idea, there is no idea of non-existence from which to differentiate it; being incapable therefore of differentiating any idea from any other, it seems impossible to acquire an idea of existence through comparisons, and *a fortiori* to explicate it in terms of a habitude (see *T*67). The key to dealing with this difficulty is to recognize that, for Hume, existence adds no content to the idea but is in fact "the same with the idea of what we conceive to be existent" (*T*66). This suggests that the correct way to interpret existence is in terms of vivacity, which likewise adds no content to the idea but instead merely colors the attitude of consciousness toward it (see *TApp*623f.). Hume equates the *possibility* of existence with having a clear and distinct idea (e.g. *T*43, *T*250), and the *actuality* of existence with belief (e.g. *T*109, *T*153); thus, the difference is merely one of the degree separating conception (minimal vivacity) from belief (impression or association-enlivened idea). Since perceptions can be compared in respect of resemblances in the degree of vivacity with which they are regarded, the abstract idea of existence common to all perceptions can be explained by the fact that all inspire some degree of vivacity simply as presences before the mind; but they differ, and so admit of comparison, in degree. The comparison that seems most relevant here is that of an ideational content *with itself* at different times, the actual existence of which may, at one time, be believed or disbelieved, and at another time, the contrary; this awareness of the possibility of increase and decrease of vivacity is thence the basis of the belief that everything we can clearly conceive is potentially an actuality. Given that an abstract idea is a habit and that habits are separable, Wilson asserts that "Hume can hold that there is a distinction of reason between a thing and existence – these two ideas are different – while also holding that the idea of a thing and the idea of existence are inseparable" ("Hume on the Abstract Idea of Existence," pp. 190f.). Since Hume does not actually hold this ("Our foregoing reasoning [in *Treatise* I/i/§7] concerning the *distinction* of ideas without any real *difference* will not here serve us in any stead," *T*67), Wilson's remark requires qualification. The abstract idea of existence is obtained not by comparison of distinct ideas, but of (ideas of) the feelings present in consciousness in regarding distinct perceptions – feelings that are not distinct perceptions in their own right (i.e. vivacity is intentional); so, it is not a true associative relation. But this is all to the good since, if existence (possible or actual) were an aspect of the perception itself, then it would be impossible for the same content to be, at different times, believed and disbelieved – see chapter 4-C.

[16] Hume's treatment of general ideas has close affinities with Wittgenstein's

treatment of concepts in terms of inductive series formed of propositions in which they are used (see especially *Philosophical Investigations* §135).

17 See *CPR* §§9–10 (A70/B95 ff.), A242-A245, A248f., B305, A321/B378, A349, B378, B428, and B431; also *Prolegomena* §28 and §39 (*AA* 3, pp. 311 and 324) and the footnote in the Preface to the *Metaphysical Foundations of Natural Science* (*AA* 4, p. 474). Wright claims that Kant felt a debt to Hume for undermining the maxim that "nothing we imagine is absolutely impossible" on the ground that Kant claimed that many ideas (= *Ideen*) do not possess objective possibility (see "Hume's Rejection of the Theory of Ideas," pp. 150f.) This seems to me mistaken. Wright's argument can only work "in spite of Hume's appeal to imagination," that is, only if we suppose that Hume admitted a faculty higher than imagination, a "pure reason" (which he denied on *T*72). When Hume says "imagination," I take him at his word (see chapter 2-D); and Kant would never have dreamed of denying that any idea (= *Vorstellung*) we can *imagine* is a possible appearance.

18 See *CPR* B141f. and the *Opus Postumum* (*AA* 22, pp. 85, 89, 93, and 96).

19 "It is a mere tautology to speak of general or common concepts, a mistake based on a wrong division of concepts into *general*, *particular*, and *singular*. Not the concepts themselves, only their use can be divided in this way," *Logic* §1 (*AA* 9).

20 I am currently preparing a paper, to be called "Universals Without Language," which will deal with this topic in greater detail. There is a striking similarity between Kant's illustration of the synthetic unity of apperception by "the unity of theme in a play, a speech, or a story" (*CPR* B114 – see reference to this passage at B131) and Hume's literary illustration of the effects of association in *Enquiry* III: "the events or actions which the writer relates must be connected together by some bond or tie: They must be related to each other in the imagination, and form a kind of *unity* which may bring them under one plan or view, and which may be the object or end of the writer in his first undertaking ... etc." (see also *TAbs*662). This passage was deleted in the final edition Hume supervised, but is present in the German translation known to Kant. So, Flew was probably very wide of the mark when he judged it as "an entirely new item" of no significance other than "an attempt to apply the notion of the association of ideas to literary criticism" (*Hume's Philosophy of Belief*, London: Routledge and Kegan Paul, 1961, p. 4).

21 *Progress*, p. 100. Baier believes that nearly all of *Treatise* I is based on language (see above, introduction note 28), as do most other "common life" interpreters (see e.g. chapter 1 note 6). This is especially so in the case of generality: "the Humean world seems to have been peopled from the start, or at any rate from the start of a thinker's language-dependent use of general ideas. Without these, causal inference could not occur" (p. 111). Of course, if this were right, then Hume could never have argued, as he in fact did, that animals reason causally; so, the assumption that he restricted generality to the language-user seems equally dubious.

22 Except in the extremely attenuated sense in which some scientists suppose higher apes capable of language (claims which have been cast in doubt by expert reviewers of their findings).

23 In my view, Livingston does violence to this passage when he equates "purposes

of life" with *social conventions*, making it impossible to extend Hume's account of generality to asocial higher animals like tigers (he even presumes to correct Hume for speaking of ideas rather than terms, thereby excluding social animals as well – see *Common Life*, p. 78).

24 Unlike his Scottish successor, Locke denied the power to form general ideas to animals. Yet, he did so not because of their lack of language, but because he deemed the mental power of abstraction beyond them – see *ECHU* II/xi/§11.

25 *Common Life*, p. 72. Contrast this with Quine: "The idea of defining a symbol in use was ... an advance over the impossible term-by-term empiricism of Locke and Hume. The statement, rather than the term, came with Bentham to be recognized as the unit accountable to an empiricist critique." ("Two Dogmas," *From a Logical Point of View*. New York: Harper Torchbooks, 1963, p. 42). Or G. Strawson: "All one has to do, in order to find out what the content of an idea or concept or word is – and, hence, in order to find out *what one is* (*really*) *talking about*, when employing the idea in thought, or equivalently *what one is* (*really*) *talking about*, when one uses the word – is to consider the impression(s) from which it is derived" (*The Secret Connexion*, p. 102). In the case of concepts or words, this would be correct only if restricted to *objective*, or better *experiential*, content.

26 *Common Life*, p. 78.

27 E.g. Kemp Smith, *The Philosophy of David Hume*, pp. 273ff.; Robert Fogelin, *Hume's Skepticism*, London: Routledge, 1985, p. 34; and Wright, "Hume's Rejection of the Theory of Ideas," p. 152. A recent exception is Michael Costa, "Hume, Strict Identity, and Time's Vacuum," *Hume Studies*, 16: 1, April, 1990, p. 3.

28 Hovering just beyond these considerations is an issue on which Hume did not take a position until *Treatise* I/iv: the vulgar identification of impressions (at least of vision and touch) with mind-independent objects, and the philosophical supposition that impressions are images of things (or, in Berkeley's case, of an order) existing outside the mind. In *Treatise* I/ii, he goes only so far as to claim that the sole objects with which we can concern ourselves in disputes concerning indivisibility, vacuum, etc., are perceptions (e.g. "whatever we may imagine of the *thing*, the *idea* of a grain of sand is not distinguishable, nor separable into twenty, much less into a thousand, ten thousand, or an infinite number of different ideas," *T*.27 – emphasis mine).

29 See especially Wittgenstein's *Philosophical Remarks*, §§ 134, 136f., 173, 178, and 205–17.

30 On *E*XII/ii.124n., Hume affirms "that there are physical points." But, as the sequel makes clear, this is not a contradiction, merely a change in terminology for the perceptible minima of the *Treatise*: " ... that is, parts of extension, which cannot be divided or lessened, either by the eye or imagination. These images, then, which are present to the fancy or senses, are absolutely indivisible, and consequently must be allowed by mathematicians to be infinitely less than any real part of extension."

31 The three-dimensionality of space Hume seems to have regarded as an object of reason, not the senses: see *T*56–58, *T*581f., and *E*V/ii.227f.

32 It would be grossly mistaken to interpret Hume's assertion that a "sound reason convinces us that there are bodies *vastly* more minute than those, which

appear to the senses" (*T*48) as applying to perceptions themselves, and in particular as implying that he deemed minima of perception to be complex rather than simple. This "sound reason" turns out, in *Treatise* I/iv, to be based on a host of fictions of imagination; and while the fictitious character of the beliefs in no way compromises their certainty, it still restricts their validity to the purview of imagination. See chapter 7–B.

[33] *Remarks on the Philosophy of Psychology*, Vol. I, §§1079–80.

[34] Nor can we be sure that Wittgenstein himself would have been unwilling to countenance *talk* of such a standard so long as no pretence was made of devising an actual *example* of such a language. His critique was directed largely against Frege, Russell, and himself in the *Tractatus*: "But, if we're to say that a proposition isn't an elementary proposition unless its complete logical analysis shows that it isn't built out of other propositions by truth-functions, we are presupposing that we have an idea of what such an 'analysis' would be. Formerly, I myself spoke of a 'complete analysis', and I used to believe that philosophy had to give a definitive dissection of propositions so as to set out clearly all their connections and remove all possibilities of misunderstanding. I spoke as if there was a calculus in which such a dissection would be possible. I vaguely had in mind something like Russell's definition of the definite article" (translated and quoted by Hilmy in *The Later Wittgenstein*, p. 219; see also his note 228 on pp. 256ff.). See also appendix 4 in *Philosophical Grammar* ("Elementary Propositions") and *Brown Book* §4.

[35] *Intentions*, p. 87f.

[36] *Locke*, *Berkeley*, *Hume*, Oxford University Press, 1971, p. 227f. Kripke too imposes a linguistic orientation on Hume: "Hume... thinks that an appropriate 'impression' or 'image' can constitute an 'idea', without realizing that an image in no way tells us how it is to be applied" (*Wittgenstein*,p. 63n.). But this is to confuse ideas with terms of a language. For Hume, ideas are not applied but associated with other perceptions, whereas terms belong to the public sphere and have their application determined by our shared needs and purposes; it thus is impossible to identify the meaning of a linguistic expression with an idea or feeling considered in isolation from the social context (contrast this with James's "but"-feeling). Kripke's confusion also reflects a deeper, more pervasive misunderstanding, namely, that when Hume concerns himself with the beliefs of the "vulgar" he means the judgments (especially verbal behavior) of "the common man." The beliefs of the latter concerned Hume in *Treatise* I only to the extent that they are shared with infants, our pre-linguistic ancestors, and higher animals; beliefs dependent on eduction and convention were only of secondary importance. See chapter 7-B.

4 BEYOND THE SENSES

[1] Hume probably borrowed it from Locke (*ECHU* II/xxi/§4).

[2] Given Hume's principle that whatever is separable in imagination is distinct in reality (see e.g. *T*18), no perception can endure beyond the temporal minimum. See chapter 6-A.

[3] In section C, when we consider relations of ideas, it will emerge that relations of quantity, and even deductive reasoning itself, owe their application to

matters of fact and real existence to causal relations. Although I agree with Winkler's general position, I think him mistaken when he asserts that, by contrast with the existence of bodies which we must take for granted in all our reasonings, Hume "makes no corresponding point about objective necessary connections ... Hume never says that the projective propensity is irresistible. It is, moreover, hard to see why our welfare should depend on the propensity" ("The New Hume," *Philosophical Review*, 100: 4, October, 1991. Cornell University Press, pp. 562 and 564). Hume repeatedly affirmed that causal connections are "always necessary" (as in the title of *Treatise* I/iii/§3; see also chapter 1 note 44) And, if not irresistable (*T*92), causal relations are of such importance that, without them, "human nature must immediately perish and go to ruin" (*T*255). For, in their absence, we could not believe in any reality beyond what is immediately present to our senses; the objective validity of identity and all other relations thus presupposes that of cause and effect (*T*74), as does memory itself (i.e. original/copy relations – see *T*4f.).

4 *Hume*, pp. 226ff.

5 *David Hume: Philosopher of Moral Science*, Oxford: Basil Blackwell Ltd., 1986, p. 31.

6 "Hume notes [on *T*73f.], the other ideas – identity of objects and relations of time and place – themselves depend on causation, since they require us to conclude something beyond the evidence of the senses (for example, that the object in front of us is the same as it was earlier)" (*David Hume and the Problem of Reason*, New Haven: Yale University Press, 1990, p. 64). Inexplicably (for they do not attempt to justify their reading), Hausman and Hausman take *T*74 to be asserting just the reverse – see "Idealizing Hume," *Hume Studies*, 18: 2, November, 1992, p. 210.

7 Costa gets things the wrong way around, in my view, when he claims: "we do ... extend 'custom and reasoning' beyond the perceptions themselves. What allows us to do this is that the constancy and coherence of some of the perceptions lead the imagination to produce dispositions to populate the gaps with appropriate ideas so as to minimize the de facto irregularities. The custom or habit that represents causal inference takes its start then from these *constructed* regularities. The point will become key when we address the signficance of Hume's views with respect to the metaphysical and epistemological questions concerning the existence of the external world" ("Hume and Belief in the Existence of the External World," *Philosophical Studies* (Dublin), 32, 1988–90, p. 104) Baier too contends that external objects are "taken for granted in his reasonings about causal inference," that *Treatise* I/iii is a "non-phenomenalist account of causal inference," and that "Hume's own 'system' needs the supposition of an external world, and one that is peopled" (*Progress*, pp. 104ff.). No doubt it is true that belief in an external world adds numerous regularities to our stock. But the causal inferences truly essential to, and characteristic of, Hume's system (especially of inference from the impression to the idea) are not those *among* the realities of the world of judgment, but those *which first make such realities possible.* The standpoint from which *Treatise* I/iii sets out is the world of the memory and senses, for one must already be in this world if one is to need causal inference to extend one's purview beyond it. Hume states explicitly that relations like identity cannot be

affirmed beyond the immediacy of memory and senses (as is required for belief in body) except on the presupposition of causal relations (*T*73f.); and *T*108 merely confirms that custom is the basis, not the consequence, of the supposition of an external world. (Nor is personal identity taken for granted as Baier supposes on p. 106; the mind of *Treatise* I/i is conceived on the model of something continuing through time, but no awareness of self – no *idea* of the mind – is premised there, nor explicable until Hume's system of *causally* related perceptions is found to make such an idea possible in *Treatise* I/iv.) Costa's key fits a quite different door than he imagines. Similarly, Baier's claim that a focus on the isolated mind is present only in *Treatise* I/iv errs not merely by being "guilty of picking and choosing" (p. 107), but also by seeing Hume's theory of cause and effect through the examples used to illustrate it (cf. Kant's remark that "examples are judgment's walker," *CPR* A134/B173); and, since it is only by denying that *Treatise* I/iv is of a piece with the rest of *Treatise* I that she can sustain her claim that Hume's system requires a world that is peopled, I see no reason not to restrict the claim to *Treatise* II and III. See chapter 7-A.

8 See Kant's Refutation of Idealism (*CPR* B274–9) and my paper "What are Kant's Analogies About?," *Review of Metaphysics*, September, 1993; *Kant's Model of the Mind*; and chapter 3-B above (especially note 20); also Nuyen, "Sense, Reason and Causality in Hume and Kant," *Kant-Studien*, 1990. Kuehn claims that Kant was closer to Reid than Hume in that he too rejected "simple apprehension" and the appearance of psychology in his philosophy was an aberration (see "Reid's Contribution to Hume's Problem" in *The 'Science of Man' in the Scottish Enlightenment*, Edinburgh University Press, 1989, edited by Peter Jones). In my view, accounting for the origin of ideas in and through psychological operations constitutive of experience was as centrally important for Kant as for Hume; and, in particular, Kant too acknowledged simple apprehension.

9 Nor was this the only occasion. Life was not made easier for Hume when, in 1754, John Stewart, in an article appearing in a volume Hume himself helped oversee, wrote: "That something may begin to exist, or start into being without a cause, hath indeed been advanced in a very ingenious and profound system of the sceptical philosophy – *Treatise of Human Nature*" (cited by Kemp Smith, *David Hume*, p. 411). The same criticism is prominent in the first reviews of the *Treatise*, for example that which appeared in the *Bibliothèque Raisonnée*, 1740: Hume "proceeds to maintain ... that it is false that everything which exists must necessarily have a cause of its existence" (cited by Ernest Mossner in *The Life of David Hume*, Oxford University Press, 1980, second edition, p. 130). Reid's agreement with this criticism is implicit in the introduction and elsewhere in his *Enquiry into the Human Mind on the Principles of Common Sense* of 1762, and explicit in chapter 6 of the sixth of his *Essays on the Intellectual Powers* of 1785 (cited below).

10 It is mentioned only once, at *E*VII/ii.60, in the section dealing with necessary connection; otherwise, it is simply stated and left unchallenged, as at *E*VIII/i.74.

11 See also Groarke and Solomon, "Some Sources for Hume's Account of Cause," *Journal of the History of Ideas*, 52: 4, October, 1991.

12 The resolvability of general claims into particular is essential to Hume's

argument; otherwise it would be vulnerable to the criticism directed against it by Anscombe: "Suppose there is a logical necessity about 'Every beginning of existence has a cause'. It would not follow that the connection between any particular cause and its effect involved any logical necessity. For 'Every beginning of existence has a cause' only says of every beginning of existence that it must have some cause or other, not that there is any given cause that anything must have" (*Metaphysics and the Philosophy of Mind*, p. 151).

13 *Metaphysics*, p. 160. Anscombe is actually countering Hume's reply to the position of Hobbes on *T*80.

14 Memory, however, is founded on a causal relation: we take an idea to be a memory only if we believe it to have derived from (and so dependent on the existence of) the past perception of which it is the present image. So, it is impossible to believe a memory to begin to exist without a cause.

15 *CPR* A760/B788 and *Prolegomena to any Future Metaphysics*, Preface, *AA* 3, pp. 257–61. See also *Critique of Practical Reason*, Pt. I, Bk. I, chapter 1, section ii. Whether he knew *Treatise* I/iii/§3 is unknown, but that he directed this remark specifically to Hume's treatment of the general causal law and the general concept of cause is clear. Since Hume's teaching in this regard is evident in the *Enquiry* as well, which (unlike the *Treatise*) had been translated into German, we can be reasonably sure that Kant was directly acquainted with it.

16 *Essays on the Intellectual Powers*, chapter 6.

17 See *CPR* A112f., A118f., and A121ff. See my "What Are Kants Analogies About?" and Beck, *Essays on Kant and Hume*, New Haven: Yale University Press, 1978, parts I, 7, and 8.

18 *Prolegomena*, Preface, *AA* 3, p. 258.

19 His theory of a priori imagination provided him the means by which to establish this point. See note 8 above.

20 Hume's treatment of possible existence and actuality as pertaining not to perceptions themselves, but our consciousness of them, so that modality predicates concern the relation of objects not to one another, but to the contemplating subject, is yet another uncanny anticipation by Hume of Kant. See *CPR* A219/B266f.

21 These may be regarded as tentative and subject to revision in the light of later evidence and "experiment" – just as we found to be the case with imagination (see chapter 2-B).

22 As will emerge in chapter 5, constant conjunction is necessary to causal relations from an *experiential/causal* point of view (i.e. where the concern is to furnish a *causal* explanation of how experience gives rise to particular causal inferences and the general maxim), but it does not enter into the content of the idea. As to content, the idea consists of (i) the impression and associated idea and (ii) the reflexive impression of necessary connection comprised of the phenomenological feelings of vivacity and customary ease of transition. It thus is possible, in principle, for the imagination of one who has just this moment come into existence to feel a causal relation.

23 A common objection, going back to Reid, is why, on Hume's account, it would not be natural to regard night as the cause of day since night constantly precedes day? See, e.g., Fogelin, *Hume's Skepticism*, Appendix B. I do not think the counterexample very good: the rising sun, not night, is naturally

regarded as the bringer of day. As for the rising sun itself, since night continues for hours on end without causing the sun to appear, it is doubtful that anyone, man or beast, would causally associate it with the appearance of the sun; rather, in the absence of anything perceptible, a cause would likely be imagined on analogy with familiar cases of raising things, e.g. an unseen hand. In any case, I am not that sure Hume would be very keen to be defended against this objection in the first place. His concern was not to supply us with a manual of good reasoning but to explain what reasoning is as such and how it comes to be. On good reasoning ("logic") one finds only a meagre section in the *Treatise* – I/iii/§15 – and a footnote in the *Enquiry* section concerned with the reason in animals. Whether the reasoning is good or not, true or false, etc., is tangential to his inquiry. So, for example, if a deer were convinced that a certain duration of night causes day, it will then know when to ready itself for the next day, and so long as this serves the purposes of its life, then the reasoning is quite "good" enough. Nor is it any different with humans: primitive man might have gotten along as well as the deer with the same belief. For it is likewise our purposes of life, as determined by our complex social organization and technology, that lead us to concern ourselves with continually refining our capacity to identify causes and distinguish them from coincidences. It seems to me that far too much emphasis tends to be placed on Hume's "logic" nowadays (e.g. Baier: "The whole enterprise is a search for norms," *Progress*, p. 97), almost to the point of treating it as the true (esoteric) subject matter of the work. That the *Treatise* should exemplify principles of sound human reasoning was surely Hume's objective; but, since he regarded this as something we more or less naturally do anyway ("philosophical decisions are nothing but the reflections of common life methodized and corrected," *E*XII/iii.130), it can be exemplified by any empirical investigation, from physics to drawing up a business plan or planning a marketing strategy. As far as subject matter is concerned, however, good reasoning is purely tangential to the *Treatise* and *Enquiry*, which focus almost entirely on the nature and origins of reasoning *as such*. It is possible for a sensitive interpreter to draw from these texts a number of important insights pertinent to the epistemology of adult, acculturated human beings, especially scientists; but one could not make a greater mistake than to suppose this to have been Hume's principal objective. For an excellent analysis, modest in pretensions, of the normative side of Hume's account of knowledge and its relation to science see Wilson, "Hume's Defense of Causal Inference," *Dialogue*, XII, 1983.

24 Letter to Lady Welby, 20 May, 1911.

25 *Hume's Philosophy of Belief*, p. 81. See also Stove, *Probability and Hume's Inductive Scepticism*, Oxford University Clarendon Press 1973, p. 43. The degree to which this judgment has become standard wisdom is evident from its inclusion in so primary a text as L. Jonathan Cohen's *An Introduction to the Philosophy of Induction and Probability*, Oxford University Press, 1989, §23.

26 *Hume*, p. 62 (Stroud credits Judith Jarvis Thompson with inspiring his solution to the problem).

27 *Hume*, p. 257n.17.

28 Fogelin follows Stroud but with a slight shift of emphasis: "The point is that the charge that someone is supposing the very matter at issue does not, *eo ipso*,

commit the person making the charge to deductivism. Perhaps an analogy will help bring out the force of Stroud's response. We can imagine a legislature that is deeply distrusted by its people. In response, the legislature undertakes an investigation and declares itself trustworthy. Clearly, the people will not be satisfied with these assurances, since the inquiry is subject to the same doubts that initiated it. It is, I think, in this sense that Hume holds that probable arguments in support of the claim that nature is uniform suppose the very thing at issue. Looked at this way, it is hard to see how deductivism comes in at all" (*Hume's Skepticism*, p. 157). Since, for Hume, a foundation of the principle of uniformity in probable reason involves reference to our *strongest*, most *firmly established* causal relations – relations with the status of *proofs* and so certain beyond any *real* possibility of doubt (one may doubt them with the lips but just try acting contrary to them! – see chapter 1 note 44), Fogelin's analogy of an *already* suspect legislature seems inappropriate. To render it viable, he needs to unpack his notion of "distrust" and explain how anything even remotely analogous to it is possible here. I cannot imagine how this might be done other than by invoking the *logical* concern occasioned by the gap separating past experience from present and future belief, thus raising again the spectre of deductive insufficiency.

29 Stroud attributes such a view to P. Strawson (see *Hume*, p. 64f.). Since I am dissatisfied with Stroud's arguments against this position (and with the correctness of the attribution as well), I shall briefly state my own reasons for rejecting it. If the analycity of the equation of "reasonable" with "proceeding in conformity with the uniformity principle" means that it holds regardless of any alteration, however complete, in our psychological, anthropological, and sociological formation, then it clearly is not analytic; for one cannot exclude the possibility that humans might have evolved, or even had inculcated in them, radically disparate responses to past experience than those familiar to us. But if this is not what "analytic" means here, then any such response to Hume would simply beg the question. For it was never his intention to deny that the behavior we *call* "reasonable" includes acting in conformity to the uniformity principle. But this is only to say he regarded it as a basic principle of human psychology; he would still deny that it has or can be given a rational foundation of any kind.

30 Beauchamp and Rosenberg believe "It was never Hume's intent to question the entire institution of inductive procedures and standards. His argument is a frontal attack on rationalist assumptions that at least some inductive arguments are demonstrative; it is not a demand for a wholesale justification of induction and *a fortiori* not a sceptical assault on induction" (*Causation*, p. 41). I agree that Hume was not concerned to question the entire institution of induction. Nevertheless, by challenging it at the most primitive level of consciousness, where causal relations first take us beyond the senses, he *ipso facto* put in question induction at the more advanced levels erected thereon. For, without our primitive instinct to believe in the reality of that which is present to the mind only in idea, all forms of non-deductive rationality would be rendered impossible. Because Beauchamp and Rosenberg fail to see Hume's problem in the context in which he framed it ("The only connexion or relation of objects, which can lead us beyond the immediate impressions of our memory and

senses, is that of cause and effect...etc." *T*89), they infer, without textual warrant so far as I can tell, that Hume's sole target was Cartesian rationalism. By contrast, on my reading, Hume is doing precisely what he claimed to be doing: challenging any attempt whatseover to found induction on empirical rationality, especially Locke's notion of the probable, rather than instinct. Owen too recognizes that Hume's principal target was Locke (see "Hume and the Lockean Background," *Hume Studies*, 18: 2, November, 1992). However, I believe he goes too far when he claims that Locke conceived of reasoning in terms of ideas rather than propositions. Locke was careful to distinguish propositions (the only bearers of the predicates "true" and "false") from the ideas, or materials, of which they consist (see *ECHU* II/xxxii/§1 and IV/v/§§2–3). Elsewhere, he asserted that "Everything which we either know or believe is some proposition" (Third letter to Stillingfleet). For Locke, there was a difference in kind between propositions, in which ideas are compared with an eye to their agreement or disagreement, and ideas themselves. Among other things, this means that, in demonstrations and proofs, truth is conveyed not from idea to idea, as Owen supposes, but from judged agreement to judged agreement (proposition to proposition). This is not to say that Owen is completely mistaken, but that he exaggerates the difference between Locke's tradition and others, including our own. One thinks of Russell's understanding of a proposition as a kind of relation, or complex, for which Wittgenstein criticized him in the pre-war years, as well as the later Wittgenstein's criticism of the *Tractatus* (see chapter 3 note 8); and today, with the renewed fashionability of isomorphisms of language/logic with mind and/or brain, the temptation to treat propositions as complexes is once again becoming great.

31 According to Nelson, Hume's argument only works if we actually experience things as distinct, isolated individuals and this in fact is not the case: "I contend that the kind as such, e.g. *gold*, is experienced" ("Induction A Non-Sceptical Humean Solution," *Philosophy*, 67: 261, July, 1992, p. 314). So, while there is a Humean gap in an inference from several occasions of seeing billiard-balls fall when dropped to the claim "all billiard-balls fall when dropped," there is none in the inference to the proposition "a billiard ball falls when dropped." The experience of a thing as a billiard-ball, as a natural kind, is *sine qua non* and irreducible to experiencing isolated, typeless individuals; thus, according to Nelson, so long as we recognize that our experience is typological, there is no need to go beyond probable reason and invoke blind instinct and custom in order to explain inductive generalization and our reliance on past experience in the present and future. But the weakness of this explanation, at least from a Humean perspective, is not difficult to find. Nelson invokes Aristotelian formal causes, e.g. the cause for something's having a craw rather than gills is its being a chicken. But what if it has no craw – does that mean it cannot be a chicken? Nelson concedes that through a genetic defect or other countervailng causes there may be crawless chickens: "where countervailing causes enter, a gap is produced but where none enter, there exists no gap" (p. 315). Here Nelson reveals his hand: if the exception has to have an efficient cause, then so too must the non-exceptions. A modern biologist, presented with a formal cause as the reason something has a craw but no gills would despair in the face of such persistent typological thinking: there is an efficient, biochemical causation that

explains this (and why it is a chicken), not some philosopher's figment of type (see e.g. Mayr, *Towards a New Philosophy of Biology*, Cambridge: Harvard University Press, 1988). Hume, too, recognizes that efficient causality is the basis of our notions of natural kinds (see *T*16). For what is it that unites in our imagination the visual form of a chicken, clucking sounds, a feathery texture, the finding of craws, etc., except constant concomitance? Even conceding that we experience them not disjointly, but as the kind *chicken*, we do so only because we refer the compresence of all these features to a prior efficient cause (a chicken creating vital force, the deity's choice, something about the egg, or, in the twentieth century, genetically based biochemistry). For, in the absence of an immediately perceptible relation between the concomitant features that combine them into our notion of the kind *chicken*, only the glue of custom can *bring* them together and, by the gentle force of association, bias imagination to *keep* them together and not randomly recombine them with other features, e.g. tusks, nectar, gills (nor can this kind of custom be the sort that underlies generality: generality is based on *immediately perceptible* resemblance relations; only the customs responsible for necessary connections can explain our experience of things as kinds). In short, experience of things as natural kinds depends on the experienced constant concomitance of various features; such concomitance can only distinguish itself as a kind if conjoined with a prior cause which makes their compresence non-random; and to account for this invocation of a cause we cannot refer again to experience of things as natural kinds, but must either find some other form of probable reason or accept that only instinct, blind custom, can explain the inference.

5 CUSTOM AND NECESSITY

1 Hume was careful to remark that this feeling becomes less noticeable the more fixed and confident we are of the pattern of transition – see *T*25, *T*99, *T*103, *T*110f., *T*133 but especially *T*258. Other passages that help shed light on this feeling include: *T*116, *T*132, *T*141ff., *T*185f., *T*203f., *T*208. *T*220, *T*237, and *T*260.

2 For Baier, custom is "a feeling of determination ... [in] the phenomenology of free and constrained association ... [I]n inference we feel that we are determined" (*Progress*, pp. 81f.). Pears proposes that we interpret it as a feeling of *powerlessness* rather than of being *compelled* (see *Hume's System*, Oxford: Oxford University Press, 1990, p. 110–14). I confess to being unable to see how this improves matters: the notions of passivity and patience are no less causal in nature than activity and agency. How could one be supposed capable of immediately perceiving powerlessness, but not its contrary? And even if one could perceive the one without the other, it still seems suspiciously like a direct perception of causality (in the form of patience); if so, then Pears' notion is no more compatible with Hume's position than compulsion.

3 "Hume and Thick Connexions," *Philosophy and Phenomenological Research*, L., Supplement, Fall 1990, p. 242.

4 *Problems and Projects*, The Bobbs-Merrill Company, Indianapolis: 1972., pp. 387–88.

5 There is a similar oversight in Pears' treatment of Hume's claim that custom is not responsible for belief in body – see chapter 7 note 9.

6 At the outset of section §14, Hume states that "we must now return upon our footsteps to examine that question, which first occur'd to us, and which we dropt in our way, *viz. What is our idea of necessity, when we say that two objects are necessarily connected together*" (*T*155). Since this query makes no mention of a cause to every beginning of existence, one could not be sure that the maxim was meant were it not for a footnote he appended referring his reader back to the question first posed on *T*78, "For what reason we pronounce it *necessary*, that every thing whose existence has a beginning, shou'd also have a cause?" Beck is therefore unjustified in saying that the question of how the maxim arises from experience, once sunk into the question regarding the inference from particular causes to effects at the end of *Treatise* I/iii/§3, "never reemerges" (*Essays*, p. 121). The whole of *Treatise* I/iii/§14 should be viewed as its answer (as is clear on *T*172 under "Thirdly").

7 Wilson, too, supposes that patterns in our own inference themselves become the subjects of causal inferences: "What makes Hume's rules the *reasonable* ones to adopt? ... Given that our end is to come to believe general truths, then, what we discover is that, as a matter of lawful fact, conformity to these rules is the best or most efficient means for achieving that end, so far as we are able ... What we discover are regularities to the effect that certain conditions bringing about law-assertive attitudes are more likely than others to yield successful law-assertive attitudes. *These regularities are inductions about making inductions.*" ("Hume's Theory of Mental Activity," pp. 112 and 117, in *McGill Hume Studies*, D. Norton, N. Capaldi, and W. Robison, editors; final emphasis mine).

8 For an example of what may occur when this is neglected see note 14 below.

9 In my view, Pears was not giving Hume his proper due when he criticized him for failing to take account of "the difference between changes attributable to the observer and changes attributable to the phenomena themselves" (*System*, p. 169). Once a custom is objectified and two objects are believed to be conjoined in a causal relation, it is no longer possible to regard the cause as posterior to the effect even if the effect is the first perceived (i.e. if I see the smoke before seeing the fire). Although itself a product of causal relations, Hume invariably grouped memory with the senses (e.g. *T*86 but especially *T*108) because his real concern, in my view, was objectivity: filling out the universe of space and *its* time (not subjective recollection but cosmological history). I would even go so far as to say that Kant's Second Analogy (*CPR* A189/B232 ff.), whether wittingly or not, is patterned after precisely this aspect of Hume's positive account of causality: the role of the concept "cause" in distinguishing the objective succession of events irrespective of the succession of perceptions of sense and memory.

10 *Intentions*, p. 75f.

11 Broughton claims that "Hume's point ... is that the mind *cannot* exercise its general spreading propensity in the particular case of the idea of necessary connection. The content of the relevant impression *cannot* be conjoined in thought with ideas of objects. But if this is so, then Hume must be denying that our impression of determination allows us to speak meaningfully of an

objective and necessary connection between events" ("Hume's Ideas About Necessary Connection," *Hume Studies*, 13: 2, November, 1987, p. 222). It is true that an impression that is "nowhere" cannot *really* be situated in the space of an extended object; but Hume made quite clear that this does not stop the imagination from doing so anyway, and the necessity impression is no exception (see *T*167). What Broughton overlooks, I believe, is the projective character of all belief generally, such that consciousness ascribes verismilitude to anything in observing which it feels vivacity – be it an isolated perception or the complex idea of a relation. The only thing Hume precluded is the application of our ideas of causal relations to objects in a manner inconsistent with their dependence (both in origin and in content) on phenomenological imagination ("we are led astray by a false philosophy ... when we transfer the determination of the thought to external objects, and suppose any real intelligible connexion betwixt them," *T*168).

12 See chapter 4-C for a consideration of which factors – spatial continuity, temporal, contiguity, constant conjunction – are indispensable to natural causal relations and which are merely usual.

13 See e.g. Penulhum, *Hume*, New York: St. Martin's Press, 1975, p. 55; Robinson, "Hume's Two Definitions of 'Cause' Reconsidered," in *Hume*, Vere Chappell, editor, Notre Dame: University of Notre Dame Press, 1966, p. 132.; and Stroud, *Hume*, p. 90. Others, like Beauchamp and Rosenberg, take the *seemingly* more cautious position that, for Hume, the relations composing philosophical cause and effect – contiguity, succession, and constant conjunction – apply uniquely to perceptions (not mind-independent entities), but are none the less independent of consciousness (imagination): "Hume finds two different impression-sources for the idea of necessity ... His reductionist account describes only the external impression-sources (impressions of sensation), as in [the definition of the philosophical relation]; while the genetic account describes both the external and the internal (reflective) impression-sources, as in [the definition of the natural relation]" (*Causation*, p. 29). I cannot imagine what else this could mean than that, in addition to sensations and reflexions, we have relation-impressions as well. But there seems to me little reason to believe and much to disbelieve that Hume ever wished to trace the ideas of relations to impressions, outside and independent of idea-relating and -enlivening imagination (see introduction and chapter 2-D). Hume's theory of relations may well be "opaque" (p. 27), but at least this much is clear: they are not copied from impressions (with the exception of a peculiar variety of resemblance relations mentioned on *T*283, their application is expressly restricted to ideas related and enlivened in imagination – see *T*13, *T*259f. and *TAbs*661f.).

14 Robison claims Hume "explicitly rejects D2 [the definition of the natural relation]" because "What it connects ... is not a cause with its effect, but a *perception* of a cause with a conception of or belief in the occurrence of its effect. It is the wrong kind of connection; it is necessary for its existence that the mind observe the relations of contiguity and succession holding between similar objects ... and that the mind react to that observation by producing it. What is foreign in D2 [as Hume requires a definition of an idea to be] is thus that natural relation. D2 makes it a condition of something causing something else that a

mind observe and react to what it observes. That Hume does not accept such a condition is clear from his claiming that there are 'secret [i.e., unobserved] causes'" ("Hume's Causal Scepticism," p. 160, in *Bicentenary Papers*, G. P. Morice, editor, Edinburgh University Press, 1977; 2nd bracketed insert Robison's). Robison thus infers that Hume regarded the proposition that the only idea we have of any necessary connection is derived from the impression of the mind's determination as false: "In the *Treatise* at least Hume was concerned not with causation, but with causal judgment" (p. 157; see also p. 161). Robison's claim that Hume was concerned only with causal judgments and not with causation itself is belied by the fact that, on *T*172, he draws a conclusion regarding the general causal maxim from the definitions (the question he had sunk into that of causal inferences on *T*82). More importantly, the contention that custom, once objectified, is the wrong kind of relation fails to do justice to the fact that the idea of necessity is copied from an impression which consists of precisely the two phenomenological elements which D2 incorporates: the *facility* of transition in custom and the *vivacity* of the idea when its associate is present in sensation or reflexion. Since necessity is an essential part of causation, D2 genuinely does explicate the meaning of cause and effect (and, despite Robison's claim to the contrary, D1 – of the philosophical relation – is likewise a genuine definition since it borrows the notion of necessity from the natural relation; and it is further dependent on the observing mind in so far as constant conjunction is simply an amalgam of associative relations of resemblance and contiguity). This, according to Hume, is the *only* idea of cause and effect we have; hence, there is nothing that can ensure the meaningfulness of philosophers' talk of imperceptible, inconceivable, unbelievable "secret causes" (see section F; also chapters 1 note 47, and 7-C). Moreover, I see no problem as Robison does in explaining Hume's "saying of [D1 and D2] that they are 'drawn from objects foreign to the cause'" (*T*170) (p. 162). The relevant sense of "foreign" is something distinct (by the *T*18 separability principle) from the idea defined: the cause and the effect are perceptions, that in virtue of which they are "necessarily connected" is a customary transition in the imagination; being in the imagination, it is therefore both foreign and extraneous to the cause and effect, i.e. these perceptions are as separable from the transition as they are from one another (since nothing but the transition conjoins them). Nor can I concur with Robison that D2 outruns Hume's "classificatory machinery – and the principles of his empiricism" on the ground that "to equate the determination with an impression is to mis-identify elements of the mind's structure as its content" (p. 159). I agree that the word is ill-chosen since it is apt to lead one to believe that determination is part of the content of the idea of cause, whereas in fact, phenomenologically, custom manifests itself only as a feeling of easy transition (see section A). The ambiguity seems unavoidable since D2 is as much a causal/experiential explanation of the natural relation as D1 is of the philosophical relation. Hume's purpose in *Treatise* I/iii was to show how experience causally generates both causal inferences and the causal maxim; since in the case of D2 this meant showing how experience causes certain phenomenological contents, the two senses of "customary determination" discussed in section A were bound to be inextricably intertwined in it. At any rate, in so far as Hume was a skeptic regarding causal relations, it was not because of a want of adequate defintions.

15 Contrary to the view of Beauchamp and Rosenberg that "Hume's analysis requires that there be two definitions, two meanings, and two senses of 'cause' ... And this is equally true of 'necessity'" (*Causation*, p. 29). It is true that Hume also says "I define necessity two ways, conformable to the two definitions of *cause*" (*T*409). But this is also the case on my reading, according to which the philosophical senses of "cause" and "necessity" are derived from, and parasitic on, the natural. There are a variety of ways of showing it, but perhaps the most direct is this: since relations of constant precedence *themselves* constantly precede natural causal relations, they must eventually, and quite *naturally*, become associated with beliefs in necessary connection (a kind of metahabit); hence, wherever there is constant precedence, the imagination will think – and believe – there is a necessary connection. This association holds true even when the judgment is so general and complex that none of the items concerned in it naturally lead the mind to any of the others: if constant precedence can be demonstrated, the custom will determine the imagination to think and believe in a necessary connection. This way of interpreting *T*409 was not considered by Fogelin, who saw it as evidence for his reading of the first definition as "a uniformity interpretation of necessity itself" (p. 40, *Skepticism*). Nor does he offer convincing readings of passages in the *Enquiry* that seem to belie this reading, e.g. the reformulation of the first definition which clearly goes beyond uniformity to full-fledged necessary connection ("where if the first object had not been, the second never had existed," *E*VII/ii.60), the reiteration of the claim that necessary connection is part of the idea of cause at *E*VIII/i.74, and, finally, the remark that the two senses of necessity "are at bottom the same" (*E*VIII/ii.75).

16 As with other standards employed in Hume's psychology, there is a gray area in the application of the separability principle as well. Intentional feelings seem to fall somewhere between, on the one hand, distinctions between shape and color in the visual field (which clearly are aspects, i.e. distinctions of reason), and, on the other hand, distinctions between discontinuous patches of color, which equally plainly are fully distinct perceptions. The feeling of vivacity I feel when confronted with a patch of red in my visual field is not merely an aspect like the shape or extension of the patch; I can imagine having the sensation without also feeling the belief. Yet, to imagine the feeling without any perception present to which it could be directed does not seem possible. See discussion of *esse* is *percipi* in chapter 6-B.

17 I construe it as imprecision on Hume's part that, on one occasion, he identifies the impression of reflexion not with a perception but with "that propensity, which custom produces, to pass from an object to the idea of its usual attendant" (*T*165). Since a propensity is not a perception, he must really have meant the felt facile transition.

18 Its purely phenomenological character belies Passmore's claim that "Hume never undertakes an analysis of mental necessity" (*Intentions*, p. 78f.). Baier recognizes that Hume intended his (causal) account to apply to the causality of thought itself in producing the idea of cause, but seems to regard constant conjunction as part of the content of the idea of necessary connection (see

Progress, pp. 90ff.). There is evidence for this, e.g. "Here then are two particulars, which we are to consider as essential to necessity, *viz.* the constant *union*, and the *inference* of the mind" (*T*400; see also *T*171). But I do not think Hume should be taken too literally: setting aside essences (which he deemed unknowable, in respect of the workings both of mind and body – see *T*xvii), the claim is that constant experience shows that a constant union of perceptions produces customary transitions; hence, the evidence for the inference from constant union to necessary connection amounts not merely to probability, but to proof (= essential). Constant conjunction is "essential" to necessary connection because *experience* proves that it is, and, more importantly, because it is that alone which *experience* reveals to be common between natural and philosophical cause and effect (i.e. the common feature which enables inferences of the latter sort to "tap into" the belief-engendering power of the former). But nowhere in these texts, or elsewhere to my knowledge, is there any explicit evidence that a *memory* of constant conjunction is an indispensable part of the *content* of the idea of necessary connection; it merely pertains to its causal explanation (i.e. is constantly conjoined with that content). Thus, an instantaneously existing consciousness could, in my view, *feel* a customary transition to have occurred, and so acquire the idea of necessity, without any memory of constant conjunction.

19 *Prolegomena*, Preface, *AA* 3, pp. 258–59.

20 *David Hume*, p. 401f. See also Robinson (in Chappell, editor, *Hume*, p. 146f.) and Fogelin, *Skepticism*, pp. 47ff. Stroud advances a considerably modified form of this view: the determination of the mind is "just a feeling that arises in the mind whenever a certain kind of mental occurrence causes another" (*Hume*, p. 85; see pp. 80–86).

21 *David Hume*, p. 135.

22 *Sceptical Realism*, p. 132 (his italics).

23 The whole paragraph is written in a mocking tone: the way Hume states the objection; his use of the analogy of the blind man; his witticism that "twill be to little purpose to prove, that an efficacy is necessary in all operations" if "we have really no idea of a power or efficacy in any object"; etc. (moreover, this humorous vein continues into the "subtility" on *T*169). To discount Hume's irony here seems to me to require a leap of faith as great as would be required to accept *Shamela* and *Joseph Andrews* as actual sequels of *Pamela.* On the other hand, I believe too much can be made of Hume's use of irony (e.g. Livingston, Baier). Even where all can agree irony is intended, its meaning, like most irony, is elusive; so, in interpreting it, we will ultimately have to rely on our understanding of his doctrine.

24 *Intentions*, p. 36. See also Winkler, "The New Hume," pp. 550ff.

25 According to Strawson, "in his Realist (or Basic Realist) linguistic practice, he acknowledged that words may have a proper use or meaning (a proper use and hence a meaning) beyond the use or meaning granted to them by the theory of ideas" (*Connexion*, p. 127). I disagree. It is one thing to hold, as I believe Hume did, that ideas are not the meanings of words, but quite another to attach objective import to words even when there is no idea to support them. In this respect, Hume's view seems to me clear: that of which we have no idea, we not only cannot conceive, we also cannot believe ("we can never have reason to

believe that any object exists, of which we cannot form an idea," *T*172). Strawson saddles Hume with a type of inference he was particularly keen to expose and discredit: "it naturally happens, that after the frequent use of terms, which are wholly insignificant and unintelligible, we fancy them ... to have a secret meaning, which we might discover by reflection" (*T*224).

26 Broughton derives her realist interpretation, in part, from a passage from Hume's *History* lauding Newton for both "admitting no principles but such as were founded on experiment" and a readiness "to adopt every such principle, however new or unusual," for he thereby "shewed ... the imperfections of the mechanical philosophy; and ... restored her ultimate secrets to that obscurity in which they ever did and ever will remain." According to Broughton, this shows that "Hume sees Newton as holding that our ignorance of underlying causes (even if our ignorance is necessary) does not imply our ignorance of the existence of gravitational forces, or the inappropriateness of investigating them empirically" ("Hume's Ideas About Necessary Connection," p. 234). In my view, Hume would never admit the existence of causes where our ignorance of them is necessary, i.e. where objects are inconceivable. Hume's praise of Newton suggests to me a condemnation of mechanists who, *on a priori grounds alone*, rule out action at a distance. Newton was bold enough to abandon a priori preconceptions and be guided by experience in his search for causes; and the *constant experience* of objects acting at a distance is simply added confirmation of Hume's belief that we have no business making a priori judgments on matters of fact. Such a view is quite incompatible with the affirmation of secret causes; on the contrary, it urges us to trust always in experience and resist any temptation to affirm the existence of that which experience can never disclose to us (i.e. that of which we can have no idea and, *a fortiori*, can never believe). Winkler said it quite well: "To ascribe power to a secret cause is to say something about the expectations we would have were we to *experience* unseen parts or mechanisms. And to ascribe power to an ultimate cause is to say something about the expectations we would have were we to *experience* the smallest objects (or fundamental parts)" ("The New Hume," p. 577 – emphasis mine).

27 "The Hume Literature of the 1980s," *The American Philosophical Quarterly*, 28:4, October, 1991, p. 259. See also "The Dogmatic Slumber of Hume Scholarship," *Hume Studies*, 18: 2, November, 1992, pp. 125f.

6 THE TRUE IDEA OF THE HUMAN MIND

1 Locke's conception of succession is perhaps his most important philosophical contribution. In addition to Hume, Kant's conception of time as the form of intuition probably would not have been possible except as a refinement (or, rather, a superseding) of Locke. Kant retained the idea that empirical apperception (consciousness) is not the observer of succession, but is *itself* the succession; however, for him, this meant that time is the *form* of inner sense, not that manifolds of perception are received into the mind in transcendentally real succession to one another (i.e. the successiveness constitutive of empirical consciousness is only an appearance in synthesizing imagination). This is like,

but not the same as, McTaggart's view (see my "Time and Change in Kant and McTaggart"; also *Kant's Model*, chapter 1).

2 In defending his thesis that Humean perceptions occupy intervals of time but without duration, Baxter completely neglects Hume's concept of succession, the implications just described, and its Lockean derivation (see "a Defense of Hume on Identity Through Time," *Hume Studies*, 13: 2, November, 1987). The Lockean subjective notion of duration (as opposed to clock time) as simply a distance (= interval) between different parts of a succession suffices of itself to show that Baxter's is a distinction without a difference (only if the idea of a time-interval could be acquired and applied independently of succession could an account like Baxter's be true, but Hume denied this – see *T*35ff.). Moreover, the charge Baxter was bent on refuting – that Hume begs the question by presupposing an idea of *real* identity relations in exposing sequences of qualitatively identical perceptions to be mere fictional identities – seems hardly to merit refutation: just as Hume did not deny we have an idea of cause but only an idea of it as metaphysically real (i.e. valid independently of associative imagination), so, too, he deduced a conception of identity that also has no application outside and independently of imagination. The charge probably rests on the supposition that, on *T*201, Hume was tracing the idea of identity to its *source* in the fiction of an unchanging object. In my view, however, this fiction is offered only as an *instance* of an identity for the purpose of showing how the incompatibility between unity and number does not prevent the imagination from forming this idea; its source in (human) nature is identified only on *T*203 (the fiction of perfect identity).

3 According to Wilson, "there is no idea of an objective necessary connection; the 'idea' is itself simply a confusion. In contrast, while the belief in the existence of a continuing particular is false and the result of a confusion, the idea of such an entity, or, what is the same, the idea of identity (i.e., identity through change), is *not* such a confusion, it is a perfectly legitimate and well-formed idea" ("Hume's Fictional Continuants," *History of Philosophy Quarterly*, 6: 1, April, 1989, p. 181). I maintain exactly the opposite. Far from being well formed, the identity fiction is a hybrid of unity and number, at once both and neither, which results from the running together of different, mutually incompatible views. As a juggling of irreconcilables, Hume deemed the very idea of identity itself a fiction (a necessary consequence of his Lockean view of succession and duration), and that of (imperfect) identity through variation still more antinomial (see chapter 7-B). By contrast, the objectification of customary transitions in the inference from the impression to the idea is a genuine idea: we conceive, and believe, in their objectivity (and universality and necessity) as causal relations – a reality which of course must never be thought of as more than verisimilitude (see chapter 5-E). Accordingly, Hume never denominated the relation of cause and effect a *fiction*.

4 Hume (Kant, too, with his notion of spontaneity) would surely have endorsed Locke's claim that the actions of thought, just as they take up no space, "require no time, but many of them seem to be crouded into an Instant" (*ECHU* II/ix/§10; see chapter 2-A). For an interesting recent account of the hidden dimension of consciousness see Colin McGinn's *The Problem of Consciousness*, Oxford: Basil Blackwell, 1991, especially chapter 4 (however, he

does not recognize that empiricists like Locke and Hume did not hesitate to venture beyond the precincts of the introspectively evident).

5 The *fiction*, not the *conviction*: the latter, explicated only on *T*208f., is not yet our concern. When Hume applies the term "fiction" to something, I take him to be dismissing it as false, incoherent, even impossible, yet grounded in the natural propensities of imagination. Saul Traiger, referring to the fiction of the duration of an unchangeable object, claims that "Nothing suggests that this fiction itself is *false*, only that it is improper or inexact" ("Impressions, Ideas, and Fictions," *Hume Studies*, 13: 2, November, 1987, p. 386). Although Hume prefaced the analysis of the fiction cited by Traiger with the words "But to be convinc'd of its falsehood" (*T*37), Traiger's claim should be adjudged in the light of his general notion of a Humean fiction: "A fiction involves an improper application of an idea" (p. 395). For Hume, however, apart from a few cases restricted to speculative philosophy (i.e. non-vulgar views), it is not the application of the idea, but the idea itself that is false. For example, that the idea of a continued, distinct existent is not copied directly from impressions does not mean that it does not properly apply to them, for that precisely is the nature of belief: a verisimilitude projected onto that which consciousness beholds. An *application* to objects is fictitious only if an idea's dependence on phenomenological feeling is ignored or denied, and it is referred to something (be it perception, substance, or thing in itself) absent from consciousness *even in idea*. Accordingly, relations are limited in their objective validity in that, while applicable to perceptions, their contents essentially include (or presuppose) phenomenological data and ideas of actions of the mind (e.g. comparison); a relation can only be considered fictitious if, as in the case of identity, it implies an impossibility (the fusion of unity with number, as distinct from the juggling of these irreconcilable viewpoints).

6 In "Continuants," Wilson contends that Hume's account of identity is defective in just such a way as to be supplanted by the account of identity made possible by Russell's theory of descriptions (see pp. 177ff.). But contrary to Wilson's belief that this does "no violence to his basic principles" (p. 186), Russellian analysis seems quite unable to satisfy the criterion Hume made the touchstone of a theory of the kind at which he was aiming, viz. applicability to reasoning in animals (the same criticism can be levelled against Wilson's application of the Russell paradigm to the case of the missing shade of blue on p. 185). For Russellian analysis applies to an item only under some description or other, and this presumably is not how inarticulate animals recognize identities. Even in humans, it can hardly be supposed to work in the case of the perfect identity experienced at the most primitive (oyster-like) levels of our imagination, and perfect identity sets the pattern for all other identities. Perhaps at far higher levels of consciousness – well beyond the ken of animals, infants, and even our prelinguistic ancestors – Russell's account furnishes the preferable analysis of identity (though I would dispute that too); but it seems useless for dealing with the primitive sorts of identity belief that were Hume's real concern. Moreover, the application of quantificational analysis to Hume presupposes an isomorphism between language and thought whereby psychological generality may be transformed into linguistic (i.e. the consideration of an individual under some description); yet, such an isomorphism seems

incompatible with Hume's insistence on the public nature of language (see chapter 3-C).

7 In "Hume, Strict Identity, and Time's Vacuum," Costa claims that Hume's analysis of the vacuum in *Treatise* I/ii/§5 sets the pattern for that of identity, i.e. identity is time's vacuum. Though an intriguing idea, I find it unconvincing for three reasons. (i) In dealing with identity, Hume's only reference to the discussion of the vacuum in *Treatise* I/ii/§5 relates not to perfect identity but imperfect, that is, it is analogous to the confusion of a sequence of resembling *relations* of ideas with the strict identity of a single idea (see *T*202f.); there is no reason to believe that Hume thought it analogous to perfect identity itself. (ii) There is a disanalogy between the cases of space and time that Costa overlooks: a vacuum in time is most plausibly construed as an unoccupied time, *which, unlike its spatial counterpart, is not a possible perception* (i.e. I cannot gaze *simultaneously* at two points of time and so take in the emptiness between them as I can two points in space separated by darkness). (iii) Most importantly, Costa seems to mistake unity for perfect identity (as Baxter before him – see "A Defense," pp. 325f.). The former he defines variously as "the idea of a continuous, unchanging perception," "invisible time," and "time without change." These characterizations seem indistinguishable from the description of perfect identity on *T*203: "we fix our thought on any object, and suppose it to continue the same for some time; 'tis evident we suppose the change to lie only in the time." Unity should not be temporalized. It is the same with conception, the simple view of an object (irrespective of duration of viewing), and might well be instantaneous; hence, everything said of existence on *T*66f. applies to unity as well (which is why Locke grouped unity with existence). Unity, like number, is a precondition for relations, including temporal contiguity (see chapter 2-B). Identity relations are no exception: before they are possible, unity has to be broken up, differentiated from itself, and this simply means we must have a *sequence* of views in which one and the same conception (idea) is repeated. With his Lockean conception of succession, a continuous perception is for Hume an impossibility ("it being impossible to recal past impressions, in order to compare them with our present ideas," *T*85); it is a *fiction* of *identity*, not an *idea* of *unity*.

8 E.g. Stroud, *Hume*, p. 17: "the theory of the mind ... he adopts without criticism from his predecessors ... He never asks himself whether the theory of ideas is correct, and he never gives any arguments in support of it." Also Fogelin, *Hume's Skepticism*, p. 104: "Hume was uncritically wedded to the way of ideas." The possibility is hardly ever considered that Hume may have provided no defense of his position because, in his day, no need for one was perceived – just as few analytical philosophers today spend much time defending their fundamental assumptions against the misgivings of outsiders. Does the scarcity of such argumentation make the latter uncritical? Does it mean they could not construct defenses of their position if called upon? Knowing their approach inside and out, and having satisfied most of demands of their own critical instincts, contemporary philosophers – the better among them at least – are presumably anything but uncritically wedded to their approach. So, why not extend the same courtesy to Hume? It seems to *us* that the way of ideas calls for defense since it has fallen into such disfavor in recent

times. But it is highly presumptuous to assume that a philosopher of Hume's calibre, for whom the way of ideas is rightly thought to have been everything, would not have invested the time and thought necessary to mount formidable defenses against most of the difficulties that occur to us so readily *had a worthy opponent made it incumbent upon him to do so.*

9 "The faculty of representing an object *even without its presence* in intuition" (*CPR* B151). See chapter 3 of *Kant's Model* for an extended discussion of this definition derived from Baumgarten.

10 Even a belief as bankable as that night will give way to morning is for Hume merely probable since, without memory and experience, it would be no more certain than its negation. See chapter 1 note 44.

11 Quite apart from being incompatible with Hume's separability principle, Baxter's thesis that perceptions are not instantaneous in their existence (see "A Defense," pp. 326ff.) runs afoul of Hume's claim that perceptions are perfectly known (where knowledge is defined, as at *T*70, to exclude reliance on retentive memory).

12 Here, too, Hume was most likely following Locke's lead: "let any *Idea* be as it will, it can be no other but such as the Mind perceives it to be; and that very perception, sufficiently distinguishes it from all other *Ideas*, which cannot be other, *i.e.* different, without being perceived to be so" (*ECHU* II/xxix/§5). However, Hume's criterion for what counts as a *distinct* perception is far stricter than Locke's – see chapters 1-C and 3-B.

13 The claim is reiterated on *T*190–92 and is implicit elsewhere, e.g. *T*65 (time), *T*207 (relation to connected heap of perceptions), *T*218 (the internal world), and *T*254. Keith Yandell supposes Hume to be maintaining that "I am directly aware of myself only if I am able, from that awareness, to offer a proper account of *being a self*," something he can see "no reason to suppose ... true" (Continuity, Consciousness, and Identity," *Hume Studies*, 18: 2, November, 1992, pp. 265f.). However, it seems clear that it is not an *account* of the self but merely an idea of it that Hume thinks is required for awareness of external objects (animals presumably have an idea of themselves, derived from the causal links between perceptions as described on *T*261, but only humans take the trouble to account for it in books like the *Treatise*).

14 See chapter 7 note 11.

15 If this could only take place by a fallacy and illusion, it would still suffice for it to make *sense* to say, even if *falsely*, that the objects of the senses are continued and distinct existents, and so *are* more than they *appear* to be. And this, according to Hume, is what happens – except that the fallacy and illusion are wrought by imagination, not the senses. See chapter 7.

16 More precisely, if one were to suppose that consciousness is itself a perception, it would then be necessary to posit yet another consciousness that is *not* in order to account for how the first comes to be associated with its object (since "distinction and difference ... are essential to [perceptions]," *T*259, the *thinking of* X and *X itself* would need to be associated). Moreover, as a distinct perception, this consciousness would have to be supposed detachable from every other and so capable of existing even without an object; and Hume gives no indication of believing that consciousness simply as such, void of perceptible contents, is conceivable as self-subsistent.

[17] Berkeley himself seems to have been inconsistent on this point (as on so many others). He held that operations of the mind are not known to us in ideas but only in notions; but what could be simpler for the imagination than to separate two things so disparate as an idea and a notion? Moreover, by affirming in *PHK* §48 that an idea present to my consciousness can continue to exist even after I cease perceiving it (just so long as another mind then perceives it), he thereby effectively concedes that there is no contradiction in imagining the detachment of an idea from my, or any, *particular* perceiving of it; and if detachable from *any* particular perceiving of it, why not also from *all*? He offers no reason. One can only suppose that *esse* is *percipi* is founded on a dogmatic affirmation of the principle of subsistence and inherence (just as he uncritically adhered to the universal law of cause and effect – see chapter 4-B).

[18] Yandell, in one of the few sustained treatments of Hume's concept of a perception, still assumes that perception is an ontological category (e.g. he interprets the "reality" of *T*190 ontologically). See "Continuity," pp. 260ff.

[19] Some may doubt that the existence of the mind (self, person), as conceived by Hume, can be neither interrupted nor discontinuous. But to suppose that its existence could be interrupted means that it could exist *even in the absence of a succession of perceptions*, and so exist unchanging. However, Hume's Lockean notions of succession and duration preclude this, and require that we take literally his claim that "they are the successive perceptions only, that constitute the mind" (*T*253). Since "the thought alone finds personal identity, when reflecting on the train of past perceptions, that compose a mind, the ideas of them are felt to be connected together, and naturally introduce each other" (*TApp*635), it is nonsensical to suppose the mind to exist in the absence of an *awareness* of that succession. It thus comes as no surprise to find him asserting that whenever succession and/or its consciousness has ceased, it is not just the perception of the self that is interrupted but its very existence: "When my perceptions are remov'd for any time, as by sound sleep; so long am I insensible of *myself*, and may truly be said not to exist. And were all my perceptions remov'd by death ... I shou'd be entirely annihilated, nor do I conceive what is farther requisite to make me a perfect non-entity" (*T*252). Bricke recognizes this, but holds that Hume deemed the existence of the self to be discontinuous, i.e. punctuated by periods of non-existence (see "Hume on Self-Identity, Memory and Causality," p. 172, *Bicentenary Papers*, Morice, editor; also Flage, *Hume's Mind*, p. 142). This, too, seems to me mistaken. In all likelihood, Bricke is confusing discontinuous existence with discontinuous memory. In the case of Locke's theory of personal identity, the two are the same, but not so for Hume: by basing his theory of identity on causal relations, Hume could suppose personal identity to continue uninterrupted through gaps in memory (see *T*262); but this is by no means to affirm a discontinued existence. Secondly, the only text Bricke cites in support of his interpretation – *T*195f. – does not refer to the *mind*, as he supposes, but to *internal impressions* and *passions* (he forgets that constant, coherent sense impressions also belong to the system of causally linked perceptions that constitute the mind). Thirdly, and most importantly, Hume's anti-abstractionist adaptation of the Lockean theory of duration forbids attributing discontinuous existence to the mind since to ascribe duration to it independently of any perceived succession would be

possible only if the idea of duration could be *abstracted* from that succession, which Hume of course denied.

20 Since substance (i.e. the permanent, invariable in it) is imperceptible, one can say its perception is always interrupted ("A substance is entirely different from a perception. We have, therefore, no idea of a substance," *T*234).

21 I am treating the identity of mind, person, and self as equivalent, just as Hume did: the section entitled "Of Personal Identity," which promises to elucidate the identity "of what we call our SELF" (*T*251), completes its task with an explanation of "The true idea of the human mind" (*T*261). Penelhum's wish to separate the notion of "person" from that of "mind" so as not to say "that the life-histories of persons have merely mental components" ("Hume on Personal Identity," p. 221, in *Hume*, Chappell, editor) seems to me a wholly misguided approach. Aside from attaching an ontological import to perceptions (as mental), it leads him to suppose that for Hume to deem personal identity a *fiction* is to deem it a *mistake* so that, *in truth*, there is a different person each time a perception changes (p. 224). Though Hume did sometimes speak of our "mistaking" certain very similar dispositions of imagination (as on *T*204), this does not mean he regarded the beliefs founded on such "mistakes" as falsehoods. Being as natural and irresistible as belief in the existence of body, quite the opposite is true: though illusory, they are none the less indubitable. What Penelhum supposes is true of mind is true only of *perfect identity* (which ceases as soon as what is considered by imagination demands "a different direction of the spirits, in order to its conception," *T*203). Person/self/mind, on the other hand, is altogether different: as constituted by a succession of causally related perceptions (see *T*261), it is quite impossible for isolated perceptions, or even successive but unrelated perceptions, to yield any idea of person, etc. Penelhum ignores Hume's analysis of perfect identity and fails to discuss the Humean concept of identity itself in light of an analysis of the Lockean conception of succession and duration.

22 On the only occasion known to me where he did venture to remark on issues of this kind it was only to say they "are to be regarded rather as grammatical than as philosophical difficulties ... we have no just standard, by which we can decide any dispute concerning the time, when [objects] acquire or lose a title to the name of identity. All the disputes concerning the identity of connected objects are merely verbal, except so far as the relation of parts gives rise to some fiction or imaginary principle of union" (*T*262). By contrast with verbal disputes about when personal identity begins or ends, Hume took the issue of personal identity as such (i.e. the source of the idea) to reflect a psychological reality ("the controversy concerning identity is not merely a dispute of words," *T*255). It is also worth noting that Hume placed language in the public realm and the external world (see chapter 3-C and -D); hence, in treating the issues of identity that engage today's linguistically oriented philosophers as mere disputes of words he was, in effect, agreeing that *these* questions fall within the framework of the external world. The real difference lies in the judgment as to what *philosophical* problems lie within the range of naturalistic solutions.

23 E.g. Pears, *System*, chapters 8 and 9; and Stroud, *Hume*, p. 125f.

24 One or both of these points tend to be overlooked in debates about Hume on personal identity. The dispute about unowned states and whether Hume is to be

criticized (e.g. P. Strawson) or commended (e.g. Ayer) is a good example. Hume's problem was neither the metaphysical reality of the self nor the epistemological problem of distinguishing true attributions of selfhood from false (which is not to deny that the theory has implications in this area). His problem was psychological: the *origin* of the idea of the identical self (not how it is *applied* by acculturated adults) and of our belief in its reality/verisimilitude (not the ontological questions of the consciousness-independent *truth* of the belief). That a state is unowned in Hume's sense of personal identity could only mean that it falls outside the system of successive causally related perceptions that constitute the mind, e.g. an impression of which no copy has been taken (and so is lost to the self for good) or an idea so completely disconnected from every other perception as to be powerless to influence our thought, passions, or actions (and so is as good as forgotten). Those who see a problem of ownership in the case of perceptions that do fall within the mind-system invariably invoke cases occurring at far too sophisticated a level of conscious identity to have any real bearing on Hume's theory. For example, an amnesiac who still is able to speak, fear a flame, or walk, is still influenced by previous experience, that is, his perceptions constitute a system of causally related existents (so, too, the sufferers from Korsakov's syndrome cited by Brennen – see "Fragmented Selves and the Problem of Ownership," *Proceedings of the Aristotelian Society*, XC, Pt. II, 1989/90, p. 157f.).

[25] I do not agree with Penelhum's view that "The self ('as it concerns the passions') is a social construction" ("The Self of Book 1 and the Selves of Book 2," p. 288): a self isolated from others would still have a passionate concern for its welfare (so, too, animals and presocialized infant children). Kemp Smith, among others, has criticized Hume for asserting in *Treatise* II that we have an impression of ourselves constantly before us, after having expressly denied there is any such impression in *Treatise* I (see *David Hume*, p. 74). This overlooks the fact that "the true idea of the human mind" is defined as a system of *causal* relations, each of which involves impressions of reflexion; so, in identifying one's person with the system of perceptions in relations of cause and effect, the idea of self is renewed by impressions of necessary connection at each passing instant (curiously, Kemp Smith acknowledged this later in his book, but failed to retract his earlier criticism – see p. 556). More importantly, belief in the idea of oneself transforms the idea into an intense image of reflexion (see chapter 7-B), and it is this image that then becomes the object of our passionate concern.

[26] Strawson comments: "We have no notion of these things. Yet no doubt there *is* such a 'place', and such 'materials'; ignorance, not non-existence, is what is in question" (*Connexion*, p. 129). But is there any more reason to affirm than to deny this? Ignorance is ignorance, no notion no notion: if Hume's claim means anything, it is that talk of such a "place" and such "materials" is empty. To claim, as Strawson does, that there no doubt is such a place and such materials is to forget "that we can never have reason to believe that any object exists, of which we cannot form an idea" (*T*172). Once again a Humean declaration of agnosticism is twisted into belief in the existence of things we cannot even conceive.

[27] According to Passmore, this is a "curious, sudden, and totally unjustifiable

shift from the problem of *our* identity to the problem of other people's identity" (*Intentions*, p. 81). Such a shift would undoubtedly be curious; but, since there is nothing in what follows to indicate that such a shift was intended, the fault more probably lies in Passmore's over-literal reading of the text. The problem is almost surely syntactical: having mentioned the identity of *person*, Hume thought the appropriate pronoun to be "his"; had he instead (as he easily might have) spoken of the identity of the *mind*, he no doubt would have used the less misleading "its."

28 Stroud has criticized Hume's bypassing of contiguity (*Hume*, p. 122) on the ground that "the contiguity of the things thought about ... leads the mind from an idea of one of them to an idea of another, and some of the perceptions we contemplate when regarding a bundle we take to be one person could be expected to be perceptions of contiguous things" (p. 260). But contiguity is not a universal relation among perceptions, one so uniform as to the give the imagination the feeling of an identity linking all its successive perceptions. Many perceptions are "nowhere" (*T*167); and while it is true that such perceptions can, in some cases, fictitiously acquire contiguity (see *T*235), this is commonly true only of sensations, rarely of reflexions, and never of thoughts.

29 This supposition has been the occasion of controversy (see Bricke, "Hume on Self-Identity, Memory and Causality," pp. 167ff., in *Bicentenary Papers*, Morice, editor). In my view, Hume's motive for directing our gaze to the perceptions of another was to help us detach ourselves from our natural, and thence inescapable, belief that we directly behold a world of continued, distinct existences (i.e. imperfect identities like physical objects, other minds, and substances); and the best means of achieving this was to ask us to imagine ourselves spectators in the theatre of another's mind.

30 Since an idea is considered a remembrance of the past only in so far as it is believed to be derived (copied) from an actual past perception, memory is also a causal relation. See chapter 2-B.

31 Concerns related to those Passmore expresses: "the original fiction and the discovery that it is a fiction are possible only if there is something which is at first misled by, and then, after reconsideration, can discover that it was misled by, a series of similar perceptions" (*Hume's Intentions*, p. 83).

32 For a view on how one might advance farther by abandoning empiricism see my paper on Hume's appendix on personal identity (*TApp*633ff.), "Hume's Quandary Concerning Personal Identity," *Hume Studies*, 18: 2, November, 1992. Its gist is the following. (i) Like everyone else, I see no incompatibility between the two principles on *TApp*636 and seek a third, equally unrenouncable principle incompatible with the other two. (ii) Unlike other commentators, I do not believe the problem is to be found in Hume's account of the identity of the mind given on *T*259ff.: even in the appendix Hume saw no other way to explain the origin of the idea except in terms of reflection, i.e. the imagination's tendency to confound its contemplation of a succession of like *relations* of ideas with the successive repetition of the same idea (characteristic of perfect identity); otherwise, he would have had to discard his entire account of imperfect identity in *Treatise* I/iv, not simply that relating to the mind. (iii) The difficulty Hume discovered after *Treatise* I went to press concerns the consciousness of perceptual succession *before* associative imagination produces

the system of causally related perceptions from which the identity derives: since his Lockean view of succession and duration committed him to supposing that perceptions exist in real succession, there seemed no way to account for the *consciousness* of their succession except by supposing either that perceptions inhere in consciousness and consciousness persists through time or that we can immediately read off the predecessors of present perceptions by means of some sort of internal connection. Since neither option was acceptable to him, he had to confess that "all my hopes vanish, when I come to explain the principles, that unite our *successive* perceptions in our thought or consciousness" (*TApp*635f. – emphasis mine). (iv) Since Hume could no more abandon his Lockean views on succession than his two unrenouncable principles, he was left with no alternative but to "plead the privilege of a sceptic, and confess, that this difficulty is too hard for my understanding" (*TApp*636). (v) I conclude by showing that Kant's transcendental idealism furnishes a way out: by abandoning Lockean realism regarding the succession of perceptions and ascribing *consciousness* of perceptual succession to the form (= pure time) in accordance with which the imagination synthesizes perceptions, Kant could preserve Hume's two principles intact.

33 Although Hume never to my knowledge explicitly ascribed the idea of the self to children or animals, he did ascribe that of bodies to them (see *E*XII/i.118). So if, as I claim (see chapter 7-A), the identity of mind is presupposed by that of external objects, then Hume must have been willing to accord the idea to children and animals as well. In any case, there is nothing in his account of the idea of the mind that would lie beyond the powers of animal psychology; and since extension to animal reasoning was, for Hume, a touchstone of any philosophical account of human understanding, the burden of proof is on those who think he would deny an idea of self to animals.

34 That Hume's "true idea of the human mind" relates to consciousness and is distinct from the notion of mind as an immaterial substance (capable in principle of continuing to exist even without a perceived succession of perceptions) is reflected in his division of topics: *Treatise* I/iv/§5 considers the identity of mind-*qua*-substance with Cartesians the principal target; while *Treatise* I/iv/§6 examines the identity of consciousness with Locke uppermost in mind. The identity of substances will be examined in chapter 7-C.

35 Fogelin (*Skepticism*, p. 104) seems to me mistaken in supposing that Hume lacks a response to Don Garrett's criticism that his account furnishes no means of assigning to different minds two simultaneous, qualitatively identical, non-spatial perceptions. Fogelin and Garrett do not attach sufficient importance to the fact that, for Hume, identity is not a real relation of the perceptions themselves, or even an associative relation of their ideas, but rests above all on the disposition of imagination in contemplating perceptions; it is only in so far as ideas are *felt* to be related in *consciousness* that personal identity is possible. Since identity can only arise out of a *perceived* succession of *causally* (reflexively) related perceptions, the possibility of Garrett's two perceptions belonging to different minds is precluded by the very fact that they fall within the same *perceived* succession of *related* perceptions. In other words, since "They are the successive perceptions only, that constitute the mind," their being perceived together and as part of the same consciously related succession of perceptions

is of itself all that is necessary to unify them in the same self or person. Conversely, if a perception in that succession were totally unrelated to any of the others by resemblance and causality in the perceiving imagination, it could not belong to the same mind they do. For Hume, personal identity, as an affair wholly of relations of perceptions in imagination, is necessarily the identity not of the perceptions taken by themselves (single or in aggregate), but of the *consciousness* of them. It thus is quite possible for many different minds to be conscious of the same successive perceptions (rather, as for Malebranche, all finite minds are conscious of the same ideas in the mind of God), and yet each incorporate them within their own individual, distinct *conscious* mind (i.e. within distinct causally interlinked systems of perceptions demarcating the consciousness of each from every other). If one finds this implausible because the word "perception" already implies the privacy of the contents concerned, Hume would surely have been happy to substitute "the name of *object*, standing for the very same thing" (*T*207), to give it a more acceptable cast.

36 Since Hume did not give a separate account of how we come to repose *belief* in the fictions of the identity and simplicity of mind, one may presume that the account of our belief in the imperfect identity of bodies given in *Treatise* I/iv/§2 carries over to the mind. I shall therefore consider Hume's views on the matter only once, in chapter 7-B.

37 The world of the senses and memory of *T*108 is also a creation of causal imagination, for it is a system formed of ties between impressions and ideas. As emerged in chapter 4-A, the world of judgment differs from it by incorporating into it causal relations able to take us beyond memories to belief in ideas as unperceived *present* existents (e.g. the idea of fire associated with the impression of smoke) or as never perceived *past* existents, prior to one's most distant memories. Since in the world of senses and memory, the imagination admits no distinct, continued existents, but believes its objects to be only fleeting perceptions, it is compatible with – if not the same as – the verdicts of immediate consciousness (which admit no necessary connections, only perceptions and phenomenological feelings *vis à vis* sensations and reflexions).

38 The answer to Passmore's question, "why, in Hume's terminology, certain of our 'perceptions' are taken to be 'ourselves' and others to be 'our object'" (*Intentions*, p. 81), is therefore this: *all* are taken to be ourselves and some are *also* – albeit inconsistently – taken to be objects external to us. Consistency is something the vulgar imagination will quite happily do without if preserving it is contrary to its natural propensities and feelings.

7 FROM MIND TO BODY

1 Hume has often been criticized for claiming that distinct existence entails continued existence, and that the conception of continued existence is prior to and produces that of distinct existence (e.g. Price, *Hume's Theory of the External World*, Oxford: The Clarendon Press, 1940, p. 18f., and Bricke, *Mind*, p. 9). This criticism would be warranted if an idea of independent existence could be acquired without reference to the mind, for there would then indeed be no entailment; but I view this simply as additional confirmation that, for Hume, the identity of mind is presupposed by that of bodies. Moreover, critics

tend to overlook the fact that Hume's claim concerns the priority not of the fiction of continued existence, but of the opinion (belief); it therefore relates to the *fourth* part of Hume's system outlined on *T*199f.

2 Hume never raised the question whether the senses might suggest the idea of *continued* existence by a kind of fallacy and illusion. Probably, he thought the proposition so manifestly implausible as not to merit the trouble of refutation. For this would be to suppose that the senses can illusorily seem to continue operating after they have *actually* "ceas'd all manner of operation."

3 Pears criticizes Hume's analysis of the case of the senses (*T*188–93) for violating the strict ontological neutrality to which he committed himself (see *System*, pp. 161ff.). There are two considerations that seem to have motivated this criticism: the argument that the impressions of the senses are not *images* of distinct existents requires the assumption that impressions are the sort of thing that can be an image of something else, i.e. dependent existents; and the argument that, so far as the senses are concerned, the reality of impressions can never differ from their appearance, prejudges the outcome. In my view, Pears is mistaken in both regards, and for the same reason: he has interpreted Hume's denial that the senses are the source of the idea of distinct existence as an implicit affirmation of their being the source of the idea of non-distinct existence. In other words, he has overlooked a crucial disanalogy between the cases of *continued* existence and *distinct* existence: the senses *are* a source of the idea of *discontinued* existence, and it requires enormous exertion on the part of imagination to disregard their testimony (e.g. if I close my eyes and then reopen them, the *appearance* is of two distinct objects separated by an interval; it is only the imagination that supposes that a single object *continued* the same through the interval – see *T*205ff. and *T*231). However, where distinct existence is concerned, *the senses yield no idea or belief either way*. One must not forget that, already in *Treatise* I/iii, Hume had gone to great length to demonstrate that the senses are not the source of the idea of necessary connection, and that all issues of existential independence *and dependence* are beyond their ken (this is what lay behind his assertion that the idea of distinct existence requires "some inference either of the reason or imagination," *T*189). We therefore should not read into Hume's *denial* that the senses convince us that impressions are independent and external an *affirmation* that they convince us of the opposite; the senses are not a source of opinions regarding existential dependence (it is reason based on causal inference that informs us of the dependence of perceptions on the mind – see *T*193). Finally, so far as Hume's supposed commitment to ontological neutrality is concerned, one must be careful how to interpret it. Pears seems sometimes to confuse *being neutral with regard to entity* and *being a neutral entity* (= neutral monism). The testimony of the senses supports the former, not the latter position (see chapter 6-B).

4 See chapter 6 note 18.

5 An additional piece of (indirect) textual evidence in favor of the thesis that Hume predicated the identity of bodies on that of the mind is the structure of *T*265, analyzed in chapter 2-B. It divides into three stages, according to the pattern that something which, at one stage, seems to be presumed as given is, at the next, subordinated to "imagination, or the vivacity of our ideas." Accordingly, if the interpretation offered here were correct, we should expect to

find the attribution of the identity of mind to imagination occur at a later (i.e. representationally more primitive) stage in the unfolding of this pattern than the attribution to it of the identity of external objects; and this is the case.

6 Pears, if I understand him correctly, is committed to both positions. Firstly, following Price, he supposes Hume to have attributed to the vulgar an ontologically neutral notion of body (see *System*, pp. 152ff.). If this means that the vulgar take no position in the philosophical debate between phenomenalists and anti-phenomenalists, then he is correct; but then it certainly does not warrant describing Hume's conception of the vulgar view as "so paradixocial" (p. 153) as to require drastic repair. Secondly, Pears thinks Hume has caricatured the view of ordinary people when he treats double existence views as confined to the extravagant speculation of philosophers and scientists (see pp. 168ff. and citation §52).

7 Pears, *System*, p. 196. Baier maintains that "if [my] claims about the language dependence of our general ideas are taken seriously... faith in a human community is still uneasily present in Part IV of Book One ... [I]f we *can* pool it, if we can treat my viewing and your viewing as both viewings *of one mountain*, at one time, at overlapping times, or at contiguous times, then we have faith in an interchangeability of perceivers, a way of getting a sort of continuous 'us' out of a plurality of different 'me's', (or different 'you's'). This merging of perceivers into a relay team of perceivers, and into a standard perceiver, is the 'fiction' which is in fact correlative to the 'fiction' of an 'external' world's containing some continuants. Without the pair of them, we would perish and go to ruin, and perish mutely, unable to comment on or theorize about our sorry end" (*Progress*, p. 121). This cannot be correct, adequate to the essentials of Hume's account: the belief in an external world that concerned him is the one we share with inarticulate animals, infants, and our pre-linguistic ancestors. Nor is Hume's account anything like what one would expect it to be if Baier were right; it is framed in exclusively psychological, subjective terms (imagination, its feelings, discomfort, etc.).

8 Bodies do, of course, undergo change; but, for simplicity's sake, Hume ignores this in much of his discussion in *Treatise* I/iv/§2 (it was not an oversight: he does, after all, acknowledge their change in his discussion of coherence). Once he had accounted for the identity of constant objects in terms of the smooth transitions involved in resemblance relations, he could apply the reasoning to other relations and thereby explain organic, artificial, and personal identity.

9 Although the fiction of body involves an advance beyond the senses and imagination, it is not a causal inference, i.e. not an inference founded on custom (see *T*197); in fact, these two propensities of imagination conflict (see *T*231). The reason for this may be seen in considering how Hume might have responded to an objection raised by Pears in connection with the claim on *T*197: "This piece of self-criticism throws a clear light on Hume's very strange formulation of the problem of unobserved objects. The trouble, as he sees it, is that it involves inferences to conclusions that are never verified. For example, he would complain that inferences from smoke to ships below the horizon remain unverifiable" (*System*, p. 174). Hume's concern was not *verification* but the conditions necessary to *produce* a custom: (i) causal inference depends on custom; (ii) custom rests on observation ("since nothing is ever really present

to the mind but its own perceptions, 'tis ... impossible, that any habit shou'd ever be acquir'd otherwise than by the regular succession of these perceptions"); (iii) only that we observe can generate a custom, and only in the relations and situations in which it is observed; (iv) since the essence of custom is a transition of thought, there must be perceptions from and to which the transition is made, which is impossible if no more than one is observed; (v) any conception and belief not founded on such observation cannot be founded on custom; (vi) since a thing's continuing to exist when no longer observed is, by definition, unobservable, our conception and belief in it cannot be founded on custom ("this supposes a contradiction, *viz.* a habit acquir'd by what was never present to the mind"); (vii) our reasoning regarding the continued existence of objects therefore cannot be based on causal inference. Verification is simply not an issue here. If I am at sea and see smoke rising up over the horizon, then, even if I never get near enough to the ship to see it, I still believe a ship to be there because repeated observation of ships' billowing smoke has created a custom in me. But my belief that the ship continues to exist (and billow smoke) even after I cease to perceive *any* sign of it cannot be produced by experience-bred custom; thus could Hume assert, without even a hint of self-criticism, that some other cause than custom must be discovered to account for belief in continued existence (in "Idealizing Hume," Hausman and Hausman miss this simple solution to the problem and so introduce unnecessary complexity into its solution). How, *once I have the belief*, I set about *verifying* it (to others, or to myself if I have reason to doubt) does not seem to have concerned Hume a great deal. In *Treatise* I, what in his time would be termed "logic" is relegated to a lone section [iii/§15] and in the first *Enquiry* to a mere footnote [section IX]; unlike some recent commentators, I try to reflect this balance by concentrating on Hume's associationalist psychology (which, though the basis of Hume's norms, is not itself normative but causal – see chapter 4 note 23).

10 Baier holds that "in calling these assumptions 'fictions,' Hume is saying not that they are false, but rather that they are unverifiable, and so unverified" (*Progress*, p. 103). Yet, for Hume, before one can make an assumption of any kind, one first has to have an *idea* to which to attach this predicate. So, if by "verify" we mean an object corresponding to the idea, then the idea of a distinct, continued existent is not unverifiable but actually falsified: "our perceptions are our only objects" (*T*213) and they are "internal and perishing existences and appear as such" (*T*194; see also *T*188f.). If "verify" means to give a psycho-phenomenological account, then the "fiction" not only is quite verifiable, but Hume would claim to have scientifically verified it: our *ideas* of distinct, continued existents correspond to *real* feelings and propensities of imagination projected onto certain sense impressions. Because these feelings are really present, we cannot but believe in the distinct, continued existence of our constant, coherent impressions; hence, there is a conflict between the verdicts of immediate consciousness and imagination, both of which carry the force of natural belief (see conclusion). The only alternative is that by "unverifiable" Baier means beliefs about things that are never given in perception. Yet, since, for Hume, this is tantamount to saying that we have no idea of them at all (for ideas are all copied from previous perceptions), there is nothing to which the predicate "unverifiable" can attach; so, far from being

unverifiable, they would be inconceivable, completely beyond our ken. See also chapter 6 note 5.

11 Given that many subsequent philosophers (especially Kant and his successors) are famous for treating self-consciousness as the condition for the representation of any object, it is astonishing that commentators of Hume have so neglected this striking claim. Since Descartes seems not to have concerned himself with questions of identity except in respect of immaterial substance, and Locke did not recognize the implications of his theory of succession/duration, Hume is apparently the first philosopher, prior to Kant, whose theory of consciousness predicates the external world of ordinary experience and scientific cognition on consciousness of *oneself*, and does so in a context prior to language and self-ascription (for the account applies to animals). Of course, from a Kantian perspective, Hume's position is marred both by its empirical idealism and by the failure to distinguish the transcendental logical *I think* (in relation to which alone material objects are conceivable – see *CPR* B152ff.) from the empirical self (which presupposes external objects – see *CPR* B275ff.).

12 This, incidentally, enables us better to resolve a question touched on earlier: in what sense, if any, identity can be regarded as a natural relation without having to add it to the ranks of resemblance, contiguity, and causation. Identity has no natural power of giving rise to belief of its own; whatever belief attaches to identities depends on causality: the relation of ideas to impressions as copies (i.e. memories) to originals; identity has no natural power of its own to engender belief. This explanation accords with Hume's claim in *Treatise* I/iii/§2 that identity, like all other relations, can *believably* extend beyond the senses and memory only given causal relations. Even perfect identity, which goes beyond the senses and *retention*, presupposes the causal relation of idea-copies to impression-originals, and so rests on experience and custom.

13 In the case of perfect identity, the imagination follows the smoothest path of thought, and so confounds the maintenance (inertia) of its feeling in contemplating the idea of an object with the maintenance of the existence of the object itself; in that of imperfect identity, it needs to relieve the unease occasioned by the opposition between its feeling of beholding an identity and the interruption in its appearance.

14 Flew (see *David Hume*, pp. 25ff.), for example, fails to appreciate that his approach is no less philosophical and remote from vulgar habits of thought than double existence or Hume's own position. After all, who among us owes their confidence in the reality of the world about them to esoteric reflections on the use of such notions as "experience," "belief," "meaning," "truth," etc.? (A similar question can be asked in respect of the analogous move of relying on a theory of language to ward off the challenge to vulgar experience posed by the analysis of matter in contemporary physics.) Thus, not only does Flew (like Pears) mistakenly equate Hume's notion of "the vulgar" with his own notion of "ordinary," he confounds (or comes perilously close thereto) his own *reasoned* "ordinary" point of view with *real* ordinary points of view.

15 "Was Hume a Subjectivist?," *Philosophy Research Archives*, 14, 1988–89, p. 258 and "Is Hume a Sceptic with Regard to the Senses?," p. 58. Wilson identifies the philosophical system with imperceptible relative ideas. Most probably, he has in mind a species of abstraction common among Hume's

predecessors, e.g., a visual impression has shape as well as color, but only in the former respect does it supposedly resemble its object cause (which has *a* shape if not necessarily *the same* shape as the visual impression it causes). So, provided that abstractions are conceded objectivity, one has *relative ideas* of objects from the impression they cause (owing to their generic similarity). By contrast, Hume treated abstractions as mere habitudes of association. He denied objective force to distinctions of reason, maintaining that they have no validity or application beyond the perceptions through whose comparison in imagination they were produced (the restriction of the idea of duration to the presence of perceptual succession and the idea of extension to the presence of arrays of visible or tactile points are merely the most prominent cases). This excludes any supposition that objects might agree with perceptions in features like shape, but differ from them in being made of matter. So, given the impossibility of applying the idea of shape in the absence of color or texture, there are only two possible ways to conceive their imperceptible causes: either they are colored and/or textured as well as shaped or they are devoid of any aspect of perceptions (duration, extension, et al.). The former is just a crude version of the double existence view; so, although consistent (since it forswears the untenable abstraction on which the distinction between primary and secondary qualities is based), Hume would still have deemed it a "confusion of groundless and extraordinary opinions" from which we may look for nothing "but error and falshood" (*T*218). The second notion of relative idea fares even worse, since it is altogether inconceivable: a relation with only one idea (that of the impression effect) is as much an absurdity as a valley without surrounding mountains (see above and chapters 1 note 47 and 3 note 10).

16 Most of the points I have raised against Wilson were made by Robison two decades previously (see "Hume's Scepticism," *Dialogue*, 12, 1973, pp. 91f. and 96f.). My disagreements with Robison are minor, e.g. I think he puts too much weight on coherence when he asserts that "What activates the principle of imagination which makes us suppose that some objects exist unperceived is thus another principle of imagination, the one that makes us reason from cause and effect" (p. 95). Constancy seems to me by far the most important quality where identity is concerned: perfect identity *is* constancy, and imperfect identity a result of confounding successively contemplating a *constant* relation of ideas with successively contemplating a *constant* idea. Coherence is important only in the general sense that identity relations presuppose causal relations in order to extend beyond the senses (see *T*73f.). That is, the derivation of continuity of existence from constancy presupposes causation as the basis for objects that "are fixt and unalterable" (*T*110), but causation by itself does not, in my view, create conditions "that *make* us suppose that objects exist unperceived" (p. 96). Without the identity fiction we might still associate perceptions in relations of cause and effect, but could not even get so far as the idea of mind, much less that of bodies external to it.

17 Microscopy can already produce fuzzy images of atoms; with new techniques to get around the limitations of electro-magnetic energy, it may eventually produce clear images of them, of sub-atomic particles, etc. For Hume, anything with spatial properties is *in principle* observable and so *presently* imaginable; atoms and their components are therefore not conceptually closed. In addition,

just as Hume admits unobservable properties at the macro-level (especially causal powers, e.g. the quantity of a force), so, too, there is room in his system for micro-level unobservable properties. Where sensory impressions are lacking, there are still reflexive impressions from which to derive necessary connections, and from these detailed functional descriptions can be given of scientific entities such as quarks. So, I doubt if there is very much that science could come up with that Humean theory could not assimilate.

18 Wilson distinguishes two senses of "natural" – what our natures make unavoidable for us and what has natural causes – and holds that "the judgments that perceptual objects involve identities are in this second sense natural, but are not natural in the first sense: Hume clearly says that philosophers, at certain times at least, can resist the confusion and can think unmistakenly about perceptual objects – how, indeed, could Hume himself make the distinction in the text if the association created an *unavoidable* confusion?" ("Continuants," p. 180). Yet, aside from occasional rhetorical hyperbole (e.g. *T*183, *T*225), Hume made clear that association is only a "gentle force, which commonly prevails" (*T*10) and principles like causation are " neither the *infallible* nor the *sole* causes of an union among ideas" (*T*92). His is not a deterministic account of understanding: *no* belief is unavoidable *all* of the time. This not merely because Hume was undogmatic but because he interpreted belief as a feeling and, like any feeling, it admits of being resisted or suppressed, if only temporarily (though in the case of disfunctions like madness its suspension might well become enduring). Moreover, Hume made quite plain that belief in external objects is as much a matter of natural instinct as belief in causes (see *E*XII/i.118); the former may rest on a confusion, but if it is like a malady, as Wilson claims, it is one no less necessary to our survival than the latter.

CONCLUSION

1 *Meditations on First Philosophy*, First Meditation, AT VII/21.

2 The First Meditation and certain other texts seem to warrant Hume's reading. Yet, in the Second Replies (AT 144–46), Descartes states that he never meant to cast doubt on the truth of what is apprehended clearly and distinctly (i.e. *while* it is being apprehended, e.g. while attending to $2+2=4$ its truth is indubitable); hence, he cannot truly be said ever to have doubted the perfection of the intellect as an *instrument* of knowledge. In general, Descartes' dualism seems to me incompatible with a thoroughgoing skepticism regarding human nature: while sense and imagination may be hostages to the constitution of human nature, intellect was, for him, prior to and independent of human nature properly so called (i.e. the substantial union with a body); so, however defective we may suppose our *human* nature might be, it is beyond our power to conceive how our *intellectual* nature could be flawed ("What is it to us that someone may make out that the perception whose truth we are so firmly convinced of may appear false to God or an angel, so that it is, absolutely speaking, false? Why should this alleged 'absolute falsity' bother us, since we neither believe in it nor have even the smallest suspicion of it?" AT 145). Hume, by contrast, rejected a pure intellect over and above imagination (i.e. the notion that imagination is

a mere mode of intellectual substance is rife with abstraction and so merely an "artifice," *T*72). Instead, "understanding ... [is] founded on the imagination, or the vivacity of our ideas" (*T*265), and so no less a hostage to human nature than any other faculty (see chapter 2-D).

[3] So far as I know only Robison has noted this contrast with Descartes: "To pursue the comparison with Descartes, it is our very faculties that are in question. But when Descartes puts our faculties in question by supposing an evil genius, the crucial suggestion is not that anything is wrong with *them* ... Hume's point, on the other hand, is ... to show that the constitution of the human mind is such that we cannot be reasonable, and he thinks there is no need to appeal to a *deus malus ex machina* to make the point" ("Hume's Scepticism," p. 99).

[4] See *Prolegomena* Preface (especially note 2, *AA* 3, p. 258).

[5] There are other kinds of conflict between natural beliefs: in addition to that within immediate consciousness to be discussed below, there is that between causality and identity internal to imagination (see *T*266).

[6] In "Naturalism and Scepticism," Bell and McGuinn consider the beliefs Hume ascribed to immediate consciousness to be mere "philosophical baggage ... that he has lifted from a wholly different [i.e. non-naturalistic] tradition" (p. 414). It never occurs to them that such beliefs are not alien to Hume's naturalism, but its very core, and that his theory of ideas, far from being taken over from his predecessors, is, thanks to its phenomenological aspect, of the highest originality. Bell and McGuinn proceed as if Hume never mentioned either the senses or imagination in connection with natural belief, yet concede that his theory is subjectivist from the outset; this is far too selective to be credible as interpretation (e.g. when they claim that Hume sought to exhibit the reasonableness of causal inference they forget that he himself expected others to take it as a portrait of "a gross absurdity," *T*168, and that such reasoning is saved from self-destructing only by a "trivial property of the fancy," *T*267f.). In my view, far from being heir to the anti-skeptical tradition of Descartes, Hume is an anti-rationalist in the tradition of Locke, for whom naturalism is a means to a skeptical end, not vice versa.

[7] Even relations of constant conjunction, in so far as they entail *natural* relations of contiguity and resemblance, are conceivable only on the basis of associative imagination and the attendant feelings of vivacity and ease of transition from one perception to another. For, despite the fact that contiguity and resemblance do not, like causal relations, derive from a special impression of reflexion, their immense power to engender feelings of easy transition (see *T*10ff.) and vivacity (see *T*107) gives constant conjunctions their significance for us. Moreover, that significance only becomes causal when given the support of the natural relation of cause and effect (see chapters 2-D and 5-E).

[8] Substance might, on the face of it, seem exempt from the Cartesian nightmare since, by definition, it is never present to consciousness. But, if this were truly so, there would have to be more to our idea of substance than a mere amalgam of causal and contiguity relations and this Hume denied (see *T*16 and *T*237). Substance is, if anything, the most obviously illusory of all philosophical fallacies since it ascribes self-subsistence to contents that, by their very nature, are dependent on phenomenological imagination.

[9] According to Kant, "No psychologist has so much as even thought that the imagination might be a necessary constituent of perception itself" (*CPR* A120n.). See Part II of *Kant's Model.*

[10] The reasoning from causes whereby the vulgar opinion that our constant, coherent perceptions are continued, distinct existents is exposed as illusion is "philosophical and study'd" (*T*214), depends on "profound and intense reflection," and is easy prey to the least "Carelessness and in-attention" (*T*218). Though "The natural consequence of this reasoning shou'd be, that our perceptions have no more a continu'd than an independent existence" (*T*211), it "has been peculiar to a few extravagant sceptics; who after all maintain'd that opinion in words only, and were never able to bring themselves sincerely to believe it"; for "the moment we relax our thoughts, nature will display herself, and draw us back to our former opinion" (*T*214). "Nature has not left this to ... choice, and has doubtless esteem'd it an affair of too great importance to be entrusted to our uncertain reasonings and speculations" (*T*187).

[11] The notion of epigenesis figures prominently in Kant's thought (see *CPR* B167 and chapter 7 of *Kant's Model*). Since Hume's thinking strikes me as no less suited to this organic analogy, I have appropriated the term.

[12] Here especially one must be careful not to falsify Hume's position by yielding to the temptation to intellectualize belief, e.g. by supposing that only propositions are fit objects of belief (thus excluding two-year olds, early man, and animals from the ranks of believers – contrary to Hume's iterated assertion). Belief, so far as it interested him, is "individually the same" (*T*116) with vivacity, whether concerning impressions, memory, or customary association (see *T*86); hence, a clashing of beliefs even at the level of pre-associative consciousness is, for him, perfectly conceivable. In the context of Hume's account of human understanding, the most primitive, least feeling-informed forms of consciousness have the strongest claim to truth (*adequatio rei et intellectus*); he may therefore be presumed to have held that it is fully within our power to know, with complete certainty, that even our firmest, most natural convictions are false – i.e. that natural belief is simply *natural illusion.* (Though Hume reduces reason to feeling and instinct, and is therefore anti-foundationalist, the fact that we can *know* that this reason is a false reason means that his anti-foundationalism has a foundation.)

Bibliography

Aaron, Richard. *John Locke*. Oxford University Press, 1967 (third edition).

Anscombe, Gertrude E. M. *The Collected Philosophy Papers. Volume Two: Metaphysics and the Philosophy of Mind.* Minneapolis: University of Minnesota Press, 1981.

Baier, Annette. *A Progress of Sentiments. Reflections on Hume's* Treatise. Cambridge: Harvard University Press, 1991.

Baxter, Donald. "A Defense of Hume on Identity Through Time." *Hume Studies*, 13: 2, November, 1987.

Beauchamp, T. and Rosenberg, A. *Hume and the Problem of Causation.* Oxford University Press, 1981.

Beck, Lewis W. *Essays on Kant and Hume.* New Haven: Yale University Press, 1978.

Bell, Martin and McGuinn, Marie. "Naturalism and Scepticism." *Philosophy*, 65, 1990.

Bennett, Jonathan. *Locke, Berkeley, Hume. Central Themes.* Oxford University Press, 1971.

Blackburn, Simon. "Hume and Thick Connexions." *Philosophy and Phenomenological Research*, L., Supplement, Fall 1990.

Brennan, Andrew. "Fragmented Selves and the Problem of Ownership." *Proceedings of the Aristotelian Society*, XC, Pt. II, 1989/90.

Bricke, John. *Hume's Philosophy of Mind.* Princeton: Princeton University Press, 1980.

Broughton, Janet. "Hume's Ideas About Necessary Connection." *Hume Studies*, 13: 2, November, 1987.

"What Does the Scientist of Man Observe?" *Hume Studies*, 18: 2, November, 1992.

Capaldi, Nicholas. "The Dogmatic Slumber of Hume Scholarship." *Hume Studies*, 18: 2, November, 1992.

Capaldi, N., King, J., and Livingston, D. "The Hume Literature of the 1980s." *The American Philosophical Quarterly*, 28: 4, October, 1991.

Chappell, V. C. *Hume.* Notre Dame: University of Notre Dame Press, 1966.

Costa, Michael. "Hume and Belief in the Existence of the External World." *Philosophical Studies* (Dublin), 32, 1988–90.

"Hume, Strict Identity, and Time's Vacuum." *Hume Studies*, 16: 1, April, 1990.

Danford, John. *David Hume and the Problem of Reason.* New Haven: Yale University Press, 1990.

Descartes, René. *The Philosophical Writings of Descartes*. Two volumes. Cottingham, Stoothoff, and Murdoch editors and translators. Cambridge University Press, 1984.

Flage, Daniel. *David Hume's Theory of Mind*. London: Routledge, 1990.

Flew, Anthony. *Hume's Philosophy of Belief*. London: Routledge and Kegan Paul, 1961.

David Hume. Philosopher of Moral Science. Oxford: Basil Blackwell Ltd., 1986.

Fogelin, Robert. *Hume's Skepticism in the Treatise of Human Nature*. London: Routledge, 1985.

Green, Thomas H. *Works of Thomas Hill Green*. I. London: Longmans, Green, and Co., 1885.

Groarke, L. and Solomon, G. "Some Sources for Hume's Account of Cause." *Journal of the History of Ideas*, 52: 4, October, 1991.

Hausman, A. and Hausman, D. "Idealizing Hume." *Hume Studies*, 18: 2, November, 1992.

Hobbes, Thomas. *Leviathan*. Harmondsworth: Penguin Books, Ltd., 1968.

Johnson, Oliver. "'Lively' Memory and 'Past' Memory." *Hume Studies*, 13: 2, November, 1987.

Jones, Peter, editor. *The "Science of Man" in the Scottish Enlightenment*. Edinburgh University Press, 1989.

Kemp Smith, Norman. *The Philosophy of David Hume*. London: Macmillan and Co., 1941.

King, James. Review of Baier's *A Progress of Sentiments*, in *Bulletin of the Hume Society*, Fall, 1991.

Laird, John. *Hume's Philosophy of Human Nature*. Archon Books, 1967.

Livingston, Donald. *Hume's Philosophy of Common Life*. Chicago University Press, 1984.

Losee, John. "Hume's Demarcation Project." *Hume Studies*, 17: 2, April, 1992.

Merrill, K. and Shahan, R., editors. *David Hume. Many-Sided Genius*. Norman: University of Oklahoma Press, 1976.

Morice, G. P., editor. *David Hume. Bicentenary Papers*. Edinburgh University Press, 1977.

Mossner, Ernest C. *The Life of David Hume*. Oxford University Press, 1980 (second edition).

Nelson, John. "The Authorship of the *Abstract* Revisited." *Hume Studies*, 17: 1, April, 1991.

"Induction: A Non-Sceptical Humean Solution." *Philosophy*, 67: 261, July, 1992.

Norton, David F. *David Hume. Common-Sense Moralist, Sceptical Metaphysician*. Princeton University Press, 1982.

Norton, D., Capaldi, N., and Robison, W., editors. *McGill Hume Studies*. San Diego: Austin Hill Press, 1979.

Nuyen, A. T. "Sense, Reason and Causality in Hume and Kant." *Kant-Studien*, 1990.

Owen, David. "Hume and the Lockean Background." *Hume Studies*, 18: 2, November, 1992.

Passmore, John. *Hume's Intentions*. Third edition. London: Duckworth, 1980 (first published 1952).

Pears, David. *Hume's System*. Oxford University Press, 1990.
Penelhum, Terence. *Hume*. New York: St. Martin's Press, 1975.
"The Self of Book 1 and the Selves of Book 2." *Hume Studies*, 18: 2, November, 1992.
Price, H. H. *Hume's Theory of the External World*. Oxford: The Clarendon Press, 1940.
Reid, Thomas. *Inquiry and Essays*. R. Beanblossom and K. Lehrer, editors. Indianapolis: Hackett Publishing, 1983.
Robison, Wade. "Hume's Scepticism." *Dialogue*, 12, 1973.
Rorty, R., Schneewind J., and Skinner, Q., editors. *Philosophy in History*. Cambridge University Press, 1984.
Ross, Don. "Hume, Resemblance and the Foundations of Psychology." *History of Philosophy Quarterly*, 8: 4, October, 1991.
Savage, Reginald. "Hume's Missing Shade of Blue." *History of Philosophy Quartery*, 9: 2, 1992.
Sesonske, A. and Fleming, N., editors. *Human Understanding: Studies in the Philosophy of Hume*. Belmont: Wadsworth Publishing Co., 1965.
Stewart, M., editor. *Oxford Studies in Modern Philosophy*. Volume I. Oxford: Clarendon Press, 1990.
Stove, D. C. *Probability and Hume's Inductive Scepticism*. Oxford University Press, 1973.
Strawson, G. *The Secret Connexion. Causation, Realism, and David Hume*. Oxford University Press 1989.
Stroud, Barry. *Hume*. London: Routledge and Kegan Paul, 1977.
Tienson, John. "Resemblance and General Terms." *Philosophical Studies*, 1989.
Todd, William B., editor. *Hume and the Enlightenment*. Edinburgh University Press, 1974.
Traiger, Saul. "Impressions, Ideas, and Fictions." *Hume Studies*, 13: 2, November, 1987.
Tweyman, Stanley. "Some Reflections on Hume on Existence." *Hume Studies*, 18: 2, November, 1992.
Waxman, Wayne. *Kant's Model of the Mind*. Oxford University Press, 1991.
"Hume's Quandary Concerning Personal Identity." *Hume Studies*, 18: 2, November, 1992.
"Time and Change in Kant and McTaggart." *Graduate Faculty Journal*, 16: 1, Spring, 1993.
"What Are Kant's Analogies About?" *Review of Metaphysics*, September, 1993.
Wilbanks, Jan. *Hume's Theory of Imagination*. The Hague: Martinus Nijhoff, 1986.
Williams, William. "Is Hume's Shade of Blue a Red Herring?" *Synthese*, 92, 1992.
Wilson, Fred. "Hume's Defence of Causal Inference." *Dialogue*, 12, 1983.
"Is Hume a Sceptic with Regard to the Senses?" *Journal of the History of Philosophy*, 27: 1, January, 1989.
"Hume's Fictional Continuants." *History of Philosophy Quarterly*, 6: 1, April, 1989.
"Was Hume a Subjectivist?" *Philosophy Research Archives*, 14, 1988–89.
"Hume's Critical Realism: A Reply to Livingston." *Journal of the History of Philosophy*, 29: 2, April, 1991.

"Hume on the Abstract Idea of Existence." *Hume Studies*, 17: 2, November, 1991.

Winkler, Kenneth. "The New Hume." *Philosophical Review*, 100: 4, October, 1991. Cornell University Press.

Wright, John P. *The Sceptical Realism of David Hume*. Minneapolis: University of Minnesota Press, 1983.

"Hume's Rejection of the Theory of Ideas." *History of Philosophy*, 8: 2, April, 1991.

Yandell, Keith. "Continuity, Consciousness, and Identity." *Hume Studies*, 18: 2, November, 1992.

Index